Black Protagonists of
Early Modern Spain

Three Key Plays in Translation

Black Protagonists of Early Modern Spain

Three Key Plays in Translation

Juan Latino
Diego Jiménez de Enciso

The Brave Black Soldier
Andrés de Claramonte y Corroy

Virtues Overcome Appearances
Luis Vélez de Guevara

Translated, with an Introduction, by
Michael Kidd

Hackett Publishing Company, Inc.
Indianapolis/Cambridge

Copyright © 2023 by Hackett Publishing Company, Inc.

All rights reserved
Printed in the United States of America

26 25 24 23   1 2 3 4 5 6 7

For further information, please address
    Hackett Publishing Company, Inc.
    P.O. Box 44937
    Indianapolis, Indiana 46244-0937

    www.hackettpublishing.com

Interior design by Laura Clark
Composition by Aptara, Inc.

Library of Congress Control Number: 2023938104

ISBN-13: 978-1-64792-142-2 (pbk.)
ISBN-13: 978-1-64792-143-9 (PDF ebook)

The paper used in this publication meets the minimum requirements of American National Standard for Information Sciences—Permanence of Paper for Printed Library Materials, ANSI Z39.48–1984.

∞

So this is what it means to be black? These are the consequences of color?
—Juan de Mérida in *The Brave Black Soldier*

CONTENTS

Title Support Webpage and Illustrations	ix
Abbreviations, Symbols, and Conventions	x
Acknowledgments	xi
Preface	xii
Introduction	1
1. **Historical and Literary Contexts**	1
The Spanish *Comedia*	1
Afro-Spaniards	4
Popular Opinion	6
Law	7
Theology	8
Language	9
Interracial Unions	10
Black Characters in Spanish Literature to 1620	11
Medieval Period	11
Early Modern Period	18
Three Plays Attributed to Lope de Vega	32
2. **Biographical Sketches**	42
Diego Jiménez de Enciso	43
Andrés de Claramonte y Corroy	46
Luis Vélez de Guevara	49
3. **Literary Analysis**	56
The Slave Scholar	57
The Servant Soldier	68
The Accidental Prince	81
Conclusions	91
4. **Translator's Note**	98
Orality and Performance	98
Poetry and Prose	99

Textual Transmission	99
Scenes and Stage Directions	101
Racial Terms and Slave Dialect	101
Puns, Jokes, and Wordplay	103
Works Cited	105
Juan Latino	*121*
The Brave Black Soldier	*207*
Virtues Overcome Appearances	*269*
Glossary	317

TITLE SUPPORT WEBPAGE AND ILLUSTRATIONS

A webpage associated with this book, www.hackettpublishing.com/bpems-resources, contains additional supplemental materials including maps of the plays' settings as well as the illustrations referred to in the Introduction:

- Figure 1: Ramón Rodríguez, reconstruction of an early modern Spanish playhouse. Also reproduced in the book, p. 3.
- Figures 2–3: Juan Bautista Maíno, *Adoration of the Magi*.
- Figures 4–5: Diego Velázquez, *Adoration of the Magi*.
- Figure 6: Diego Velázquez, *Portrait of Juan de Pareja*.
- Figures 7–8: Scenes from Alfonso X's *Songs of Holy Mary*: A Black Moor, the Virgin, and the Devil.
- Figure 9: Titular hero of the *Book of Zifar the Knight*.
- Figure 10: Jan Mostaert, *Portrait of an African Man*.

Scan the QR code below to visit the Title Support Webpage.

ABBREVIATIONS, SYMBOLS, AND CONVENTIONS

I refer to the corpus of plays translated in this volume as the "Triad," used in the sense of three loosely related works that lack the common authorship or continuous story arc of a trilogy. Throughout the supplemental materials, and especially in the Biographical Sketches and Glossary, I occasionally abbreviate the names of the Triad authors and their play titles as follows:

- Diego Jiménez de Enciso (DJE), Andrés de Claramonte y Corroy (ACC), Luis Vélez de Guevara (LVG).
- *Juan Latino (JL), The Brave Black Soldier (BBS), Virtues Overcome Appearances (VOA)*.

In referencing dates, I use the abbreviations c. for *circa* (approximately), b. for *born*, d. for *died*, and, when even approximate birth and death dates are unknown, fl. for *flourished*. All years are CE (Common Era) unless specified as BCE (Before Common Era). In referring to the illustrations, I use fig. for *figure* and TSW for Title Support Page. In cross-referencing subsections of the Introduction, I use the symbol § followed by the relevant section title.

While I capitalize *black* in my own discussions when referring to people, I follow the lowercase originals of the Spanish plays as well as of the primary sources quoted in the Introduction. For details on the racialized language of the translations, see the Translator's Note as well as Glossary items such as *African, Darkskin, Ethiopian, Guinean, Mandinga, Manicongo, Moor, Morisco, Negro, Paleface, Swarthy,* and *Zape*. All translations in the supplemental materials are my own unless otherwise noted.

In the plays, stage directions in square brackets are ones that I have added for clarification purposes; those that appear in parentheses are original to the Spanish texts.

ACKNOWLEDGMENTS

I am grateful to all those who contributed to this endeavor: the Provost and Board of Regents of Augsburg University, who granted me a crucial semester of sabbatical leave; my editor at Hackett, Rick Todhunter, and the anonymous peer reviewers; a scholarly translation group at the University of Minnesota, run by Emily Groepper and Jim Parente; a personal writing group including Becky Boling, Scott Carpenter, and Greg Johnson; librarians at Augsburg University, the University of Minnesota, the British Library, the Biblioteca Nacional de España, the Biblioteca Palatina di Parma, and the Universitätsbibliothek Regensberg; and all the students, colleagues, friends, family members, and other loved ones who provided crucial moral support. A special thank you goes to Professors Evangelina Rodríguez and José Luis Canet of the Universidad de Valencia, who gave permission to use the drawing by Ramón Rodríguez reproduced in Figure 1.

I bear full responsibility for any errors, omissions, or misinterpretations.

PREFACE

This volume brings together, in modern American English translations, three Spanish plays from around 1620 that feature exemplary—meaning admirable or commendable in some important sense, often implying nobility or heroism—Black protagonists:

1.) *Juan Latino*, by Diego Jiménez de Enciso
2.) *The Brave Black Soldier*, by Andrés de Claramonte y Corroy
3.) *Virtues Overcome Appearances*, by Luis Vélez de Guevara[1]

Among the plays of this Triad, only the second has ever appeared in English translation: V. B. Spratlin's *Juan Latino: Slave and Humanist* (1938). Spratlin's volume, which includes an excellent set of supplemental materials, deserves much credit for placing this important play—and the historical figure at its center—on the map for English-speaking readers.[2] Nonetheless, Spratlin's translation, which he referred to as an adaptation, takes many liberties with the Spanish text, and its language has acquired a dated feel. In contrast to *Juan Latino*, the works by Claramonte and Vélez de Guevara have never appeared in English.

The primary purpose of the present volume is to introduce English-language readers to the works of this remarkable Triad. While they are not the only early modern Spanish plays to feature exemplary Black protagonists, they *are* the only ones in which the main characters end up, in each case, marrying white noblewomen. A striking feature of the marriages, and one that is not sufficiently appreciated in the growing body of criticism on the plays, is that they do not appear to trigger any severe punishment for the Black protagonists who dare to desire white noblewomen, in contrast to Othello's tragic death "upon a kiss" (Shakespeare 1997, 5.2.369), for example, or to the destinies of several Black protagonists in medieval and early modern Spanish literature that will be examined in the Introduction. The second purpose of the volume, then, is to ponder the significance of these interracial marriages and what they might have meant for Spanish audiences of the early 1600s. To that end, I have prepared a wide-ranging

---

1. The Spanish titles are (1) *Juan Latino*, (2) *El valiente negro en Flandes*, and (3) *Virtudes vencen señales*. Though *Juan Latino* is sometimes referred to by the longer title *The Famous Comedy of Juan Latino*, almost every Spanish play published in the 1600s began with "The Famous Comedy of" as a selling point, so it should not be considered a unique part of the title.
2. Prior to Spratlin, English speakers would have been most likely to come across references to Juan Latino in English translations of *Don Quixote*, which makes an oblique reference to him in its satirical prefatory poems (Cervantes 1987, 1:61).

Introduction that includes a historical survey of Afro-Spaniards and their representation in Spanish literature, succinct biographies and chronologies of the Triad authors and their plays, and a literary analysis focusing on the Triad's Black and minority characters. I have also included a Translator's Note in which I outline my approach to the plays and the challenges I encountered. A Works Cited and full Glossary complete the supplemental materials.

I need to conclude this Preface with an unsettling observation. Though the world these plays represent and the world in which I have translated them are separated by four centuries, there are several disconcerting parallels between the two. In *Juan Latino*, a Black scholar faces pervasive institutional discrimination in his studies and subsequent candidacy for a teaching position. In *The Brave Black Soldier*, a Black servant is told to "go to Guinea" when he volunteers for the Spanish army. In *Virtues Overcome Appearances*, a Black prince spends twenty years in prison for no reason other than his skin color. A full and proper accounting of such parallels to our contemporary world would take me far beyond the scope of the Introduction as well as my own expertise. I will say simply that I believe the similarities are more than superficial, and I leave it to readers to ponder them and draw their conclusions.

Michael Kidd
Minneapolis, Minnesota
July 2023

INTRODUCTION

1. Historical and Literary Contexts

The Black characters at the center of *Juan Latino*, *The Brave Black Soldier*, and *Virtues Overcome Appearances* first appeared on Spanish stages, probably in Madrid or Seville, around 1620, at the peak of the genre known as the *comedia*.[1] How would the majority-white audiences have reacted to these characters? What were the playwrights hoping to achieve by bringing them to the stage? A brief account of *comedia* conventions followed by a survey of Afro-Spaniards (Spaniards of sub-Saharan African descent) and their representation in medieval and early modern Spanish literature will be an essential prerequisite to answering these questions.

The Spanish *Comedia*

Comedia is a generic term in Spanish literary criticism—not to be confused with the Italian *commedia dell'arte*—that refers to all Spanish secular drama during the century from approximately 1580 to 1680. Widely recognized as the most prolific national theater in world literature, the *comedia* followed a formula crafted by the most successful playwright of the period, Lope Félix de Vega Carpio (1562–1635). In his *New Art of Writing Plays in Our Time* (1609), Vega explains that plays are divided into three acts and written exclusively in verse; they favor plot over character; they freely mix serious and comic elements; they disregard the unities of time, place, and action; and they favor happy endings (which is one reason *comedia* became a universal term). Thematically, Vega's formula draws from history, legend, classical mythology, and hagiography. Issues of love and honor, especially the latter, are particularly privileged "because they move everyone deeply" (Vega Carpio 2002, lines 327–28). By the time of the Triad, the immense success of Lope de Vega's model had ensured the *comedia*'s dominance, and its formulaic nature enabled prodigious output.

---

1. The exact dates of composition of the Triad plays are unknown, but the weight of evidence points to the period between 1618 and 1625. I have chosen 1620 as a rhetorical simplification (as with the term *Triad*). While performance records are scanty, all three Triad authors were active in Madrid and Seville, which had the most important theaters of the period. I address chronology in greater detail in the Biographical Sketches.

The ideology of the *comedia* is conservative by modern standards, reflecting pre-Enlightenment values such as deference to royal power and acceptance of social hierarchies; its view of Spain's multicultural communities is thus deeply skewed in favor of the dominant white majority. However, I believe it is a mistake to go as far as those who consider the *comedia* a mere propaganda tool of the state (Maravall 1990, 13). Such views cannot account for creativity, individuality, or subtlety, all of which play important roles in the creation of the Triad's Black protagonists.

The language of the *comedia* is a product of the exclusive verse format in which it is written. Playwrights of the period were known as poets rather than dramatists, and all poetic figures, including many of the excesses of baroque poetry, were incorporated into drama; in particular, the use of metaphor and simile was stretched to the limit. Various metrical forms were cultivated, but the traditional eight-syllable verse in assonant rhyme, a favorite of the classical ballad, was beginning to predominate by the time of the Triad. When read aloud, this form is not far from the rhythms of prose and was easily understandable to early modern Spanish audiences, who were practiced listeners and spoke of hearing plays rather than seeing them.

Given the emphasis the *comedia* placed on the spectator's ability to listen, elements such as costume, scenery, and special effects became secondary, and staging techniques were modest. Initially, public plays were performed in the courtyards of charity hospitals, where space and mobility were extremely limited. The first permanent theaters arose around 1580, just as Lope de Vega's formula was taking hold. Similar in blueprint to the hospital courtyards, the new theaters were built into the inner patios (*corrales*) of preexisting buildings. While more advanced than their predecessors, they still did not favor elaborate staging techniques, and being open-air like the courtyards, they were at the mercy of the elements.

Excellent historical scholarship from Allen (1983), Varey (1985), Ruano de la Haza (1988), and Ruano de la Haza and Allen (1994) has allowed for a plausible reconstruction of the public theaters, as hypothesized in the accompanying illustration (Fig. 1). A platform stage was about six feet high and typically twelve feet deep by twenty-four wide. At each end, lateral platforms could be used for seating or additional staging areas if required. Across the back of the central stage ran a four-tiered façade whose bottom level provided access to the dressing area. Each level of the façade was probably about eight feet high and several feet deep. Balconies with detachable railings projected from the second and third levels and were supported by columns rising from the stage. The fourth level, hidden from the audience, was used for stage machinery. The lower three tiers were each partitioned into three, creating a total of nine independent niches, each with its own curtain, that could be used for a variety of scenic effects. The left and right curtains of the bottom tier generally served

Figure 1. Reconstruction of an early modern Spanish playhouse. The nine recesses of the back façade were used to stage entries and exits, discovery settings, window and balcony scenes, mountaintops, and so on. The design would have been in place at the time of the Triad. Illustration by Ramón Rodríguez, from *Ars Theatrica: tramoyas y decorados*, courtesy of Evangelina Rodríguez and José Luis Canet.

as the main entrances and exits, while the middle curtain (but sometimes the left or right one) could be drawn back to reveal an inner stage or discovery space such as a dream, cave, prison cell, or the hiding place from which Juan de Mérida reveals Doña Leonor at the end of *The Brave Black Soldier* (3.2). Trapdoors were located in the main stage and the central niche. The second level of the façade could be used to perform balcony or window scenes such as those of *Juan Latino* 1.2 and 3.3, while the third might represent additional windows, a castle wall, or a mountain peak. Climbable mountains such as those in *Virtues Overcome Appearances* 2.1–2 or *Juan Latino* 2.2 could be simulated by ramps leading to one of the balconies. Free niches could be closed off or employed for additional effects.

Because the plays were performed in broad daylight (local statutes prohibited night shows), the recessed niches of the back façade would have provided a distinct lighting contrast to the brighter surroundings of the main stage. Costumes, gestures, and textual cues were used to compensate for the general lack of scenery, requiring a strong suspension of disbelief on the part of the audience in order to complete the theatrical illusion. Although Italian innovations in set design had made possible more elaborate staging techniques by the 1620s, the stage directions indicated by the Triad authors do not appear to call for anything beyond the stage described above, whose multidimensional flexibility permitted a wide variety of adaptations.

The rowdy, heterogeneous audiences that attended the public theaters were segregated by sex and class (Rennert 1963, 117–19). Onstage, women seem to have been allowed to perform alongside men from the beginning; though concerns about licentiousness led to a ban on women actors in 1586, it lasted only about eighteen months and was never reinstated (Shergold 1967, 507–8). Regarding Black characters, the normal approach seems to have been white actors in blackface (Beusterien 2006a, 102–4; Jones 2019, 29–47), as indicated in the stage directions of *Virtues Overcome Appearances* (1.2), or possibly in masks, as suggested in a document from Toledo in 1525 (Cotarelo y Mori 1911, clxxi). Nonetheless, there may have been a small number of Afro-Spanish actors for these roles (Ruano de la Haza and Allen 1994, 309). Where would they have come from?

Afro-Spaniards

Black Africans formed part of a complex tapestry of minority communities in medieval and early modern Spain. Defined by interlocking factors such as skin color, religion, and emerging senses of national identity, each of the communities has its own history of marginalization and persecution, especially following the establishment of the Spanish Inquisition in 1478. Jews, who inhabited the Iberian peninsula since at least the Roman period, faced slavery and forced conversions under the Germanic Visigoths in the 600s, "clean-blood" statutes that limited their livelihoods under Christian rule in the 1400s, and, finally, an ultimatum from Christian monarchs Ferdinand and Isabella to either convert or leave the peninsula in 1492. North African Muslims, known as Moors, entered the peninsula in 711 and occupied most of it within a decade, but Christians regrouped and gradually clawed back territory in a long process known as the Reconquest, culminating in the fall of the last Iberian Muslim kingdom, Granada, in 1492. Soon after that point, Muslims, like Jews, were forced to convert to Christianity, becoming known as Moriscos, a group that twice rebelled against Spanish authority, in 1500 and 1568 (the latter year forming the historical backdrop to *Juan Latino*), and was ultimately expelled from the country in 1609. Across the ocean, Native Americans faced decimation, slave-like conditions, and mass conversions soon after the Spanish arrival in 1492.[2]

Unfolding against this backdrop, the history of Afro-Spaniards is inseparable from the story of slavery itself. From a steady but limited presence in the Middle Ages, when human chattel entered the peninsula through the ancient trans-Saharan trade route, slavery in Spain surged with the economic expansion of the early modern period and reached its peak during the time of the Triad.[3] In raw numbers, one historian (Domínguez Ortiz 2003, 9) estimates a total of 100,000 Spanish slaves around the year 1600. But the distribution was extremely uneven, so while it probably did not surpass 1 percent nationwide and never met the classic definition of a "slave society" (Finley 1980, 67–92), it may have reached 10 to 20 percent in certain urban areas (Phillips 2014, 10–11). Granada's slave population, for example, jumped from 5 to 14 percent after the 1568 Morisco rebellion was suppressed, resulting in widespread captivity (Martín Casares 2000a, 208). Cádiz's slave population approached 15 percent in the late 1600s (Stella 2000, 52) while Seville's, which registered 7 percent in 1565 (Pike 1972, 172), eventually grew into the largest in Spain and second largest in Europe after Lisbon (Domínguez Ortiz 2003, 9). In the New World, Cartagena de Indias's slaves made up an astonishing 70 percent of the population (von Germeten 2008, 10).

It is crucial to note that though there were Black slaves in the peninsula prior to the early modern period, it was equally if not more likely that a Spanish slave in the Middle Ages would have been light-skinned, captured from populations of Slavs (so numerous that they gave origin to the word *slave*), Greek and Balkan peoples, Sardinians, Canary Islanders, and Moorish captives from the Reconquest (Martín Casares 2014, 414–22). But by the dawn of the early modern period (late 1400s), it was becoming increasingly likely for a Spanish slave to be differentiated by skin color, with slave owner preferences trending steadily toward darker and darker complexions. This growing correlation led to devastating consequences for Black Africans.

---

2. I follow scholarly practice in using the term *Moors* and its derivation *Moorish* to refer to medieval Muslims of Spain and North Africa. Originally, the term *morisco* appeared in Spanish as a synonym of *moro* ("Moor"), as documented in the thirteenth-century *Poem of the Cid* (*Poema de Mio Cid* 1990, lines 178, 796). But after the forced conversions, *morisco* came to designate those Moors who remained in Spain, now presumably baptized. In the absence of an acceptable alternative term for this group, I use *Morisco* with the same historiographical intent that I use *Moor*, though I share the reservations of Harvey (2005, 4–5), whose history of the Moriscos is fundamental. On the history of the Jews in Spain, see Gerber (1992). On Muslim Spain, see Catlos (2018). On the Spanish treatment of Native Americans, see Todorov (1984). On the Spanish Inquisition, see Kamen (1998).

3. See J. Wright (2007, 18–40) for the trans-Saharan route in the medieval period. Verlinden (1955) provides additional documentation of medieval Spanish slavery among the Visigoths (61–102), Muslims (181–247), and the various Christian kingdoms (103–80 and 249–545).

As early modern trade strengthened capital markets, the old trans-Saharan trafficking route became insufficient to supply Europe's demand for slaves. Meanwhile, Portuguese explorers, starting with the voyages of Henry the Navigator in the 1430s, began inching down the West African coast. The first Black slaves arrived in Europe via this new route in 1444, in a traumatic scene on a Portuguese beach recounted by a contemporary chronicler (Zurara 1841, 132–35). In the following decades, many thousands of Black slaves were imported into Spain, some still along the old trans-Saharan conduit but the vast majority via the new Atlantic route, on which Portugal acquired a monopoly in 1479.

Though the slave population reflected a wide diversity of West African nationalities, Spaniards of the period tended to refer to all of them as "Guineans" or, less frequently, "Ethiopians," who were considered of higher social status owing to their country's long history of Christianity (Martín Casares 2014, 423). Both terms became essentially synonymous with "African." Significant anxieties and ambivalences developed toward this new, highly visible population, leaving deep imprints across four broad areas of Spanish culture.

Popular Opinion

Black stereotypes took off in the public imagination. Kate Lowe (2005, 26–47) details the most common of these prejudices across Europe: (1) the laughing Black, "too stupid to understand the misery of his or her situation"; (2) the lazy and irresponsible Black, native of "an Edenic land of plenty whose inhabitants did not have to work"; (3) the drunken and criminal Black, ignorant of "civilized or European behaviour" and lacking in self-discipline; (4) the lascivious and promiscuous Black, "incapable of restraint and sexually uncontrolled," perhaps in association with Muslim polygamy; (5) the physically exceptional Black, expert at horsemanship, swordplay, and wrestling; (6) the musical Black, whose innate sense of rhythm led to irrepressible urges to sing and dance; and, finally (7) the uneducated and illiterate Black, forced to learn the vernacular as best as possible and excluded from the scholarly language of the early modern period, Latin. Santos Morillo (2011) provides important documentation of these same trends in the case of Spain.

Not all stereotypes were vicious in nature. An important counterexample comes from the biblical story of three magi (singular: *magus*), said to have followed a star to the site of Jesus's birth in Bethlehem (Matthew 2:1–12). In a long tradition beginning perhaps as early as the year 800, one of the magi is represented as a Black man, often named Balthasar. By the time of the Triad, the tradition had become a widespread European phenomenon, amply documented in visual art including two important

Spanish paintings. Juan Bautista Maíno completed his *Adoration of the Magi* (TSW, Figs. 2–3) for a church in Toledo in 1614, while Diego Velázquez finished his own *Adoration* (TSW, Figs. 4–5) five years later in Seville, perhaps also for a religious interior. While Maíno represents the Black magus as clearly African and Velázquez as essentially a European with black skin, they both seem to treat the subject with sympathy. It is tempting to wonder, given the dates of their paintings, whether the Triad authors would have had the opportunity to view them.[4]

Because the Black protagonists of the Triad are generally exemplary, many of the stereotypes detailed by Lowe and Santos Morillo are applied to them in affirming ways. Juan de Mérida, as examined in an insightful article by Olmedo Gobante (2018), is an excellent swordsman. Juan Latino is recruited as a tutor for his musical talent. Prince Filipo of Albania nobly suppresses his sexual appetite. All three characters speak an impeccable classical Spanish indistinguishable from that of the noble white characters, and Juan Latino goes as far as to become a teacher of Latin. All three also benefit from positive—if occasionally comedic—allusions to the figure of the Black magus. Nevertheless, negative Black stereotypes are not lacking in the plays, as evidenced in the fiendish Moor Cañerí from *Juan Latino* and the buffoonish Antón from *The Brave Black Soldier* (both to be examined in the Literary Analysis). In the end, the authors draw from almost all the popular stereotypes of the period.

Law

A defining legal principle of the period is the concept of the slave as a nonentity, a view that stretches back to an influential thirteenth-century law code.[5] In Jiménez de Enciso, the principle is repeated by Juan Latino's antagonist Villanueva: "Slaves are not men. They are nothing but inert bodies whose names, works, and dealings have no value" (2.4). The inferior if not inhuman status of the slave—who, to repeat, was increasingly likely to be Black by the late 1400s—enabled a legalized discrimination that enshrined many of the anxieties and stereotypes outlined above. Blacks were not allowed to move freely at night or to purchase alcohol at any time (Cortés López 1989, 90); nor were

---

4. In some English translations of the Bible, the magi are called "wise men," but the precise meaning of the Persian *magus* may be something closer to "sorcerer" or "astrologer." Later Christian writings begin to call them kings, which becomes standardized in the Spanish tradition as *reyes magos*. See Young (1933, 31) for the Latin text in which a Black Balthasar is first thought to appear (though the Latin *fuscus* is ambiguous). For the tradition of the Black magus overall, Kaplan's monograph (1985) is indispensable; Koerner (2010) and Fracchia (2019, 60–66) are also helpful. Stoichita (2010, 207–9) offers an insightful comparison of Maíno and Velázquez.
5. The relevant passage from King Alfonso X's *Seven-Division Law Code* states that the master has "full power" over his slave and may do with him "whatever he wishes," though he may not kill him without permission from a judge (Alfonso X 1807, 120); see the discussion in Cortés López (1989, 76–77).

they permitted to learn any craft regulated by a guild, and a master craftsman who took one as an apprentice was subject to punishment (Martín Casares 2005, 256–57).

An important exception to the guild restriction was made for painters, as evidenced by a Black apprentice of Velázquez's, Juan de Pareja, whom Velázquez immortalized in a stunning portrait shortly before manumitting him (TSW, Fig. 6). It is worth noting, additionally, that freed Black slaves were allowed to form confraternities and hospitals, as happened in Valencia (Blumenthal 2005), Granada (Martín Casares 2000b, 422), and Seville (Moreno 1997). In 1475, Juan de Valladolid, a Black freedman, was appointed by Queen Isabella as head of the Black community in Seville (Rout 1976, 18).

Theology

Distinct from legal arguments, an important debate emerged in the Catholic Church regarding the place of Blacks in God's creation. The traditional view, with conceptual roots in Aristotle and elaboration by Thomas Aquinas, is that physical characteristics such as skin color—including white skin—are "accidental."[6] An authoritative Spanish dictionary from the period of the Triad captures this meaning, defining *accidente* as "any quality that can be added or subtracted to a thing without damaging it, or the quality that can be present or absent in a substance with no effect, such as color, whiteness, etc." (Real Academia Española 1990, 1:41a). This is an essentially egalitarian argument: all *souls* are equal before God and worthy of salvation, whereas the *body* is subject to variations and flaws ("accidents" in theological terms) that act as a corrupting force. But as Black slavery grew and worked its way into everyday life, serious challenges arose to the egalitarian argument.

In the mid-1400s, the Portuguese chronicler Zurara argued that black skin was a mark of the curse of Ham, which justified enslavement (Zurara 1841, 93).[7] In 1573, the Spanish translation of Gaius Julius Solinus's late-classical *Polyhistor* (Beardsley 1970, item 86), added fuel to the fire with its representation of an African continent teeming with excess and monstrosity: springs that freeze by day and steam at night, dust that repels serpents and scorpions, lions that mate with hyenas, ants shaped like dogs, apes

---

6. In *Metaphysics* 6.2, Aristotle defines the accidental as that which is "neither always nor for the most part," that is, not an inherent quality. "And it is an accident," he continues, "that a man is white (for this is neither always nor for the most part so), but it is not by accident that he is an animal" (Aristotle 1984, 2:1621). In his commentaries on Peter Lombard's *Sentences*, Thomas Aquinas explains that color is an accident and that the soul cannot be the subject of accidents; it is rather the individual body that is the subject of skin color; black and white are thus nonessential properties of humans (LeNotre 2018, 305).

7. Zurara references Cain rather than Ham, which is a common confusion in the period, but his context makes it clear he had the latter in mind. The curse of Ham as a justification for slavery had an earlier origin in Near Eastern sources (Goldenberg 2005, ch. 12).

with tails, men with wolf heads, others who drink wolf's milk, others who are twelve feet tall and feed on elephants, others with atrophied mouths who eat through straws, others who lack tongues and use nods and gestures instead of speech, others who feed on serpent flesh and shriek rather than talk (Solinus 2011, chs. 27–30). In 1599, books 7 and 8 of Pliny's *Natural History*, on which much of Solinus's work was based, also appeared in Spanish translation (Beardsley 1970, item 121), confirming Africa as a land of excess and monstrosity (Pliny the Elder 1991, 73–127).

With the image of the homeland of Blacks thus cemented in the popular imagination, the Church maintained its principle, though with a significant accommodating stance in practice. The Jesuit priest and missionary Alonso de Sandoval is typical. In his 1627 treatise *On Restoring the Salvation of the Ethiopians*, Sandoval argues that Blacks (as usual, the word *Ethiopian* refers to all Black Africans [von Germeten 2008, xxii]) possess rational souls and are worthy of salvation. Perversely, however, Sandoval's premise leads him to the same conclusion Zurara reached: slavery is permissible. Sandoval's logic is not that Blacks carry the mark of Ham but that they must be *rescued* from Solinus's monstrous continent: slavery, in other words, is the instrument of their salvation (Sandoval 1956, 99). For reasons such as this, Blacks never achieved the legal protections against slavery that, in the case of Native Americans, were to become enshrined in the so-called New Laws of 1542 (Kamen 1991, 94–95).

Language

Anxieties toward Afro-Spaniards left an imprint on both literary and everyday Spanish. Perhaps inspired by the stereotype of the illiterate Black (Lowe 2005, 41–47), late fifteenth- and early sixteenth-century writers began representing the language of Black characters in an exaggerated dialect known as *bozal*, whose fragmented syntax and distorted phonology contrasted with the more polished Spanish of slaves referred to as *ladinos*.[8] The earliest surviving *bozal* texts come from late fifteenth-century Portugal, reflecting that country's importance in the slave trade. The convention then spreads, whether spontaneously or through conscious imitation, to a series of Spanish poems by Rodrigo de Reinosa from the late 1400s or early 1500s (Santos Morillo 2020, 27–37). As it becomes more popular, the dialect appears in well-known authors such as Gil Vicente, Lope de Rueda, and Lope de Vega, where, as will be seen shortly, it is almost always

---

8. The word *bozal* was applied to newly arrived slaves of any race, but today the dialect is mostly associated with Black slaves. Frida Weber de Kurlat (1962) pioneered the linguistic study of the phenomenon. Subsequently, John Lipski (1986, 10) concluded that *bozal* was primarily a literary convention but later acknowledged (Lipski 2005, 93) that it might reflect historical reality to some degree. Much more recently, studies by Jones (2019) and Santos Morillo (2020) tend to support Lipski's revised opinion. Beusterien (1999) provides a helpful glossary of *bozal* Spanish. On *ladinos*, see Martín Casares (2000a, 210).

employed for comic effect. Unique among characters of the Triad, the slave Antón in *The Brave Black Soldier* speaks in a *bozal* dialect that I examine in the Literary Analysis.

More broadly still, the words for Black (*negro*) and slave (*esclavo*) become virtually interchangeable in the period. In a bill of sale from 1577, the seller revokes all rights "to said *negro*" (Martín Casares 2000b, 145). In 1663, the Spanish Capuchin missionary Antonio de Teruel reported that the Congolese "do not wish to be called blacks, but swarthy. Only slaves are called blacks. And so, as far as they are concerned, it is the same thing to say black as to say slave" (qtd. in Wynter 1977, 10). The slippage in language undoubtedly reflects assumptions people made about skin color. In a will from 1566, a widow left her estate to two Black siblings, noting that the "colour of their faces gives rise to the suspicion that they are slaves, but I say and declare that they are not, and that they have never been but free people" (qtd. in Martín Casares 2005, 252).

In a striking literary parallel, Juan de Mérida, protagonist of *The Brave Black Soldier*, feels compelled to declare: "For though I am black, I have not known slavery, and the sun in the sky is a liar if it thinks otherwise" (1.2).[9] Slavery, in fact, is a prominent theme throughout the Triad. Juan Latino remains unfree throughout the play that bears his name, and Prince Filipo of *Virtues Overcome Appearances* spends twenty years in chains for no reason other than his skin color. A major goal of the Literary Analysis is to interrogate these themes against the backdrop of Spanish slavery, whose peak coincided with the lives of the Triad playwrights.

Interracial Unions

Given the marriages with which the Triad plays end, a word about interracial unions in early modern Spain is in order. In the New World colonies, mixed-race unions were common from the very beginning given the mathematics of settlement and colonization. In the Spanish Caribbean, for example, European women constituted only a tiny fraction of the female population (Altman 2013, 228). Bowing to the inevitable, the law officially sanctioned white-Indian marriages in 1514. Black-white marriages, though discouraged, faced no legal impediment in the colonies until a law in 1687 limited them in Santo Domingo (Rout 1976, 140). Soon a panoply of new terms had entered common parlance—with some local variation—to describe the offspring of interracial unions: *mestizo* (Indian-white), *zambaigo* (Indian-Black), and *mulato* (Black-white).

The situation was quite different in Spain, where Native-white unions were unheard of (Natives themselves being virtually nonexistent on the peninsula) and Black-white

---

9. Several critics appear to ignore this statement from Juan's own mouth and proclaim him a slave. I do not believe he is, though I recognize that the language around his status is ambiguous. I return to this important issue in the Literary Analysis.

ones, extremely rare. Most Blacks in early modern Spain were slaves, and Black slaves, when they married, showed a strong preference for marrying other Black slaves (Martín Casares 2000b, 363). Records from seventeenth-century Granada, for example, show that of all marriages involving at least one slave, 91 percent were between two slaves, 5.9 percent were between a male slave and a free woman, and 1.3 percent between a female slave and a free man. Moreover, when marriages between slave and free did occur, the free party was usually destitute (Martín Casares 2000b, 364).

These historical data suggest that the unions with which the Triad plays end—three Black men, one of whom is a slave, joined in legal marriage to three white noblewomen—are surprising not only to us today: they would have surprised and quite possibly shocked the audiences of 1620 as well. What led to their sudden appearance in three different plays? A review of Black characters in Spanish literature prior to the Triad will help to answer that question.

Black Characters in Spanish Literature to 1620

The word *characters* in this survey refers to figures that appear in a recognizable story arc in prose, narrative poetry, popular song, and drama. I leave aside lyric poetry as well as mixed-race characters of any genre. The overview is intended, in any case, as representative rather than exhaustive.

Medieval Period

Medieval Iberian literature features a paucity of Black characters given the limited African presence in the social reality of the peninsula during the period. Howard Jason's bold claim (Jason 1977, 29–30) that Baltasar in the *Act of the Magi* is a Black man would make this anonymous mystery play, which probably dates from the late 1100s (Pérez Priego 1997, 39), the earliest Spanish source of a Black character by far. Sylvia Wynter (1977, 14–15), tentatively supporting Jason, finds a skepticism in Baltasar that she identifies as the mark of an outsider. Panford (2001, 237), meanwhile, repeats Jason's claim without qualification. These are all risky arguments. The lone manuscript that contains the *Act of the Magi* is completely lacking in stage directions and gives no indication of the characters' skin color or physical appearance; and while the tradition of the Black magus may be alluded to as early as the year 800 (Young 1933, 31), it does not gain widespread popularity until well after the *Act of the Magi* (Kaplan 1985, 2). Secondly, the manuscript does not indicate speakers, and the considerable disagreement among textual critics in assigning the dialogue (Pérez Priego 1997, 248–49) makes it impossible to know with certainty who speaks which lines. As a result, though the claims of Jason, Wynter, and Panford cannot be refuted, it is prudent to treat them with caution while recognizing the importance of the Black magus in later periods.

The earliest definitive Black characters in Iberian literature appear, in fact, at the margins of the Spanish-language tradition. A minor example occurs in the *Poem of Joseph*, a fourteenth-century text that falls within a tradition of works composed in primitive Romance with Arabic or Hebrew characters, reflecting the widespread diglossia of the period. The poem in question, based on Quranic sources and written in Aragonese with Arabic script, tells the story of the Jewish patriarch Joseph. Sold into slavery by his brothers, he is entrusted to the vigilance of an unnamed Black man. When Joseph escapes, the Black character hunts him down and punishes him, then faces punishment himself. Ultimately pardoned, he does not reappear in the story, though the text seems to end inconclusively.[10]

Much more significant than the anonymous *Poem of Joseph* is a work sponsored and perhaps partially written by Spain's King Alfonso X (1221–1284). The *Songs of Holy Mary* was a decades-long project that collected, embellished, and invented folktales of miracles associated with the Virgin Mary and recorded them in poetic form accompanied by musical notation. Though Alfonso was king of Spanish-speaking Castile, he chose to compose the songs in Galician Portuguese, which at the time had a more prestigious lyric tradition than Spanish. While the language itself may not have been completely accessible to Spanish speakers of the time, Alfonso's great cultural authority combined with the charming music of the songs would probably have been enough to hook most audiences. Moreover, at least three codices of the work were lavishly illustrated, further bridging whatever linguistic divide the songs may have created.[11]

Black characters—always Moors—figure prominently in several of Alfonso's tales and the codex illustrations. In song 186, a Moorish servant is commanded to lie in the bed of a married white woman to frame her for adultery. When the sleeping partners are discovered, they are dragged to the public square to be burned alive. The woman, a devotee of the Virgin, is saved from harm while the "treacherous Moor" (Alfonso X 2019, song 186, line 55) is consumed in flames, as depicted in the illustration (TSW, Fig. 7). Though the Moor's religion probably weighs most heavily in the final judgment

---

10. The *Poem of Joseph* is estimated to have been written in the late 1300s (Menéndez Pidal 1902, 2–3). The episode with the Black character occurs in stanzas 46–57 (Menéndez Pidal 1902, 34–36). Joseph's owners, in fact, may have all been Black. The Bible associates them with the Midianites or Ishmaelites, who were traditionally represented as Black in Byzantium and the West (Kaplan 1985, 8).

11. Spanish and Portuguese, considered 50–60 percent mutually intelligible today (Jensen 1989, 851), would have been even more so in the medieval period. Known by his epithet "the Wise," Alfonso authored or sponsored an astonishing diversity of texts, not only literary but also legal, historical, and scientific (including translations from Arabic). For a complete English version of the *Songs of Holy Mary*, see Kathleen Kulp-Hill's excellent translation (Alfonso X 2000).

of his "treachery," it is significant that he is described as "black as pitch" (line 50). The language recalls the demons and devils that are compared to pitch, coal, ink, or mulberries in the rest of the collection (songs 3, 47, 68, 74, 75, 85, 115, 219, 298, and 404) and depicted in the illustrations, as in song 47 (TSW, Fig. 8). Though religion is the primary source of Christian hostility toward Moors, skin color cannot be ruled out as a contributing factor, especially in the case of a Black man who finds his way into the bed of a white woman: even when the transgression happens against his will and with apparently no sexual contact. Moors with black skin also appear in songs 185 and 329 of Alfonso's collection.[12]

Leaving behind the non-Hispanic traditions of the peninsula, we come to Alfonso's nephew Don Juan Manuel (1282–1348), who is responsible for arguably the most important figure in medieval Spanish literature's limited cast of Black characters. Juan Manuel's *Book of Exemplary Tales of Count Lucanor and Patronio* (1335) shares the folkloric dimension of his uncle's work but lacks the central theme of the Virgin or miraculous events. It is instead a book of practical wisdom directed toward noble readers: fifty-one stories, each ending with an explicit moral, propose solutions to problems of power, leadership, and estate management. Tale 32, "On What Happened to a King with the Fabric Swindlers," became the basis, five centuries later, of Hans Christian Anderson's now famous "The Emperor's New Clothes" (1837). In Juan Manuel's version, the magical cloth can be seen only by those actually sired by the men they claim as their fathers. Seeing the cloth, in other words, amounts to a confirmation of paternity in an era in which family and clan are paramount. In the story's madcap final scene, as the duped king rides through town on horseback during a public festival, everyone claims to see his nonexistent clothes "until a black man, who tended the king's horse and had nothing to lose, went up to the king and said, 'Sir, it matters not to me whether you consider me to be son of the father I claim or of any other, and thus I say to you: either I'm blind or you're parading around stark naked'" (Juan Manuel 1990, 218).

This lowly Black stable attendant with "nothing to lose" fits the profile of non-Muslim African slaves imported into medieval Spain via the ancient trans-Saharan trafficking route (J. Wright 2007, 18–40). If he had been a Moor, his identity would almost certainly have been specified as such, and he would have been vulnerable to the trick that he successfully eludes, for the narrator specifies that the Moors "cannot inherit anything from their fathers unless they are truly their sons" (Juan Manuel 1990, 215). That only a Black man of dubious faith can speak truth to power and expose the king's

---

12. Importantly, there are also many instances in which Moors are mentioned with no reference to skin color at all; and in two songs (324 and 406), they are specifically described as white. The illustrations support these varied depictions, which seem to suggest that Moors were often indistinguishable in appearance from Spanish Christians and Jews.

ridiculous charade is at once funny and tragic. His sparse but poignant characterization is closer to that of Triad protagonists Juan Latino and Juan de Mérida than anything else in all of medieval Spanish literature.

In the subordinate roles they assign to Black characters, *Count Lucanor*, the *Songs of Holy Mary*, and even the *Poem of Joseph* reflect, to varying degrees, the sociohistorical reality of Africans in medieval Spain. In contrast, the Black characters in three other works from the period exist in the realm of pure fantasy, a world more akin to that of the *Act of the Magi*. The ambiguity of Baltasar's skin color in the latter, in fact, applies equally to the hero of the first of these works. The *Book of Zifar the Knight* (c. 1300), which holds distinction as Spain's first chivalric romance (a novel-length fantasy centered on the adventures of a knight), features a hero said to be from the "First India, populated by Gentiles, [which] is the one that borders on the land of the blacks" (*Libro del caballero Zifar* 1983, 95). Given that medieval writers often referred to India in the plural and imagined it divided into three separate realms including lands as diverse as Mongolia and Ethiopia (Kaplan 1985, 64), the narrator of *Zifar the Knight* may be alluding to the latter in the phrase "the India of the Blacks." Nevertheless, though he makes a point of noting that the Indians "are dark and close to blacks in color, since they border on them" (*Libro* 1983, 97) and though black-skinned knights are not unheard of in medieval literature (as evidenced in the Middle Dutch Arthurian romance *Moriaen*), Zifar himself is never described that way. His skin color, in fact, remains entirely irrelevant to the plot, and a fifteenth-century illuminated codex represents him with an olive complexion (TSW, Fig. 9). As in the case of the *Act of the Magi*, it is probably impossible to determine how the author of *Zifar the Knight* visualized his hero.

The ambiguity of skin color disappears in the next two examples, which bring us to the close of the medieval period in Spain. At the beginning of Diego de San Pedro's short allegorical novel *Prison of Love* (1492), the author-narrator observes a Black man dressed in yellow who repeatedly strikes the main character Leriano with a halberd, while the latter "received the blows on a shield that suddenly emerged from his head and covered him to his feet" (Diego de San Pedro 1989, 57). Leriano later explains that the unnamed Black man is a personification of Despair, which incites him to end his tragic love by committing suicide, while the shield represents Judgment, which protects him from mortal sin (60). Although the Black man never reappears directly, his presence is crucial, for at the end of the novel Leriano indeed kills himself. While the example is but a brief one, it is an excellent illustration of the bias at the heart of color symbolism in European culture: a bias that routinely privileges white over black (Goldenberg

2009, 93–97).[13] Given the enormous success of Diego de San Pedro's novel, which saw multiple editions and translations well into the 1600s (Moreno Báez 1989, 40–41), its allegorical Black character should not be overlooked.

The final example is perhaps more fantastical still. Garci Rodríguez de Montalvo's *The Exploits of Esplandián* was a sequel to the same author's immensely popular *Amadís of Gaul*, a four-part Arthurian-style saga that Rodríguez de Montalvo had elaborated from a now lost original dating back to at least the 1300s. While the earliest surviving edition of *Esplandián* dates from 1510—two years after that of *Amadís*—it was almost certainly printed earlier and was probably completed between 1495 and 1497 (Sainz de la Maza 2003, 23). Despite the judgment of Don Quixote's village priest, who condemns *Esplandián* to the flames (Cervantes 1987, 1:112), the novel enjoyed considerable success in the early modern period (though not as much as *Amadís*), and its representation of Black characters, generally overlooked by critics, deserves attention in this survey.

Toward the end of the eight-hundred-page tome—chapter 157 of 184—as the hero Esplandián and his father Amadís defend Constantinople from a siege by the Ottoman Turks, Rodríguez de Montalvo introduces a bold new ally of the infidels:

> At the right hand of the Indias, very close to the realm of earthly Paradise, there was an island called California, populated entirely by Black women.[14] Without a single man among them, they led a lifestyle almost like that of the Amazons. They had strong bodies, robust and fiery hearts, and great strength. The island itself was the rockiest and craggiest on earth. Their weapons were all gold, as were the trappings of the wild beasts they rode about after domesticating them, for on the whole of the island there was no other metal. They dwelt in well-constructed caves and had many ships with which they sailed to other regions to conduct raids. The men they captured they took with them, killing them in the manner you will soon hear. And at times, when there was peace with their enemies, they circulated freely among them and had unions, from which many of them became pregnant; and if they had a girl they kept it, and if it was a boy they killed it. (Rodríguez de Montalvo 2003, 727–28)

---

13. Though Goldenberg (2009, 93) suggests that the privileging of white over black is "universal," Doniger (2003, 33–35) cites compelling evidence that the reverse phenomenon—a favoring of black over white—is normative in non-European cultures. I return to this topic in my discussion of Lope de Vega's Black saint plays, where the European norm undergoes a significant inversion that anticipates the Triad.

14. The plural *Indias* continues the medieval usage found in the *Book of Zifar the Knight*. Hale (1945, 3–8) speculates that Hernán Cortés named the territory now called Baja California, which Cortés believed to be an island, after Rodríguez de Montalvo's fictitious land.

The inhabitants of this fanciful island are said to be ignorant of Christianity and unaware of any lands "except the closely neighboring ones"; and their queen, Calafia, in rallying them to the Turkish cause, cites not religion but rather the honor and fame to be gained from such an endeavor (729). Nevertheless, the broad brushstrokes with which the Californians are painted seem to identify them with Islam. On multiple occasions they are referred to as "pagans" and "infidels," which is the same language used for the Turks. The queen wears a headdress that suggests Islamic practice and rides a beast that is compared to a dromedary (757–58). Finally, as Hale notes (1945, 10), the words *California* and *Calafia*, which are apparently of Rodríguez de Montalvo's invention, are suggestive of the Muslim *caliphate* and its supreme leader or *caliph* (*califato* and *califa* in Spanish).

Rodríguez de Montalvo's fictitious island would thus seem to represent a dystopian nightmare for Spanish Christian readers, carefully crafted to instill terror and revulsion with its provocative name and its Black women inhabitants who practice infanticide, strut about on enormous beasts (eventually identified as griffins), and ally themselves with the mortal enemy of medieval and early modern Christendom. Remarkably, however, the women are never represented as villainous or degenerate but instead in rather admiring terms. They are described as striking in appearance, though the phrasing is careful: they have "strong bodies and robust and passionate hearts" (727) while the queen is "very beautiful in their company" (729). Skin color is not even mentioned following the initial reference. Moreover, after the siege of Constantinople fails (in defiance of historical reality) and Queen Calafia is defeated in single-handed combat by none other than Amadís of Gaul, she falls in love with Amadís's son Esplandián. The obstacle to their union, however, is not the queen's skin color but the fact that Esplandián is already betrothed to a Byzantine princess and, additionally, that Calafia is not a Christian. The latter problem is solved when the queen converts amid much fanfare, at which point she is rewarded with betrothal to Esplandián's cousin Talanque. What may be the first interracial marriage of premodern Spanish literature is all the more astonishing because it is never remarked on as such. But rather than indicating a truly "color-blind" author, the silence may be a way of shielding readers from an uncomfortable situation. Indeed, in what will become a pattern across the very limited number of such marriages in premodern Spanish literature, Calafia and Talanque are never shown participating in domestic life or even interacting in the way all-white couples are.

Rodríguez de Montalvo's treatment of Black women characters is not limited to the mythical Californians. Around the same point in the novel, he introduces an unnamed messenger woman who delivers letters to the Christians, first from the Turks and then from their new allies. Initially appearing with a knight outfitted in black armor, the new character is described as being "of black face and hands yet very kindly in appearance, and she was so beautiful that there were [Christian] knights there who would have counted themselves lucky to serve her" (699). Later, when the messenger delivers a joint letter from Queen Calafia and the Turkish sultan, the narrator recalls her as "that beautiful black damsel," now described as "richly attired atop her savage beast" (754). She is at once "scrutinized by all [in the Christian camp], seeming to them, according to their judgment, to be very beautiful and quite extravagant in all her rich accoutrements and dress" (754). In turn, she is "astonished to see [Esplandián's] beauty" (755), a point she emphasizes upon rejoining the queen: "O queen! What can I tell you other than the fact that if he were of our law, we would believe that our gods had fashioned him with their own hands, using up all their power and knowledge in the endeavor?" (756). After thus sparking the queen's fascination with Esplandián, the messenger disappears from the narrative.

Several contrasts between this unnamed character and Queen Calafia's warrior tribe are noteworthy. To begin with, the narrator signals a disjunction between the messenger's dark skin and her kindly and beautiful appearance with an all-important *yet* ("of black face and hands yet very kindly in appearance, and she was so beautiful that . . ."). This type of "black but beautiful" judgment is absent in all references to the Californians. Additionally, though her nationality is never stated, the description of the messenger suggests a native Turk or perhaps a sub-Saharan African slave. Her mention of "our law" hints at the law of Muhammad, that is, Islam, and the subsequent reference to polytheism ("our gods") would be consistent with medieval Christianity's wildly inaccurate representations of the Muslim faith (Akbari 2009; Heng 2018, ch. 3). Thus, though she moves in the same fictional universe as the queen, the messenger might conjure for Rodríguez de Montalvo's readers a more plausible historical reality than the mythical Californians.

Finally, the messenger draws a distinctly more fetishizing gaze than the queen. The male characters ogle her exotic appearance while the narrator reiterates her blackness: a detail that apparently ceases to be worthy of comment in the queen's case. This contrast may in fact flow from the first: the messenger, being closer to the contemporary reality of the novel's readers, many of whom would have been male (Eisenberg 1973), is perhaps in a position to play a more titillating role than the illusory queen.

∽

Rodríguez de Montalvo's *The Exploits of Esplandián*, written at the close of the Middle Ages, provides an intriguing coda to this review of Black characters from Spanish literature of the period. The author's anonymous messenger, and especially the Californians, are as close to exempt from color prejudice as anything in the medieval or early modern period. This is not to argue that they *are* exempt from color prejudice, as becomes clear in a final twist to be discussed below. Nevertheless, the Californians are portrayed in the generally positive terms reserved for noble enemies. Their skin color, mentioned only once, seems to be a secondary consideration, and their queen goes on to marry a powerful white nobleman, setting an important precedent for the plays of the Triad. The representation of the messenger certainly mobilizes orientalist tropes, but it is worth noting that the erotic dimension of her character could have as much to do with her subordinate status—either servant or slave—as with her skin color.

This point signals a theme that will consistently reappear in works with Black characters. The entanglement of skin color with gender and social standing occurs in complex and unpredictable ways that both challenge and accommodate preconceived notions. In the case of the messenger, the mostly positive representation of her skin color is nonetheless subject to a fetishizing gaze, perhaps aided by a perception of lower social standing. Additionally, Rodríguez de Montalvo ends the fable of his warrior women with a twist that seriously undermines the near exemption from color prejudice mentioned above. At the end of the California episode, upon converting to Christianity and marrying Talanque, Calafia readily submits to his male authority: "You shall be lord over me and all that is mine, which is a considerable fiefdom" (801). The remaining Californians also convert, the queen's sister is married to another of Esplandián's cousins, and everyone returns to the island, which, in a final nod to the patriarchal norm, is opened to male residents so that "the natural generation of men and women" may be restored (801). While the reinstatement of traditional gender roles seems to be the focus of this ending, the submission of women to men in this case also implies that of Blacks to whites, rupturing the nearly color-free narrative.

Lastly, it is worth mentioning that the representation of Black women in *The Exploits of Esplandián* channels two distinct traditions: both of which have appeared, separately, in the previously reviewed works. On the one hand, the Black and potentially Black characters of *Prison of Love*, the *Book of Zifar the Knight*, and the *Act of the Magi* exist in a realm of mystery, fantasy, and allegory that is severed from the sociohistorical reality of Africans in medieval Spain. This is the world of the Californians. On the other hand, the servitude and slavery so central to that reality are reflected, to one degree or another, in the *Poem of Joseph*, the *Songs of Holy Mary*, and *Count Lucanor*. This is the world of the Black messenger. Though the following survey charts the consolidation of the latter trend in the early modern period, it bears remembering that the first does not disappear. It will reemerge, in fact, transformed and updated, in *Virtues Overcome Appearances*.

Early Modern Period

The rise of slavery, which begins in earnest in the early 1500s, transforms the social reality of early modern Spain, dragging the literary representation of Black characters along with it. In this overview, which will bring us up to the period of the Triad, I examine representative examples from popular song, prose fiction, and, most importantly, theater.

Two songs by Rodrigo de Reinosa, published as broadsides in either the late 1400s or early 1500s, are best known for marking the appearance in Spain of the *bozal* dialect discussed above. "Song to Black Men and Women" (Reinosa 2020a) takes the form of a lewd and insulting dispute between a Wolof man and a Guinean woman in Seville. While the dispute genre was a popular medieval form, the presumably unfree status of both characters introduces a uniquely early modern concern, as the spread of slavery prompted anxieties among white Spaniards and a proliferation of demeaning stereotypes about Blacks. In a second example, "Another Song to Black Men and Women" (Reinosa 2020b), Reinosa's description of the mistreatment and deprivation suffered by the Black slave narrator might suggest a more sympathetic perspective. However, as in the first song, the comically distorted Spanish betrays a parodic if not malicious intent.

The most daring representation of a Black character from all the 1500s comes in another song. "How a Lady Begs a Black Slave to Woo Her through Song, and How the Slave Lets Himself Be Begged until Finally the Lady, Won over by his Charm, Offers Him Her Body" was published anonymously in Seville, in another broadside, in either 1520 (Lawrance 2005, 74, n. 14) or 1524 (Fra Molinero 1991, 441). Though authorship is impossible to prove, some critics suspect Reinosa as well, but the song is so different from the previous two that I share Russell's skepticism (1978, 386) about that attribution. The use of *bozal* is limited in this song, appearing only in a short refrain that seems to sample a previously circulating nursery rhyme (Covarrubias 2006, 206a). Otherwise, the slave—named Jorge, as in the lullaby—speaks quite elegantly, using witty, erotic language to respond to the bold advances of his white mistress, who repeatedly asks him to "sing" for her while her absent husband returns from the Holy Land. Jorge replies with a clever retort, "A captive can't sing" ("Coplas" 2005, line 18), alluding to his unfree status through a central conceit of courtly love: the lover's "captivity" (Lawrance 2005, 75). At the same time, in refusing his lady, he inverts the model of courtly love in which the male is typically rebuffed by his female beloved (Fra Molinero 1991, 442). Nonetheless, the slave begins to tease the lady with responses that signal a change of heart: "I was always a crossbowman and a miller in my homeland; thus do I shoot and grind so surely that I leave those I fancy in shock" ("Coplas" 2005, 53–56). The increasingly desperate lady promises Jorge "whatever you command" (60) if only he will "scratch this itch of mine" (105), finally pledging to "take the irons from your feet and the ring from your neck" (114–16). Jorge's change of heart is tracked by the refrain, which, on two occasions including the final line of the song (112, 177), switches from "don't wanna sing" to "wanna sing now."

It is easy to understand why "How a Lady Begs" was published anonymously: the song's representation of Jorge is astonishing for the early 1500s. In the first place, while the wife who cheats on her absent husband was a popular folksong motif (Lawrance 2005, 93, n. 77), the implication that a white noblewoman would do so with a Black slave is nothing short of scandalous. Second, the refined speech of the Black character challenges the growing use of the *bozal* dialect as a literary convention. Third, the lack of punishment Jorge receives forms a strong contrast to the Black Moor from the *Songs of Holy Mary*, for example, and to other examples that we shall soon see. At the same time, the song does not appear to argue for the humanity of Blacks but instead adroitly combines two stereotypes discussed by Lowe (2005, 29–35), the musical Black and the lascivious Black, to poke fun at the figure of the lustful mistress. Nonetheless, the refined Jorge holds a unique place in sixteenth-century Spanish literature, and though it is unclear how well known the song became, its Black character could potentially have served as a model for the exemplary protagonists of the Triad.

Moving to the genre of prose, we come to a novella from 1554, *Little Lazarus of Tormes* (*Lazarillo* in Spanish), which launched the rich literary tradition known as the picaresque, a satirical genre focused on antiheroic figures from the lowest rungs of society. The eponymous narrator of *Little Lazarus* is a young rogue whose poverty and misfortune have led him through the underbelly of early modern Spain. After recalling his biological father, who was banished for petty theft and eventually died in a military operation, Lazarus recounts a brief period when a Black stepfather enters his childhood. Given its brevity and significance, I translate the episode in its entirety:

> My widowed mother, finding herself with no husband and nowhere to turn, determined to test her luck with the good people, counting herself among them. She came to town, rented a tiny house, and started cooking for several university students. She also did laundry for some stable hands of the Knight Commander of Magdalena Church, so she began frequenting the stables.
>
> She and one of the dark-skinned men who tended the horses came into acquaintance. Sometimes he'd come to our house and leave in the morning. Other times he'd arrive at the door during the day, with the pretense of buying fresh eggs, and come inside. When he first started appearing, I was alarmed and scared of him, fixated on his color and ugly features. But once I realized his arrivals meant we ate better, I started liking him, for he always brought bread, strips of meat, and, in the winter, firewood that we warmed ourselves around.
>
> As the acquaintance and conversation developed, my mother ended up giving me a cute little black boy, who I bounced on my knee and helped to keep warm. And I remember how, when my poor stepfather played with him, the little one,

seeing that my mother and I were white and the man wasn't, would point and say: "Mama, it's the boogeyman!"

And my stepfather would laugh and say, "You little son of a whore!"

And though just a boy, I was struck by my little brother's words and said to myself: "So many people there must be in the world who flee from others because they can't see themselves!"

As luck would have it, our acquaintance with Zayd—for this was his name—reached the ears of the Knight Commander's steward. An inquiry was launched, which found that he'd been stealing half the barley they gave him for the horses; pretending that bran, firewood, currycombs, towels, blankets, and sheets had been lost; and, when all else failed, prying horseshoes off the animals. All of which he used to help my mother raise my little brother. Can we be surprised that a priest or friar raids the collection box or monastery to support his sweetheart or his who-knows-what, when love inspired a poor slave to the same?

They proved him guilty of all of it and more, for they interrogated me with threats and, being just a child, I revealed everything I knew out of fear, even the horseshoes that my mother had asked me to sell to a smith. They whipped and scalded my unfortunate stepfather while my mother's punishment, on top of the customary hundred lashes, was to be forbidden from entering the above-mentioned Knight Commander's house or from receiving the wounded Zayd into hers. (*Lazarillo* 1987, 15–20)

This episode is striking, in the first place, for its realistic portrayal of the cycles of poverty that ensnared the lowest ranks of Spanish society. Upon her husband's absence, Lazarus's mother is forced into odd jobs such as cooking, laundry, and "frequenting the stables": a possible euphemism for prostitution that would enable a literal reading of Zayd's "son of a whore" outburst. The mother's desperate circumstances not only usher Zayd into Lazarus's life but also lead to his exit, for it is in trying to ameliorate the family's living conditions that he is apprehended and so horrifically punished.[15] In the second place, then, the episode demands attention for the role played by its central character.

While one critic (Fra Molinero 1993) has rightly pointed to the anti-Black discourse of the "boogeyman" incident and the moral ambiguity of the lesson that Lazarus draws from it, the passage as a whole represents racial issues with a fair degree of complexity. On the one hand, certainly, it suggests that black skin is terrifying in and of itself, holding up as proof the "natural" reaction of an innocent toddler as well as Lazarus's remark

---

15. The Spanish verb I have translated as "scalded" (*pringaron*) literally means to pour hot grease (*el pringue*) onto skin flayed by a whip.

about his stepfather's "ugly features." On top of this, Lazarus's accusation of hypocrisy against those who "flee from others because they can't see themselves" would seem to suggest that if only Blacks were only honest, they would identify against their own color. On the other hand, it is precisely this Black man with the Arabic name who provides Lazarus with the only sense of security and belonging of his entire childhood.[16] His disappearance from the boy's life precipitates the core narrative for which the novella is best known: the narrator's meager, peripatetic existence at the mercy of one terrible master after another. His recollection of Zayd is thus tinged with fondness and sympathy for the "poor slave" whose crimes were inspired only by love for his family.

Zayd's miserable standing in Spanish society recalls the Black stable hand from *Count Lucanor* who had "nothing to lose" in exposing the duped king. The *explicit* parallels between the two characters—skin color and occupation—lend support to an *implicit* parallel: that the *Count Lucanor* figure is also a slave even though the word *esclavo* is absent from that story. Far from coincidental, this convergence of skin color, occupation, and servitude brings us to the second important Black character of early modern Spanish fiction.

The Jealous Extremaduran is among the most discussed prose works of Miguel de Cervantes (1547–1616) outside *Don Quixote*. Published in the *Exemplary Novels* in 1613 with a draft manuscript dating to 1604/1606 (Lambert 1980, 219), this work—more accurately classified as a novella than a novel—closely coincides with the composition window of the Triad. It tells the story of Felipo de Carrizales, a gentleman of the low nobility from an unnamed village in the Spanish region of Extremadura. In Cervantes's time, Extremadura was known for the large numbers of its inhabitants (among them the conquistadors Cortés and Pizarro) who found their way to the great melting pot of "indigents," "murderers," "swindlers," and "loose women": that is to say, America (Cervantes 2000, 99). The New World is the natural destination for Carrizales, who, having squandered his inheritance by age forty-eight, finds himself penniless as the story begins. He sails to Peru and rebuilds his fortune, returning to Spain twenty years later and settling in Seville, where he marries a young girl, Leonora, "who appeared to be thirteen or fourteen years old" (102). The bulk of the story revolves around Carrizales's obsessive jealousy of Leonora along with the absurd and ultimately unsuccessful measures he takes to protect his "honor."

A key figure in the story is Luis, an elderly Black man who is not only a slave but also a eunuch, presumably so he cannot violate the women of the household. Even with

---

16. The name *Zayd* (*Zaide* in Spanish), suggestive of Arabic origin, has an unclear etymology, though it was common among African slaves of the period (*Lazarillo* 1987, 18, n. 28). While no mention is made of Zayd's religious beliefs, it is interesting that Lazarus's biological father, in a rather ambiguous passage, is also associated with Islam (*Lazarillo* 1987, 14).

this precaution, Luis is never allowed into his master's house—not even male animals are permitted inside (106)—but lives instead in the barnlike vestibule that Carrizales has configured in the entryway. Enclosed in this space, which is locked to both the street and the main house with a master key, Luis spends his time tending a mule and sleeping in a hayloft. His one passion is music, which is soon discovered by a handsome young neighborhood slacker, Loaysa, who has fallen for Leonora. Loaysa claims a spot outside the street door to the vestibule, singing ballads and strumming "a grimy little guitar that was missing a few cords" while Luis, on the inside, "placing his ears to the crack between the entry doors, would hang on every note of the young punk's music, and he would have given an arm to be able to open the door and listen to him at leisure: such is the attraction that blacks have to music" (107–8). With the promise of teaching him to sing and play guitar, Loaysa convinces Luis to pick the lock to the street door, allowing him into the vestibule. From there, while Carrizales sleeps, he serenades Leonora through a revolving panel in the wall of the main house. He eventually convinces her to steal the master key and open the door to him, sealing Carrizales's dishonor.

There is no doubt that Cervantes's construction of his character traffics in several demeaning Black stereotypes of the period. Like the *Count Lucanor* stable hand and Zayd, for example, Luis is tasked with caring for beasts of burden. But what most defines him is his love of music, a common cliché discussed by Lowe (2005, 35–40) that will resurface in *Juan Latino*. It is this passion, in fact, that paves the way for the ruin of Carrizales, who dies of fright shortly after discovering Loaysa and Leonora locked in a dreamy embrace. Yet Cervantes's representation is a complex one that, even more than the narrative voice of *Little Lazarus*, demonstrates a degree of warmth and sympathy toward his Black character. It is telling, for example, that Luis—unlike Zayd—is never punished, either literally or poetically, for his actions. On the contrary, he is rewarded with manumission upon his master's death while blame for the tragedy—the exemplarity of the "exemplary" tale—is laid squarely on Carrizales's trust in "keys, revolving panels, and walls when human will remains free" as well as on Leonora's "green and tender age" (135).

Two additional Black characters in *The Jealous Extremaduran* are worthy of attention. Though slaves like Luis, they contrast with him in significant ways. In the first place, both are women who, unlike Luis, inhabit Carrizales's house and interact with Leonora along with four white slave women that Carrizales is also said to have purchased (104). Second, whereas Luis speaks a standard (though colloquial) dialect of Spanish, both slave women are described as recent arrivals in the country who speak in the broken *bozal* dialect (104). Guiomar, the only one of the two to receive a name, is said to be "Portuguese and not very eloquent" (128), and Cervantes does not miss the opportunity to poke fun at her verbal miscues in the few scenes in which she speaks

(123, 125, 128). But his tone is far from the malicious one he directs at the white governess, Marialonso, who uses Leonora as bait to try to seduce Loaysa herself. Ultimately, while he does not show the same degree of warmth toward Guiomar that he does toward Luis, he nonetheless has Carrizales reward her (and the other slave women) with the same prize at the end of story: freedom. Coming from an author who spent five years in a prison in Algiers and who wrote frequently about the significance of freedom, the humanity implied in this final gesture should not be overlooked.

The traces of sympathy toward Black characters that begin to emerge in the prose of the early modern period, as evidenced in *Little Lazarus* and *The Jealous Extremaduran*, are almost entirely lacking in the sixteenth-century theater. The fact that comedy was the main form of Spanish theater seems to have doomed Black characters to constant scorn and ridicule throughout the first century of the art form, with a few important exceptions.

Gil Vicente (c.1465–c.1536) was not one of the exceptions. Still considered Portugal's most famous playwright, he wrote in both Portuguese and Spanish and had a significant impact on the development of early Spanish theater. Because of his bilingualism, he was well placed to facilitate the importation into Spain of the *bozal* literary convention, and he also helped define Black characters as comic types (Fra Molinero 1995, 24). *The Forge of Love*, the earliest of his plays to feature a Black character, is representative of these trends.

This curious play was written for performance at the wedding of King John III of Portugal and his Spanish cousin Catherine of Austria (sister to Emperor Charles V), who were married in 1525. The language of the text reflects the international audience. While the title and stage directions are in Portuguese, 68 percent of the dialogue is spoken in Spanish by Greco-Roman gods (Venus and Cupid) and "planets" (Mercury, Jupiter, Saturn, and the Sun). Another 19 percent is in Portuguese, assigned to characters representing different segments of society. The remaining 13 percent corresponds to a Black slave, who is described as speaking "the language of his homeland" (Vicente 1912, 160), meaning the *bozal* dialect. The central conceit seems to be that the love between John and Catherine has the power to dignify the Portuguese nation. To enable this process, Cupid has created a great forge that people may enter to have their imperfections melted down and refined by smiths, who are represented by the four planets. After flirting with Venus, "queen of music" (156), the Black slave, who calls himself Furunando, is the first to arrive at the forge. When Mercury asks how he wishes to be transformed, he replies, in *bozal* Spanish: "Make me white, I beg you" (164). He enters the forge and soon reappears as "a very elegant white gentleman" (166), but he discovers that his *bozal* dialect has not undergone a corresponding transformation: "If I speak like a black man, what good does it do me to be white?" (166).¹⁷ Despairing that he will be spurned by Black and white women alike, he asked to be transformed back into his original state. At this point Furunando disappears from the story, and a host of other characters pass through the forge, each requesting a different "improvement."

In his other plays that feature Black characters, Vicente continues the degrading representation begun with Furunando, establishing a powerful precedent even for authors who, like Diego Sánchez de Badajoz, may have wished to return to the egalitarian message of medieval theology explored above (see §Theology). A parish priest who died in the mid-1500s, Sánchez de Badajoz left twenty-eight short dramatic works of a mostly religious or allegorical nature, written between 1525 and 1547 (Pérez Priego 1985, 19–20). At least five of them feature Black characters (presumably slaves, though their status is never specified), making Sánchez de Badajoz among the most important sources of such characters in early Spanish theater. Significantly, while Black characters are represented as silly and quarrelsome in three religious pieces, the proposition that all souls are equal before God becomes a consistent theme in these works, reiterated in one instance by Saint Paul himself:

> THEOLOGIAN (*Theological Farce*). O sacred and divine Word, O eternal mysteries, even in *bozal* blacks do you reveal your path. (Sánchez de Badajoz 1968, 98, lines 769–72)

*

> KNIGHT (*Farce of Fortune*). Embrace, brothers. Since God is love, let not the brotherhood between his Christian children be severed: for his peerless embrace is open to all. (390, lines 233–38)

*

> SAINT PAUL (*Farce of Moses*). Peace, brothers! For God wishes brotherhood for everyone: blacks, whites, poor, rich, healthy, and handicapped. (419, lines 265–68)

---

17. While I render *bozal* into a distinctly different idiom in the speech of Antón in *The Brave Black Soldier* (see the Translator's Note for details), I refrain from doing so in translating other sources in my introductory materials; instead I simply note the use of dialect wherever it comes into play. Furunando's very name, however, cannot but reflect the dialect as it appears intended as a comic distortion of *Fernando*.

Yet in all three cases, the egalitarian message is undermined by not only the Black characters' petty behavior but also the distorted dialect in which they speak, prompting the theologian to "laughter for an entire week" (98, lines 761–62).

In the only two of Sánchez de Badajoz's pieces that are considered "entirely secular" (Wiltrout 1987, 155), there is an interesting turn in the author's representation of Black characters. While the *bozal* dialect is still employed to comic effect and the egalitarian message of the religious pieces is no longer explicitly stated, the characters seem crafted to demonstrate that white skin is not inherently superior to black. In the *Farce of the Innkeeper*, a Black woman vocally objects, in *bozal*, when her white mistress (the innkeeper of the title) steals from an impoverished guest: "May the Devil take you if you steal from this poor man!" (Sánchez de Badajoz 1968, 503, lines 259–60). At the end of the work, the Devil indeed appears and drags the unscrupulous innkeeper down to Hell, sparing the Black woman and prompting another character to comment: "The Black woman shows good judgment" (504, line 313). In the *Farce of the Sorceress*, an unnamed white suitor, pushed to desperation by unrequited love (a favorite plot device of the period), contemplates committing the mortal sin of suicide. As he pulls out his knife, a Black woman appears and, speaking in *bozal*, attempts to stop him: "Jesus, Jesus, I am astonished! Why do you cut your throat, lovely one? Oust the evil spirit and abandon the knife" (486–87, lines 73–76). The stage directions indicate that she then "draws her face to his with sweet flatteries" (487), but the suitor's reaction leaves little room for interpretation: "You black whore! You would dare to kiss me? [. . .] You have revealed your true nature, O curse of Muhammad!" (487, lines 84, 91–92). Thus insulted, the Black woman exits and does not return. Like the *Farce of the Innkeeper*, the play ends with the appearance of the Devil, in this case summoned by the titular sorceress to validate a love spell she has cast on the suitor's lady.

When read carefully, Sánchez de Badajoz's short plays provide an important antidote to the anti-Black virulence of an author like Vicente. His religious pieces offer a doctrinal basis for the principle of equality, while the secular counterparts show the manifestations of that doctrine, dramatizing white characters who fall into corruption and sin even as Black characters attempt to warn or save them. Several characteristics of the plays, however, blunt the impact of the positive message. First is the use of the *bozal* dialect, which portrays those who speak it in a ridiculous light. In Sánchez de Badajoz's defense, his Black characters are not the only ones to speak a substandard form of Spanish. His white shepherds, for example, speak a rustic dialect known as *sayagüés*, which was equally well known in the literature of the period. Nevertheless, the *bozal* dialect probably obscured the content of the Black characters' dialogue for many audience members, who would have interpreted it mainly for its comic value.

The second mitigating circumstance is genre. Sánchez de Badajoz applies the label *farce* (*farsa*) to twenty-seven of his twenty-eight dramatic works. While this term, along with *act* (*auto*) and *eclogue* (*égloga*), was employed rather loosely in the 1500s, sometimes with the neutral meaning of "skit" or "play," it could also conform to our modern notion of a comic or satirical sketch. In the latter sense, the actions of Black women who attempt to counsel or save white characters could easily be interpreted as farcical. In the *Farce of the Sorceress*, for example, the attempt by a Black woman—and a Muslim, at least according to the suitor's outburst—to save a white man from losing his soul runs counter to the primary symbolic and iconographic trends of the period, which, as seen in the *Songs of Holy Mary* (TSW, Figs. 7–8), associate blackness with evil, sin, and the Devil.[18] Additionally, the violation of interracial taboos implied in the suitor's accusation that the woman has tried to kiss him points to the type of comic, topsy-turvy world that was a favorite theme of early modern satirists such as Rabelais (Bakhtin 1984). Sánchez de Badajoz may have intentionally mobilized this world, along with the *bozal* dialect, to soften through comedy the rather radical implications of his egalitarian message.

While Sánchez de Badajoz's pairing of a white man with a Black woman may have drawn laughs, Juan Pastor (of whom almost nothing is known), writing around the same time, appears to do the reverse in his *Farce of Lucretia: Tragedy of the Chaste Lucretia*. As the incongruous title indicates, this play has more of a tragic tone than the *Farce of the Sorceress*, though it does not avoid attempts at humor. Its subject, recounted in ancient authors such as Livy and Dionysius of Halicarnassus, comes from Roman legend: the chaste wife Lucretia, coerced into sexual submission by Tarquin, son of King Tarquinius Superbus, commits suicide out of shame, provoking a popular revolt that leads the Romans to depose the king and abolish the monarchy in favor of a republic (Livy 1960, 98–101; Dionysius 1961, 475–527). Pastor follows the sources fairly closely, with one important substitution. In the ancient authors, Tarquin, who is cousin to Lucretia's husband, coerces her with a threat: if she refuses him, he will kill her along with one of her male slaves and report that he found them together and murdered them to avenge his cousin's honor. Pastor adds a twist to Tarquin's threat: "And if [you refuse me], know that I intend to kill you right here and now, along with this black slave, and lay you down in that bed together. And then I'll make it known that I found you with him and killed you both immediately to avenge the offense to my relative" (Pastor 1912, lines 556–65).[19]

---

18. An additional example of the association between blackness and the Devil comes in an anonymous sixteenth-century mystery play on the figure of Job, in which the Devil appears with Africanized features. See the analysis in Ndiaye (2022, 64–65).
19. I use Bonilla y San Martín's transcription (Pastor 1912) for the line numbers of Pastor's text, but I base my translation off the facsimile edition (Pastor 1914).

It is interesting to ponder why Pastor, contrary to ancient sources, makes his slave a Black man: an innovation that the play's modern editor believes "does not accredit Juan Pastor's creativity" (Bonilla y San Martín 1912, 6). One answer may come from contrasting the work's apparently tragic intent, indicated in the title, to that of the *Farce of the Sorceress*. For white audience members of the period, the suggestion of a Black man lying with a white noblewoman—even when explicitly framed as a lie, in the form of the rumor that Tarquin threatens to spread—may well have been seen as inherently tragic. Conversely, Sánchez de Badajoz's pairing of a white man with a Black woman may have proved less threatening and more conducive to comedy. As in the case of *The Exploits of Esplandián*, it becomes difficult to disentangle skin color and gender in these short plays.

This point becomes even more apparent when Pastor's Lucretia, following the sources, gives in to Tarquin's demands. As the rape takes place offstage, the slave stands guard and pronounces an unsettling soliloquy in the *bozal* dialect: "I stand guard here until master exits, and a black slave never flees, though I'd like to. Wait, I hear her scream" (594–98). The soliloquy hints, whether intentionally or not, at a parallel that might prove awkward for white audiences of the period: both the slave and Lucretia are being forced to do something against their will. Does the explicit parallel with the much-admired Lucretia spark a glimmer of sympathy for the slave's predicament? If so, it is surely undermined by the character's broken Spanish, verging on the unintelligible and sprinkled with crude references. Furthermore, once the rape is completed, the slave exits with Tarquin and does not reappear, so whatever pangs of conscience he may have inspired are quickly buried. Nevertheless, it seems clear that Pastor does not engage in the degree of ridicule to which Vicente subjects Furunando.

Like Sánchez de Badajoz and Pastor, Feliciano de Silva (1491–1554) refrains from a wholesale adoption of Vicente's model of Black characters. Silva's *Second Celestina* (1534), the most successful of the sequels to Fernando de Rojas's enormously popular *Celestina* (1499), was not intended for the stage, but its exclusively dialogic format and unique Black characters argue for its inclusion in this survey. Amid the numerous erotic intrigues of the noble main characters, two Black Muslim servants—the male Zambran and his female love interest Boruca—play minor roles, appearing in scenes 2 and 6 of the sprawling forty-scene work. While they speak in a *bozal*-like dialect, their language is, according to one critic, "more evocative than parodic," registering authentic Arabic words and phonological features characteristic of Hispano-Muslims (Santos Morillo 2020, 44). Zambran swears that he loves Boruca "more than all other women" (Silva 1874, 58) while she accuses him of "whoring around" with his master's prostitute (58), but the tone is one of playful banter that never reaches the invective of Reinosa's characters in "Song to Black Men and Women." Moreover, Zambran is represented as loyal to his mistress (22) as well as astute, and he quickly sees through the flattery of another servant who tries to dupe him (61). Silva thus challenges two common stereotypes—disloyal servants and simpleminded Blacks—in the character of Zambran. His depiction is perhaps all the more surprising given that he is not only Black but Muslim and openly invokes Muhammad and Allah.

The mid-century works of Sánchez de Badajoz, Pastor, and Silva stand in the shadow of the most important Spanish dramatist of the pre-*comedia* period: Lope de Rueda (c. 1510–1565). First as an actor and then as an author, Rueda was active from the late 1530s until around the time of his death (González Ollé and Tusón 1992, 9–10). Cervantes himself, who was born in 1547, claims to have attended performances of Rueda's plays as a boy, offering an intriguing description:

> In the time of this distinguished Spaniard, [. . .] plays were just dialogues or eclogues between two or three shepherds and maybe a shepherdess. They spiced them up and stretched them out with a few interludes: the black woman, the pimp, the clown, and the Basque were four roles, among many others, that Lope de Rueda himself did with the greatest distinction and naturalness imaginable. (Cervantes 1989, 91–92)

If Black women figured as prominently among the stock characters of Lope de Rueda's theater as Cervantes suggests, it would show the extent to which sub-Saharan Africans had entered mainstream Spanish consciousness. It is, furthermore, both revealing and plausible that they would have shared this position with pimps, clowns, and Basques: all frequent objects of ridicule and thus ideal comic characters. Basques, for example, were often mocked for their broken Spanish in the same way as speakers of the *bozal* dialect. And if Rueda indeed "blackfaced and cross-dressed in his own theater company" (Jones 2019, 121), as the passage seems to suggest toward the end (though the language is ambiguous), it may have added another layer of humor to the performance.[20]

Cervantes's memory seems to be vindicated by the historical record. Black women are found in Lope de Rueda's urban comedies *Eufemia* and *The Deceived* as well as his pastoral plays *Timbria* and *Gila*. In all four cases, the scenes with the Black women are largely superfluous to the plots of the plays in which they are inserted. Rueda's sixteenth-century editor, in fact, identifies the relevant scene from *Eufemia* as one of

---

20. Given that female roles were usually played by women on the Spanish stage, a violation of that norm, especially in a comedy, is likely to have been interpreted as humorous. And though blackface seems to have been routine (Beusterien 2006a, 102–4; Jones 2019, 29–47), when combined with cross-dressing in the same character, it may have added to the madcap atmosphere. The ambiguity comes from the word "did" (*hacía*) in the last sentence: Does Cervantes mean that Lope de Rueda *performed* the roles or simply *wrote* them?

a group of interludes "that can be lifted from the present comedies and dialogues and placed in other works" (Rueda 1567, pt. 3, fol. 55r). It is plausible that all four scenes could have been inserted into other plays to "spice them up" or "stretch them out," as Cervantes appears to have grasped.

Rueda's construction of Black characters owes much to Vicente, with none of the countercurrents found in Sánchez de Badajoz, Pastor, or Silva. Caricatures at best, his Black women share several characteristics meant to provoke humor. In *Eufemia* and *The Deceived* they harbor aristocratic pretensions, while in *Timbria* and *Gila* they are insufferably vain. All four speak in the *bozal* dialect, which is nearly impossible to understand on several occasions. Likewise, they all prompt condescension or outright verbal abuse from other characters, often involving animal-related insults. Despite the distastefulness, Rueda's importance in this period justifies a close look at one example.

In scene 7 of *Eufemia*, the Black slave Eulalla responds to the advances of the white Polo, who is servant to one of the main characters. Their courtship is among the few elements that tie the scene to the rest of the play, through an implicit comparison with the love interests of the noble characters. While this type of parallel romantic structure is typical of early modern comedy, Rueda pushes it to a parodic extreme. The sketch begins in the street, with Polo approaching Eulalla's window as she is heard singing a ballad in the *bozal* dialect: "Gil González / pays a visit from town. / I don't know, mothers, / if I should open to him. / Gil González / knocks at the tower door. / Open your voice to him, / daughter Leonor, / for thus do the horses / bespatter the falcons. / I don't know, mothers, / if I should open to him" (Rueda 2001, 117–18). All the ideals of chivalric romance are here: the knight in shining armor; the reticent damsel in the tower; the role of poetry and song ("Open your voice to him"); the animals most emblematic of nobility (horses and falcons). But in Rueda's version the elements are deformed into a scene that would have functioned, for spectators of the period, as a madcap inversion of courtly love. This interpretation is invited by the poem's opening verses, which sample a previously circulating popular lyric: "Gil González Dávila pays a visit: / I don't know, mother, if I should open to him" (Frenk 1987, 90). In Eulalla's version, the surname "Dávila" is transformed into "de la villa" (from town) and the singular "mother" becomes plural, thus distorting the well-known lyric in ways that were likely to provoke hilarity. The imagery is also crudely sexual, with the voice that is commanded to "open" functioning as a metonymy for the mouth and the horses that "bespatter" the falcons suggesting insemination.

The historical Gil González Dávila was the first Spanish explorer to enter the region of modern-day Costa Rica and Nicaragua (Fowler 1985, 43), reportedly baptizing more than thirty thousand Indians (Meyer 1972, 135). Eulalla's opening song thus idealizes the courtship of a conquistador well known enough to appear in popular lyric, in an allusion whose full irony will become clear only at the end of the scene. In the meantime, Polo arrives and presses his courtship of the "lady," who rejects his advances with the requisite fussiness. The parody reaches an extreme as Eulalla reveals that she bleaches her hair blond to look like "other women" (Rueda 2001, 118–19), claims to have aristocratic lineage that entitles her to marry a nobleman (119), and demands that Polo buy her a parrot and a monkey to prove his fidelity (120). Finally, in an aside, Polo reveals his true intentions toward Eulalla: "What an insufferable dog! I'm planning to sell her at the next village I come to, claiming she's my slave, and here she is playing princess. I'm surprised she didn't ask me for a canopy and a comfy chair! I haven't a penny to my name, yet she thinks I can pull one from thin air and buy her a parrot and a monkey" (121). Not surprisingly, an interlude that seems constructed to turn the Black character into the butt of one joke after another concludes by suggesting that she will be sold into slavery: presumably a hilarious resolution for spectators of the period and perhaps an allusion to the actions of conquistadors like González Dávila in the New World.[21]

As Rueda's Eulalla is perfectly representative of his Black women characters, it is unnecessary to examine the others in detail; nevertheless, the context of this survey demands a brief mention of the character Sofía from his play *Gila*. In only the second interracial marriage registered thus far, Sofía is the wife of an unnamed white man, a point that clearly surprises the white character Tenoria: "Since he's white and you're a bit dark, you made me suspect he wasn't your husband" (Rueda 2006, 172). Sofía reveals that her husband is a public torturer and executioner (176), considered to be "always a disgraceful profession" (Covarrubias 2006, 1522a). The thinly disguised implication is that only a man who occupies such a shameful position would marry a Black woman, who is mocked for believing that she was desired for her beauty (Rueda 2006, 173). Like Queen Calafia and Prince Talanque in *The Exploits of Esplandián*, Sofía and her husband are never represented together, which would perhaps have represented an even bigger taboo in the visual medium of theater than in Rodríguez de Montalvo's novel. And though they are not noble like Calafia and Talanque but mere commoners, given

---

21. González Dávila, however, was a somewhat atypical conquistador who has been praised for his humane treatment of the Indians (Fowler 1985, 43). Rosenbaum (2016) claims, without documentation, that he owned two hundred Indian slaves. I must dissent from Jones's reading of this scene, in which he argues that Eulalla's desire for blond hair is not the product of an anti-Black trope but evidence of a powerful "diva" who fashions her own image in a supposed parallel to the contemporary singer Beyoncé (Jones 2019, 125–47). He questions the "canonical interpretation" (149) of Polo as a slave trader, yet it is no "interpretation" but Rueda's text itself, in the passage cited above—which Jones omits from his reading—that establishes this point. Jones offers a similar reading of Guiomar from *The Deceived* (151–58), with which I also disagree. My interpretations are more in line with those of Hermenegildo (2001, 33–34, 45–46) and Ndiaye (2022, 76).

the scarcity of interracial marriages in Spanish literature and the fame of this particular play, it cannot be discounted as a precedent for the Triad authors.[22]

To summarize, the representation of Blacks in the first hundred years of early modern Spanish literature includes a daring depiction in song (the anonymous "How a Lady Begs"), a pair of sympathetic portrayals in prose (*Little Lazarus* and Cervantes's *The Jealous Extremaduran*), and a wide range of characterizations in theater, from the egalitarian message of Sánchez de Badajoz to the degrading representations of Gil Vicente and Lope de Rueda. Theater was, by far, the most prolific genre in the production of Black characters, and despite the variety of depictions, the enormous success and popularity of Vicente and Rueda led to the dominance of their demeaning model, establishing an unfortunate norm across much of the 1500s.

Three Plays Attributed to Lope de Vega

This brings us to the beginning of the 1600s—the threshold of the Triad—and to three plays often attributed to the second great Lope of Spanish theater. As a rhetorical convenience, I assume that the plays—(1) *The Black Saint Rosambuco of the City of Palermo*, (2) *The Marvel of Ethiopia*, and (3) and *Black Slave to the Greatest Master: Antiobo of Sardinia*—are indeed Lope de Vega's, but it is important to note that questions exist about their authorship as well chronology.[23] What matters most is that the protagonists

---

22. The work was apparently well-known enough in the period to be cited directly by Lope de Vega, possibly from memory (Cátedra 2006, 19–20). Subsequently considered lost for many years, it was recovered and published in 2006, in the edition from which I have cited.

23. *The Black Saint* was published in 1612 (Vega García-Luengos 2008, 22) and *The Marvel of Ethiopia* in 1645 (Beusterien 2005, 9), while *Black Slave to the Greatest Master* exists in a single undated manuscript whose handwriting has been traced to the early 1600s (Restori 1891, 28). The most widely accepted chronology suggests that *The Black Saint* was authored before 1607 (Morley and Bruerton 1968, 393) and *Black Slave to the Greatest Master* between 1599 and 1603 (265). The same study declines to offer a date of composition for *The Marvel of Ethiopia* and also casts doubt on its authorship (540). In the introduction to his edition of the latter play, John Beusterien (2005, 9) indicates that it was originally written "probably in 1600," though he provides no evidence for such a specific claim. Regarding authorship, the most likely scenario, maintained by both Menéndez Pelayo (1894, lxix–lxx) and Beusterien (2005, 11), is that the text we possess today of *The Marvel of Ethiopia* is a heavily retouched version of a Lope de Vega original that has since been lost. While doubts have also been cast on the authorship of *Black Slave to the Greatest Master*, critical opinion is now unanimous in attributing this work to Vega (Weber de Kurlat 1970, 344; Fradejas Lebrero 1984, xviii). Meanwhile, a very recent study using digital analysis has questioned the authorship of *The Black Saint* (Vega García-Luengos 2021, 100–101). For the purposes of tracing the evolution of Black characters and establishing possible influences on the Triad, chronology is much more important than authorship. Crucially, the balance of critical opinion dates all three plays to before 1607, meaning that they would have been available as models to the Triad authors. For the convoluted transmission history of these plays, which involves a web of titles, authors, and cheap imitations including Vélez de Guevara's own *Black Slave to the Seraphim* (c. 1643, a revision of Lope de Vega's *The Black Saint* that gets attributed to Mira de Amescua as *Black Slave to the Greatest Master*), see the discussions in Vega García-Luengos (2008, 22–23), González Martínez (2012), and Belloni (2019, 80).

of these three plays represent a quantum leap in the development of Black characters. While not completely avoiding the insulting epithets and stereotypes of previous authors, Vega's representations are unprecedented in several ways. First, in contrast to the Black characters of the sixteenth-century theater, who are shuffled about the stage with a narrow and primarily comedic intent, Vega's characters are true protagonists: integral to the plot, psychologically complex, and, most importantly, dignified in bearing and language. While a few secondary Black characters in *The Black Saint* and *Black Slave to the Greatest Master* speak in the *bozal* dialect, the protagonists of all three plays speak in an elegant classical Spanish indistinguishable from that of their noble white counterparts, and there is no use of *bozal* at all in *The Marvel of Ethiopia*. Finally, all three protagonists are saints (at least two of them based on historical figures), launching what one critic (Profeti 2005, 233) has identified as a subcategory—the Black saint play—within the well-known genre of Spanish hagiographic drama. In assigning holy status to Black characters, Lope de Vega goes much further than Sánchez de Badajoz's timid egalitarianism, completely repudiating the models of Vicente and Rueda that had dominated sixteenth-century theater.

Because the chronology of the plays has given rise to conflicting critical opinions, I discuss them in an order that reflects my assessment of their innovations in Black characters and themes, from least to most advanced. First in this reckoning, *The Black Saint Rosambuco of the City of Palermo* is loosely based on the life of Saint Benedict the Black, who was born to enslaved African parents near Messina, Sicily, in 1526 and freed at an early age. Insulted on account of his color, he joined a group of Franciscan hermits as a young man and later became a lay brother at a friary in Palermo, where he achieved the post of guardian. Though not canonized until 1807, he acquired considerable fame during his lifetime as a religious counselor and healer of the sick (Attwater 1995, 57–58; Fracchia 2019, 70–76, offers an iconographic analysis). It may have been with his death in 1589 that he came to the attention of Lope de Vega, who transforms him into the awkwardly named Rosambuco, a Turkish slave reputedly descended from Ethiopian royalty. After proving his valor, Rosambuco is entrusted with command of a Turkish galley and captured by Christians in a naval battle off the coast of Sicily. He becomes a slave to the Palermo town constable, who promptly orders him to execute his wife, Laura, for a minor indiscretion. When an icon of Saint Benedict performs a miracle that saves Laura's life, Rosambuco is inspired to abandon Islam for Christianity. He adopts the name Benedict (Benito) and joins a Franciscan monastery where he cures the sick, exorcises a demon, and raises the dead, dying at the end of the play amid an aura of saintliness.

Notwithstanding Menéndez Pelayo's judgment of this play (1894, ci) as a "barbaric debacle, unworthy of such a great poet," the representation of Black characters and the ensuing racial dynamics deserve more attention than they have received.[24] Rosambuco is a complex figure, represented sympathetically from the beginning despite his devotion to Islam, "the law that I adopted in my tender years, [which] I ever intend to honor" (Vega Carpio 1965, 145b). Despite the religious difference, he experiences great distress when he is ordered to kill his white Christian mistress, recalling the Black slave from the *Farce of Lucretia* who was forced to stand guard during the rape scene: "Allah knows, my lady, the suffering and anguish with which I do this; but I am a slave, and bound to obey" (148a). It is noteworthy that Vega's Black male character threatens a white woman only as a result of the flawed judgment of the constable, who represents the legal and moral heart of Spanish society. Is the play pointing a finger at the latter? It is, nonetheless, a miraculous intervention by Saint Benedict that derails the constable's barbaric judgment and, in a clever twist, brings about Rosambuco's conversion. If Vega's message is that white society is flawed, he seems to suggest that its religion is beyond reproach.

An important secondary character in *The Black Saint* is Laura's Black female slave, Lucrecia, fashioned from the stereotype of the lascivious Black (see §Popular Opinion) and ironically named after the same chaste Roman matron who inspired Pastor's *Farce of Lucretia*. Vega's Lucrecia lusts after Rosambuco and openly flirts with him, providing an important test of the budding saint's ability to resist temptation: "It is torture listening to you," he tells her, adding that "I must depart, for I give a poor account of myself" (146a). In a later scene, she approaches him in his sleep and tries to kiss him, recalling the young Black woman from Sánchez de Badajoz's *Farce of the Sorceress*, but the stage directions indicate that "from beneath the stage a serpent's head emerges with a firecracker in its mouth, or the firecracker alone may be used, and the black girl is stunned and retreats in terror" (Vega Carpio 1965, 153b). Lucrecia also flirts with a minor character named Ribera, described as a "lecherous old [white] man" and, in what may be the first physical display of interracial affection in Spanish drama, locks herself in a passionate embrace with him onstage (146b). While Sánchez de Badajoz, in the scene just recalled, comes close to representing an interracial embrace, his suitor violently rejects the Black girl's advances. The boldness of Vega's scene should thus not be underestimated. Even the interracial *marriages* in Rodríguez de Montalvo's *The Exploits of Esplandián* and Lope de Rueda's *Gila* are never directly represented. But Vega does not allow his lustful couple's audacity to stand. When the constable walks in on the pair, he has Rosambuco tie them up, back-to-back, to be punished, though they are eventually set free with a warning. Thus Rosambuco, in an indication of his moral authority, serves

---

24. Apart from ch. 4 of Fra Molinero's seminal study (1995) and a pair of unpublished dissertations (Panford 1993; García Otero 2013), the play has been ignored by critics.

as the punisher of transgressive women: the constable's wife, who has the temerity to speak to another man in the street, and her Black slave, who embraces one onstage.

Unlike Rosambuco, Lucrecia speaks in the *bozal* dialect, setting up an opposition of Black characters that will be repeated in the Triad's *The Brave Black Soldier*. And not only Lucrecia. When the Sicilian viceroy's daughter becomes possessed and Rosambuco arrives to perform the exorcism, she mocks him by speaking to him in *bozal*. "She speaks Latin, Black, Basque, and all tongues," one of the witnesses explains (168a). The Devil also hurls a series of vile racial epithets at the protagonist, as does Pedrisco, a lay brother who becomes jealous when Rosambuco is elected guardian of the Franciscans. As objectionable as they are, it is significant that these insults are placed in the mouths of the play's antagonists, including the Devil himself, in contrast to the sixteenth-century theater, where such verbal abuse is typically spoken by main characters with impunity. Additionally, Rosambuco eventually triumphs over both the Devil and Pedrisco, though only after suffering physical abuse from the latter. Apparently weakened from the encounter, he dies in the act of resuscitating the constable, who has perished in a fire.

While Lope de Vega goes to great lengths in *The Black Saint* to show that a Black African and convert from Islam can become not only a legitimate member of the Christian community but an authentic saint, he does so by validating an anti-Black trope at the heart of medieval and early modern Christianity. "My honor do I now solicit," Rosambuco explains in a monologue, "and seek to become Christian. In this law I now rejoice, with white soul and black body, all on account of you, Benedict" (150b). A few scenes later, an angelic choir confirms the sentiment: "A black slave sends roses to God, whom he understands is white [. . .]. For though you [Rosambuco] are black, there will come a day when you are lovely, beautiful, and white" (152b). It is immediately after this confirmation of the Black man's white soul that he is protected from Lucrecia's attempt to kiss him, in a scene that effectively isolates him from his own race.

The notion that a beautiful white soul can exist in a body considered deformed by blackness, that is, that Black people can be good and noble *despite* their appearance, is not unique to *The Black Saint*. On the contrary, it is a concept that lingers over the entire early modern period and that will form the central conceit of Vélez de Guevara's *Virtues Overcome Appearances*. Nevertheless, its indulgence by Lope de Vega in this play together with the plethora of vile racial insults and liberal use of the demeaning *bozal* dialect lead me to rank *The Black Saint* last in the author's treatment of Black characters. But it is far from an easy judgment, as the next play shows.

The Marvel of Ethiopia finds inspiration in a historical figure from early Christianity. Saint Moses the Black (c. 330–c. 405) was an Ethiopian servant who turned to a life of crime after dismissal from his master's household; repenting of his ways, he converted to Christianity and joined a group of monks in the Desert of Sketis (Attwater 1995,

257). In Vega's play, the Black protagonist becomes a slave when the Egyptian general Alejandro conquers Ethiopia and brings him back home as a war trophy. Calling himself Filipo, the slave falls in love with Alejandro's (white) lover Teodora and eventually tricks her into running away with him to the countryside, where they both join a band of robbers. Pressed to offer her hand to Filipo in marriage, Teodora literally cuts it off and delivers it to him in protest. Stunned by her self-mutilation, Filipo repents and joins an anchorite community, gradually acquiring an air of saintliness. He is martyred and dies in the final scene, when his salvation is confirmed and his true name is revealed to be Moses.

At the center of this play is the racial dynamic between Teodora and Filipo, which the latter perfectly encapsulates in a rhetorical question: "Yet what black slave ever loved a highborn subject who wasn't black?" (Vega Carpio 2005, lines 226–27). Filipo, in literally embodying the answer to that question, provokes twin episodes of violence that anchor act 3 of the play. First, a white noblewoman prefers to cut off her hand rather than promise it in marriage to a Black "monster" (2153). As if that message were not clear enough, the Devil then appears to shoot Filipo through the chest with an arrow, onstage, repeatedly claiming that he is doing God's work: "God allows me, for secrets only he knows, to shoot this arrow through you" (2555–58); "God frees my hands against you" (2569–70); "God orders it so" (2579). These two moments—one that destroys the object of Filipo's desire and another that annihilates the desirer himself—seem intended to atone for the audacity of the desire and to restore the order it disrupted. The purifying violence—blood as a cleansing agent is a frequent metaphor in the period—both paves the way for Filipo's sainthood and enables Teodora's reconciliation with her father (whom she had disobeyed in running away with Filipo). An angel confirms the resolution in a closing speech:

> *[Addressing the other characters.]* You who witness this moment and this terrible spectacle the Devil created with Moses, be neither frightened nor astonished. For God works in mysterious ways and wishes to resurrect this Black man as a wonder to the world, this white swan that sang so sweetly at its end. *[Addressing the Devil.]* You, horrible monster, will no longer torment and persecute him. He who was the wonder of Egypt, a second Moses they say, is now an anchorite martyr in a wondrous place. *[Addressing Teodora's father.]* And you, Leopoldo, as Teodora already walks the path of sacred religion, will allow her to wear the blessed habit so that her life may serve as an example for many to follow. (2641–62)

It is significant that the word *monster*, which Teodora had used to refer to Filipo, is now reserved for the Devil. Though the stage directions do not indicate the Devil's skin color, noting only that he is dressed as a gallant, audience members would have been familiar with medieval and early modern iconography that represented the Devil as a Black man (as in TSW, Fig. 8). Filipo, by contrast, is compared to a swan, confirming a description he gives of himself upon arriving at the hermitage: "A black man who desires a pure white soul; a sad and dark night that seeks the light; he who wished to become eternal in the marble of Lysippus" (2368–73). The conceit of the Black man with the white soul, already noted in *The Black Saint*, is validated in *The Marvel of Ethiopia* in a message that seems clear: the Devil, in killing Filipo, has liberated his white soul and usurped his "monstrous" qualities, perhaps even including his skin color.

While the optics of a Black man shot down onstage by the Devil only to become white are troubling in the extreme, the language of this play represents an advance with respect to *The Black Saint*. There is no use of the *bozal* dialect at all, no mocking of Black speech, no Black servant who, like Lucrecia, exists essentially to cast the main character's language (and conduct) in better light. The long list of racial slurs in *The Black Saint*, pronounced by both the lay brother Pedrisco and the Devil (speaking through the mouth of the viceroy's daughter) is mostly absent from *The Marvel of Ethiopia*. The one exception is the word *monster*, which is spoken twice by Teodora in reference to Filipo (1008, 2153) before the angel uses it as an insult against the Devil (2650). Yet even this word, as I will explain in my discussion of *Virtues Overcome Appearances*, indicates surprise as much as contempt and thus does not channel the same degree of malice as the epithets used in *The Black Saint*.

A final advance comes in the representation of Islam. In *The Black Saint*, Rosambuco is explicitly described as a devout Muslim, and when he converts to Christianity, he identifies strongly against "the perverse Quran" and "the lying Muhammad" (Vega Carpio 1965, 150b). In *The Marvel of Ethiopia*, Filipo's religion prior to his conversion is never specified, though Islam is suggested when the bandits call him a "new sultan" (Vega Carpio 2005, 1948). The play's fanciful setting, vaguely reminiscent of late-Roman Egypt, may have kept the author from going further than that in referencing Islam. At any rate, when Filipo converts, there are no imprecations against any religion; the focus instead is on Teodora's severed hand as a "celestial instrument" (2340) that points him to truth. The restraint is notable, for Christian authors of the period rarely miss the opportunity to expose other religions as fraudulent. The next play, however, follows *The Marvel of Ethiopia* in marking a pleasant exception to this tendency.

For many years following its discovery in the late 1800s (Restori 1891), *Black Slave to the Greatest Master: Antiobo of Sardinia* was thought to lack any historical basis, for there is no record of any saint with such a name. More recently, it has been suggested (Fradejas Lebrero 2008, 98; Belloni 2019, 83–85) that the play could be based on the life of the obscure Antiochus of Sulci, who was martyred in the early Christian era according to a hagiography published in Lope de Vega's lifetime by Dimas Serpi (Serpi 1600, fols. 8v–26r). While there are some interesting parallels to support this theory, the most important one is missing: Antiochus is not described as Black in Serpi's account, despite Belloni's insistence to the contrary. Ultimately, it is probably unknowable what sources Vega used for this intriguing play.

Set in the contemporary period (another important detail that diverges from the story of Antiochus of Sulci), the play centers on the Muslim prince Antiobo, son of a white Moorish king and a Black Libyan princess. Despite his parentage, the protagonist is consistently described as Black rather than of mixed race. Harboring unexplained affinities toward Christians, he discovers that he was secretly baptized as a child by his nurse. When his father gives him command of a fleet sent to assist in the Ottoman invasion of Sardinia, Antiobo turns on the Turks and rallies the Christians to victory. Announcing his intent to devote himself to the Virgin and become a hermit on Sardinia, he performs miracles and overcomes temptation from the Devil. Even after his death, his body continues to perform miracles and attract pilgrims.

The representation of skin color and national origin in *Black Slave to the Greatest Master* reflects several problematic elements. The title itself is a prominent reminder of the near interchangeability of the words *negro* (black) and *esclavo* (slave) in early modern Spanish; thus *El negro del mejor amo* requires two words in English to communicate the double meaning of *negro*. There is also a religious dimension to the wordplay when, upon his conversion, Antiobo tells the Virgin, "I wish to be your *negro*" (Vega Carpio 1995, 473).[25] And while the conceit of the Black man with the white soul is not exploited to nearly the same degree as in the previous two plays, it underlies the eulogy offered by Antiobo's stepbrother Alí: "His saintly soul has now ascended to become a white host at the chaste altar of the holiest lamb" (504). In a similar but more secular vein, the African king Aufrido describes his people as Black but "with a white way of thinking; here envy and flattery have no home" (459).

The issue of nationality also reveals a problematic logic that flows from the previous two plays, with perhaps an attempt at a correction. In both *The Black Saint* and *The Marvel of Ethiopia*, the protagonists have fully Ethiopian origins: Rosambuco is born in Ethiopia and enslaved by Turks before being captured by Sicilians while Filipo, also born in Ethiopia, is enslaved by Egyptians. Given Ethiopia's well-known Christian tradition (Martín Casares 2014, 423), an Ethiopian origin makes characters more familiar and relatable: in a sense, more European. Lope de Vega appears to take a step away from this familiarity in making Antiobo only half Ethiopian, his father being a white Moor from Libya.

---

25. See the Translator's Note for my approach to translating Spanish *negro*.

While the *bozal* dialect in *Black Slave to the Greatest Master* is limited to act 1, the implications are troubling. Instead of characterizing the language of Black slaves in European settings (as in the case of Lucrecia from *The Black Saint*), *bozal* appears in sequences that take place in Africa (the setting of the first two acts), among Black Africans, where it differentiates commoners such as the soldier Febo (445–47, 452–53, 457, 460) and a group of musicians (448) from royalty such as Antiobo's parents. It is, undoubtedly, an insulting absurdity to ascribe a pidgin Spanish to characters who would be speaking native African languages among themselves (rather like American films that assign heavily accented English to "foreign" dialogue). While the main purpose may be to elevate the protagonist's parents, a demeaning comic intent cannot be discounted.

In the representation of interracial unions, the record of *Black Slave to the Greatest Master* is rather mixed. In act 1, the protagonist's parents, the white Dulimán and the Black Sofonisba, represent only the third interracial marriage of this survey, following Queen Calafia and Prince Talanque in *The Exploits of Esplandián* and Sofía and her unnamed husband in Lope de Rueda's *Gila*. But it is merely implied. Following the pattern of the previous two cases, Lope de Vega minimizes the characters' interaction, showing a fleeting moment of their courtship and nothing at all of their married life. One explanation for this reticence is that the parents are there simply to explain Antiobo's ancestry, given that traditional hagiographies emphasized genealogy (Weber de Kurlat 1970, 344–45). But there seems to be a lingering squeamishness about representing Black-white relationships onstage. Indeed, a very odd dynamic characterizes acts 2 and 3, in which Dulimán continues to make appearances but Sofonisba disappears completely. Though she continues to be referred to, she is never shown interacting with Antiobo; it is not even clear if she remains alive. In addition to shielding the spectators from an interracial marriage, Sofonisba's prolonged absence (and perhaps her death) helps to justify the presence of the white nurse who will be instrumental in Antiobo's conversion. Though it is never stated, there may be an anti-Black trope at work here: only a white woman can provide the (white) milk needed to nourish a Black Christian saint and save him from his beautiful but Black mother, who is also described as "pagan" (77). Whatever the case, Antiobo's conversion (484–85) is closer to Filipo's and wholly lacking in the Islamophobic imprecations of Rosambuco's.

The protagonist's relationship with his childhood nurse, who dies in his arms when he is reunited with her (act 2), is but one in a series of problematic relationships with white women. In act 3, after he has devoted himself to the Virgin, the Devil incites the shepherdess Dórida to make advances toward him. Claiming a pain in her chest, she asks him to touch it; when he does so, she collapses and dies, presumably of shock, and he resuscitates her (495–97). At the end of the play, when the saint has perished, the pilgrim Doña Juana visits his body and attempts to place a ring on his finger, which the body rejects and hurls to the ground (508). Only after Doña Juana repents of her dubious past—there is a suggestion of prostitution—does the body accept the ring (512–13). Such are the protagonist's relationships with white women: a childhood nurse who dies in his arms, a shepherdess whom he startles to death, and a reformed prostitute who is allowed only to place a ring on his dead finger. All three encounters occur within the narrative of the protagonist's saintliness, but in purely visual terms—and of course the theater is a visual medium—the message is more problematic: white women, even those of questionable character, are not meant to touch or be touched by Black men.

Notwithstanding these flaws, *Black Slave to the Greatest Master* has a number of characteristics that signal a new orientation toward Black characters, perhaps creating a precedent for the Triad authors. It is significant, for example, that the protagonist's mother, Sofonisba, is repeatedly described as beautiful or lovely. While Rodríguez de Montalvo's Queen Calafia and her women warrior tribe are also described in physically admiring terms, the characterization is limited to a couple of occasions and phrased in rather careful language; and the Black messenger, it will be recalled, is described with a "black but beautiful" formulation. In contrast, Lope de Vega, who may well owe his inspiration for Sofonisba to the Californians of Rodríguez de Montalvo, goes far beyond the latter in having the princess's beauty lauded effusively on at least seven separate occasions (451, 457 [twice], 459, 470 [twice], 488) by both Black and white characters, Christian and Muslim. Antiobo too, even after his death, is described as beautiful by Doña Juana: "Such great love I conceived for him that in order to see his beautiful face, to love him and to know him, I embarked on this journey" (506). Only the Devil, in comments that recall the viceroy's possessed daughter in *The Black Saint*, insults Antiobo and derides his color (497–500).

Not only are the play's Black characters admired for their beauty, but the white ones emphasize that there is nothing inherently more beautiful about their own color. Antiobo's Moorish attendant Armindo notes that "Heaven pays no attention to nuances [of color]" (463), leading to the following exchange between Antiobo and his white stepbrother Alí:

> ANTIOBO. Why do you call me *sir*?
> ALÍ. Well, am I to consider myself the equal of a prince of Algiers?
> ANTIOBO. No, for your color is superior.
> ALÍ. What is my color?
> ANTIOBO. White.
> ALÍ. Well, I'm going to prove to you that color is not the most important quality in a man. Listen then: What do we say to a man to make him the equal of a king?

ANTIOBO. That he has royal blood.
ALÍ. Does blood have color?
ANTIOBO. Yes.
ALÍ. What color?
ANTIOBO. Red.
ALÍ. Which proves that whiteness is not the most admired color in a man.
(465)

Though it may seem sophistical to the modern reader, the dialogue is significant in offering a *secular* argument—as opposed to doctrinal statements from authors like Sánchez de Badajoz—to debunk the Black caricatures popularized by Gil Vicente and Lope de Rueda. Antiobo appears to internalize this lesson in a monologue that glosses the play's title: "Heaven is no more stained by blacks than by whites. I am God's black slave, a black slave to the greatest master" (485–86).

But Lope de Vega goes a step further than equality and privileges black over white through a consistent internal symbolism that inverts traditional European color hierarchies and favors images such as night and coal over daylight and snow. In act 1, the protagonist's white father tells his Black mother: "What a beautiful and immaculate night . . . may the day never dawn if the nights are such" (451). Her Black suitor then complains in jealousy: "Your beautiful face will be stained by African snow" (459). In act 2, Costancio tells Antiobo that he considers his mother's face "superior to snow" (470). The inversion culminates in act 3 when the Devil, who arrives to tempt Antiobo, refers to himself as "the Morning Star" and "whiter than the sun" (498), effectively identifying whiteness with evil in contrast to Antiobo's saintly blackness. This bold new schema challenges centuries of European iconography and symbolism that favored white over black, such as the Black man in *Prison of Love* who serves as an allegory of despair (see §Medieval Period) or the black Devil in Alfonso X's *Songs of Holy Mary* (TSW, Fig. 8). It is Lope de Vega's greatest innovation in his development of Black characters, and it will not go unnoticed by the Triad authors.

∽

The Black Saint, *The Marvel of Ethiopia*, and *Black Slave to the Greatest Master* occupy an important place in the history of Black characters that I have traced through early modern song, prose, and theater. The humanity of these plays' protagonists more closely reflects the prose creations of Zayd in *Little Lazarus* and Luis in *The Jealous Extremaduran* than anything from sixteenth-century theater, with the possible exception of Sánchez de Badajoz. Any of these plays on its own would represent a frontal assault on the prototype of Black characters established by Gil Vicente and Lope de Rueda; the three of them together smash the old mold to bits. Rosambuco, Filipo, and Antiobo are complex characters who speak elegantly, act ethically, and drive the plots of full-length plays, not interludes. Each of them is differentiated not only by color but by birth outside the Christian community: Islam explicitly in the case of Rosambuco and Antiobo, and perhaps by implication in the case of Filipo. Given the antagonistic relations between the two religions in the period, fictional characters associated with Islam would have faced a significant negative bias from the audience; and if the taint of Islam in Filipo's case is not enough, he turns to a life of crime. Nevertheless, each character overcomes the obstacles placed in his path, converts to Christianity, and achieves the status of saint, establishing an important model of redemption that runs counter to what Noémie Ndiaye (2022, 70) has identified as a "diabolical script of blackness."

The plays are not without flaws. The *bozal* dialect as well as insulting racial epithets appear extensively in *The Black Saint* and in more limited fashion in *Black Slave to the Greatest Master*. The conceit of the Black man with the white soul underlies the conversion of each character to a greater or lesser degree (even as *Black Slave to the Greatest Master* challenges the black-white bias of traditional color symbolism). Perhaps most importantly, all three characters are quite literally walled off from society: Rosambuco in a monastery, Filipo in a desert hermitage, and Antiobo in an insular cave. This is the flip side to the positive image of their saintliness: the men are barred from community with greater society, from marriage, and, significantly, from reproduction. All three, moreover, all killed off in the end, quite barbarically in the case of Filipo. A cynical interpretation might even claim that such isolation and death are the price that must be paid for representing the saintliness of a Black man onstage. It is significant, finally, that none of the plays takes place in Spain (two are set in Italy and one in Egypt). Is this a defensive gesture, designed to spread the blame for slave trafficking?

In short, Lope de Vega's contribution to the evolution of Black characters in Spanish literature is best described as two steps forward, one back. His syncopated advances, while stopping short of the next logical step, nevertheless silently point to it: integration. And nothing suggests integration more than interracial marriage. This is the challenge that will be taken up by the authors of the Triad.

2. Biographical Sketches

This section of the Introduction provides brief biographies of the Triad authors followed by informed speculation regarding the composition dates of their plays. A concluding reflection highlights common threads that may offer clues to interpreting the plays.

Diego Jiménez de Enciso, 1585–c. 1634[26]

Of the three Triad authors, we have the fewest intimate details about DJE. His early life is a mystery, and if he ever had a wife or children, they have become invisible to posterity. Nonetheless, he was praised by lofty contemporaries such as Lope de Vega as well as by fellow Triad author Claramonte. If the suspicions detailed below about his family's attempts to suppress its genealogy are correct, they may explain the scarcity of historical detail. DJE's known dramatic output—only seven authentic plays and three more of doubtful attribution (Juliá Martínez 1951, xiii–xiv)—suggests he was not nearly as prolific as some of his contemporaries, but his work has been praised for emphasizing quality over quantity. He is particularly known for his attention to historical detail, as reflected in *Juan Latino*, and for his psychological insights.

Chronology

1584   DJE's parents are married in Seville. There is evidence that both had descended from a line of converted Jews and that the paternal grandfather was a street peddler and the maternal great-great-grandmother a Moorish slave. The family becomes closely associated through marriage and mercantile activities with the ruling elites of Seville, many of whom are of converted Jewish backgrounds.

1585   DJE is baptized August 22 in Seville, suggesting a birthday shortly prior.

1606   DJE reads a pair of satirical poems at a banquet in Seville attended by major Spanish poets.

1609   In his *Jerusalem Conquered*, Lope de Vega, referring to the poems read at the banquet of 1606, calls DJE a poet whom his native land "sweetly praises" (Vega Carpio 1611, fol. 495r).

1612   DJE is appointed lay member of the Inquisition in Seville and named to the Brotherhood of Santa Ana.

1613   At the end of his *Moral Litany*, Claramonte praises DJE as a "renowned Sevillian intellect and valiant gentleman" as well as a "discreet courtier and very sharp-witted poet" (Claramonte y Corroy 1613, no page; also qtd. in Gallardo 1863–1889, 2:473). DJE is appointed to the city council of Seville.

1615   DJE is named representative of the Alhóndiga neighborhood of Seville.

---

26. Drawn from Cotarelo y Mori (1914a), Spratlin (1938), Juliá Martínez (1951), Pike (1990, 1991, 1993), Cobos (1998), Urzáiz Tortajada (2002a), Huerta Calvo et al. (2005), Cerezo Rubio (2010), and Fra Molinero (2014).

1618   DJE has moved to Madrid by this point (possibly the year before), where he becomes associated with the court of Philip III and a literary academy called either La Peregrina or the Academy of Madrid, which is also attended by Lope de Vega and Vélez de Guevara.

1621   The Spanish throne passes from Philip III to his son, Philip IV. The new king's favorite, Count-Duke Olivares, will become a powerful patron and protector of DJE.

1622   Two of DJE's plays—*The Medicis of Florence* and *The Hidden One*—are performed at court in Madrid this year and the next.

1624   From this point until 1626, DJE becomes deeply involved in genealogical investigations of two cousins nominated for knighthood in the Order of Santiago. He seems to have used his influence with Olivares to falsify the family's genealogy and obtain a favorable decision.

1625   DJE returns to Seville and is named to several sinecures as a result of his friendship with Olivares.

1627   DJE arranges the marriage of his niece with an ample dowry that includes "a female slave named María Marta, of the Indian people, somewhat dark in color and twenty years old, valued at two hundred ducats." The slave has two daughters, aged seven and four, whom DJE initially "reserves for himself." But he then grants them to the newlyweds for approximately one hundred ducats with the condition that they be freed upon turning twenty-five.

1629   In failing health and unable to travel by coach or horse, DJE is given license by the king to travel about Seville on a litter. He works as a judge in the city's Indies Trade Office.

1631   Gravely ill, the niece whose marriage DJE arranged writes a will in which she frees the three slaves she had received as part of her dowry.

1632   DJE's play *Jupiter Avenged* is performed at court for the swearing-in of Prince Balthasar Charles, though it is unknown if the playwright attended. His niece dies and he launches a lengthy lawsuit to recover the dowry from her husband.

1634   DJE dies in September, buried on the 14th, leaving a will that indicates no spouse or children.

1637   A shipping document links DJE's cousin Pedro to slave trafficking in Angola. Given the household slaves that DJE included with his niece's dowry in 1627 and the family's mercantile history, it is likely that slave-trafficking ventures had occurred during his lifetime with his knowledge.

DATING OF *JUAN LATINO*

Given the scarcity of detail on DJE's life, dating the composition of *Juan Latino*, which was not published until 1652, has proved difficult. I begin by correcting several misunderstandings that have become embedded in the critical record.

Weissbourd (2013, 534), citing Gates and Wolff (1998, 36), identifies a composition window of 1610 to 1621, while E. Wright (2016, 178), citing no evidence at all, seems to split the difference with "circa 1615." The 1610–1621 window, it turns out, goes back to Spratlin (1938, 206), where it is not a window at all. Spratlin's argument is that *Juan Latino* had to be written prior to Claramonte's *The Brave Black Soldier* because of a passage near the end of the latter in which the main character, Juan de Mérida, references Juan Latino. Spratlin cites two possible years for Claramonte's death: 1610 and 1621. In his opinion, these years suggest two mutually exclusive terminal points for the composition of the play, *not* an inclusive window. At any rate, we now know, as detailed in the next biography, that Claramonte died in 1626, not 1610 or 1621. Thus, even if we accept Spratlin's premise that *Juan Latino* preceded *The Brave Black Soldier*, it proves only that it was written before 1626.

Given that the frequently cited window of 1610–1621 is invalid, I suggest dating *Juan Latino* based on internal criteria and what is known of DJE's life and literary influences, with the caveat that any conclusions are necessarily speculative. The earliest I believe the play could have been written is 1615: the year that Ambrosio de Salazar's curious *Mirror of Grammar* was published in Rouen, France. Toward the end of Salazar's book, a lively biography of Juan Latino involves an extended, complex pun on the Spanish word *manera* (Salazar 2015, 484–85). The exact same pun, which I fully explain in my discussion of wordplay in the Translator's Note, appears in act 3 of *Juan Latino*. The length and specificity of the puns in both texts make it virtually impossible that they could have arisen independently. So either Salazar copied DJE, or DJE copied Salazar. Stoichita (2010, 371, n. 73) suggests the former scenario without entertaining the latter, which I believe is more credible. There is no evidence that *Juan Latino* was published during DJE's lifetime, so Salazar would have had to learn of the pun by attending a performance of the play, presumably in Madrid or Seville. But he was already living in Rouen by the early 1600s (Morel-Fatio 1900, 22), well before DJE would have begun writing for the theater. It seems more likely that DJE would have come across Salazar's book, which went through several editions including a second in 1622 (Menéndez Pelayo 1907, lxxxii; Gallardo 1863–1889, 4:324–25).

Another important date is 1618: the year that DJE, now living in Madrid, began attending La Peregrina literary academy, which was formed the year before (Gibson 1964, 176). This is a key moment. While DJE shows strong literary inclinations early on, there is no evidence of specifically theatrical endeavors on his part before this point. Attendance at the academy may have focused his dramaturgical interests by bringing him into frequent contact with many of the foremost playwrights of the day including Lope de Vega, who, whether or not he authored all the Black saint plays thought to be his (see §Three Plays Attributed to Lope de Vega), would almost certainly have been able to talk intelligently about the topic. Act 1, scene 4 of *Juan Latino* portrays a literary academy in the Duke of Sessa's palace in which Juan Latino demonstrates his prodigious intellect. I believe the scene may well have been modeled on DJE's experience at La Peregrina.

Odds are, however, that DJE did not write the play his very first year at the academy or even his second. La Peregrina lasted until 1622, which is precisely the date of the first performance record of a play authored by DJE: *The Medicis*, which was followed by *The Hidden One* in 1623. With the academy experience behind him and two plays under his belt, and perhaps inspired by the second edition of Salazar's *Mirror of Grammar* (1622), I believe it was around this time that he would have begun writing *Juan Latino*, which shows considerable technical progress with respect to the previous two plays (Juliá Martínez 1951, lxi). The year 1624 marks the beginning of the genealogical inquiries into DJE's cousins, which soon demands all his attention. Meanwhile, 1626 marks the death of Claramonte, which represents, if we accept Spratlin's premise, the true outer limit for the composition and performance of DJE's play.

Perhaps this is why Baltasar Fra Molinero, in two recent articles (2014, 16, and 2016, 184), offers an approximate date of 1625 for *Juan Latino*. Though he does not explain his reasoning, I believe he is closer to the mark than the misleading 1610–1621 window. My best guess would be 1623–1624.

Andrés de Claramonte y Corroy, c. 1580–1626[27]

ACC's life is a dizzying swirl of activity befitting the restlessness of an ambitious theater professional. Actor, company director, and playwright, he left his mark on all of Spain's major theatrical centers including Valencia, Seville, and Madrid. He lacked the powerful patrons of his fellow Triad authors, never gained the status of a first-tier playwright, and was often accused of plagiarism: judgments that have lingered over his reputation in the modern period. Nevertheless, in recent years, several critics have worked to rehabilitate

---

27. Drawn from Leavitt (1931), Hernández Valcárcel (1983), Ganelin (1987), Castillejo (2002), Urzáiz Tortajada (2002a), Huerta Calvo et al. (2005), Rodríguez López-Vázquez (2010a), Ferrer Valls et al. (2012a), and García-Reidy (2019).

his image, attributing major works to him such as the original Don Juan play (traditionally ascribed to Tirso de Molina). ACC's plays—numbering around twenty authentic, full-length titles—are characterized by a wide variety of subject matter, an easy unfolding of action, an emphasis on the supernatural and miraculous, and a predilection for surprise endings that sometimes strain credulity.

Chronology

1578   A shoemaker named Pedro de Claramonte takes up residence in the city of Murcia in southeastern Spain. If he is ACC's father, it would confirm the humble origins that the playwright alludes to in his *Moral Litany* of 1613 (see below).

1580   ACC is born in or slightly prior to this year, probably in Murcia, though Valencia and Cartagena have also been suggested.

1592   ACC may have begun a precocious acting career by this point.

1602   ACC may have written plays by this point and is perhaps living in Valencia.

1603   ACC is recognized in theater circles as both actor and playwright, his name appearing in a well-known catalog of playwrights (Rojas Villandrando 1972, 158).

1604   ACC marries a Valencian, Doña Beatriz de Castro y Virués, on February 4. No children are known to have issued from this union or from any other. He performs in Valladolid in a theater troupe for the king and in Salamanca in a play written by Lope de Vega.

1605   ACC resides in Seville from this point until possibly 1607, joining Alfonso de Heredia's theater troupe in August and Antonio Granados's in December.

1606   ACC visits Zaragoza with Granados's troupe.

1607   ACC forms a theater troupe with Alonso de Olmedo y Tofiño. First documentation of his activities as a playwright.

1608   ACC performs with his and Olmedo's troupe in Valencia.

1609   ACC forms his own theater troupe.

1610   ACC becomes a congregant at the Convent of the Barefoot Trinitarians in Madrid in March, perhaps making a brief return to Murcia. He performs in Toledo and Segovia in December.

1611   When theaters close in mourning of Queen Margarita's death, ACC begins frequenting a literary academy at the home of the Count of Saldaña in Madrid, which is also attended by Lope de Vega and Vélez de Guevara.

1612   Three ballads from this year are ACC's first published works. The manuscript of *The Catholic Princess Leopolda*, perhaps his earliest play, bears this year's date but was probably written earlier. When theaters reopen, ACC returns to Seville and forms a new theater company. *The Brave Black Soldier* may have been performed in Murcia this year (but see below on dating *BBS* for an important caveat).

1613   ACC performs in Cordova. In a prologue to his *Moral Litany*, he anticipates criticism of his "lowborn" status and defends himself with biblical citations (Claramonte y Corroy 1613, no page). At the end of the same book, he praises the work of Jiménez de Enciso and Vélez de Guevara (see the year 1613 in their chronologies).

1614   ACC is back in Madrid, preparing for a theater tour through Alcalá de Henares, Algete, and Guadalajara. He forms three new theater troupes and performs in Valencia from September to October.

1615   According to a royal decree dated this year, ACC's company is one of only twelve authorized to perform in Spain for a two-year period. He resides mainly in Seville from this point on and concentrates on writing.

1623   ACC takes up residence in Madrid, for unexplained reasons, at some point prior to this year. He writes two mystery plays for the Corpus Christi celebration in Seville.

1624   ACC writes two more mystery plays for Seville's Corpus Christi. He produces a play in Seville and appears before a notary in Madrid to claim license for his last known play.

1626   ACC dies on September 19, leaving no will.

Dating of *The Brave Black Soldier*

The play was first published in 1638, well after ACC's death. Two nineteenth-century historians hint of a performance in Murcia in 1612. One calls it "the second part of that famous play," while both say it was performed by the theater troupe of Manuel Vicente Guerrero (Fuentes y Ponte 1872, 339; Díaz Cassou 1895, 113). These claims must be treated with skepticism. Neither cites any documentation, and Fuentes y Ponte insists that ACC died in 1610, which we know to be false. Furthermore, it is now clear that Manuel Vicente Guerrero lived in the following century, dying in 1753 according to Spain's Royal Academy of History (Herrera Navarro n.d.; see Guerrero 2003 for the lively "sequel" to ACC's play).

At a minimum, there seems to have been a confusion of names and dates. It is not impossible that the year 1612, cited by both nineteenth-century sources, could have marked a performance of *The Brave Black Soldier* in Murcia. ACC was active as a playwright as early as 1607, and the manuscript of *The Catholic Princess Leopolda* is dated 1612. All of Lope de Vega's Black saint plays would probably have been performed by this point, perhaps creating an inspiration for ACC, who would also have had direct contact with Lope de Vega through the Count of Saldaña's literary academy. The year 1611/1612 may thus be considered the earliest possible inception date of the play; however, that would place it among ACC's earliest works, and I find it unlikely that he would begin his career with such a risky endeavor. Ferrer Valls et al. (2012a, item 1), moreover, indicate that 1612 could be an error for 1712 given Guerrero's death in 1753. I thus agree with critics who suggest a later date in ACC's life for the original performance of *The Brave Black Soldier*, ranging from 1617 to his death in 1626.[28]

To narrow things down even more: if we agree that ACC's play responds to *Juan Latino* and accept the date I have proposed for the latter (1623–1624), *The Brave Black Soldier* could well belong to the same period given the swiftness with which plays were written and performed.[29]

Luis Vélez de Guevara, 1579–1644[30]

Two identities define LVG's amply documented public life: writer and courtier. Inextricably linked, the twin professions kept him at the forefront of the literary scene as well the very nerve center of the Spanish state. Despite success in both, he never achieved financial independence, perhaps because of a teeming private life that included at least

---

28. Castillejo (2002, 363) says it was performed in 1617, though he offers no proof and Rodríguez López-Vázquez (2010b, 131) disputes the claim. Both Beusterien (2006a, 114, and 2006b, 175) and Olmedo Gobante (2018, 69) suggest a date of approximately 1620, also without evidence. Rodríguez López-Vázquez (2010b, 131) believes it was written "close to 1625" based on metrical analysis, but metrical analysis leads the same critic to conclude that Calderón de la Barca's *Life Is a Dream* preceded *Virtues Overcome Appearances* (Rodríguez López-Vázquez 2017), a claim contradicted by documentary evidence (Ferrer Valls et al. 2012b, item 1; see also Ruano de la Haza 2010, 16). Rennert (1907, 55), citing another nineteenth-century source, says Claramonte's play was performed in 1626, but Shergold and Varey (1963, 231) refute this point.

29. Lope de Vega famously bragged that he wrote some of his plays in less than a day each, an astonishing pace that a recent biographer has found to be plausible (Sánchez Jiménez 2018, 176–84). Not all *comedia* authors could match his speed, but briskness of composition was the norm. It was not uncommon for a play to be performed only once (Ziomek 1984, 33–35).

30. Drawn from Cotarelo y Mori (1917), Morley and Bruerton (1936), Spencer and Schevill (1937), Entrambasaguas (1973), Rodríguez Cepeda (1975), Davies (1983), Peale (1983), Bolaños Donoso (2001), Urzáiz Tortajada (2002a, 2002b), Peale and Urzáiz Tortajada (2003), Huerta Calvo et al. (2005), Peale (2009), and Valdés Gázquez (2010).

three wives and nine children. He repeatedly requested financial assistance from his benefactors, leading to inside jokes about his neediness. He was by far the most prolific of the Triad playwrights, with some contemporary accounts—including one by his son Juan, which should be treated with skepticism given the obvious bias—claiming over four hundred plays, though today we possess only around eighty-five. His dramaturgy was widely admired during his lifetime, but assessment of it in the modern period has varied considerably.

Chronology

1573 LVG's parents, Diego Vélez de Dueñas and Francisca Negrete de Santander, both from families of modest means, are married in the town of Écija, about fifty miles from Seville. An ancestor of Francisca's, Luis de Santander, was reportedly accused of "judaizing" and burned at the stake by the Inquisition in the 1550s.

1579 LVG is baptized on August 1 in Écija, suggesting a birthday shortly prior, though his son Juan claimed he was born in 1578. The name on his baptismal certificate is Luis Vélez de Santander, which incorporated, as was traditional, surnames from both parents.

1596 LVG graduates from the University of Osuna with a bachelor of arts degree. His academic record includes a request to waive expenses on account of financial hardship.

1597 Around this time, LVG becomes a page to the Archbishop of Seville, presumably accompanying him to the wedding of King Philip III in 1599.

1600 The archbishop dies, leaving LVG without a patron. He completes several years of military service that takes him all around the Mediterranean.

1603 Still using the name Luis Vélez de Santander, LVG contributes a prefatory sonnet to a famous miscellany (Rojas Villandrando 1972, 56). A murky period of four to five years follows, in which LVG's presence is documented in Valladolid, Seville, and Madrid. A family friend suggests that a brief marriage during this time ended in the wife's death, but there is no documentary proof of the assertion.

1608 By this point LVG has established himself at the court in Madrid, in the service of the Count of Saldaña, son of King Philip III's powerful minister, the Duke of Lerma. In a poem published in praise of the king's son (the future Philip IV), he now signs his name Luis Vélez de Guevara, presumably to mask the connection to the accused judaizer in his genealogy. This same year he marries Úrsula Ramisi

Bravo, whom he also requires to change her name, to Úrsula Bravo de Laguna. Despite the suggestion that he was previously married, LVG will always refer to this marriage as his first. Also this year, Lope de Vega intervenes on behalf of LVG in a dispute with Saldaña and will remain, from this point on, a close friend.

1611   LVG's wife gives birth to Juan, his first son and primary successor. Two additional children by this wife, a son and a daughter, will both precede their father in death. LVG begins attending the Count of Saldaña's literary academy, which is also attended by Lope de Vega and Claramonte.

1613   At the end of his *Moral Litany*, Claramonte praises LVG as the "fully flowering intellect of Écija from whom we expect great works, and who has already written many famous plays" (Claramonte y Corroy 1613, no page; also qtd. in Gallardo 1863–1889, 2:476).

1615   Cervantes praises the "greatness of Luis Vélez de Guevara's plays" (Cervantes 1989, 93).

1616   LVG's wife Úrsula Bravo de Laguna dies.

1618   LVG remarries, to Ana María del Valle, falsifying his father's name as Diego Vélez de Guevara in the official records. Around this time he leaves Saldaña's service, enters that of the Marquis of Peñafiel, and begins attending the literary academy known as La Peregrina or Academy of Madrid, also attended by Lope de Vega and Jiménez de Enciso.

1619   LVG's new wife gives birth to a daughter and dies shortly afterwards. The daughter does not survive childhood.

1621   Lope de Vega praises LVG's "flowery and eloquent lyre, worthy of Orpheus" (qtd. in Cotarelo y Mori 1917, 40).

1623   LVG serves as usher to the Prince of Wales in his visit to Madrid.

1624   LVG becomes majordomo to the Archduke of Austria, but the latter dies shortly afterwards.

1625   LVG becomes usher at the palace of King Philip IV, a position that will keep him at the center of power until 1642, when he passes the job on to his son.

1626   LVG marries his last wife, María López de Palacios, with whom he will have four daughters and a son over the next eighteen years.

1630   Lope de Vega praises LVG as the town of Ecija's "new Apollo" (qtd. in Cotarelo y Mori 1917, 54).

1635   Death of Lope de Vega. LVG composes a laudatory sonnet praising him as "a comet unto himself" (qtd. in Cotarelo y Mori 1917, 55).

1638   LVG participates in an improvised play in the royal palace with Pedro Calderón de la Barca, who has become, upon Lope de Vega's death, the most important playwright of Spanish theater.

1641   LVG publishes *The Limping Devil*, a short prose satire with picaresque elements that will ultimately gain him more fame than his theater. In this work and elsewhere, the author appears to poke fun at his own obsession with the "wardrobe of grandfathers" (Vélez de Guevara 1981, 47), that is, lineage and surnames.

1644   LVG dies in November from a sudden illness, leaving behind his last wife, two of the five children he fathered with her (one of whom was born only four months earlier), and his son Juan, now in his early thirties.

Dating of *Virtues Overcome Appearances*

First printed in Zaragoza in 1640, LVG's play stands on firmer ground than the other two Triad plays in terms of dating, thanks to an intriguing document from Salamanca in 1625. On January 9 of that year, the theater company director Juan Jerónimo Valenciano deposited, along with various clothes and jewels, a group of play manuscripts including *Virtues Overcome Appearances* as collateral for a loan he used to move his company from Salamanca to Madrid (Ferrer Valls et al. 2012b, item 1). It appears that he was successful in his venture, for there is evidence that Valenciano's company performed the play in Seville during the 1626–1627 season (Bolaños Donoso 2011, 317). It thus seems reasonable to conclude, if the play existed in manuscript in January 1625, that it was written no later than 1624.

The question remains: Exactly when? Was it before or after *Juan Latino* and *The Brave Black Soldier*? Peale and Urzáiz Tortajada (2003, 938) give a precise date of 1617 with no explanation; seven years later Peale, in his critical edition with Manson (Vélez de Guevara 1640–2010 [E]), offers no new information. Fra Molinero (1997, 344) believes it was "some fourteen years" after the Morisco expulsion, which would mean 1623, though he does not explain his reasoning. Davies (1983, 31) says it was "perhaps not long after the death of Philip III," which occurred in 1621. He does not explain his reasoning either, but it may have to do with the fact that the king in power at the beginning of the play dies as well. Citing themes and versification, Schevill (1933, 190) and Profeti (1965, 40) suggest windows of 1618–1622 and 1615–1628, respectively. My guess is that it belongs to the same 1623–1624 period as *Juan Latino* and *The Brave Black Soldier*. I will return shortly to the question of exactly where in that two-year span it might fall.

~

While DJE, ACC, and LVG led different lives, a surprising number of common threads in their biographies may help us understand the genesis of their plays.

First comes the issue of ancestry. While the historical record is not entirely clear, it appears that all three authors came from non-noble or questionable backgrounds. DJE's grandfather may have been a converted Jewish street peddler and his great-great-grandmother a Moorish slave. ACC's father appears to have been a shoemaker. LVG had an ancestor, or at least someone with the same surname (which at that time was just as damning) who was accused of judaizing and burned at the stake, and his work has often been interpreted through this lens (Entrambasaguas 1973, Rodríguez Cepeda 1975, Peale 1983). Moreover, we know that all three issues were important enough to prompt responses: ACC confronted his origins in the prologue to his *Moral Litany* while DJE and LVG tried to cover theirs up, and LVG seemed to parody his own efforts at doing so. It is reasonable to wonder whether the authors' Black protagonists came about as additional responses to these issues. Do the challenges faced by the characters represent the social stigma the authors may have felt on account of their ancestry?

Second, all three playwrights had significant connections to the city of Seville. DJE was born and raised there; LVG was born in nearby Écija and served as page to the Archbishop of Seville; ACC lived there, for significant stretches, from 1605 on. As noted above (see §Afro-Spaniards), Seville had the largest number of Black slaves in Spain. In contrast, the relatively low incidence of slavery in northern Spain made the institution virtually undetectable to residents of those regions. Even in the Spanish capital, Madrid, slavery was limited and not highly visible (Domínguez Ortiz 2003, 14–17). Thus an alarmed visitor to Seville from the northern city of Valladolid warned that Black and Morisco slaves appeared to outnumber Seville's free white citizens, while another compared the city's residents to the contrasting pieces of a chessboard (Domínguez Ortiz 2003, 9–10). The importance of Seville's highly visible slave population should not be underestimated in assessing the intentions of the Triad authors, who seem intent on bringing a Black minority with "no place in the social imaginary" (Herzog 2012, 5) before the eyes of white spectators.

It must be remembered, furthermore, that DJE—unique among the Triad authors, it seems—owned household slaves and that his family seems to have been involved in the triangular trade. Does his decision to free his slaves when they reached the age of twenty-five reflect "a humane attitude" toward them (Spratlin 1938, 205): perhaps some sort of moral reckoning on his part? That might be the only way to reconcile his slave ownership with his apparent sympathy toward the plight of slaves in *Juan Latino*. These are complicated questions to which I will return in the Literary Analysis. For now, I simply echo Fra Molinero's observation (2014, 17) that "the contradiction is typical of the Baroque."

Of equal if not greater importance than Seville is Madrid. Seat of the Habsburg court during the lifetimes of the playwrights, Madrid was not only the political but the literary capital of the Spanish Empire. One of the most valuable resources it offered writers, both established and aspiring, was a plethora of literary "academies" or venues where writers could meet to read samples of their work: "The central importance of this series of academies to the literary life of the capital cannot be overstated" (Robbins 1997, 26). The Triad authors must have sensed this opportunity, for all three moved to Madrid at some point during the reign of Philip III: LVG by 1608, ACC by 1610, and DJE by 1618. And their instincts seem to have paid off. The Count of Saldaña, who became LVG's patron soon after the latter's arrival in Madrid, established a literary academy in which both LVG and ACC rubbed elbows with giants like Lope de Vega and Cervantes (both of whom, it will be remembered, had contributed important Black characters to Spanish literature). Several years later, by the time of DJE's move to the capital, another academy was up and running. Named either La Peregrina or the Academy of Madrid, it was attended by DJE and LVG in addition to Lope de Vega (Cervantes had died by that point). Finally, when the throne passed from Philip III to Philip IV (1621), the arts found a lavish patron in the new king, who apparently attended some sessions of La Peregrina himself. It is during these exciting initial years of Philip IV's reign that I believe the Triad plays were written.[31]

Madrid's literary academies provided writers with venues not only for practicing their craft but also for discussing the burning issues of the day, often organized around the favorite "arms and letters" motif (Sánchez 1961, 12–13). Given the heady times and proximity to the seat of power, there could have been no lack of inspiration. At the same time that the Count of Saldaña was running his academy, for example, his father and Philip III's favorite, the Duke of Lerma, was in charge of implementing the king's controversial edict expelling the Moriscos (1609–1614). In part 2 of *Don Quixote* (1615), Cervantes channels something akin to a national sense of shame in the character of the expelled Morisco Ricote, who claims that he and his people "weep for Spain wherever

---

31. On La Peregrina, see Cotarelo y Mori (1914a, 25), Cotarelo y Mori (1914b, 14), Sánchez (1961, 113–16), Gibson (1964, 176), and Robbins (1997, 26).

we go, for it is, after all, our birthplace and natural homeland" (Cervantes 1987, 2:451). It seems likely that a policy that generated such public debate and that was being carried out by the academy founder's father would prompt discussions, perhaps intense, among attendees. In a private letter to the Duke of Sessa, Lope de Vega describes a heated exchange at Saldaña's academy in which LVG and a minor poet from Granada practically drew swords on each other (Vega Carpio 1985, 111). He does not explain what caused the altercation, and I do not mean to suggest it was the edict of expulsion, though it is worth noting that the expulsion decimated LVG's hometown of Écija (Fernández Zorrilla 1996). At a minimum, the great moral and political issue of the day would almost certainly have arisen in debate and provided the academy's attendees with ample opportunity for reflection. It may be that LVG's and ACC's Black protagonists reflect a certain sensitivity to the tragedy of the Moriscos in addition to speaking directly to the plight of Blacks in Spain.

DJE's biography is particularly perplexing in this regard. While he was not a member of Saldaña's group, he could hardly have been ignorant of the issues raised by the expulsion. Indeed, he is unique among the Triad authors in incorporating an extensive cast of Morisco themes and characters into his play, often from a seemingly sympathetic perspective that I explore in the Literary Analysis. At the same time, his appointment to the Inquisition in Seville in 1612 would seem to indicate downright hostility toward the Moriscos. Though his status as lay member (*familiar*) of the institution may suggest a bureaucratic and largely ceremonial role (Kamen 1998, 145), antagonism toward religious minorities cannot be ruled out, perhaps as a way of proving his orthodoxy (a documented pattern in Jewish converts). If hostility motivated him, it would be, as with the question of slavery, another glaring contradiction between the life and work of this author. In any case, his role at the Inquisition in Seville, as different as it may seem from LVG's and ACC's participation in Saldaña's academy in Madrid, suggests an interesting parallel: the experiences likely brought all three close to the beating heart of power on a difficult issue, providing ample opportunity for literary inspiration.

Finally, what Madrid offered the writers of the Triad is something that should be obvious by now but that perhaps should be stated directly: one another. It is almost certain the authors all knew each other *on paper* by 1613, the date in which ACC praises both DJE and LVG in his *Moral Litany*. What Madrid gave them was the opportunity to meet, converse, and perhaps even collaborate *in person*. We know for a fact that ACC and LVG attended the same academy in 1611 and that LVG and DJE began attending another in 1618. And though ACC had departed for Seville by this point, his constant travels would have brought him back with frequency to the capital, where by 1623 he had returned to live, albeit briefly. Then there is the common thread of Lope de Vega, the central figure of Madrid's literary life, who attended both academies, was a close friend of LVG's, praised DJE's writing early on, and had at least one work performed by ACC. While there is no evidence that places all three Triad authors in the same place at the same time, it is very likely to have occurred, perhaps on multiple occasions.

This brings us back to the chronology of the plays and the probable dates I have proposed: 1623–1624. With such a narrow window of composition for authors who inhabited the same circles, knew each other's work, and were quite possibly collaborating or engaging in friendly competition, it becomes almost a metaphysical question which play came "first." Does the honor belong to the author who first had the idea, the one who first put words to a page, or the one who first brought his work to the stage? I believe it makes sense to treat the three plays as part of a creative whole that represents the integration of Black characters into white society through intermarriage, a topic to which I return in my conclusion to the Literary Analysis. As for a precise chronology, if pressed I would cite the order in which I have placed the translations: *Juan Latino*, *The Brave Black Soldier*, and *Virtues Overcomes Appearances*. The first two works, firmly rooted in the lived Iberian experience, I see as existing in close dialogue with each other. I believe that LVG was aware of both plays, perhaps even saw them performed, and decided to adopt a fresh approach to the topic of Black characters: an approach that would take him back to the fantasy world of medieval works such as the *Book of the Zifar the Knight*, *Prison of Love*, and *The Exploits of Esplandián*.

3. Literary Analysis

The plays of the Triad have value beyond their extraordinary protagonists. *Juan Latino* dramatizes the proceedings of a literary academy (1.4) and of a major early modern university (3.6). It also provides important historical perspective on the Morisco issue, representing the uprising of 1568 through the lens of the 1609 expulsion. *The Brave Black Soldier* offers valuable insights into the Spanish infantry and its military campaign against the rebellious Low Countries. *Virtues Overcome Appearances* reveals political thinking on kingship and succession, promulgates a popular pseudoscientific theory of the period, and reveals significant parallels to Calderón de la Barca's *Life Is a Dream*.

Nevertheless, it is the plays' Black protagonists that attract our attention today, just as they almost certainly captivated audiences at the time of their creation. My analysis focuses on the main characters through the critical lens of race in a contemporary sociological sense. While early modern spectators would not have shared the same critical framework, they would certainly have recognized the tangled issues of skin color, religion, and nationality that I trace in the pages that follow.[32]

(To avoid spoiling plot details, readers may wish to proceed directly to the plays at this point, returning to the remainder of the analysis afterwards.)

The Slave Scholar

Of the three plays, Jiménez de Enciso's is the most deeply enmeshed in the early modern Iberian reality. At its center stands the historical figure of Juan Latino, an Afro-Spanish slave who rose to prominence as a poet and Latin instructor (hence his nickname, which has nothing to do with our contemporary usage of *Latino*), eventually marrying the white noblewoman Doña Ana de Carlobal. The details of Latino's long life (c. 1516–c. 1597) have been the subject of much speculation. In the only autobiographical statement known to have survived, he reports that he was "taken out of Ethiopia in early childhood" (E. Wright 2016, 23, fig. 3); but the chronicler Fernández de Córdoba (1954, 198) claims he was born in Baena, Spain.[33]

The main plot of *Juan Latino* is defined by a dual quest on the protagonist's part: courtship of the white Doña Ana and pursuit of a teaching position at Granada's all-white cathedral school, a position that requires not only a formal application process but also an advanced university degree. A subplot involves the Morisco uprising of 1568 (1569 in the play), linked to the main story through the character Don Fernando de Válor, who becomes a rival suitor to Doña Ana. Meanwhile, in his application for the teaching position, Latino's opponent is Magister Villanueva, a character strongly associated with a converted Jewish ancestry. Issues of skin color, religion, and nationalism are thus deeply rooted in the play's basic conflicts.[34]

---

32. There is a long and polemical debate about whether it is appropriate to refer to "race" in texts from premodern periods, when the concept was not fully formed. Representatives of the "discontinuity" theory include Appiah (1990) and Foucault (1997). Heng stands at the opposite pole, finding race and racism across all of medieval literature including, for example, in interactions between the English and Irish (Heng 2018, 38–39). Bartlett (1994, 199–242; 2001; 2009) and Nirenberg (2007, 2009) represent intermediate positions closer to my own, which is that early manifestations of race-based thinking are observable in the period of the Triad, where they are deeply embedded in concepts of religion, skin color, and nationality or ethnic origin (I use *nationality* and *ethnicity* as rough synonyms).

33. Modern biographies of Juan Latino include those of Marín Ocete (1925), Green (1968, 136–37), Masó (1973), Gates and Wolff (1998), Sánchez Marín and Muñoz Martín (2009), Mira Seo (2011), Martín Casares (2016), and E. Wright (2016). Separately, Gates (1988, 90) points to Latino as a predecessor of the African American cultural tradition he calls *signifyin(g)*. Biographical sources from the early modern period include Bermúdez de Pedraza (1608), Fernández de Córdoba (1954), and Salazar (2015, 482–87).

34. Jiménez de Enciso does not unequivocally identify the institution from which Latino seeks his teaching position, but the cathedral school is the most logical candidate; the University of Granada, which grants his degree

Latino's courtship of Doña Ana is enabled when he demonstrates his prodigious erudition at a literary academy held in the Duke of Sessa's palace, where he serves as a household slave. Both Doña Ana and her brother, Dr. Carlobal, are present at the session and witness his intellectual display.[35] Suspicious of the white suitors who wish to tutor his sister, Dr. Carlobal proposes Juan Latino instead: "Why not? Is he not a man? Is his soul less pure or less rational because his skin is black? A man is shaped only by his soul. Color is an accident that does not change it. It is insulting to compare a wise, discreet, virtuous, and devoutly Christian black man to a white man ruled by vice" (2.3). Carlobal's justification reprises the classic theological argument reviewed above (see §Theology) and the corresponding principles revealed in the drama of Sánchez de Badajoz (see §Early Modern Period): color is "accidental," that is, not an essential quality of souls, which are equal before God. Carlobal's confirmation that Latino is a devout Christian is also important, for Doña Ana has already rejected Don Fernando as suspect in this regard: "How can you suspect I'd be interested in Don Fernando, a Morisco? His grandfather was a Moor, his father a Berber!" (1.1). Nevertheless, she seems to want further confirmation of this point during her first meeting with Latino, asking him directly, "Juan, are you a Morisco?" (2.3). Curiously, Juan's laconic reply, "I am black," does nothing to rule out his being a Moor or a Morisco, as demonstrated by the presence in the play of the Black Moor Cañerí. Nevertheless, his answer seems to satisfy Doña Ana, and she never returns to the issue.

On the contrary, the tutoring sessions lead to a romantic entanglement that culminates in a pair of eye-opening scenes. In the first, Latino, while teaching Doña Ana numbers and counting, grabs her hand and begins writing on it with a quill. "It's so fair I took it for paper" (2.3), he explains, implicitly identifying himself with the black ink of the pen. The second scene (3.1) breaks even greater ground:

> JUAN LATINO. Does white snow really wish to be touched by soot?
> DOÑA ANA. Why wouldn't it? Love has bitten my soul.
> JUAN LATINO. You no longer fear my stain?
> *(JUAN LATINO and DOÑA ANA embrace. Enter CARLOBAL.)*

---

at the end of the play, is also a possibility. (On the historical relationship between the cathedral school and the university as well as the real-life Juan Latino's apparent membership on both faculties, see E. Wright 2016, 53–55.) A less likely candidate is the University of Osuna, which the play claims was founded by Dr. Carlobal (3.2). See the Translator's Note for explanation of the title *Magister*.

35. In real life, Carlobal was governor of the second Duke of Sessa's estate and *father* to Doña Ana. His son, the third Duke of Sessa—Don Gonzalo in the play—was served by Juan Latino, who reportedly carried his books to school. Before adopting *Latino* as a surname, Juan was known, in both real life and the play, as Juan de Sessa.

While Lope de Vega stages an interracial embrace in *The Black Saint* (see §Three Plays Attributed to Lope de Vega), he does so between characters of the lower class whose skin color and gender configurations—white man, Black woman—concentrate the dominant terms in the same subject (white man). Jiménez de Enciso disrupts this pattern, staging an interracial embrace between a Black male slave and a white noblewoman that is virtually unprecedented in Spanish literature and theater.[36] When Carlobal walks in on the embrace as indicated in the stage directions, he is so shocked that he arranges to have his sister sent off to a convent, setting up one of the most astonishing scenes of the play.

Swapping places with a soot-covered coal merchant who supplies the convent—with the pretext that they look alike—Juan Latino breaks Doña Ana out of her cloister and marries her before an ecclesiastical judge. This detail alone, absent from other sources of Juan Latino's life and thus presumably of the playwright's own invention, represents a breathtaking transgression by any reckoning. From a Black slave pursuing a white noblewoman, it is almost unthinkable. As a point of comparison, it will be recalled that when the Black protagonist of Lope de Vega's *The Marvel of Ethiopia* runs away with his master's white lover, he is shot through the chest with an arrow by the Devil. There are unsettling parallels outside Spain as well. In Shakespeare's *Othello*, written around 1603, marriage between the Black "Moor of Venice" and the white Desdemona—a union described as "an old black ram / [. . .] tupping [a] white ewe" (Shakespeare 1997, 1.1.88–89)—ends in the disastrous murder-suicide of the final scene. Yet Juan Latino faces no such lethal consequences to his behavior, though that may be partially due to the historical record the author wishes to follow.[37]

Latino's erudition and teaching ambitions also reveal the racial politics of the period. In act 1 of the play, as the protagonist accompanies the duke's son and his friends, he is ridiculed with vile racial epithets and spit at for reciting phrases in Latin. Later in the same scene, he is forced to kneel and kiss Magister Villanueva's hand, declaring in an aside, "Oh, color, what I suffer because of you!" (1.4). But when he attends the duke's literary academy in the same scene, he establishes his erudition and begins to gain respect. In act 2, he applies for the teaching post and is immediately challenged by Magister Villanueva, who argues that Latino is inferior and should be barred from a publicly funded position. Yet when Villanueva, in his application speech, uses insulting racial terms against Latino, he is fined by the moderator in the amount of one gold coin "for each word uttered outside the bounds of propriety and courtesy" (2.4). This

---

36. One possible precedent is the song "How a Lady Begs," which imagines a risqué dialogue between a Black male slave and a white noblewoman (see §Early Modern Period). But as an anonymous song, it lacks the very public and visual nature of theater, and it ends with only an anticipation of physical contact between the characters.
37. See Weissbourd (2013) for an excellent comparative analysis of *Othello* and *Juan Latino*.

is a fascinating moment that appears to indicate a certain degree of institutional reaction to anti-Black discourse. It also marks a tipping point in the way other characters respond to Latino, who now feels empowered to hit back with a series of antisemitic smears associating Villanueva and his supporters with the blood of converted Jews, a point also hinted at in the magister's last name.[38] In a dynamic that will be repeated in *The Brave Black Soldier*, Latino's participation in anti-Jewish discourse identifies him with the Christian majority, increasing his appeal to white Spanish audiences of the period.

A remarkable scene in act 3 seems crafted to enhance this appeal. The powerful prince, Don Juan of Austria, arrives in Granada to lead the campaign against the Morisco rebellion (a historically accurate detail) and invites Juan Latino to his quarters. After allowing his guest to return his hat to his head—an honor normally reserved for peers—Don Juan reveals that, by commission of his brother the king, an official portrait of Juan Latino will hang in the royal palace. In a move that was surely played to great effect, the painter arrives and unveils the portrait. The historicity of the characters in this scene (Latino, Don Juan, and the prince's attendant Quijada) has invited speculation that the unnamed painter as well as his painting may also have a basis in reality (Martín Casares 2016, 133–50). Be that as it may, it is certainly a dramatic "teaching moment" that would have modeled for audience members, in the figures of the prince and his brother the king, the esteem in which Latino should be held.

The scene in Don Juan's quarters does not end with the painting. The prince goes on to say he has composed a poem in Latino's name, which he proceeds to recite:

> Son of a slave, I was born in Baena,
> Where I first learned the alphabet.
> I grew up seeking the depths of truth:
> A prize that Heaven bestows on virtue.
> As a result of my labors of love
> I have become Granada's public servant:
> Its Orpheus, Mars, Cicero, and Homer
> In song, in arms, in Latin, in poetry.
> I became a prized professor of Greek,
> An illustrious man by all rights,

---

38. Villanueva means "new town," a possible allusion to the term *New Christian* that was applied to Jewish and Moorish converts to Christianity. It is important to remember that Jiménez de Enciso's family was also accused of having converted Jewish blood, and though it appears the accusation was accurate (Pike 1990), there may be a subtle critique in this scene of the way that innuendo and hearsay were used in the period. As there is never any objective confirmation in the play of Villanueva's ancestry, it is problematic to accept it as established fact as do Ivory (1979, 615) and Barrios (2002, 293).

Worthy of a stipend from this town.
And just as ancient Rome
Called Emperor Hadrian *the Greek*,
Noble Spain has dubbed me *the Latin*. (3.2)

It is significant that Jiménez de Enciso places this "biographical" sonnet in the mouth of Don Juan and not Juan Latino, contrary to assertions from a steady stream of commentators.[39] The effusively laudatory content is, in fact, questionable or exaggerated on several points. First, Don Juan indicates Juan Latino's birthplace as Baena, Spain. Though that assertion squares with a chronicle from the period (Fernández de Córdoba 1954, 198) and with other comments in the play, it is contradicted by the historical Juan Latino's autobiographical statement (E. Wright 2016, 23, fig. 3), which claims Africa as his birthplace: a conclusion that white audience members might have been inclined to draw about any Black man. Crucially, Don Juan's poem confirms Latino as a native-born Spaniard. Second, the poem alludes to military prowess ("Mars . . . in arms") and excellence in Greek ("I became a prized professor of Greek"), both of which seem to be exaggerations. There is no record that Latino served in the military, and while it seems he was competent in Greek (Green 1968, 136), he was best known as a Latinist. It all appears to be a clever sleight of hand on Jiménez de Enciso's part, sealing a sort of tacit collusion between the two characters: a wink and a nod through which the prince, as a gesture of magnanimity, validates a respectable identity for the slave, whose clever reply—"Silence is all I can manage"—neither confirms nor denies the torrent of hyperbole. Jiménez de Enciso brandishes the moral authority of the beloved Don Juan to aggrandize the figure of Juan Latino for the audience, fashioning an impressive pedigree that includes a European birthplace, military honors, and near-native conversance with the classics.

The playwright also makes clever use of this scene to dramatize the genesis of *The Austriad*, the epic poem in Latin hexameters that the real-life Latino penned to commemorate Don Juan of Austria's victory in the Battle of Lepanto (1571). One of the largest naval clashes in European history, Lepanto pitted an alliance known as the Holy League (Spain and the Italian states) against the Muslim Ottomans; the Holy League's resounding victory halted the Ottoman advance into the western Mediterranean and served as a Christian rallying cry in the struggle against Islam for years to come. In the scene in question, Latino tells Don Juan he will record his "memorable deeds" (3.2) in a poem he plans to compose in his honor, revealing the title as *The Austriad*. There is

---

39. Marín Ocete (1925, 7), Gates and Wolff (1998, 16), and Naveros Sánchez and Santos Flores (2000, 99) all insist that the poem is recited by Juan Latino. For a salutary correction, see Sánchez Marín and Muñoz Martín (2009, 242–43).

a glitch, however: Lepanto occurred in 1571, *after* the setting of this scene, so a direct mention of the battle would be an anachronism. The playwright avoids that blunder with the vaguely worded "memorable deeds": knowing, of course, that audience members would think of Lepanto and that, in any case, the reminder of Latino's authorship of *The Austriad* would further dispose them to sympathy for the main character.[40]

The scene in Don Juan's quarters mobilizes the two great representational arts of the Renaissance, poetry and painting, to create a flattering portrait of Juan Latino, further enhanced by the elegant classical Spanish spoken by the protagonist throughout the play.[41] But a final assessment of the author's attitude toward his character must reckon with several details that demean or diminish the protagonist. First, Doña Ana is described as having a face that "may limit [her] options" (1.1) and a "homely appearance" (2.3), and she tells her servant Juana: "Only intelligence is beautiful to me" (1.1). The thinly disguised implication is that only such a woman would be interested in a Black scholar who describes himself, at the duke's literary academy, as "a beautiful soul in an ugly body" (1.4), recalling the trope of the Black man with the white soul (see §Three Plays Attributed to Lope de Vega). Second, in the graduation scene at the end of the play, Juan Latino is mercilessly ridiculed in a long string of racially offensive terms, though they come in the context of a satirical university tradition that spares no one.[42]

The most important detail that diminishes Juan Latino and certainly the most troubling for modern readers is his slavery, which presents a major hurdle in his pursuit of Doña Ana as well his application for the teaching position. The scholar begs for his freedom five different times from the duke and duchess, even slipping in a bold universal claim that will find more robust development in *The Brave Black Soldier*: "Blacks are noble" (2.1). When his entreaties fall on deaf ears, he asks Don Juan of Austria, in the

---

40. The composition of *The Austriad* in Latin hexameters was meant to recall Virgil's *Aeneid*, a model for epic poets of the period. In her excellent analysis, E. Wright (2016) demonstrates that Latino wrote the poem in part to make his loyalties clear and position himself as favorably as possible in the rapidly shifting sands of Granada following the Morisco uprising. Jiménez de Enciso is thus perhaps not far off base when he has Doña Ana quiz Juan about his ethnicity in the scene analyzed above. On Latino's literary output, see also Sánchez Marín and Muñoz Martín (2018).
41. The claim that Juan Latino speaks in "black slang" (Martín Casares 2000b, 389) is incorrect. Nothing the protagonist says falls outside the register of classical literary Spanish, except the lines he recites in Latin.
42. As José Sánchez (1961, 15) explains, the traditional *vejamen* "is a satirical and festive scolding in which a person's physical and moral defects are brought to light and examined. [. . .] It constitutes the final part of the program [. . .] a good-natured and humorous satire directed at all those who have attended the event and at members of society." Sánchez's description applies perfectly to Castle's madcap final speech. Thus, while several critics (Gates and Wolff 1998, 39; Fra Molinero 1995, 159; Panford 1999, 6) have focused on the speech's merciless treatment of Juan Latino, which indeed rechannels all the play's racial animus, it is important to note that it also pillories officers of the university, noble members of the audience, and a motley assortment of "citizens and townspeople," "beautiful and discreet ladies," "judges of the Audiencia and Chancery Court," and "weapons, books, quills, and staffs" (3.6).

scene just analyzed, to intervene on his behalf. But the duke delivers a final, crushing response:

> DUKE. You have grown tiresome, magister. What need have you for freedom? Did you not win the teaching chair? Are you not respected by all? Are you not in charge of your house, your property, your servants? Have I not given you my word that I will facilitate the conferral of your degree?
> JUAN LATINO. Sir . . .
> DUKE. Not another word. My titles of Duke of Sessa and Count of Cabra are less important to me than having you as my slave. What prince or monarch can claim what I can? My fame will live in you more eternally than in the ancient and awesome deeds of my illustrious grandparents. Do not bring this matter up again. All you need to know is that I do not wish it. (3.2)

It is a difficult scene for modern readers to stomach: a slave, begging on bended knee for his freedom, only to have his hopes crushed because his master wishes to remain associated with the fame he has earned by his own merit. For many readers today, it is probably safe to say that reception of the play will turn on this one scene and on our understanding of Jiménez de Enciso's intentions. After seemingly taking such care to create an exemplary protagonist, why does he not free him when the historical Juan Latino reports that he was manumitted? Critics have professed bewilderment on this point, with Spratlin (1938, 17) complaining that "we constantly expect a liberation that never comes" while Gates and Wolff (1998, 39) opine that "it is either a sign of Enciso's artistry or of his lack of artistry that the play, despite its happy ending, strikes so many incongruous notes." Other critics, apparently unable to process these "incongruous notes," insist that Latino earns his freedom at the end of the play.[43] These reactions are understandable. Juan Latino's slavery raises complex and emotionally fraught questions that are probably impossible to answer satisfactorily, but I will try to provide some guidance.

One possibility is that Jiménez de Enciso is simply reflecting the historical reality as he understood it (Spratlin 1938, 17). While we know from Juan Latino's autobiographical statement (E. Wright 2016, 23, fig. 3) that he was freed in real life, we do not know exactly when it happened. Many biographers assume it would have occurred before he married, but there is no proof of that, and the historical Latino's use of the word *finally*

---

43. Ticknor (1882, 582, n. 12); Woodson (1935, 225); Williamsen (1981, 202, and 1982, 66); González Echegaray (1998, 424); Stoichita (2010, 218).

(Latin *tandem*) to refer to his manumission "insinuates that freedom was a long struggle" (E. Wright 2016, 50), perhaps well after his marriage. Jiménez de Enciso may have accurately incorporated information that we no longer have access to. The problem with this theory is that the author significantly alters the chronology elsewhere in the play: for example, in setting Latino's romance with Doña Ana a generation after it actually happened to allow it to coincide with the Morisco uprising. Had he really wanted to, it seems he could have freed his protagonist before the corresponding moment in the historical record.

There may also be literary and dramatic principles behind Jiménez de Enciso's preservation of Juan Latino's servitude. There is the old conceit of the lover as captive of the beloved, employed for example in "How a Lady Begs" (see §Early Modern Period). In fact, after he is denied his freedom by the duke, Latino tells Doña Ana: "My body is another's property, but you shall have my soul" (3.4). Second, though Spratlin (1938, 17) suggests the play is anticlimactic because Latino is never freed, is it not perhaps more dramatic that way? If the author was trying to shine a spotlight on the injustice of slavery, the "incongruous notes" observed by Gates and Wolff might have appealed to him precisely because of their jarring effect. I do not, however, find this idea entirely convincing given that it assumes an abolitionist inclination in an author who, as revealed in the Biographical Sketches, belonged to a slave-trafficking family and owned slaves himself.

We are thus forced to consider the disconcerting possibility that Jiménez de Enciso's personal life blinded him to the injustices faced by Juan Latino and led him to side with the duke's position. Spratlin (1938, 205) attempts to preempt this conclusion by suggesting that Jiménez de Enciso's decision to free his own slaves shows a "humane attitude" toward them and is thus consistent with a "dramatist who could write so sympathetically of Juan Latino." But this argument has two problems. First, the decision to free the slaves was made in 1627, almost certainly after the play was written, and thus does not necessarily reflect the author's thinking at the time. Second, Spratlin's argument assumes that Jiménez de Enciso *intended* to "write so sympathetically" of his character. But what if Juan Latino's repeated requests for freedom are not intended to generate sympathy but rather exasperation? This appears to be exactly the reaction that informs an aside from the duchess as he begs for his freedom: "He's an insistent one!" (2.1). If the duchess's comment is meant to enable the audience to think the same way, any "incongruities" disappear and the work becomes an apology for slavery. We are thus left with a thematically incongruous play or a morally repellent one. Either way, interpretation of *Juan Latino* runs aground on this original sin of early modern society.

Any discussion of racial politics and the question of sympathy in *Juan Latino* would be incomplete without consideration of two additional figures, inextricably tied to the main character through a web of associations involving skin color, religion, and nationality: the white Morisco Don Fernando and the Black Moor Cañerí.

A well-known historical figure, Don Fernando de Válor, claimed noble lineage going back to the caliphs of medieval Spain's Umayyad dynasty. Born in post-1492 Granada and thus obligatorily Christian, he held a hereditary position on the town council but became disgruntled over mistreatment of the Morisco people, adopting the Arabic name Aben Humeya and leading them to revolt in 1568. In Jiménez de Enciso's play, he is a charismatic but brooding figure, alluded to in the first scene as a suitor to Doña Ana, who reassures her brother that she could never be interested in a man who is "barely even a Christian" (1.1).[44] In interpreting comments such as this one, it is crucial to remember that Jiménez de Enciso sets his work during the Morisco revolt of 1568–1570, an event that would appear to have garnered little sympathy among Christians. Ironically, however, the revolt coincided with a Moorish craze in Spanish literature and culture, dubbed *Maurophilia* by later critics (Cirot 1938–1944; Fuchs 2007 and 2011), which peaked in the second half of the 1500s. In novellas such as *The Abencerraje* (1561) and *Ozmín and Daraja* (from the first part of Mateo Alemán's *Guzmán de Alfarache*, 1599), Moorish characters appear as noble and sympathetic figures, often tragically doomed by history's steady march toward Christianity. This perspective seemed to find confirmation in the expulsion of 1609–1614, occasioning much sympathy and soul-searching: Cervantes's character Ricote and his Morisco people "weep for Spain" (Cervantes 1987, 2:451), while as late as 1626 a commentator calls the expulsion a "most malign policy of state" (qtd. in Kamen 1991, 220). Is Don Fernando de Válor a late expression of Maurophilia? Does Jiménez de Enciso engage in the soul-searching of his contemporaries, connecting the dots between Doña Ana's contemptuous "barely even a Christian" comment and the hostility that would lead to the expulsion? Or is the author attempting to *justify* the expulsion by reenacting, through the play's historical dimension, an event that Christian Spaniards viewed as an act of treason? As with the question of slavery, it is exceptionally difficult to assess the author's intentions, and all options must be kept in mind in considering the play's Moorish characters.

A key development in Don Fernando's character comes in an extraordinary speech he delivers to the duke, who, acting on behalf of the king, is attempting to suppress Morisco language and culture. Historically, these assimilationist measures, passed in 1567 (1569 in the play's telescoped chronology), were a direct cause of the Morisco uprising, and Don Fernando's speech is modeled on the real-life speech of Francisco

---

44. Jiménez de Enciso borrows heavily from Mármol y Carvajal's account of Don Fernando (Mármol y Carvajal 1852, especially bk. 4, ch. 7), but the detail of his courtship of Doña Ana is a product of the playwright's imagination.

Núñez Muley following passage of the measures.[45] Cutting across the tangled issues of religion, national origin, and skin color in early modern Spain, Don Fernando's speech is at once a righteous defense of Morisco identity and a highly problematic statement on Black slavery. Arguing that his people should be allowed to continue speaking Arabic and wearing traditional dress, he also rejects as "deeply offensive" the idea that they be forced to give up their right to own "Guineans." This position, which comes straight from Núñez Muley's speech, plays perfectly into the complicated dramatic structure that Jiménez de Enciso has created, in which one of the play's male rivals for Doña Ana (Don Fernando) is associated with the dominant group through skin color and the other (Juan Latino) through religion. At the center of this Venn diagram stands the white Christian duke, wielding an enormous institutional power that forces both men to beg him for freedom: Latino on behalf of himself and Don Fernando on behalf of his people. Ultimately, the duke denies both requests.

The parallels that link Don Fernando to Juan Latino are striking. Both men are suitors to Doña Ana; both are constructed with what appears to be a good bit of sympathy (though there are lingering questions in each case); both are locked out of the dominant group, by either religion or skin color, and severely restricted in their freedom (Latino by literal slavery and Don Fernando by house arrest); both are denied their fondest wish by the duke. But these parallels begin to recede as Don Fernando's character is consumed by the Morisco issue. At the beginning of act 2, the duke reports that after being captured and imprisoned, Don Fernando was liberated from the tower by a band of Moorish outlaws and has escaped into the wilderness. In a dramatic scene in the Alpujarras region, he adopts his Arabic name, Aben Humeya, and is proclaimed king of the Moriscos (2.2). At this point his main antagonist is no longer the Black Christian, Juan Latino, but the Black Moor, Cañerí: the third and final piece in the play's complex ethnic puzzle.

Cañerí first appears in act 1, where he slips unnoticed into Don Fernando's house and interrupts him as he reads a letter from his uncle. Dressed in animal skins and carrying a staff, he is portrayed as a savage and terrifying figure that plays off many Black stereotypes of the period. As noted by Gates and Wolff (1998, 39), he comes across as a powerful and larger-than-life figure, a sort of specter that haunts Don Fernando in scenes imbued with philosophical resonance. The following dialogue, from their second encounter, is particularly noteworthy:

---

45. Jiménez de Enciso probably came across Núñez Muley's speech in Mármol y Carvajal (1852, bk. 2, ch. 9). The original manuscript of the speech, complete with Núñez Muley's signature, was discovered in Spain's National Library in the late 1800s. See the excellent translation and commentary by Vincent Barletta (Núñez Muley 2007).

DON FERNANDO. Shadow, demon, or vision: What do you want with me?
CAÑERÍ. To help you.
DON FERNANDO. Help me?
CAÑERÍ. And to harrow you.
DON FERNANDO. Why?
CAÑERÍ. Because I must serve you in order to overthrow you.
DON FERNANDO. Who are you?
CAÑERÍ. He who shall give you a kingdom.
DON FERNANDO. *[Aside.]* I tremble! *[Aloud.]* Tell me: Who are you?
CAÑERÍ. I am he who shall kill you. *(Exit.)* (1.3)

Importantly, Cañerí does not speak in the *bozal* dialect but in an elevated, oracular manner characterized by riddles. How can his purpose be at once to help, harrow, serve, overthrow, and kill Don Fernando? The clue lies in the phrase "he who shall give you a kingdom," the literal meaning of which becomes clear when Cañerí, citing ancient Muslim prophecies known as *jofores*, enables Don Fernando to become king of the Moriscos.[46] Figuratively, there is an unmistakable parallel with the Devil, who tempts Jesus in the wilderness with all the kingdoms of the inhabited earth (Matthew 4:8; Luke 4:5). I do not mean to suggest that Cañerí is the Devil incarnate but rather a sort of diabolic alter ego of Don Fernando who leads him to his act upon his worst impulses. While Jesus resists, Don Fernando gives in and, soon recognizing the sinister bargain that has put him in power, orders Cañerí assassinated. "Take heed," warns his uncle, "that you order the death of he who delivered you a kingdom" (2.2), confirming the biblical parallel.[47] Thus does Jiménez de Enciso refashion the old trope of the Devil as a Black man (as in TSW, Fig. 8) to explain how the upstanding young Don Fernando, suitor to the noble Doña Ana and member of the Granada town council, could come to lead the treasonous Morisco rebellion.

The implicit racial hierarchy that Jiménez de Enciso projects onto Juan Latino, Don Fernando, and Cañerí shows that while skin color is an important marginalizing factor in early modern Spain, religion is still more important in this regard. On the one hand, the white Don Fernando never misses an opportunity to draw distinctions between himself and the Black characters based on skin color: "O vengeful heavens, bring me black omens and black fortune, black life and black death, black love and black jealousy!

---

46. The *jofores* are treated in bk. 3 of Mármol y Carvajal, including the crucial prophecy of the Cave of Castares in 3.3. For an excellent analysis, see Morabito (2020).
47. The key word is *reino* (kingdom), which appears in the Spanish text of *Juan Latino* and in both Spanish translations of the Bible that Jiménez Enciso would have had access to (*Biblia* 1569 and *Biblia* 1602).

I am pursued by one *negro* [Cañerí], intent on killing me, while another [Juan Latino] flaunts my ribbon" (1.4). On the other hand, Don Fernando is soundly rejected by Doña Ana in favor of the Black Juan Latino because, while the latter's faith is beyond reproach, the former is "barely even a Christian" (1.1). And once Don Fernando follows Cañerí into treachery and becomes Aben Humeya, he is no longer even "barely" a Christian. With both characters seen as betraying Spain and Christendom, any distinctions between the two based on skin color become irrelevant. The leveling is completed in dramatic fashion at the end of the play, as reported by an ensign: "After killing Don Fernando, the barbarian [Cañerí] fled to a tower, where his African heart told him there was no escaping our Christian Achilles. He hurled himself onto the rocky cliffs below, where his body was smashed into a thousand bits" (3.6).

In a final twist, the grisly end to Aben Humeya and Cañerí is reported just after Juan Latino's vicious lampooning in the university graduation ceremony and just before Don Juan of Austria reconciles him with Doña Ana's brother—still angry over the interracial marriage—with the observation that the Latin scholar is "not black but rather a man whom the sun has struck more vigorously than everyone else, for he has spent much time staring at it" (3.6). What are we to make of this bewildering juxtaposition? Is the death of the villains meant to make Juan Latino's public ridicule, and perhaps even his slavery, more palatable by comparison? Does Don Juan of Austria, after essentially conferring Spanish nationality upon the protagonist through his laudatory poem, complete his "whitening" by affirming that he is not Black but simply suntanned? Has Juan Latino become a safe, sanitized version of Cañerí and thus more fit for domestic consumption (Beusterien 2006a, 110)? If so, has he become bland in the process, making Don Fernando and Cañerí ultimately more interesting as characters (Gates and Wolff 1998, 39–40)?

Such are the complexities of Jiménez de Enciso's representation of race in *Juan Latino*, to which I shall return after examining the companion plays.

The Servant Soldier

Like *Juan Latino*, Claramonte's *The Brave Black Soldier* is firmly rooted in Spanish history, coinciding with the Duke of Alba's intervention in the revolt of the Low Countries: precisely the same moment (c. 1570) as Don Juan of Austria's suppression of the Morisco uprising. Unlike Jiménez de Enciso's protagonist, however, it is not clear that Claramonte's Juan de Mérida has a solid historical dimension. While there is some suggestion he could be based on the early sixteenth-century Black conquistador Juan Valiente, the connection is a tenuous one that would imply, at best, heavily altered biographical details. I do not assume any connection in the interpretation that follows.[48]

The plot of Claramonte's play reads like a streamlined version of Jiménez de Enciso's. Juan Latino's double goal of marriage and a teaching position becomes a singular focus in Juan de Mérida, who wishes nothing more than to serve his king on the battlefield in Flanders. Like Juan Latino, he faces obstacles to his ambition, which come into focus in the play's startling first line: "Beware the dog!" Directed at the protagonist as he approaches a group of soldiers in Mérida to request a position in their company, it is the first of many variations of the word *perro* (a common racial slur of the period, also used for converted Jews and Muslims) that will be hurled at Juan over the course of the play. The situation quickly escalates and he is forced to defend himself at sword point. Eventually arrested and condemned to garroting, he is saved only when the play's main female character, Doña Leonor, recognizing him as the "son of the slave Catalina who belongs to my cousin Doña Juana de Vera," appeals for clemency. Juan thus returns home, where a key exchange takes place between him and Doña Leonor's cousin:

> JUAN DE MÉRIDA. Consider that my valor is yours, for I am a dog of your house, madam, and I wish to go forth to conquer the globe.
> DOÑA JUANA. And go forth you may, for my father grows weary of your mischief.
> JUAN DE MÉRIDA. Heaven has a hand in my behavior; do not fret if it seems madness to you. It behooves me to take quick leave of this land, where I live at the mercy of fools. Give me license to turn the coal discarded from your house into a torch. *[Pause.]* Content and prosperous I depart with this letter, for it attests to my freedom. I shall use it to rebrand the vile rebus of fate and bring an end to the infamy of color. My valor I shall represent to the world, for though I am black, I have not known slavery, and the sun in the sky is a liar if it thinks otherwise. Madam, please continue to show kindness to my mother, Catalina, and I beg your father and my lord to forgive me, for my presence in his house brought him no advantage. And when I return wealthy and satisfied by fortune, I shall repay the favor that I do not speak of today, and he shall find in me a loyal slave.
> DOÑA JUANA. Such eloquent madness! *(Exit.)* (1.2)

---

48. On Juan Valiente, see Restall (2000). On the supposed connection to Claramonte's character, see Spratlin (1934, 64), Panford (2003, 55–58), Lawrance (2005, 77), Beusterien (2006a, 114), and Ndiaye (2022, 276–77).

Dense with crucial, complicated information about Juan's background and the treatment he receives as a result of his skin color, these initial scenes require a careful analysis.

A key question is the issue of Juan's freedom, complicated by a subtle but significant divergence of language in the textual history of the play. The variation I follow has Juan use the present perfect tense in his declaration, "I have not known slavery" ("No *he sido* esclavo"). The other variation uses the simple present tense: "I am not a slave" ("No *soy* esclavo"). Not only is the first variation more textually authoritative; its sweep into the past is confirmed at the end of act 1 when Juan tells the Duke of Alba, "[I am] Juan de Mérida, for in that province I was born a free man. And so that no one may insult me further, here is my letter of freedom, which I carry about my neck like an indulgence" (1.6). This assertion, however, would appear to contradict the normal practice of the period, which followed Roman law in making slavery matrilineal: that is, children of enslaved mothers such as Juan's were born slaves themselves.[49]

Juan's letter of freedom, an important prop that visually confirms his liberty at two key moments in the play, may be Claramonte's attempt to resolve this ambiguity, but it only raises an additional question: Where does the letter come from? Its origin is of no small consequence. If Doña Juana produces it as a result of Juan's request ("Give me license . . ."), it means that she frees him as he speaks. If Juan pulls it from a pocket or perhaps a pouch around his neck, it means he is already free and the "license" he requests is simply a matter of courtesy. The second interpretation seems to be confirmed in his dialogue with the duke and the remarkable comparison to an indulgence carried about the neck. Furthermore, it seems improbable that Doña Juana would write a letter authorizing Juan's freedom on the spot, without consulting with her father; nor is there anything in the dialogue to telegraph that she does so.[50]

An additional complication comes in Juan's reference to the "vile rebus of fate": that is, the brand often carried by slaves on their faces, which Cervantes references in *The Jealous Extremaduran* (Cervantes 2000, 104) and which Juan Latino also mentions in requesting his freedom (2.1). But if Juan de Mérida was born free, why would he be carrying a brand? Given that no other character ever remarks on it (in either *Juan Latino* or *The Brave Black Soldier*), I believe the reference is best understood as a metaphor that serves to enable the complex pun I examine in my discussion of wordplay in the Translator's Note.

---

49. On matrilineal slavery in Roman law, see Buckland (1908, 397–401). On the practice in medieval and early modern Spain, see Martín Casares (2000b, 76) and Domínguez Ortiz (2003, 47). The variation of the play containing the present perfect tense in Juan's mention of slavery is found in Claramonte y Corroy 1636–2016 [A], [B], [H], [I], [J], [L], [N], [O], and [P].

50. In my translation of the scene, I insert a stage direction indicating a pause before the letter is referenced to mark the important moment, but I follow all versions of the text in not indicating where the prop comes from.

A final area of ambiguity is the frequent and unavoidable use of the word *negro*, which, as noted above (see §Language), can mean both *black* and *slave*. When Juan tells Doña Juana at the end of the play, "I have always prided myself, my lady, on being your *negro*," does he mean *slave*? That interpretation, while enabled by the language, would contradict all of act 1, scene 2, and I have thus translated *negro* in this case as *servant*. Similarly, several lines later, when Doña Juana tells Juan, "I wish to promote you from *negro* to *dueño*," one interpretation of the last four words could be "from slave to master." But *dueño* is not the word normally used for a slave master (that word is *amo*). *Dueño* literally means owner, and with human subjects it usually appears in the context of courtly love and means something like "owner of my heart." Accordingly, I have translated this line as "from servant to husband," and I believe the most accurate interpretation of Juan's role in the play is that of domestic servant.

The ambiguous representation of Juan's freedom, tangled up in the text's complicated transmission history and semantic slippage, makes it difficult to reach consensus on this important issue. While several critics describe the main character as a slave without qualification, I feel confident in saying that Claramonte insists on his freedom at several key moments of the play, chief among them the scene with Doña Juana.[51] He has two reasons for doing so. First, he wishes to show that the treatment his character receives is based on skin color, not slavery. In Jiménez de Enciso's play, the obstacles faced by Juan Latino are framed as a technical issue, with both Doña Ana and Magister Villanueva citing his unfree status as a pretext for denying his requests. While Latino seems to recognize the real reason in his comment, "Oh, color, what I suffer because of you!" (1.4), he does so only in an aside, leaving unchallenged the public position that the issue is his slavery. By dramatizing Juan de Mérida's freedom in the scene with Doña Juana, Claramonte strips away this pretext, making it clear that the challenges and abuse his character faces are a direct result of his skin color. With his free status validated in a letter that is waved about as a prop, there can be no doubt what his mistreatment is about.

The second reason for Juan's freedom is that it enables full development of his titular character trait: bravery. Despite being an object of ridicule at the beginning of the play, he gradually gains respect through demonstration of this trait. His main rival is the infantry captain Don Agustín, source of the "Beware the dog" comment. After the skirmish of the first scene, however, the captain comments to Doña Leonor, whom he is courting, that Juan "lacks only the right color to be a knight" (1.1). The comment sets up a story arc that will culminate in its refutation. Stowing away on the Duke of

---

51. Woodson (1935, 228), Fra Molinero (1995, 163, and 2000, 125), Rodríguez López-Vázquez (1997, 5), González Echegaray (1998, 409), Fradejas Lebrero (2008, 98), and Ndiaye (2022, 79) all claim that Juan is a slave. Fra Molinero modifies his position, without explanation, in a later article (2014, 11).

Alba's ship to Flanders, Juan proves himself on the battlefield with many daredevil feats including the single-handed capture of the Prince of Orange, an astounding accomplishment that forces the enemy into a negotiated surrender. When a bewildered Flemish captain asks who was responsible for the bold move, Juan's answer—"I, for only a black man would risk such a thing because only a black man is nothing" (2.4)—recalls *Count Lucanor*'s lowly Black stable hand who had "nothing to lose" in confronting his king (see §Medieval Period).

Juan's bravery enables a meteoric rise through the ranks, from private to sergeant (1.6) to ensign (2.2) to captain (2.2), with a final surprise promotion that comes upon his return home. Invited to an audience with the king, he makes such an impression that the monarch names him lieutenant general. But that is not all:

> DUKE. He who, through honorable actions, shows the ability to rule over great lords has earned a lordship. His majesty offers you a seat in the Order of Santiago.
> JUAN DE MÉRIDA. *[Stunned.]* But how do I qualify for the order with Guinean blood?
> DUKE. Your deeds here in Flanders qualify you, for such an outstanding captain needs no qualification other than his valor. You are the product of your accomplishments, through which fortune accredits your color. (3.1)

Juan's knighthood in the military-religious Order of Santiago not only validates his bravery and debunks the captain's initial comment to Doña Leonor; it also makes a profound statement about the origin of bravery, confirming the protagonist's very first line in the play: "Defect does not reside in blood, nor does courage" (1.1). Juan's African blood is not a defect or impediment to his induction into the order. The duke's language is key in this regard: the protagonist's *deeds* qualify him; he is the product of his *accomplishments*. Given that induction into orders such as Santiago *did* routinely require not only deeds and accomplishments but extensive investigations into family genealogy and proof of "pure" blood, as shown by the case of Jiménez de Enciso's cousins (see the Biographical Sketches), the significance of this scene cannot be overstated.

The emphasis on deeds and behavior sets up a dichotomy between Juan and the play's noble characters. In the first scene of act 3, while waiting to meet the king, Juan is confronted by four noblemen who hurl racial insults at him and, reflecting a practice of the period, sneeze and fart in his direction.[52] While Jiménez de Enciso represents

---

52. On this vile behavior toward Blacks, see Pike (1972, 187–88), Lowe (2005, 20), Ogallas Moreno (Claramonte y Corroy 1636–2016 [R], n. 46), and Moreno (1997, 85).

their behavior somewhat humorously, it is significant that he gives Juan the last laugh. Attacking all four of the noblemen at once, he easily overpowers them, forcing them to cry out for help to the palace guards, whom Juan proceeds to take on as well. When the duke arrives to quell the madcap scuffle, he recognizes Juan and pardons him, leaving the four noblemen humiliated.

A much more significant example comes in the contrast between Juan and his main rival, Don Agustín. Having promised to remain in Mérida and marry Doña Leonor, the blue-blooded captain instead deflowers her and slips out of town in the dark to return to his military post (1.3), later accepting a proposal from his father (2.2) to marry her wealthier cousin, Doña Juana de Vera: none other than the daughter of Juan de Mérida's former employer. Meanwhile, Doña Leonor makes her way to Flanders, where she eventually requests Juan's help in restoring her honor. The female cousins thus bring out the innate contrasts between the two men: perfidy and greed motivate the "noble" captain to abandon Doña Leonor for Doña Juana, while boldness and chivalry lead the lowborn Juan to leave Doña Juana's service and come to the aid of Doña Leonor. The contrast is also enhanced on the battlefield, where Juan proves his bravery time and again while the captain is exposed as a coward and a hypocrite. In a pair of telling scenes at the end of act 1, Don Agustín disguises himself as an enemy "Teuton" to carry out a mission he has usurped from Juan, but the latter, also in disguise, captures him, steals his insignia, and humiliates him before the duke.[53]

Validation of Juan's bravery through his contrast with other noble characters and his astonishing induction into the Order of Santiago enables an even more astonishing ending. Back in Mérida and now Don Agustín's superior officer, Juan refuses to let him forget their past:

> In this very place, if you remember, incited by my lowliness, you refused to grant me a position in the army; and in the same spot you now recognize me—who would have believed it!—as your general. For thus does time transform fortune. And while I could take black vengeance on you here for your offenses, I wish to honor your person so you'll see me as a black man who both acts white and targets whites . . . for promotion! And thus I name you to my regiment as a three-star colonel, though it's insufficient for so great a soldier. (3.2)

---

53. What Juan's disguise is meant to look like is an interesting question. The text indicates that he wears a mask but provides no description. Beusterien (2006a, 115) assumes a white mask, but I do not see why that has to be the case. White would certainly create some irony (especially if the captain's "Teutonic" disguise is black), but a mask of any color would serve the purpose of disguising Juan for the mission.

With a clever pun on Spanish *blanco* ("white" and "target": see the Translator's Note for a full explanation) that will reappear in *Virtues Overcome Appearances*, Juan kills his formal rival with kindness as a prelude to forcing him to honor his word and marry Doña Leonor. But this good deed leaves Doña Juana without a husband, prompting a remarkable dialogue:

> DOÑA JUANA. *[To JUAN DE MÉRIDA.]* You betray me.
> JUAN DE MÉRIDA. On the contrary, madam: I look out for your good name. For if Don Agustín had given you his hand in deception, you would have looked foolish and lost all honor. And if I have stripped you of your husband—though your complaint is without justification— choose another from Mérida to your liking, and I shall, through my position and my income, offer him to you.
> DOÑA JUANA. Well since I am to be married under your sponsorship, and Heaven has bestowed upon you an honor that equals my nobility, I wish to promote you from servant to husband. (3.2)

It is a stunning conclusion by any measure. Juan has gone from the lowly son of a slave to the rank of lieutenant general, a seat in the Order of Santiago, and marriage to the white noblewoman whom he had previously served as a domestic. Don Agustín, meanwhile, is forced to marry Doña Leonor and watch idly as Doña Juana chooses the Black man he had tried to execute in the first scene. So controversial was the interracial marriage that it was deleted, along with Juan's induction into the Order of Santiago, from the 1638 edition of the text, though it was included in most later editions and taken for granted in Guerrero's eighteenth-century sequel.[54]

Emphasized throughout the play and culminating in the explosive conclusion, Juan's bravery and chivalry work to counteract suspicions audience members might have about his black skin. In an unsettling way, several reactionary character traits serve

---

54. The first modern editor to restore the missing scenes to the play text was Rodríguez López-Vázquez in 1997 (Claramonte y Corroy 1636–2016 [P]), though Treviño Trejo included them in an appendix to his dissertation in 1977 (Claramonte y Corroy 1636–2016 [O], 287–335). Whether the scenes were performed in seventeenth-century productions of the play is an open question. The only manuscript edition of the work (Claramonte y Corroy 1636–2016 [B]), which seems to include the annotations of an acting company, leaves intact Juan's induction into Santiago but scratches through key lines of the marriage scene with "no" written in the margin. The same manuscript includes official approval for public performances of the play in Zaragoza in 1651 and 1652. The play was also performed before King Philip IV in 1637 (Ferrer Valls 2012a, item 2) with additional palace performances in Madrid in 1675 and 1688 (Ferrer Valls 2012a, items 4–5), suggesting considerable popularity. Additionally, Juan de Mérida makes an appearance in a farcical skit performed for Princess Margaret's birthday around 1660 (Restori 1903, 142–54).

a similar purpose. Channeling a popular antisemitic poem known for its insinuation that the blood of Jews could be smelled by animals (Gillet 1926 and 1928), Juan refers to himself as "Alba's dog" and exclaims to the duke, "Bring on the Jews!" (2.2). There is also an extended homophobic joke when Doña Leonor, in order to travel to Flanders, disguises herself as an effeminate male page, prompting an ominous comment from Juan about "charred flesh" (2.1).[55] While distasteful to modern readers, these qualities would have enhanced the character's appeal to early modern Spanish audiences, aligning him with the sentiments of the white majority in a parallel to Juan Latino's insinuations about Villanueva's Jewish blood.

An additional reactionary character trait of Juan's is a strong anti-Protestant streak, which comes into focus through an extended mix of allusions, color symbolism, and cultural references. It bears remembering that the Reformation's entrenchment in the Low Countries dovetailed with resistance to Spanish rule, which dated back to the inheritance of Holy Roman Emperor Charles V in 1516. By the time of the play's setting in the 1560s, the resistance had boiled over into open revolt. From the Spanish point of view, then, the Reformation was not only heresy but treason, and though it is never directly named in Claramonte's play, Protestantism informs the background every bit as much as Islam does in *Juan Latino*. The basic optics of Juan de Mérida's service under the Duke of Alba's banner are clear enough: in fighting on the side of Catholic Spain, in murdering enemy captains and capturing princes, he is a defender of the faith. But Claramonte goes a step further. Following Lope de Vega's model in *Black Slave to the Greatest Master* (see §Three Plays Attributed to Lope de Vega), he inverts traditional color hierarchies and associates whiteness with the Protestant rebels and blackness with Juan's loyal Catholicism.

Midway through the play, as the war takes a difficult turn for Spain and the duke contemplates withdrawal, his soldiers offer a grim assessment:

> The winter has turned brutal with the snow's assault, which the sky unleashes in copious quantities. It's all a frozen chaos. [. . .] The barracks sink into the bog; the troops are up to their necks in water and muck. The bulwarks do nothing against this muddy fate. Every day we bury soldiers the dawn finds frozen in their beds. [. . .] The rebels, offspring of the snow, have the advantage of home turf. The water does not bother them, no matter how much it rains. Nor does the ice, to which they have inbred resistance. (2.2)

---

55. Punishment for sodomy in early modern Spain included burning at the stake. Seventy-one men in Seville suffered this fate between 1567 and 1616. See Perry (1990, 124) and Berco (2008, 356–57).

The bleak, colorless landscape of the Low Countries—which anticipates the symbolism of Albania in *Virtues Overcome Appearances*—spawns rebels with "inbred resistance" to the elements: and, by extension, to Catholicism. The arresting description is confirmed when the enemy captain Vivanblec—perhaps a scrambling of Spanish *blanco* (white)—marches into the Spanish camp atop a snow-white horse and challenges any Spaniard willing to fight him. Accepting the challenge, Juan promises to make him "vomit up with your soul all the beer you've drunk, assuming you didn't gulp down Rhine." Dragged offstage, Vivanblec is heard screaming as Juan dispatches him (2.2). With a wordplay on *Rhine* (*Rin*) / *wine* (*vin-o*), the imagery of this scene suggests a grotesque, inverted communion: the Protestant captain, associated with whiteness through his snowy horse, is forced to vomit up pale beer rather than swallow the dark wine of the sacrament.

Parallel to Juan's religious intolerance is a supercilious Spanish nationalism that mocks and muddles the cultural differences of the Low Countries. Vivanblec is variously referred to as a German, a Fleming, and a Teuton, while his horse is a Frisian. When he introduces himself with his full name, Monsieur de Vivanblec et Raballac, Juan quips, "A name as dreadful as your appearance." Juan also mocks the language of the locals, comparing it to *bozal* Spanish: "Their language sounds worse than my own, assuming I spoke like a newly arrived black slave. It's as if Guinea started breeding white people" (2.1). With this comment, Juan turns Flanders into Guinea, channeling the racial animus against Black Africans toward the white Protestant rebels.

The religious and cultural malice, anchored in the negative portrayal of whiteness, continues when Juan promises to become a "black dog" to any "white lions" the enemy sends out to avenge Vivanblec (2.2). While lions were traditionally associated with the heraldry of the Prince of Orange, they were not routinely depicted as white. Juan's description cements the connection between whiteness and the Protestant enemy while recasting in positive terms—"black dog," which also recalls "Alba's dog"—the insult he received in the first scene. The inversion reaches its climax in the following scene, when the protagonist sets out on a mission on Christmas Eve: "This is the night that outshines the day, sovereign in God's divine hierarchy, for with his resplendent and beautiful star, he guides me like a magus. I am the black man in the nativity scene, and on this holy night, as the angel chants of glory, I respond with my instrument: a hoarse and unsteady voice that celebrates the night with songs from Guinea" (2.3). With whiteness linked to political rebellion and Protestant heresy, blackness is now shown to be guided by God and present at the birth of Jesus. The character who was told to "go to Guinea" if he wanted to fight responds with "songs from Guinea" that, in addition to welcoming the Savior, will lead him to capture the Prince of Orange and change the course of the war. Once he is in Juan's captivity, the prince remarks, "I would much prefer your jet, captain, to my noble ivory," completing the color inversion at the heart of Juan's anti-Protestant bias (2.3).

A final element that must be considered in a racial analysis of *The Brave Black Soldier* is the slave Antón, who appears in five of the play's twelve scenes. For the most part, he is a throwback to the demeaning representation of Blacks in the theater of Gil Vicente and Lope de Rueda (see §Early Modern Period). He speaks in *bozal*, behaves cartoonishly, and contributes little of substance to the plot, constrained by the double role of Black character and clownish lackey (the latter a staple of the *comedia*). Nevertheless, his character adds depth and complexity to the play around the themes of skin color and slavery, often providing important contrasts to Juan de Mérida or spotlighting issues in ways the main character cannot. Though shuffled in and out of scenes in obedience to a narrow, mainly comedic intent, he injects a startling seriousness into the play on several occasions.

It is disappointing that Claramonte resorts to the *bozal* dialect to represent Antón's speech. Given that Jiménez de Enciso scrupulously avoids it in *Juan Latino*, as does Lope de Vega in *The Marvel of Ethiopia*, it comes as something of a regression. But it is not without purpose. In the first place, Antón's barbaric Spanish, which I have rendered into a scrambled, vaguely Elizabethan idiom (see the Translator's Note for more detail), calls attention to Juan de Mérida's perfect classical register, further elevating the main character. Second, the opacity of some of his formulations parallels the playwright's representation of the languages of the Low Countries, as when Juan brings back two prisoners from his first mission:

> (Enter JUAN DE MÉRIDA with two FLEMING soldiers and their harquebuses.)
> FLEMING 1. Nee-tay!
> FLEMING 2. Nee-tay!
> JUAN DE MÉRIDA. Nee-tay, schmee-tay. Even Beelzebub is at a loss to understand your gibberish! (1.6)

On the one hand, this exchange further reinforces Juan's nationalistic disdain for the culture of the Low Countries. On the other, it is significant that it comes only seconds after Antón's first appearance in the play. While the slave's garbled Spanish is bound to provoke befuddlement in the audience, it is quickly proved to be more intelligible than the language of the Flemings. Juan makes this point explicit: "I want to bring back two or three halberds along with their sergeants chattering away: *gran bot, moltuyn, butir, estricot, zerbeza, flin flan*. Their language sounds worse than my own, assuming I spoke like a newly arrived black slave" (2.1). The gibberish of the Flemings, in an ironic twist, has the same elevating effect on Antón's language that Antón's does on Juan's.

Nevertheless, buried within the string of nonsense that Juan spouts in imitation of Flemish is the word *zerbeza*: beer (*cerveza* in modern Spanish), which becomes imbued with meaning in the encounter with Vivanblec.[56] The tiny sequence of "Flemish" that Juan utters represents Antón's Spanish through the looking glass, for the slave's garbled vocabulary and ungrammatical constructions contain similar nuggets of meaning: at intervals funny, poignant, even unsettling. It is certainly funny when he refers to Don Agustín as *dung* instead of *don* (1.6). But when he calls the king a "mighty dong" in the palace scene (3.1), it may well have a different effect.[57] Similarly, some of the language seems intended to corrode Juan's carefully curated image. Antón refers to him as the "flower of Mérida, stink of *merda*" (1.6), punning on the name of Juan's hometown and the Portuguese word for shit.[58] On a related but more serious level, Javier Irigoyen-García (2005, 157–58) focuses on the prepositional phrase *in Juan* in Antón's line "Why in Juan twere killing little Antón?" (2.1) to suggest that Antón is a sort of inner projection of Juan's consciousness. While it is a risky reading of this particular passage given that the line appears *without* the preposition in most versions of the text, it does accurately highlight the potential of Antón's language, in both comic and serious contexts, to reveal unintentional truths.

Perhaps the most important—and disturbing—way in which Antón contributes to *The Brave Black Soldier* is through the theme of slavery. When he first appears in the play, in the last scene of act 1, he is in the service of Doña Leonor as she arrives in Flanders. In contrast to the case of Juan, there is no ambiguity about Antón's slavery: "I will grant you freedom if you keep the secret I've entrusted to you" (1.6), Doña Leonor tells him. The "secret" is presumably the fact that she is a woman disguised as a boy, as part of her plan to make Don Agustín honor his marriage commitment. She repeats her promise about freedom when she begins baiting Juan de Mérida's homophobia: "In this way I'll keep him confused and distracted. Play along, Antón. [. . .] Your freedom hangs in the balance" (2.1). In the course of the prank, however, Juan comes to believe that Antón is responding to the page's advances and threatens him with death. As a result, Antón leaves Doña Leonor and enters Juan's service.

Once Antón changes masters, it is unclear where Doña Leonor's promise of freedom stands, unless we are to conclude that she freed him before he entered Juan's service.

---

56. The different versions of the text vary in their representation of the nonsense string, but they all include some spelling of *zerbeza*. My translation follows the 1638 text exactly.
57. See the discussion of wordplay in the Translator's Note for the details of these formulations.
58. One of the characteristics of *bozal* Spanish is its incorporation of linguistic features meant to suggest Portuguese (Weber de Kurlat 1963, 387–88), given that many Black slaves arrived in Spain via the Atlantic trafficking route monopolized by Portugal.

Juan mentions no such arrangement, however, and as he is dividing the spoils obtained from the Prince of Orange's surrender, the following exchange occurs:

> ANTÓN. And twere Antón to get what?
> JUAN DE MÉRIDA. I shall pay you well, *negro*. Since you serve me, do not ask for a reward from anyone else. (2.4)

Is Antón hinting in this dialogue at the freedom he has been promised? If so, it seems to be in vain, as there is never any mention of compensation for him, whether in the form of liberty or otherwise. The last we hear from him comes as he delivers Doña Leonor in the final scene, seemingly delighted for his former mistress when Don Agustín is forced to honor his word: "Into the trap twere falling, a mouse man forsooth!" (3.2). Loyal to the end yet apparently still unrewarded, Antón forms an unsettling parallel to Juan Latino: while the latter is the slave who *begged* for his freedom and never got it, the former is the slave who was *promised* his freedom and never got it. The example of Cervantes, whose protagonist in *The Jealous Extremaduran* frees his slaves upon his death (see §Early Modern Period), does not seem to have caught on.

It is, of course, not Antón but Juan de Mérida who stands at the center of *The Brave Black Soldier*: not a slave in my reading (though not far removed from slavery either) but a servant who faces obstacles based on the color of his skin and who triumphs through a remarkable combination of character traits. As a concluding reflection, it is worth reviewing not only the many qualities that Juan de Mérida shares with Jiménez de Enciso's protagonist—a comparison invited by his metatheatrical reference to "Juan Latino and Juan Soldado" in the palace scene (3.1)—but also the features that distinguish them.

Both Juan Latino and Juan de Mérida overcome color-based prejudice through hard work and virtue, one in an academic setting and the other in the military. Both participate in well-developed historical contexts. Both employ nationalistic and antisemitic rhetoric. Both have important counterparts in secondary Black and Moorish characters. Finally, both marry white noblewomen in startling ways: one by breaking his bride out of a convent, the other through a bombshell last-minute announcement. What distinguishes Juan de Mérida from his counterpart is a philosophical tendency (perhaps a bit ironic since Latino is the scholar) that expresses itself in an energetic defense of early modern Black identity. In contrast, Latino's desire to escape slavery only occasionally extends into universal territory, as with his claim that "blacks are noble" (2.1). Such assertions are far more frequent and robust in *The Brave Black Soldier*. Four extraordinary speeches from act 1—three monologues and a soliloquy—reveal this tendency:

What is a darkskin? He is fortune's inkblot, cruelly spilt onto the pages of the world. Yet there is no fault in color itself, for nature is universal and variety makes her beauty greater. Blacks and whites are both children of men, animated by the same essence. Only geography and climate differentiate them. If whites excel over blacks and rule over them, it is the result of misfortune. Whites would be equally lowly and incomplete if they lived subject to the will of blacks. (1.1)

*

It is a cape that delights the soul cloaked in it, for those of highest rank always wear black. Jet adorns the fairest neck, while the ink with which the world communicates is also black. Pitch fashions feet that flee the advances of the sea. Black gunpowder is the soul of empires. Beautiful porphyry is black, as is ebony, which is enriched by the sun. Black is the pantarbe jewel, which protects against the destruction of fire. Even the whale has a glossy black beard that brings honor to the ocean. (1.1)

*

To choler and rage am I provoked when I contemplate, in my lowliness, thoughts worthy of eternal fame despite the color that defames me. To live in a world where blackness is infamy! Are blacks not men by chance? Is their soul more base, clumsy, or ugly? Is that the reason for their poor renown? What makes Spain any better than Guinea? (1.2)

*

So this is what it means to be black? These are the consequences of color? I hold all who made me black responsible for this injustice: fortune, time, Heaven itself. Oh, what a burden color is when no one pays attention to souls. I'm losing my mind. [. . .] Oh, heavens, that blackness should be so shameful! (1.4)

In the first speech, Juan de Mérida argues for the innate equality of Blacks and whites, with an important hypothesis that I shall return to in my reading of Vélez de Guevara: "If whites excel over blacks and rule over them, it is the result of misfortune." In the second, he expounds on the innate beauty and nobility of blackness, playing into the inverted color hierarchy I have examined. In the third and fourth, he shows a mix of rage and shame at the injustice he suffers: raw emotions that will motivate his extraordinary accomplishments.

There are certainly countercurrents and contradictions to these forceful statements. In a soliloquy to fortune, for example, the protagonist declares, "Having made me black, you must correct the imperfection" (1.5). Nevertheless, when taken together, the four speeches above represent the strongest formulation of Black identity in all of medieval and early modern Spanish literature.

The Accidental Prince

Virtues Overcome Appearances features a Black protagonist who speaks elegantly, behaves honorably, and ends up marrying into white nobility: in this case, the highest echelons of nobility. Yet despite the obvious parallel with the other two works of the Triad, it is a decidedly different play. It does not dramatize the sociological reality of Afro-Spaniards or closely track any period of Spanish history. It features no Latin scholars, soldiers (though there is a vaguely defined "admiral"), or secondary Black characters. It makes no references, polite or vulgar, to Islam or Judaism. The key to understanding how such a similar protagonist could inhabit such a different context lies in the work's symbolic dimensions and fable-like qualities.

Vélez de Guevara's play is a thought experiment that posits a country, Albania, in which Black people do not exist: until, that is, a Black prince is born to the white king and queen. The author's Balkan kingdom, while perhaps vaguely corresponding to "a region in the East between Colchos and Armenia" with some clever allusions to the House of Habsburg, plays a primarily symbolic role.[59] Recalling the snowy horizons of Flanders, Albania radiates whiteness in its very name, which suggests Latin *albus* (white) as well as Spanish *albo* (white) and *alba* (dawn) and, flowing from the latter, the now familiar Duke of Alba. But Albania's whiteness goes beyond etymology. Following the model of Lope de Vega and Claramonte, Vélez de Guevara builds the symbolism of his play around an inverted color hierarchy. If whiteness in *Black Slave to the Greatest Master*

---

59. At the time of the Triad, Albania was part of the Ottoman Empire, which is mentioned nowhere in the play; on the contrary, the king speaks of baptizing the prince (1.1). The description cited above comes from a well-known lexicon of 1611, which continues: "Named thus from the color white (*albo*), inasmuch as its inhabitants are born with white hair. The dogs of Albania are most ferocious, killing bulls and lions, and the breed we call *Alanos*, according to some, should be pronounced *Albanos*, as explained in the definition of *Alano*. There is a city called Albania and a river named Albanio. Besides having white hair, the Albanians have light blue eyes, are somewhat shortsighted, and see better at night than during the day. Pliny (bk. 7, ch. 2) also notes that the island of Britain which the Latins call *Scocia* was in ancient times called Albania and Albion. Albania is also a city in Greater Armenia where Saint Bartholomew the Apostle suffered martyrdom" (Covarrubias 2006, 80b–81a). The curious definition, drawn from a jumble of classical and medieval sources, seems to confuse Albanians with albinos and ancient Britons. Whether Vélez de Guevara was juggling these various definitions is impossible to say, but the central meaning of *white* is undeniable. Zugasti (2017, 49) confirms the imprecision of the setting in *Virtues Overcome Appearances*, noting that the author wrote several other plays more firmly anchored in Albanian geography and history.

is associated with the Devil (the "Morning Star") and in *The Brave Black Soldier* with Protestantism, in Albania it comes to represent lack, infirmity, and death. The symbolism appears, in varying degrees, in the three members of the royal family.

The princess, Leda, is identified with whiteness through two central metaphors: the sun and the swan. While both have traditionally positive associations of light and beauty, they are represented with ambiguity in the play. When Filipo meets Leda for the first time, he is awestruck by her beauty, implying that she outshines the sun (2.1). Yet in a sinister play on the Spanish world *blanco* ("white" and "target": see the Translator's Note for a full explanation) that recalls Juan de Mérida's more lighthearted pun at the end of *The Brave Black Soldier*, he describes himself as "a black man, breached by . . . bleached by [Leda's] heavenly shafts" (2.1). Given that Leda often appears in hunting gear, it is an ominous reference that thankfully goes unfulfilled.

More significant perhaps is Leda's association with swans, which is made explicit when Tirrena asks: "Leda? The one from the poem who turned into a swan?" (2.1) The shepherdess's reference is a humorously garbled version of Leda's mythological namesake, who was seduced by Jupiter in the form of a swan. In any case, the association with swans becomes undeniable. And while swans suggest a certain graceful beauty, they are also known for muteness until the moment of death when, in a legend that stretches back to the ancient Greek poet Aeschylus (2011, lines 1651–52), they are said to sing a beautiful song before expiring. It is this muteness, feebleness, and biological *lack* that Leda, through her association with the swan, most strongly contributes to the symbolism of whiteness in the play.[60]

The princess's mother, Margarita, is the second member of the royal family. In his long speech before the court, Lisandro says he married his queen in Hungary. The two historical figures named Margaret of Hungary—a Byzantine empress and a Dominican nun, both from the 1200s—do not share many details with Filipo's mother. A closer parallel may be Margaret of Austria (1584–1611), queen of Spain during Vélez de Guevara's lifetime. While this is a legitimate connection that I discuss below, I believe the author was equally drawn to the symbolic value of Margarita's name, which means *pearl* in both Latin and early modern Spanish. It also suggests the more common Spanish word for pearl, *perla*, which served as a common metaphor of the period for a lady's tears (Correas 1906, 601) and was, moreover, long associated with moonlight and occult knowledge (Biedermann 1994, 259). All these connotations—tears, moonlight,

---

60. Biedermann (1994, 334) notes that swans are depicted in medieval bestiaries with "snow-white plumage" but "utterly *black* flesh" (author's emphasis). If Vélez de Guevara had this association in mind, it would add a whole new dimension to Leda's swan symbolism.

secrecy—seem fitting for the mysterious Margarita, who gives birth to a baby that must be hidden from public view. We do not know the timing or circumstances of the queen's demise, only that in the present frame of the play she "reclines eternally in my memory as if preserved in jasper" (1.1). Did she die in childbirth like her counterpart Clorilene in Calderón de la Barca's probable rewriting of the story?[61] Or perhaps from pearls of grief when her child was taken from her and locked away in a tower? These questions are never answered. After the king's speech, the ghostly Margarita vanishes from the text.

Finally, there is the king. Lisandro's most direct link to the symbolic color of Albania is his long white beard: also a universal sign of old age and infirmity. These qualities have three distinct manifestations in the king, each linked to a crucial moment in the narrative of his paternity. The first is *impotence*. Describing the early years of his marriage, the king says that "Heaven, in the green [i.e., opposed to white] years of our union, refused to give me children, for reasons only it knows" (1.1). When he does have a child, in his "more mature [i.e., white] years," it is a princess defined by her lack. The birth of a male heir—Filipo—is enabled only when the king, in a remarkable passage to be analyzed below, fixates during coitus on the image of an Ethiopian queen.

Filipo's birth precipitates the second manifestation of the king's hoary old age: *incompetence*. While the name Lisandro means *liberator* in Greek, the king does just the opposite and decides that he must hide the "aberration" and imprison his son, failing one of the basic leadership tests of the Christian monarch: raising and training a competent heir, as documented in an important manual from the period (Saavedra Fajardo 1942, 17–18). When he finally lives up to his name, the prince has already freed himself from the tower. This leads to the third manifestation of the king's weakness: *surrender*, embodied in the white flag he authorizes Ricardo to raise in their encounter with Filipo. While Lisandro does not literally surrender in this scene, the symbolic raising of the prince's "black flag" (2.2), coming as a culmination of the paternity narrative, signals the defeat of the colorless king.

The mute swan, the tearful pearl, the feeble white beard, the truce flag: these are the tokens of the Black prince's country of birth. In disclosing his existence to the court, twenty years later, the king reveals his shocking origin:

> Many times desire sought to engender its likeness, a natural inclination in all animals. On one such night, I happened to have before my eyes, in a gold and silk

---

61. On the numerous parallels between *Virtues Overcome Appearances* and *Life Is a Dream*, see Schevill (1933), Kirk (1957, lxxii–lxxxiv), Ruano de la Haza (2010, 13–18), and Rodríguez López-Vázquez (2017), who all insist on a conscious rewriting. Profeti (1965, 45–50), however, argues that the similarities can be explained by the common "intellectual, religious, and theatrical life" of the period.

tapestry, the astonishing figure of Queen Saba of Ethiopia: she who, to satisfy her curiosity, journeyed from the scorched climate of the phoenix to visit the Hebrew king. So intently were my eyes cast upon the jet-black skin, brought to pulsing life by the white hand of some Belgian Timanthes, that the visual cues triggered my imagination to engender what was being seen. For in such cases all natural historians confirm that what is seen is reproduced through communication with the imaginative faculty of the soul. [. . .] Thus, when nine months had passed—oh, heavens!—the queen gave birth, and from my imagination sprouted such a garish copy of myself that, though beautiful Margarita was its dawn, it looked to us more like Queen Saba than its mother: so dark black that those present suspected something disgraceful. To understand the extraordinary violation that had produced such an abominable birth in Margarita, I thought about where my concentration had been the night of the conception. I reasoned that either I'd looked at Saba at the key moment or that Heaven had refused to allow Margarita's innocence to suffer injury. With these explanations of the aberration, I satisfied the doubts of those present so they wouldn't spread unfounded rumors. (1.1)

The remarkable speech, of which the above passage is but a sample, serves several purposes. First, it mobilizes the erotic power of the Black woman, documented in texts dating back to Albertus Magnus in the 1200s (Groebner 2009, 218–19; see also Gilman 1985, 79–93) and here fetishized to allow the king to consummate the sexual union. Second, it points to the geographical origin of the prince. The tapestry the king refers to, apparently within reach of the nuptial bed, acts as a portal to the faraway kingdom of Ethiopia. Long the African country most respected in Europe owing to its ancient Christian tradition (Martín Casares 2014, 423), Ethiopia is also the homeland, in one way or another, of the Black saint protagonists attributed to Lope de Vega. Both exotic and familiar, it is the natural location from which to pluck a fantastical Black prince.

Finally, the passage reprises a popular pseudoscientific belief to lend credibility to the king's story. The theory of "pregnancy imprinting," according to which images that enter the eyes are rendered by the imagination for corporeal purposes including conception, was known across Eurasia well into the modern era (Doniger and Spinner 1998). Vélez de Guevara would have found accounts of it in a famous Spanish sonnet (Garcilaso de la Vega 1984, 75), an Italian courtier's manual (Castiglione 1959, 337), and an ancient Greek novel (Heliodorus 2019, 505) that was available in two Spanish translations (Beardsley 1970, items 66 and 110). Awkwardly, the king references this bizarre theory to swat down "unfounded rumors": presumably that the queen has cuckolded her husband with a Black man. It turns out that Vélez de Guevara's Albania may not be all white after all.[62]

Thus is a Black prince born to the ghostly king and queen of Albania, causing much consternation among those present. The king's reaction is dramatic: "After baptizing him, I locked him away forever, charging a nurse with his care and telling no one else of the matter, instead announcing that the child was a stillborn" (1.1). In a miserable tower that "rises above the woods like a mute sentinel" (1.1), the prince is held prisoner with only his jailer for company. Silenced and hidden from view, he "languishes like a soulless giant," reenacting the impotence of his father, the tears of his mother, the muted echoes of his sister. The banishment, which lasts twenty years, ends only when the prince hurls himself "like a miscarried infant, from his cell window into the woods below, cleverly tying his sheets into a rope to reach the ground" (1.1).

Through this startling "miscarriage," Filipo begins to encounter the world from which he was banished. In the fable-like setting, his first discovery is himself. In a scene fittingly characterized as an "anti-Narcissus" moment (Zugasti 2017, 56), he comes upon a pool of water in which he sees his image for the first time: "But good heavens! Am I this ugly monster in the water, equal in appearance to the night? It is indeed myself that I see! Even as I stare at the copy of myself that you show me, O silvery fount, I can't believe it, for it would seem impossible for such a proud soul to inhabit such a crude and clumsy casing" (1.2). This is a foundational moment in the prince's self-perception, akin to the so-called mirror stage of infant development (Lacan 1977). In Filipo's case, it is infused with the shame and self-loathing of a Black man in a white world, which may reflect Vélez de Guevara's own shame over his Jewish ancestry.[63] But the anti-Narcissus moment is not over. A few lines later, Leda appears on a cliff above the prince. Seeing her image reflected in the water behind his, he wonders if it could be his soul: "What new deity shines its rosy light upon the water? Next to my shadow stands the sun; next to my night, the day. Could it be my own soul, desiring to show me its immortal essence?" (1.2). Thus is the old trope of the Black man with a white soul, already exploited by Lope de Vega and Jiménez de Enciso, integrated into this formative moment of the protagonist's development. It is a key scene not only in the prince's self-perception but in his first encounter with the Other: in this case a beautiful woman upon whom he will form, without knowing she is his sister, a perilous erotic fixation.

---

62. Because the cuckolding suggestion is never returned to and because everyone who meets the prince in the course of the play is dumbfounded by his appearance, suggesting that no one has ever seen a Black man, the "unfounded rumors" may represent a glitch in the author's world-building: a lapse through which the sociological reality of seventeenth-century Spain intrudes for just a few lines.

63. Kidd (1998, 129); Bernstein (2021, 58–59). On the concept of Jewish self-hatred, see Gilman (1986).

As Filipo interacts with Leda and other Albanian citizens he was meant to rule, language becomes a key register of his characterization. One crucial term in this regard has already appeared, in the prince's description of himself at the fount: *monster*. At the time of the Triad, *monster* (Spanish *monstro*) signified "any departure from natural law and order, such as a man born with two heads, four arms, and four legs [. . .]" (Covarrubias 2006, 1294b). A monster is a creature that violates the boundaries set by nature: a two-headed man, a Black child born to white parents. *Monster* becomes central to descriptions of Filipo, employed by a range of characters including the king (1.1), Leda (1.2), Tirrena (2.1), Sergesto and Timbreo (2.2), and the admiral (3.2). A related set of descriptors reinforces this meaning: *aberration, barbarian, brute, freak of nature, giant, minotaur, Orcus, phantasm,* and *savage*.[64]

Filipo's "monstrosity" has led José María Ruano de la Haza (2010, 21–32) to suggest that the shock value of his appearance stems from his unfamiliarity rather than his blackness. But these qualities are impossible to disentangle: Filipo is unfamiliar to white Albanians *precisely because* he is Black. So while I question the conclusion that *Virtues Overcome Appearances* is free of anti-Black prejudice, I do believe it is useful to compare its language to that of *Juan Latino* and *The Brave Black Soldier*. In this regard, it is striking that Filipo is only rarely referred to as Black, and *never* in direct address, which occurs on countless occasions in the other two plays. More telling still, never once is the insult most commonly directed at those protagonists—*dog*—applied to the prince. Instead, the secondary characters refer to him (and he sometimes to himself) using the terms listed above, *monster* being the most prominent. Conversely, Juan Latino and Juan de Mérida are *never* referred to as monsters.[65] I want to be clear: *monster* and *dog* are both dehumanizing terms, and modern readers will understandably find distinctions between the two irksome. Yet the words do signal two very different focuses, corresponding to the two approaches to Black characters that I have identified in medieval Spanish literature (see §Medieval Period). On the one hand, Jiménez de Enciso and Claramonte, in the tradition of Black characters found in the *Poem of Joseph*, the *Songs of Holy Mary*, tale 32 of *Count Lucanor*, and most of sixteenth-century literature, seek to represent the reality of Afro-Spaniards in the Iberian peninsula. This goal results in language, such as *dog*, that reflects contempt toward Black people. On the other hand, Vélez de Guevara's setting is an ahistorical fantasy kingdom in the tradition of the *Book of Zifar the Knight*, *Prison of Love*, and *The Exploits of Esplandián*. This snow-white kingdom—the inverse

---

64. See the Translator's Note for these terms in Spanish and my approach to translating them.
65. Instead, Don Fernando uses *monster* to refer to Cañerí (1.3, 2.2); Juan Latino uses it to refer to Doña Ana (2.3); and Juan de Mérida uses it in an abstract sense to describe envy (2.1).

in many ways of Rodríguez de Montalvo's all-Black California—necessitates language, such as *monster*, that reflects surprise at the prince's divergence from the norm.

The surprise only grows as the monster-prince overcomes, one by one, all the challenges placed in his path. The first of these is personal: his erotic fixation on Leda. Only at the end of act 2 does he learn that the woman he loves—the first woman he set his eyes upon—is his sister:

> Lovely Leda, I was yours, but now I am your brother. I was mad for your beauty, but now I've come to my senses and recognize its peril. Resisting the intensity of your flashing eyes, I summon my willpower and turn my back on the charms that call to me. Only thus do I avoid the shipwreck of your beauty. I flee in freedom and return as captive, but in the contradiction between fear and bravery, between hesitation and affection, virtues overcome appearances. Through reason or force, blood must conquer desire and courage must win out over love. (2.2)

It is a key moment in which Filipo not only alludes to the delicate issue of slavery, suggesting the freedom he has gained is a paradox because it has only led him to the "captivity" of love: an old conceit examined above (see §Early Modern Period). He also pulls back from the brink of incestuous desire, rejecting an inclination that, in trampling over accepted kinship boundaries, reflects the dictionary definition of *monster* as a "departure from natural law and order" (Covarrubias 2006, 1294b).

Filipo's second challenge is political: Lisandro's death between acts 2 and 3 sets up a crucial leadership test for the new king. But the personal dimension intrudes again when Leda storms into court and accuses Filipo of violating her will by arranging her marriage to the aging King Rodulfo of Hungary, "a foreigner unequally matched to my young years" (3.1). Filipo fends off her accusations with understanding but firmness, winning her admiration and even showing a progressive orientation in his comment that "nothing in the world is more destructive than the frequency with which highborn women are married against their will." With Leda on his side, he uncovers a foreign plot against him and exposes the conspirators, leaving them groveling at his feet for forgiveness. In this way he turns Albania's hostilities with Sicily, with which the play had opened, into a mutually beneficial alliance, sealed with the *comedia*'s traditional double wedding.

The weddings offer final proof of the triumph of Filipo's leadership. The first, between Leda and King Enrico of Sicily, was rejected by the princess at the beginning of the play on the grounds that it would hand Albania over to a foreigner. But that was when the heir apparent (Leda) was a woman, for even a queen was expected to be submissive to her husband. Now that an Albanian male has become king, there is no threat to succession from foreigners, allowing the wedding to go forward. More importantly, Filipo's proposal to marry Leda to Enrico further removes her as an object of temptation to him, validating the promise he made to himself at the end of act 2.

The second marriage is Filipo's to Alfreda: another political union as well as an interracial one. Vélez de Guevara's representation of it offers an interesting synthesis of the approaches of his fellow Triad authors. In the marriage between Juan de Mérida and Doña Juana, Claramonte takes the sensationalistic route of a surprise announcement on the last page of the play, with no anticipation and no courtship. Jiménez de Enciso, in contrast, includes several finely drawn courtship scenes that detail the progress of Doña Ana's affection for Juan Latino. Vélez de Guevara's approach is closer to Jiménez de Enciso's but more dramatic, telescoping the whole courtship into the last scene of the play. While Doña Ana's initial attitude toward her "tutor" can best be described as a friendly distance, Princess Alfreda is downright hostile to the idea of marrying a "savage Ethiopian" and embraces her brother's plan to murder him. But upon meeting the king in person, she is quickly won over: "I feel the pull of love . . . Enrico will have to forgive me, for not only am I unable to murder this man, but I will act to defend him. For his soul, so akin to God's beautiful image, makes his whole body beautiful" (3.3). Alfreda's vertiginous about-face—in line 2741 of the Spanish text she is in tears at the thought of the marriage, in 2805 she is agreeing to murder, and in 2886 she is confessing her love—compresses the drawn-out courtship of *Juan Latino* into a sensationalistic ending akin to that of *The Brave Black Soldier*.

In seeking to understand Vélez de Guevara's play, at once outlandish and unsettling, I propose two parallel interpretations. The first is a moral one that recalls Juan de Mérida's hypothesis in *The Brave Black Soldier*: "If whites excel over blacks and rule over them, it is the result of misfortune" (1.1). Filipo's imprisonment at birth for no reason other than his skin color seems almost tailor-made to test this hypothesis. The extreme misfortune of the scenario, extricated and defamiliarized from the everyday context of slavery, challenges spectators to open their eyes to the injustice of an institution that was all around them, especially in Vélez de Guevara's hometown of Seville. I have already noted the allusion that Filipo draws in calling himself a captive of love (2.2). He makes an even more direct comparison in his farewell letter to his jailer: "Tebandro, by virtue of my reason, I was born free of this cell in which I've been held prisoner for crimes that my baffling fortune refuses to reveal. Today I break free to become my own owner; twenty years in captivity are enough" (1.1). The parallel to *The Brave Black Soldier* 1.2, where Juan de Mérida waves his letter of freedom in front of Doña Juana, is striking.

The second interpretation I propose is a political one, centered on the issue of succession and the concern with unfit rulers. If my speculations about chronology in the Biographical Sketches are correct, *Virtues Overcome Appearances* was written shortly after

Philip IV's accession to the throne in 1621. A particularly smooth transition, unmarked by the kinds of complications that arise in the play, it must have called attention to the many historical instances when that was not the case. One such notable example was the prince Don Carlos (1545–1568), heir apparent to Philip II, whose mental instability led him to attempt to murder both the Duke of Alba and Don Juan of Austria. He died under house arrest, locked away by his grieving father (Kamen 1997, 120–23). The episode not only caused stupefaction at home and abroad; it also attracted the attention of the Triad authors. Jiménez de Enciso made it the subject of an excellent play, *The Prince Don Carlos*, written between 1621 and 1627. Vélez de Guevara took note as well, turning both Don Carlos and Don Juan of Austria into characters in a curious play, *The Water Eagle*, dated to the period 1632–1633.[66] I would argue that *Virtues Overcome Appearances* shows the playwright grappling with the issue several years earlier.

Albania's desire to keep its crown "in the family," so to speak, finds an unsettling parallel in the Habsburg family, source of Spain's kings for two centuries. In the 150-year period from the reign of Philip II to that of Charles II, the House of Habsburg celebrated three royal marriages between uncle and niece, three between first cousins, and two between second cousins.[67] The devastating results of this inbreeding have been scientifically proved (Alvarez et al. 2009), but they were also plainly visible to contemporary observers, who did not fail to note the unfortunate Don Carlos's sickly appearance (Kamen 1997, 120). The prince's untimely death in 1568, furthermore, set in motion a chain of succession that would result, thirty years later, in the coronation of Philip III: son of Philip II and his niece. This "pallid, anonymous creature" (Elliott 1963, 296), widely viewed as an incompetent failure (responsible for the expulsion of the Moriscos, for example), was king during much of Vélez de Guevara's adult life. Did he serve as a model for Lisandro? It is tempting to think so, especially given his marriage to Margaret of Austria (his second cousin). Is she Vélez de Guevara's Margarita? And Margaret's cousin, Holy Roman Emperor Rudolph II, may be reflected in the aging King Rodulfo of Hungary about whom Leda complains in her outburst to Filipo (Holy Roman Emperors were simultaneously kings of Hungary). The correspondences are not precise, nor are they ever in the quasi-fantasy genre of palace dramas the play belongs

---

66. I rely on Platt (1956, li) for the dating of Jiménez de Enciso's play and on Peale (2003, 46–52) for that of Vélez de Guevara's. Juliá Martínez (1951, xxxix) calls *Don Carlos* "the most valuable gem" of Jiménez de Enciso's theater. The Don Carlos story went on to inspire the likes of Friedrich Schiller and Giuseppe Verdi.

67. *Uncle and niece*: Anna of Austria and King Philip II of Spain; Maria Anna of Bavaria (b. 1551) and Archduke Charles II of Austria; Mariana of Austria and King Philip IV of Spain. *First cousins*: Maria of Austria and H.R.E. Maximilian II; Maria Anna of Bavaria (b. 1574) and H.R.E. Ferdinand II; Maria Anna of Spain and H.R.E. Ferdinand III. *Second cousins*: Renata of Lorraine and Duke William V of Bavaria; Margaret of Austria and King Philip III of Spain.

to (Zugasti 2017, 46–47), but I believe the parallels are too numerous to be dismissed as coincidence.

Thus does the consumptive Habsburg line, teetering on the brink of genetic implosion, find expression in Vélez de Guevara's play.[68] And thus Albania's feeble whiteness takes on a new meaning: the pallor and sickliness that are the unmistakable mark of endogamy. Something is rotten in the state of Albania, and Filipo's blackness, ironically rejected as monstrous, would appear to be the remedy. To fully grasp this point, we must return for a moment to the king's description of the night of Filipo's conception: "So intently were my eyes cast upon the jet-black skin, brought to pulsing life by the white hand of some Belgian Timanthes, that the visual cues triggered my imagination to engender what was being seen" (1.1). Timanthes, a noted Greek painter from the 300s BCE, is transformed in this description into a Belgian, recalling the cold whiteness of Flanders. The pale, disembodied hand crafts the figure of a Black queen, Saba, identified with the biblical queen of Sheba (I Kings 10:1–13 and II Chronicles 9:1–12). The image is then helpfully placed within view of the nuptial bed. The strategy apparently works: the pulsing black skin of the queen sets the king's imagination ablaze and leads to the birth of a Black prince. Robust, vital, and potent, he embodies the antidote to Albania's feeble, shrunken whiteness. He is the king the country desperately needs, and everything he does after his emancipation from the tower proves it: his triumph over adversity in the wilderness, his prudent exercise of power in the palace, his arrangement of auspicious marriages in the final scene, and, crucially, his resistance to incest with his sister. Filipo's imprisonment—the result of misfortune, to quote Juan de Mérida again—is thus not only a moral wrong but a political mistake. The two interpretations I have offered are actually one and the same. *Virtues Overcome Appearances* is a fable of kingship, of slavery, and of the Black man whose improbable life joins the two.

There is a glitch in this interpretation, however. While Filipo's blackness saves Albania, Lisandro suggests that his color will not last: "And in his offspring, as is natural and inevitable, the white color will return to offer restitution for the injury suffered by the father for the grandfather's error, if *error* be the correct term for a powerful imaginative faculty, the source of this remarkable aberration" (1.1). As noted in the historical survey of Afro-Spaniards (see §Theology), and as Dr. Carlobal confirms regarding Juan Latino's blackness, color is an *accident* in theological terms, not an inherent characteristic. And while that means all souls are equal before God, it also means that blackness, like injuries, errors, aberrations, and all the other terms applied to Filipo, is meant to be

---

68. The Spanish Habsburg line did in fact go extinct in the year 1700, upon the death of its second unfortunate Carlos, the wretched Charles II. Product of his family's third marriage between uncle and niece, this "bewitched" king proved incapable of reproducing, bringing the line to an end and igniting a European-wide war of succession.

corrected. Overcome. "Virtues overcome appearances," in fact, was a popular refrain in the period, used to suggest that "someone acts or may act virtuously despite an appearance or outward signs that logically argue the contrary" (Real Academia Española 1990, 3:496–97) or that "sometimes virtue overcomes evil inclinations and the evil appearance of the face" (Correas 1906, 436b). As an inner principle of the soul, virtue can overcome or even erase outward signs or appearances. Accidents can be corrected.

Nevertheless, *Virtues Overcome Appearances* does not quite conform to the theological concept of *accident* in the early modern period, that is, "any quality that can be added or subtracted to a thing without damaging it, or the quality that can be present or absent in a substance with no effect, such as color, whiteness, etc." (Real Academia Española 1990, 1:41a). In theological terms, all colors are accidental *including whiteness*. Yet Vélez de Guevara seems to suggest that the erasure of blackness will restore things to their natural (white) state: "Restitution for the injury," in the king's words. Nor is there ever any suggestion that souls are anything other than white. Here is where the author's color prejudice comes through most clearly, and for this reason I must agree with Bernstein's observation (2021, 56) that Filipo's triumph "cannot be interpreted as a story of the acceptance of a different racial identity or the proof of equality of those who are of African descent."

How on earth, then, is it to be interpreted? On the one hand a Black man reaches the summit of power and resolves his country's dynastic crisis and endogamic tendencies by marrying a foreign white princess, all within a symbolic order that represents blackness as potent and vital and whiteness as frail and diseased. On the other hand, it is suggested that blackness is freakish and monstrous and that the accidental prince, after serving his purpose, will have his color erased.

The apparent contradictions of *Virtues Overcome Appearances* may represent an extreme case, but they are not incompatible with the messages of the other two Triad plays, providing a useful vantage point from which to offer final reflections on all three.

Conclusions

The Triad is the product of the Spanish *comedia*, a broadly popular art form as heterogeneous as contemporary American film. Like all drama, the *comedia* at heart is about conflict, and racial difference in early modern Spain, no less than in contemporary America, is a perennial source of conflict. This is the starting point for the three plays, which all follow a similar pattern: a talented Black man, shunned or even banished for his appearance, overcomes color-based obstacles and injustice to attain the pinnacle of success in his vocation, eventually marrying into the white nobility.

An important point sets the Triad protagonists apart from their immediate predecessors, the main characters of the trio of plays attributed to Lope de Vega around 1600. While the latter are all revered as saints, the Triad heroes have imminently *secular* roles: scholar, soldier, prince. It is a significant distinction. The saintly quality of Vega's characters serves a crucial purpose in showing the audience that the Christian community is open to everyone, but there is a flip side to their holiness. Untouchable and literally lethal in some cases (Dórida collapses and dies when Antiobo touches her), the saints are kept from communion with society at large and, most importantly, barred from marriage and reproduction. The Triad protagonists, one by one, break through that barrier. Their integration into society makes them more human and more vulnerable, ultimately allowing for greater identification by the audience.

A related point has to do with ethnicity or national origin. Lope de Vega's saints are of full or at least half (in the case of Antiobo) Ethiopian ancestry. Ethiopia's ancient Christian history gives the playwright a leg up in creating Black characters the audience could respect and identify with. But a leg up can start to feel like a crutch, which all the Triad authors move away from in differing degrees. Jiménez de Enciso says nothing about the Ethiopian origin that the historical Juan Latino claimed, instead making his character, through the poem recited by Don Juan of Austria, a native-born Spaniard. Claramonte follows the same model: Juan de Mérida boldly declares his birthplace as Mérida in the first scene of the play, later referencing his "Guinean blood" (3.1). Whether Guinea is meant in a strict sense or as a synonym for Africa, it is significant that Juan does not claim Ethiopian ancestry. Claramonte pushes the envelope even further in suggesting that if honor is truly defined by deeds rather than genealogy, then there is no difference between Ethiopia and Guinea or, in fact, between Guinea and Spain: "What makes Spain," the protagonist asks, "any better than Guinea?" (1.2). Both Claramonte and Jiménez de Enciso, furthermore, buttress their main characters' blackness with antisemitic sentiments, investing them more fully in mainstream (white) Spanish ideology. Vélez de Guevara avoids the latter trait in Filipo and also regresses to the Ethiopian myth of origin, but he does so with the fantastical device of ancestry through a painting, essentially laughing at the cliché of Black characters with Ethiopian blood.

Secondary characters add to the sociological complexity of the protagonists. In *Juan Latino*, Don Fernando's eloquent defense of Morisco culture, set during the uprising of the late 1560s, inevitably comes into dialogue with the post-expulsion (1609) soul-searching that was happening at the time of the Triad. Yet the genteel and charismatic Don Fernando, at one point a rival to Juan Latino for Doña Ana's love, slowly transforms into the mutinous Aben Humeya, losing his mind and soul to the Black Moor who stalks him in his own home. Cañerí, for his part, is a larger-than-life, quasi-mythical figure who speaks in elegant prophetic language and stirs up rebellion among the Moriscos, eventually destroying both himself and Don Fernando in the process. In Claramonte's play, it is the Black slave Antón who provides a counterpoint to Juan de Mérida, his garbled Spanish laden with scatological humor, malapropisms, and unintentional truths that do not always reflect kindly on either the protagonist or other powerful characters. Antón's participation in a long, homophobic joke with Doña Leonor likewise results in the ridicule of Juan de Mérida. In *Virtues Overcome Appearances*, while there are no secondary characters from minority communities, gender plays a similarly synergistic role. In the zero-sum game of monarchical succession, Filipo's triumph is Leda's loss, his male privilege overriding her claim to the throne and overcoming the "monstrosity" of his color.

The theme of monstrosity brings us to the issue of language, where there is a clear divide. On the one hand, *Juan Latino* and *The Brave Black Soldier*, in seeking to represent the lived reality of Afro-Spaniards, make copious use of racial epithets that reflect contempt toward Blacks. On the other, *Virtues Overcome Appearances* creates a fantasy-like setting in which Black people do not exist, its language gravitating toward terms that register the unfamiliarity and surprise of the Albanians at the sight of black skin. An interesting variation in the first two plays comes in the use of the term *darkskin* (*moreno*), which is completely absent in Vélez de Guevara's text. Given that it appears to function as a polite substitute for *black*, the word *darkskin* shows that Spanish *negro*, while sometimes neutral, could also be applied with offensive intent. Juan Latino makes this point explicit in his appeal for freedom to the duke: "It is malicious the way they call me *negro*" (2.1). The archbishop even fines Villanueva for using the term (2.4).

A final point regarding language has to do with the slave dialect known as *bozal*. First associated with Black characters in the early 1500s, it became nearly universal in the theater, where it was employed as a humorous device that was almost always demeaning. Lope de Vega rejects its use in *The Marvel of Ethiopia*, though he returns to it in limited fashion in *The Black Saint* and *Black Slave to the Greatest Master*. Alone among the Triad authors, Claramonte uses *bozal* consistently with his character Antón. This is an unfortunate regression, though it is worth noting that Antón is a richer and more complex figure than the *bozal* characters who precede him, and sometimes his language, whether intentionally or not, escapes the narrow limitations of the convention. (See the Translator's Note for a discussion of my approach to translating racial vocabulary and the *bozal* dialect.)

These preliminary remarks all converge on a central issue of the plays: the stain of slavery and, by implication, its role in the geopolitical success of early modern Spain. The military might of the Spanish navy, including the famous victory over the Turks at Lepanto in 1571—alluded to in *Juan Latino*—depended on the use of galley slaves. The financial might of Spain's New World colonies, which bankrolled its political might in Europe, depended on the use of field slaves in the harvesting of cash crops such as Caribbean sugarcane. I contend that early modern Spaniards grasped these points and intuited the connections between religion, skin color, segregation, slavery, and empire. And while they wielded a cowardly distinction—that slavery was "legally permissible but morally objectionable" (Domínguez Ortiz 2003, 40–41)—we should not lose sight of the objections they marshaled. A few examples will suffice.

In the ancient world, Aristotle's discussion in the *Politics*, continually cited as a justification for slavery in the medieval and early modern periods and beyond, begins by acknowledging conflicting opinions on the matter: "Others affirm that the rule of a master over slaves is contrary to nature, and that the distinction between slave and freeman exists by convention only, and not by nature; and *being an interference with nature is therefore unjust*" (Aristotle 1984, 2:1989, my emphasis). Writing in the early medieval period, Isidore of Seville (2010, 125) calls slavery "the most extreme of all evils"; while in the thirteenth century, King Alfonso X's *Seven-Division Law Code* reaches essentially the same conclusion as the anonymous authorities cited by Aristotle: "Slavery is the belief and practice, founded by ancient peoples, through which men who were naturally free became slaves and subjected themselves to the rule of another, *against the law of nature*" (Alfonso X 1807, 117, my emphasis; see also Doerig 1966, 341–42). Nearer to the period of the Triad, Saint Teresa writes in her autobiography (1560s) that her father "could never be convinced to own slaves because he felt great pity for them, and once, when a slave girl of his brother's was at the house, he doted on her like one of his children, for he said he *could not bear the fact that she wasn't free*" (Teresa de Ávila 1990, 120, my emphasis). Finally, Don Quixote's words—"it seems harsh to me to make slaves of those whom God and Nature made free" (Cervantes 1987, 1:273)—might be cited to round out this catalog, with the caveat that the knight's madness together with the disastrous consequences of his liberation of the galley slaves in this episode tinges his words with irony and makes Cervantes's intention harder to discern than those of the previous examples.

I do not cite these passages as proof that they were normative or even that they were universally expressed by the authors cited. Cervantes, in fact, elsewhere refers to a slave as a "nobody" (Cervantes 1966, 208). Nor do I seek to read a post-Enlightenment ideology into the Triad authors, whose attitudes toward their protagonists, even at their most modern, are full of ambivalences, contradictions, and backsliding. The fact is that 1620 was not a revolutionary moment on the question of Black slavery (nor was 1776, for that matter), which had been in place for over five hundred years, long before the triangular trade. In a conformist society such as early modern Spain, no one was bold enough to throw off the weight of such a tradition, preferring instead to hide behind the "legally permissible but morally objectionable" distinction. This fecklessness is disappointing, to be sure, but if that is the only conclusion we are prepared to draw, we miss the opportunity to discern important nuances and shifts in attitudes.

The Triad authors and the startling interracial marriages they dramatize represent one such shift: a point that can be fully appreciated in light of the prior tradition of Black characters in Spanish literature, whether it is the diminished figures of the 1500s or Lope de Vega's more human but still segregated saints. The plays of the Triad reveal an attempt, however halting and imperfect, to reckon with the shame of slavery through the creation of exemplary Black protagonists who break through the last remaining barrier to integration: marriage. Ranging from an actual slave (Juan Latino) to the son of a slave (Juan de Mérida) to a prisoner of fortune or metaphorical slave (Filipo of Albania), the Black protagonists enact a sort of liberation and integration allegory, attaining ever higher entry into white society: Juan Latino into the low nobility of the Carlobals, Juan de Mérida into the upper nobility of the Veras coveted by Don Agustín, and Filipo into the echelons of European royalty. None of the Triad protagonists, furthermore, suffers corporal or capital punishment for desiring or marrying a white woman, in contrast to the public burning of the Black Moor in the *Songs of Holy Mary*, the flogging of Zayd in *Little Lazarus*, the martyrdom of Filipo in *The Marvel of Ethiopia*, and the murder-suicide at the end of *Othello*. The happy endings seem to represent the culmination of a series of inversions of traditional color hierarchies, with black, by virtue of being male, consolidated into a superior position over white. They also bring about the opposite of the color dynamic seen at the end of *The Exploits of Esplandián*, in which Black women are married and subjugated to white men.

There are a number of important qualifications to this allegorical reading of slavery and skin color culminating in "integration." I begin with the white wives of the Black men. I have touched only briefly on gender in the plays, but it is worth considering how the constraints placed on women create a sort of parallel captivity to that of the protagonists. Princess Leda directly compares herself to a slave, "my tongue bound in chains, my words silenced behind walls" (*VOA* 3.1). Doña Ana's brother sends her to a nunnery from which Juan Latino must free her (*JL* 3.4). And Juan de Mérida, while plotting revenge on Don Agustín for dishonoring Doña Leonor, orders her to "discreetly sequester yourself in the Convent of Saint Eulalia" (*BBS* 3.1). These passages leverage a good bit of irony into the endings of the plays, where women freed from their convents and metaphorical chains end up in subordinate positions as wives.

A particularly stubborn challenge to the liberation and integration allegory is the fact that Jiménez de Enciso's protagonist remains a slave at the end of *Juan Latino*. This is the "incongruity" noted by Gates and Wolff (1998, 39), which I am unable to resolve. Nor is it the only one of the Triad. Juan de Mérida, in offering his hand to Doña Juana, tells her: "Consider me, my ladyship, your slave" (*BBS* 3.2). It is a standard trope of the "captive lover" to speak in this manner, to which Doña Juana replies in kind, but given the trajectory of this character, it may also be a way of taking him down a notch. Meanwhile Filipo, as we have seen, will find the "error" of his blackness erased in his offspring, according to Lisandro's prediction.

A disturbing quality of all three protagonists, furthermore, is the strong current of self-loathing in which they participate, often through recourse to the tired trope of the white soul. Filipo is repulsed by his own image in the pool and speculates that Leda is his immortal essence. Juan Latino looks forward to the day when he can show "proof of a beautiful soul in an ugly body" (*JL* 1.4). Juan de Mérida begs the (white) heavens to "correct the imperfection" of his black skin (*BBS* 1.5). All three characters experience a "whitening" that is made explicit at various points. Don Juan of Austria refers to Juan Latino as suntanned rather than Black (*JL* 3.6), and Filipo finds himself "bleached by [Leda's] heavenly shafts" (*VOA* 2.1). Castle refers to Juan Latino as "whitened by learning" (*JL* 3.2), and Juan de Mérida hopes to "illumine" himself in the Duke of Alba's "glorious dawn" (*BBS* 1.2). This "whitening" brings us back to the underlying message of blackness as an outward sign or "accident" that can be "overcome." "Triumphant virtue," says Juan de Mérida, "is a heavenly liquor that pays no heed to the material of the vessel" (*BBS* 1.2). "Virtue and letters [i.e., interior qualities rather than appearances] are the grandees in my home," Don Juan of Austria replies when Juan Latino expresses surprise that his black skin does not bar him from the home of a white prince (*JL* 3.2). Vélez de Guevara crystallizes the message in the title of his play. While the fantasy setting allows him to magnify the contradictions we have noted, they are in fact an underlying feature of all three plays.

Given the many incongruities, it is no surprise that critical opinion on the Triad is quite fractured. One camp views the representation of blackness in the plays as unremarkable and generally in conformity with the racial animus of the period.[69] Another interprets the same plays as exceptional and a bold challenge to the ideology of the period.[70] Some even try to have it both ways, resulting in often contradictory statements.[71] Ultimately, interpretation of the plays comes down to the essential question of

---

69. Marquina (1938, 564a); Williamsen (1981, 205); Panford (1999, 8); Irigoyen-García (2005, 162); Lawrance (2005, 76, n. 21); Beusterien (2006a, n. 111); Ndiaye (2022, 81).

70. Rodríguez López-Vázquez (1997, 5); Barrios (2002, 302–3); Fradejas Lebrero (2008, 112); Ogallas Moreno (Claramonte y Corroy 1638–2016, [R], n. 57).

71. Fra Molinero claims that Juan Latino becomes the "typical Black man of the *comedia*" and an "object of ridicule" (1995, 159) but that the play is "unique" (2014, 22) and "should not be underestimated" (2005, 329). The same critic says that Juan de Mérida serves to "justify slavery as an institution" (1995, 194) but that he "does not accept the reigning social discourse on his natural inferiority (1995, 183). Finally, Fra Molinero asserts that the ending of *Virtues* "concedes defeat [because] Filipo's children will be white" (1997, 349–50) but that nonetheless the play is meant as a warning against "the obsession with *limpieza de sangre*" (1997, 350).

sympathy. Are the authors creating characters to be admired, ridiculed, or both? And if the answer is both, how is that possible?

I do not have a perfect response to these difficult questions, but I want to offer a few parting thoughts. First, the Triad authors are engaged in something that today strikes us as paradoxical at best: arguing for the humanity of Black characters by erasing blackness or, to phrase it in the language of the period, by favoring souls over bodies. The Triad protagonists, in this view, are not Black men but rather men who are black, product of an era in which racial categories and race-based identities had yet to be cemented and color was thought of as "accidental." I would hasten to add, as a caveat, that Andrés de Claramonte comes close to forming an exception to this mentality. While I tend to view him on the same continuum as Jiménez de Enciso and Vélez de Guevara, the bold formulations of Black identity that he assigns to Juan de Mérida place him at the very vanguard of early modern views on race and only a few steps from the Enlightenment.

Finally, I want to circle back to the idea of genre with which I opened this conclusion. It is significant that early modern Spanish audiences spoke of going to hear a play rather than to see it, which reflects the primary importance of dialogue. What, then, did the audiences of the Triad *hear* in the performance of these plays? Many things, to be sure, but among those offered in the manner of moral lessons, they would have heard: slaves do not deserve freedom; black bodies are home to white souls; beautiful interior virtues overcome monstrous external appearances.

At the same time, the visual element of theater is undeniable. So what did audiences *see* in the performance of these plays? In attempting to answer this question, I must begin by noting that the stage directions to *Virtues Overcome Appearances* indicate, upon Filipo's first appearance (1.2), a white actor in blackface: a practice that was also employed in Elizabethan performances of *Othello* (Strausbaugh 2007, 62) and that may well have been used in staging the other two plays of the Triad. Indeed, part of the "joke" in the scene in *Juan Latino* with the coal merchant (3.3) is that his face is blackened with soot: possibly the same makeup worn by the actor playing Latino (Beusterien 2006a, 103). Notwithstanding the shameful history of blackface in American minstrel shows and film, it is worth wondering whether the butt of the joke in scenes such as this may have been the crudeness of the theatrical illusion as much as the Afro-Spaniards it represented. It should also be noted that Spanish theater companies, unlike their English counterparts, may have benefited from a limited pool of Black performers for roles such as these (Ruano de la Haza and Allen 1994, 309), especially in cities like Seville with relatively high concentrations of Afro-Spaniards.

Even if we concede that blackface was the norm in performances of the Triad plays and that it was meant to provoke laughter at Black characters rather than at a stage convention, it was not the only visual cue offered to audiences. It is hard to imagine performing these plays, in fact, without mobilizing a whole range of redeeming visual narratives. A Black slave who wears a scholar's cape, has his portrait painted for a king, graduates from a prestigious university, and marries a white noblewoman. A Black soldier, son of a slave, who captures an enemy prince on the battlefield, shakes hands with a king, is inducted into a prestigious military order, and marries a white noblewoman. A Black prince, imprisoned at birth, who breaks free of his chains, becomes king of a white country, rules with benevolence and wisdom, and marries a white princess. Three Black *men*—not villains, clowns, or saints—who are praised and rewarded for their behavior rather than burned at the stake, flogged, betrayed, or shot through the chest with an arrow. Regardless of the performers' skin color or makeup, audiences may well have interpreted the Triad's Black protagonists as dignified characters worthy of respect: similar to the one that Jan Mostaert, roughly a hundred years earlier, appears to have represented in his *Portrait of an African Man* (book cover and TSW, Fig.10; see the analysis in Lowe 2005, 44–47).

I confess that I am not completely comfortable with the interpretation I have just proposed, nor am I confident that the production and reception of the Triad plays in 1620 will ever be fully knowable. What I will venture to say is that the theater's inherent tension between seeing and hearing is pushed to the limit in these extraordinary plays. Long after curtains fell on early modern performances, the compelling images may have lingered, disrupting and perhaps even undoing the carefully constructed verbal cues. Even today, the incongruities that arise from this tension have the potential to captivate and unsettle.

4. Translator's Note

Like most literary translators, I aim for a balance between the twin principles of accuracy and readability. There is no good consensus definition of either of these concepts, much less a formula to calculate the proper balance. Translators can and do have honest disagreements over what the final equilibrium should look like. I believe my own approach is best explained through examples. Below are the most significant challenges I confronted in my translations of the Triad, from broad principles that affect an entire work down to specific passages.

Orality and Performance

Like all works of theater, the Triad plays consist of written texts that are, to borrow from a fellow translator (Bassnett 1991, 121), "indissolubly linked" to performance. Whether or not stage representations are viable today, I have tried to respect the oral intent of the works by producing clean, footnote-free texts that aim to be intelligible through oral delivery, in real time, without the benefit of reading or rereading. I am aware, of course, that the texts will also—perhaps primarily—be accessed in their written form, giving rise to questions that require clarification and interpretation. I have addressed such issues in the Introduction and Glossary.

Poetry and Prose

Like all plays of the Spanish *comedia*, those of the Triad are written almost exclusively in verse (a notable exception is the case of letters read out loud). For the most part, however, I have opted to translate everything into prose. Having explained the reasoning behind my choice in great detail elsewhere (Kidd 2004, 45–50), I will offer only a short summary here. First, I believe prose allows for greater accuracy and readability. Second, because Spanish and English poetry are based on incompatible metrical systems, there is no axiomatic approach to reproducing the forms of one in the other. To do so well, across the three thousand or so lines of the typical *comedia*, requires a translator who is also an accomplished poet, which I do not claim to be.

I do make one exception to this principle: I believe that poems or songs that appear as independent units, separate from dialogue, should be marked as such in the translation. In this case I do translate into verse, aiming for a pleasant rhythm and, where appropriate, a smattering of rhyme.

Textual Transmission

All translations begin with a source text, but in the case of medieval and early modern literature, identifying an authoritative source can prove challenging. Many texts have complicated histories that involve various printed and manuscript versions across centuries of transmission. In working to establish a reliable text, scholars often represent the transmission history as a tree. The more branches, stems, and leaves the tree has—in the form of the various iterations, each of which includes its own unique characteristics—the more complicated it can be to find one's way to the trunk from which everything sprouts.

The challenges in this area varied considerably by play. The case of *Juan Latino* was the simplest, for there is only one surviving source of the text, a printed edition from 1652 (Jiménez de Enciso 1652–1951 [A]), which I consulted directly from a digital copy that is widely available on the internet. I also consulted Juliá Martínez's modern edition of the play (Jiménez de Enciso 1652–1951 [B]), but because he makes several transcription errors, I relied on the original in areas of doubt.

The case of *Virtues Overcome Appearances* proved to be only slightly more complicated, involving two seventeenth-century printings, one dated and one undated (Vélez de Guevara 1640–2010 [A], [B]). I consulted digital copies of both texts, which I obtained from the libraries in which they are housed (the British Library and the Biblioteca Palatina di Parma). Text [B] is clearly the superior of the two, so I used it as my base, occasionally relying on [A] to resolve obscurities or supply missing passages. I also consulted the three modern editions of the play to date (Vélez de Guevara 1640–2010 [C], [D], [E]), the best of which I found to be [D], edited by Maria Grazia Profeti. In the case of discrepancies between texts [A] and [B], which are all fairly minor and do not alter the play in significant ways, I followed Profeti's choices 95 percent of the time.

The transmission history of *The Brave Black Soldier* presents considerable challenges. The earliest dated edition is a printing from 1638 (Claramonte y Corroy 1638–2016 [A]), followed by a handwritten manuscript from no later than 1651 (Claramonte y Corroy 1638–2016 [B]). Five additional printings, believed to be from the 1600s but all undated (Claramonte y Corroy 1638–2016 [C], [D], [E], [F], [G]), and six more from the eighteenth century, three dated and three undated (Claramonte y Corroy 1638–2016 [H], [I], [J], [K], [L]), [M]), round out the early modern transmission history. (The libraries that house these editions are listed in the Works Cited.) Additionally, there are five modern editions of the text to date (Claramonte y Corroy 1638–2016 [N], [O], [P], [Q], [R]). I have consulted copies of all the texts, both early modern and modern, either digitally or in print. Acquiring all the early modern editions proved to be the greatest challenge, but most are publicly available on the internet, and the few that are not I acquired from the relevant libraries.

Regarding the modern editions, none of them takes into account all the early modern ones to my satisfaction. For example, several short passages that appear only in Claramonte y Corroy 1638–2016 [F] nicely round out the end of act 2 with an allusion to the play's title, but no modern editor includes them. Another text, Claramonte y Corroy 1638–2016 [K], which I discovered at Spain's National Library, has apparently been overlooked by all modern editors, none of whom mention it. The unreliability of the modern editions combined with the great variability among the early modern ones—most significantly, Claramonte y Corroy 1638–2016 [A] eliminates Juan de Mérida's induction into the Order of Santiago as well as his marriage to Doña Juana—has led me to base my translation on my own reading of the earlier texts. In resolving discrepancies, I have followed two principles. First, I give priority to the seventeenth-century sources, using text [A] (the earliest known exemplar) as my base. Second, I tend toward inclusivity, incorporating significant passages even when they do not appear in a majority of versions, such as the segments from [F] mentioned above. Instead of trying to find my way back to the mythical "trunk" of the tree, I aim for a composite reconstruction that incorporates meaningful variations as seamlessly as possible.

Scenes and Stage Directions

Early modern editions of the Triad texts mark divisions only between the customary three acts. For the convenience of readers and potential directors, I have also subdivided each act into scenes. As opposed to the so-called French scene, which is marked by the entry or exit of any actor and is still in common use in Spanish-speaking countries, I follow the conventions of Anglo-American theater and define a scene by its setting, which, in the *comedia*, is typically understood to change when all players exit the stage and a new group enters. I supply a description of the setting in brackets as best as can be determined.

Play texts from the period frequently skimp on stage directions. Often the author was the director and did not feel the need for explanations, which then might be supplied by the printer. Interestingly, both Jiménez de Enciso and Vélez de Guevara represent something of an exception to this trend according to Schevill (1903, 200) and Peale (2004, 80). Even in the best cases, however, stage directions are erratic and inconsistent, especially with entrances, exits, and asides. I have supplied the latter three cues as necessary and added additional stage directions where it seemed helpful. Those that do not appear in at least one of the early modern editions are indicated in square brackets.

Racial Terms and Slave Dialect

This was by far the greatest challenge I encountered in this project. There are two basic issues: specific racial terms and the slave dialect known as *bozal*. In both cases, it comes down to the tension between accuracy and readability with which I began, when readability is understood to include the sensitivities of the modern reader. Arguably, a text is not readable if it is full of language that drives the reader away. Yet the idea of censorship is inherently offensive as well. Below I explain my attempts to strike an appropriate balance between these principles.

Regarding specific terms, in most cases I opt to translate directly. The most common word in *Juan Latino* and *The Brave Black Soldier* that is universally offensive is *perro*, which I consistently translate as "dog." The augmentative variation, *perrazo*, I render as "dirty dog." The more literary *can* becomes "canine." In *Virtues Overcome Appearances*, as discussed in the Literary Analysis, these types of insults are absent, replaced with terms that signify a violation of natural boundaries. The most common of these, *monstro*, I always translate as "monster" to be consistent, though I think in some cases "monstrosity" could work as well. The variation *monstro de naturaleza*, which occurs only once, I translate as "freak of nature." Other terms in this semantic field along with my translations include *bruto* (brute), *fiera* (barbarian or beast), *gigante* (giant), *minotauro* (minotaur), *Orco* (Orcus), *portento* (phantasm or vision), *prodigio* (aberration or marvel), and *salvaje* (savage). Context necessitates variation in certain cases, but I try to maintain as much consistency as possible.

Two ethnic terms that presented a challenge are *moro* and *morisco*. Despite my reservations about these words, the traditional English form of the first, "Moor," proved to be the best option when occurring as a noun. *Morisco*, as a noun, has no single-word anglicized form, and compound terms that get at the meaning, such as "Christianized Moor" or "Converted Moor," are too awkward in dialogue. I thus leave *morisco* untranslated, with capitalization and without italics, when it is a noun; I use *Moorish* for both *morisco* and *moro* when they occur as adjectives.

The two racial terms that represented the greatest challenge were *negro* and *moreno*. In Spanish, *negro* has a wide and ambiguous semantic field ranging from the neutral "black" to "slave" to the taboo N-word in English. *Moreno* means "dark," "brown," or "brunette" and is often a polite substitute for *negro* in the Triad texts. It is not normally offensive, though it is derived from *moro*, which often is. An additional issue is grammatical: in Spanish, one may nominalize almost any descriptive adjective in direct address. In English, conversely, we do not normally say, "Hello, short," or "Hey, blond"; instead, some modification to the adjective, such as the addition of an *-ie* suffix, is required for the word to function in direct address. Considering all these factors, I typically translate *moreno* as *dark* or *brown* when it appears as an adjective and as *darkskin* in nominalized form. *Negro* as an adjective I translate as "black." In nominalized form, when I feel the meaning is deliberately offensive, I leave it as *negro*, italicized (which should be pronounced with a short *e* as in *met*); otherwise I translate it as "black man" or "slave," according to context. A final term for dark skin, limited to *The Brave Black Soldier*, is the Spanish word *prieto* (or *preto* in Antón's speech), which appears to carry the more innocent connotation of *moreno*, perhaps with a slight comic intent. I have consistently translated it as "swarthy." Lastly, when Spanish *blanco* and Portuguese *branco* (the latter limited to Antón's speech) refer to people in nominalized form, I translate them as "paleface."

The context of slavery that lingers behind all the plays led to an additional complication. In *Juan Latino*, several characters, including the protagonist, earn the title of *maestro*, a university rank indicating the bearer of a master's degree or a general title for a teacher. The most logical English equivalent, *master*, is a synonym of *slave owner*: an unfortunate ambiguity that does not exist in Spanish. I thus translate *maestro* as "tutor" when appropriate or with the Latin term for master or teacher: *magister*. I reserve *master* in the sense of "slave owner" for certain instances of the word *amo*, which I also translate as "lord" when it means the master of servants rather than slaves.

The final challenge in this category is the slave dialect of Spanish known as *bozal*, which, in the case of the Triad, is spoken only by the character Antón in *The Brave Black Soldier*. Carefully studied by linguists such as Weber de Kurlat (1962) and Lipski (1986 and 2005), *bozal* Spanish was originally thought to be a mainly literary convention employed for humorous purposes. Recent insightful studies, however, such as those by Jones (2019) and Santos Morillo (2020), suggest that it bears traces of the lived experiences of early modern Afro-Spaniards. I thus decided it was important to signal the difference, which is particularly evident in Spanish, between Antón's speech and that of the other characters. The challenge was to do so in a way that maintained the marked, humorous quality of the dialect without slipping into a version of African American Vernacular English, which would be not only ahistorical but deeply offensive. My solution is a scrambled, zany, and deliberately inaccurate version of the Elizabethan idiom associated with Shakespearean texts, including invented words such as *twere* and *meesieur*. In my introductory materials, however, when citing *bozal* dialogue from texts outside the Triad, I render it into standard English and note the presence of dialect in an observation.

Puns, Jokes, and Wordplay

The *comedia* being comedic, its authors reveled in all types of humor and wordplay, from highbrow classical allusions to earthy sexual and scatological references. The plays of the Triad are no exception. Wordplay, furthermore, typically represents one of the biggest challenges for translators because the double entendres that enable the humor in the source language often do not sort out the same way in the target language. A workaround must therefore be found if the humor is to be preserved, which I normally feel is important. But I have no universal approach to the issue. Everything depends on the particularities of the passage in question. For curious readers with a working knowledge of Spanish, I conclude this Translator's Note with a few representative examples.

A SEALED POCKET (*JL* 3.1). The Spanish word *manera* means both "way" and "pocket." When Doña Ana sews up the pocket in her gown to keep out Juan Latino's roaming hands, he threatens to stop tutoring her. When she asks why, he replies, "No hay manera," meaning both "There's no way" and "There's no pocket," with clearly sexual implications. Because English has no word with the same double meaning as *manera*, I create a pun based on a conceptual comparison: "A mind is a receptacle ... like a pocket. How can I teach to a pocket that's sewn shut? There's no way in." Not only is this pun amusing, but it also provides an important clue to the dating of the play (see the Biographical Sketches).

THE REBUS OF FATE (*JL* 2.1 and *BBS* 1.2). In a barbaric practice, Spanish slaves were often branded on the face with the telltale "*S* overlaid with an *I* shaped like a nail (*clavo*)" (Hutchinson 2002, 38). The resulting rebus (*S* plus the nail—or *clavo*-shaped *I*) spelled out, in pictorial form, *es-clavo* (slave). When Juan Latino and Juan de Mérida speak of driving a nail through fate ("ponelle a mi fortuna el clavo" and "un clavo al eje vil de la fortuna aplico"), there is a clear reference to this practice. In Juan de Mérida's case, there is an additional sound play between the word *eje* ("axle," which suggests the nail of the rebus), pronounced *EH-shay* in early modern Spanish, and the word for the letter *S*, pronounced *EH-say*. To get at the meaning of this extremely complicated pun, I use the phrase "to rebrand the rebus," which both hints at the practice of branding and incorporates a bit of sound play with the alliterative *reb-* in both words.

DUNG AND DONG (*BBS* 1.6, 2.1, 3.1). This pun is a good example of the slave dialect known as *bozal*. The character Antón mispronounces the Spanish word *caballero*, which straddles the line between English *knight* and *gentleman*, as *cagayera*, which suggests *cagar* (to shit). In my translation, I use the word *don* as an approximate synonym for *knight/gentleman* and have Antón variously mangle it as *dung* and *dong*. He thus refers to Don Agustín, who has dishonored Doña Leonor, as a "falsehearted dung" and to the king of Spain, whom he meets along with Juan de Mérida, as "a mighty dong."

TARGETED (*BBS* 3.2 and *VOA* 2.1). This pun strikes at the heart of the themes of race and slavery in the Triad, playing on the double meaning of *blanco* in Spanish: "white" and "target." In his triumph over Don Agustín, Juan de Mérida says he wishes to be gracious and reward his rival with a promotion to colonel so that he will see him as a Black man who is white (*blanco*) on the inside and who "a los *blancos* afrenta," which means both "damages his targets," that is, accomplishes his goals, and "offends white men." To capture the double meaning and veiled threat, I have translated the passage as follows: "I wish to honor your person so you'll see me as a black man who both acts white and targets whites . . . for promotion!" In *Virtues Overcome Appearances*, Vélez de Guevara uses the same pun in reverse, so to speak, making the Black protagonist a "*blanco* de los rayos de sus cielos," meaning both "*target* of her [i.e., Leda's] heavenly rays" and "*whitened* by her heavenly rays." My translation aims for a similar double meaning by putting into play a different set of words: "Tell her that a black man, breached by . . . bleached by her heavenly shafts, is being driven mad by the sight of her."

CARD SHARKS AND ENEMAS (*VOA* 3.1). Card games were a favorite pastime in early modern Spain, and the various suits, moves, and tricks made for many rich and complex instances of wordplay. When Filipo becomes king and begins rewarding his most loyal followers, Bugle expects his share but is quickly disabused of the notion. To express his disappointment, he makes a complicated pun that digresses across ten lines of verse using technical card terms such as *chacho* (a type of penalty) and culminating in a medical metaphor about an enema (*melecina*). This is a rare example of a passage where the two seventeenth-century sources of the play differ significantly, and I believe textual corruption has added to the difficulty. Focusing on the elements common to both passages, I have translated as follows: "Back then it was mutually beneficial, for we had a silent pact between us, like a pair of card sharks. But now, with a king in my hand and favors to be accrued, I fear I'm getting a-screwed."

Works Cited

Note on the Triad texts: In preparing my translations, I consulted all known Spanish editions of the plays. The bibliography below includes the various editions, each identified by a unique letter and in chronological order as far as it could be determined, beneath the relevant author and title. The early modern editions (1600–1800) include a brief description (handwritten, printed, bound, etc.) and, if the text is available online, a web link.

Aeschylus. 2011. *Agamemnon*. *The Complete Aeschylus*, edited and translated by Peter Burian and Alan Shapiro, vol. 1, Oxford UP, pp. 43–103.

Akbari, Suzanne Conklin. 2009. *Idols in the East: European Representations of Islam and the Orient, 1100–1450*. Cornell UP.

Alfonso X. 1807. L*AS* S*IETE* P*ARTIDAS* *del Rey Don Alfonso el Sabio*. Edited by Real Academia Española, vol. 3, Imprenta Real.

———. 2000. S*ONGS OF* H*OLY* M*ARY* *of Alfonso X, the Wise*. Translated by Kathleen Kulp-Hill, Arizona Center for Medieval and Renaissance Studies.

———. 2019. *Cantigas de Santa María for Singers*. www.cantigasdesantamaria.com. Accessed 5 March 2023.

Allen, John J. 1983. *The Reconstruction of a Spanish Golden Age Playhouse: El Corral del Príncipe, 1583–1744*. UP of Florida.

Altman, Ida. 2013. "Marriage, Family, and Ethnicity in the Early Spanish Caribbean." *The William and Mary Quarterly*, vol. 70, no. 2, pp. 225–50.

Alvarez, Gonzalo, et al. 2009. "The Role of Inbreeding in the Extinction of a European Royal Dynasty." *PLoS ONE*, vol. 4, no. 4, doi.org/10.1371/journal.pone.0005174. Accessed 5 March 2023.

Appiah, Kwame Anthony. 1990. "Race." *Critical Terms for Literary Study*, edited by Frank Lentricchia and Thomas McLaughlin, U of Chicago P, pp. 274–87.

Ares Queija, Berta, and Alessandro Stella, editors. 2000. *Negros, mulatos, zambaigos: derroteros africanos en los mundos ibéricos*. Consejo Superior de Investigaciones Científicas.

Aristotle. 1984. *The Complete Works of Aristotle*. Edited by Jonathan Barnes, 2 vols., Princeton UP.
Attwater, Donald. 1995. *The Penguin Dictionary of Saints*. With Catherine Rachel John, 3rd ed., Penguin.
Bakhtin, Mikhail. 1984. *Rabelais and His World*. Translated by Hélène Iswolsky, Indiana UP.
Barrios, Olga. 2002. "Entre la esclavitud y el ensalzamiento: la presencia africana en la sociedad y en el teatro del Siglo de Oro español." *Bulletin of the Comediantes*, vol. 54. no. 2, pp. 287–311.
Bartlett, Robert. 1994. *The Making of Europe: Conquest, Colonization and Cultural Change 950–1350*. Penguin.
———. 2001. "Medieval and Modern Concepts of Race and Ethnicity." *Journal of Medieval and Early Modern Studies*, vol. 31, no. 1, pp. 39–56.
———. 2009. "Illustrating Ethnicity in the Middle Ages." Eliav-Feldon et al., pp. 132–56.
Bassnett, Susan. 1991. "Translating Dramatic Texts." *Translation Studies*, rev. ed., Routledge, pp. 120–32.
Beardsley, Theodore S. 1970. *Hispano-Classical Translations Printed between 1482 and 1699*. Duquesne UP.
Belloni, Benedetta. 2019. "Lope de Vega y la tradición hagiográfica hispano-sarda: sobre una fuente de la comedia *El negro del mejor amo*." *Anuario Lope de Vega: texto, literatura, cultura*, vol. 25, pp. 75–102.
Berco, Cristian. 2008. "Producing Patriarchy: Male Sodomy and Gender in Early Modern Spain." *Journal of the History of Sexuality*, vol. 17, no. 3, pp. 351–76.
Bermúdez de Pedraza, Francisco. 1608. *Antigüedad y excelencias de Granada*. Luis Sánchez.
Bernstein, Beth. 2021. "A 'Monstrous' Problem: Examining Issues of Race in *Virtudes vencen señales*." *Exploring Race, Ethnicity, Gender, and Sexuality in Four Spanish Plays: A Crisis of Identity*, Lexington, pp. 53–88.
Beusterien, John. 1999. "Talking Black: An Unfinished Black Spanish Glossary." *Bulletin of the Comediantes*, vol. 51, nos. 1–2, pp. 83–104.
———. 2005. "Introducción." Vega Carpio 2005, pp. 9–32.
———. 2006a. *An Eye on Race: Perspectives from Theater in Imperial Spain*. Bucknell UP.
———. 2006b. "Teaching Race and the Performances of Whiteness in *El valiente negro en Flandes*, by Andrés de Claramonte." *Approaches to Teaching World Literature*, vol. 90, pp. 174–81.
Biblia, La. 1569. Translated by Casiodoro de Reina. No place or publisher.
———. 1602. Translated by Casiodoro de Reina, revised by Cypriano de Valera. Casa de Lorenço Iacobi.
Biedermann, Hans. 1994. *Dictionary of Symbolism: Cultural Icons and the Meanings Behind Them*. Translated by James Hulbert, Meridian.
Bindman, David, and Henry Louis Gates, Jr., editors. 2010. *From the "Age of Discovery" to the Age of Abolition: Artists of the Renaissance and Baroque*. Vol. 3, pt. 1 of *The Image of the Black in Western Art*, Harvard UP.
Blumenthal, Debra. 2005. "'La Casa dels Negres': Black African Solidarity in Late Medieval Valencia." Earle and Lowe, pp. 225–46.

Bolaños [Donoso], Piedad. 2001. "Semblanza biográfica de Luis Vélez de Guevara." *La serrana de la Vera*, by Luis Vélez de Guevara, edited by Piedad Bolaños, Clásicos Castalia, pp. 9–21.

———. 2011. "Nacimiento del Corral de la Montería (Sevilla) y actividad dramática, 1ª etapa (1626–1636): Diego de Almonacid, el mozo, al frente de la gestión." *XXIV y XXV jornadas del teatro del Siglo de Oro in memoriam Ricard Salvat*, edited by Elisa García-Lara and Antonio Serrano, Instituto de Estudios Almerienses, pp. 291–369.

Bonilla y San Martín, Adolfo. 1912. Introduction (no title). Pastor, pp. 1–8.

Buckland, W. W. 1908. *The Roman Law of Slavery: The Condition of the Slave in Private Law from Augustus to Justinian*. Cambridge UP.

Castiglione, Baldesar. 1959. *The Book of the Courtier*. Translated by Charles S. Singleton, Anchor-Doubleday.

Castillejo, David. 2002. *Guía de ochocientas comedias del Siglo de Oro para el uso de actores y lectores*. Ars Millenii.

Cátedra, Pedro M. 2006. "Noticia de un ejemplar único." *Tres colloquios pastoriles de Juan de Vergara y Lope de Rueda (Valencia, 1567)*, edited by Pedro M. Cátedra, Cilengua, pp. 19–32.

Catlos, Brian. 2018. *Kingdoms of Faith: A New History of Islamic Spain*. Basic Books.

Cerezo Rubio, Ubaldo. 2010. "Diego Jiménez de Enciso y Zúñiga." Jauralde Pou, vol.1, pp. 426–33.

Cervantes, Miguel de. 1966. *El gallardo español*. *Teatro completo*, edited by Agustín Blánquez, vol. 1, Editorial Iberia, pp. 139–220.

———. 1987. *El ingenioso hidalgo Don Quijote de la Mancha*. Edited by Luis Andrés Murillo, 2 vols., Clásicos Castalia.

———. 1989. *Entremeses*. Edited by Nicholas Spadaccini, Cátedra.

———. 2000. *El celoso extremeño*. *Novelas ejemplares*, edited by Harry Sieber, 19th ed., vol. 2, Cátedra, pp. 97–135.

Cirot, Georges. 1938–1944. "La maurophilie littéraire en Espagne au XVIe siècle." *Bulletin Hispanique*, vol. 40, no. 2, 1938, pp. 150–57; vol. 40, no. 3, 1938, pp. 281–96; vol. 40, no. 4, 1938, pp. 433–47; vol. 41, no. 1, 1939, pp. 65–85; vol. 41, no. 4, 1939, pp. 345–51; vol. 42, no. 3, 1940, pp. 213–27; vol. 43, no. 3, 1941, pp. 265–89; vol. 44, no. 2, 1942, pp. 96–102; vol. 46, no. 1, 1944, pp. 5–25.

Claramonte y Corroy, Andrés de. 1613. *Letanía Moral*. Seville, Matias Clavixo. R/7891, Biblioteca Nacional de España.

———. 1638–2016. *El valiente negro en Flandes*.

[A] 1638. *Parte treynta vna de las meiores comedias qve hasta oy han salido*, Barcelona, Emprenta de Iayme Romeu, fols. 152v–179r. R/23484, Biblioteca Nacional de España, bdh-rd.bne.es/viewer.vm?id=0000073191&page=1. Accessed 5 March 2023. [Does not list author's name.]

[B] c. 1651. Handwritten and bound manuscript, no place or publisher. MSS/15690, Biblioteca Nacional de España, bdh-rd.bne.es/viewer.vm?id=0000014478&page=1. Accessed 5 March 2023. [Final pages indicate approval for performance in Zaragoza in 1651 and 1652.]

[C] 1600s (no date). Single-play printing, no place or publisher. T/55273/1, Biblioteca Nacional de España.
[D] 1600s (no date). Single-play printing, no place or publisher. T/55273/2, Biblioteca Nacional de España, bdh-rd.bne.es/viewer.vm?id=0000266082&page=1. Accessed 5 March 2023.
[E] 1600s (no date). Single-play printing, no place or publisher. T/55273/3, Biblioteca Nacional de España, bdh-rd.bne.es/viewer.vm?id=0000056605&page=1. Accessed 5 March 2023.
[F] 1600s (no date). Single-play printing, no place or publisher. T/55273/12, Biblioteca Nacional de España, bdh-rd.bne.es/viewer.vm?id=0000056612&page=1. Accessed 5 March 2023.
[G] 1600s (no date). Single-play printing, no place or publisher. 58961, Institut del Teatre de Barcelona, books.cdmae.cat/visorpdf/?recurs=SL%2058961. Accessed 5 March 2023.
[H] 1745. Single-play printing, Madrid, Imprenta de Antonio Sanz. A 250/187(19), Biblioteca de la U de Sevilla, archive.org/details/A25018719. Accessed 5 March 2023.
[I] 1751. Single-play printing, Valladolid, Imprenta de Alonso de Riego. FOLL 306 3, Biblioteca de la U de Santiago de Compostela, hdl.handle.net/10347/207. Accessed 5 March 2023. [Lists author as Pedro Calderón de la Barca.]
[J] 1764. Single-play printing, Valencia, Imprenta de la Viuda de Josef de Orga. T/969, Biblioteca Nacional de España, bdh-rd.bne.es/viewer.vm?id=0000056606&page=1. Accessed 5 March 2023. [Title reverses noun-adjective sequence: *El negro valiente en Flandes*.]
[K] 1700s (no date). Single-play printing, Valladolid, Imprenta de Alonso de Ri[e]go. T/55329/14, Biblioteca Nacional de España. [Not cited by any previous scholars. Lists author as Francisco de Rojas.]
[L] 1700s (no date). Single-play printing, Salamanca, Imprenta de Santa Cruz. Bueno FA 10 COM val, Museo Nacional de Teatro, bvpb.mcu.es/es/consulta/registro.do?id=411963. Accessed 5 March 2023.
[M] 1700s (no date). Single-play printing, Seville, Joseph Padrino. T/14798/16, Biblioteca Nacional de España, bdh-rd.bne.es/viewer.vm?id=0000056610&page=1. Accessed 5 March 2023.
[N] 1881. Edited by Miguel de Mesonero Romanos, *Biblioteca de Autores Españoles*, vol. 43, Madrid, Rivadeneyra, pp. 491–509.
[O] 1977. Edited by Alex Treviño Trejo, PhD Diss., U of Southern California.
[P] 1997. Edited by Alfredo Rodríguez López-Vázquez, U de Alcalá de Henares.
[Q] 2007. Edited by Nelson López, Edition Reichenberger. [Reproduces editor's PhD diss. from the U of Florida, 1998.]
[R] 2016. Edited by Ana Ogallas Moreno, Clásicos Hispánicos, clasicoshispanicos.com/ebook/el-valiente-negro-en-flandes. Accessed 5 March 2023.

Cobos, Mercedes. 1998. "El testamento, la partida de defunción, el inventario de bienes y otros documentos inéditos relativos a los últimos años de la vida del dramaturgo Diego Jiménez de Enciso." *Actas del IV Congreso Internacional de la AISO*, U de Alcalá, pp. 449–58.

"Coplas de cómo una dama ruega a un negro que cante en manera de requiebro." 2005. Lawrance, pp. 86–93.

Correas, Gonzalo. 1906. *Refranes y frases proverbiales y otras fórmulas comunes de la lengua castellana*. Establecimiento tipográfico de Jaime Ratés.

Cortés López, José Luis. 1989. *La esclavitud negra en la España peninsular del siglo XIV*. Ediciones U de Salamanca.

Cotarelo y Mori, Emilio. 1911. *Colección de entremeses, loas, bailes, jácaras y mojigangas desde fines del siglo XVI á mediados del XVIII*. Bailly-Ballière.

———. 1914a. *Don Diego Jiménez de Enciso y su teatro*. Tipografía de la Revista de Archivos, Bibliotecas y Museos.

———. 1914b. "La fundación de la Academia Española y su primer director D. Juan Manuel F. Pacheco, Marqués de Villena." *Boletín de la Real Academia Española*, vol. 1, pp. 1–127.

———. 1917. *Luis Vélez de Guevara y sus obras dramáticas*. Tipografía de la Revista de Archivos, Bibliotecas y Museos.

Covarrubias, Sebastián de. 2006. *Tesoro de la lengua castellana o española*. Edited by Ignacio Arellano and Rafael Zafa, U de Navarra/Iberoamericana/Vervuert/Real Academia Española/Centro para la Edición de Clásicos Españoles.

Davies, Gareth. 1983. "Luis Vélez de Guevara and Court Life." *Antigüedad y actualidad de Luis Vélez de Guevara: estudios críticos*. John Benjamins, pp. 20–38.

DeCosta, Miriam, editor. 1977. *Blacks in Hispanic Literature: Critical Essays*. Kennikat.

Díaz Cassou, Pedro. 1895. *Serie de los obispos de Cartagena: sus hechos y su tiempo*. Establecimiento Tipográfico de Fortanet.

Diego de San Pedro. 1989. *Cárcel de amor*. Edited by Enrique Moreno Báez, 5th ed., Cátedra.

Dionysius of Halicarnassus. 1961. *The Roman Antiquities*. Translated by Earnest Cary, vol. 2, Harvard UP.

Doerig, J. A. 1966. "La situación de los esclavos a partir de las Siete Partidas de Alfonso el Sabio." *Folia Humanística*, vol. 4, no. 40, pp. 337–61.

Domínguez Ortiz, Antonio. 2003. "La esclavitud en Castilla durante la Edad Moderna." *La esclavitud en Castilla en la Edad Moderna y otros estudios de marginados*, Editorial Comares, pp. 1–52.

Doniger, Wendy. 2003. "The Symbolism of Black and White Babies in the Myth of Parental Impression." *Social Research*, vol. 70, no. 1, pp. 1–44.

———, and Gregory Spinner. 1998. "Misconceptions: Female Imaginations and Male Fantasies in Parental Imprinting." *Daedalus*, vol. 127, no. 1, pp. 97–129.

Earle, T. F., and K. J. P. Lowe, editors. 2005. *Black Africans in Renaissance Europe*. Cambridge UP.

Eisenberg, Daniel. 1973. "Who Read the Romances of Chivalry?" *Kentucky Romance Quarterly*, no. 20, pp. 209–33.

Eliav-Feldon, Miriam, et al., editors. 2009. *The Origins of Racism in the West*. Cambridge UP.

Elliott, J. H. 1963. *Imperial Spain: 1469–1716*. New American Library.
Entrambasaguas, Joaquín. 1973. "Haz y envés de Luis Vélez de Guevara." *Estudios y ensayos de investigación y crítica: de la leyenda de Rosamunda a Jovellanos*, CSIC, pp. 129–40.
Fernández de Córdoba, Francisco. 1954. *Historia y descripción de la antigüedad y descendencia de la Casa de Cordoua*. Edited by the Real Academia de Córdoba de Ciencias, Bellas Artes y Nobles Artes, Tipografía Artística.
Fernández Zorrilla, José Miguel. 1996. "Los bienes raíces de los moriscos ecijanos en vísperas de su expulsión." *Luis Vélez de Guevara y su época: IV Congreso de Historia de Écija*, edited by Piedad Bolaños Donoso and Marina Martín Ojeda, Ayuntamiento de Écija/Funcación El Monte, pp. 337–43.
Ferrer Valls, Teresa, et al. 2012a. "*El valiente negro en Flandes*: noticias de representación." *CATCOM*, catcom.uv.es/consulta/browserecord.php?id=1953&mode=indice&letter=v. Accessed 5 March 2023.
———. 2012b. "*Virtudes vencen señales*: noticias de representación." *CATCOM*, catcom.uv.es/consulta/browserecord.php?id=551&mode=indice&letter=v. Accessed 5 March 2023.
Finley, M. I. 1980. *Ancient Slavery and Modern Ideology*. Viking.
Foucault, Michel. 1997. *Il faut défendre la societé: Cours au Collège de France, 1976*. Seuil/Gallimard.
Fowler, William R., Jr. 1985. "Ethnohistoric Sources on the Pipil-Nicarao of Central America: A Critical Analysis." *Ethnohistory*, vol. 32, no. 1, pp. 37–62.
Fra Molinero, Baltasar. 1991. "La formación del estereotipo del negro en las letras hispanas: el caso de tres coplas en pliegos sueltos." *Romance Languages Annual*, vol. 3, pp. 438–43.
———. 1993. "El negro Zaide: marginación social y textual en el *Lazarillo*." *Hispania*, vol. 76, no. 1, pp. 20–29.
———. 1995. *La imagen de los negros en el teatro del Siglo de Oro*. Siglo Veintiuno.
———. 1997. "The Play of Race and Gender in Vélez de Guevara's *Virtudes vencen señales*." *Bulletin of the Comediantes*, vol. 49. no. 2, pp. 337–55.
———. 2000. "Ser mulato en España y América: discursos legales y otros discursos literarios." Ares Queija and Stella, pp. 123–47.
———. 2005. "Juan Latino and His Racial Difference." Earle and Lowe, pp. 326–44.
———. 2014. "Los negros como figura de negación y diferencia en el teatro barroco." *Hipogrifo*, vol. 2, no. 2, pp. 7–29.
———. 2016. "Woman, Learning, and Fear: Racial Mixing in Diego Ximénez de Enciso's *Juan Latino*." *Prismatic Reflections on Spanish Golden Age Theater: Essays in Honor of Matthew D. Stroud*, edited by Gwyn E. Campbell and Amy R. Williamsen, Peter Lang, pp. 183–92.
Fracchia, Carmen. 2019. *"Black but Human": Slavery and Visual Art in Hapsburg Spain, 1480–1700*. Oxford UP.
Fradejas Lebrero, José. 1984. "Prólogo." *El negro del mejor amo*, by Lope de Vega Carpio, edited by José Fradejas Lebrero, U.N.E.D., pp. i–xxvii.
———. 2008. "Notas sobre la relación de *El valiente negro en Flandes* de A. Claramonte." *Murgetana*, no. 119, pp. 95–114.

Frenk, Margit, editor. 1987. *Corpus de la antigua lírica popular hispánica (siglos XV a XVII)*. Editorial Castalia.
Fuchs, Barbara. 2007. "The Spanish Race." Greer et al., pp. 88–98.
———. 2011. *Exotic Nation: Maurophilia and the Construction of Early Modern Spain*. U of Pennsylvania P.
Fuentes y Ponte, Javier. 1872. *Murcia que se fue*. Imprenta de la Biblioteca de Instrucción y Recreo.
Gallardo, Bartolomé José. 1863–1889. *Biblioteca de libros raros y curiosos*. 4 vols., Rivadeneyra/ Imprenta y Fundición de Manuel Tello.
Ganelin, Charles. 1987. "Introduction: Biography." *La infelice Dorotea*, by Andrés de Claramonte, edited by Charles Ganelin, Tamesis, pp. 13–23.
García Otero, María J. 2013. *Hag(e)ografía: propaganda ideológica y política geográfica en los discursos hagiográficos peninsulares: la construcción de la nación española (siglos XIII a XVII)*. PhD Diss., U of Kansas.
García-Reidy, Alejandro. 2019. "La presencia escénica de Andrés de Claramonte en el Siglo de Oro a partir de las bases de datos *Manos* y *CATCOM*." *Bulletin of the Comediantes*, vol. 71, nos. 1–2, pp. 135–54.
Garcilaso de la Vega. 1984. *Obras completas*. Edited by José Rico Verdú, Clásicos Plaza y Janés.
Gates, Henry Louis, Jr. 1988. *The Signifying Monkey: A Theory of Afro-American Literary Criticism*. Oxford UP.
———, and Maria Wolff. 1998. "An Overview of Sources on the Life and Work of Juan Latino, the 'Ethiopian Humanist.'" *Research in African Literature*, vol. 29, no. 4, pp. 14–51.
Gerber, Jane S. 1992. *The Jews of Spain: A History of the Sephardic Experience*. Free Press.
Gibson, M. Carl. 1964. "Spanish Academies of the Golden Age." *Brigham Young University Studies*, vol. 5, no. 3/4, pp. 169–82.
Gillet, Joseph E. 1926. "The 'Coplas del perro de Alba.'" *Modern Philology*, vol. 23, no. 4, pp. 417–44.
———. 1928. "The 'Coplas del perro de Alba.'" *Modern Philology*, vol. 26, no. 1, pp. 123–28.
Gilman, Sander L. 1985. *Difference and Pathology: Stereotypes of Sexuality, Race, and Madness*. Cornell UP.
———. 1986. *Jewish Self-Hatred: Anti-Semitism and the Hidden Language of the Jews*. Johns Hopkins UP.
Goldenberg, David. M. 2005. *The Curse of Ham: Race and Slavery in Early Judaism, Christianity, and Islam*. Princeton UP.
———. 2009. "Racism, Color Symbolism, and Color Prejudice." Eliav-Feldon et al., pp. 88–108.
González Echegaray, Carlos. 1998. "Dos negros notables en España a través del teatro del Siglo de Oro." *Boletín de la Biblioteca de Menéndez Pelayo*, vol. 74, pp. 407–34.
González Martínez, Javier J. 2012. "La transmisión impresa de un manuscrito dramático censurado: el caso de *El santo negro*, *El negro del Serafín* o *El negro del mejor amo*." *Castilla: Estudios de Literatura*, vol. 3, pp. 403–17.
González Ollé, Fernando, and Vicente Tusón. 1992. "Introducción." *Pasos*, by Lope de Rueda, edited by Fernando González Ollé and Vicente Tusón, 6th ed., Cátedra, pp. 7–70.

Green, Otis H. 1968. *Spain and the Western Tradition: The Castilian Mind in Literature from El Cid to Calderón*. Vol. 3, U of Wisconsin P.

Greer, Margaret R. et al., editors. 2007. *Rereading the Black Legend: The Discourses of Religious and Racial Difference in the Renaissance Empires*. U of Chicago P.

Groebner, Valentin. 2009. "The Carnal Knowledge of a Coloured Body: Sleeping with Arabs and Blacks in the European Imagination, 1300–1550." Eliav-Feldon et al., pp. 217–31.

Guerrero, Manuel Vicente. 2003. *El negro valiente en Flandes*. Edited by Moses E. Panford, Jr., Society of Spanish and Spanish-American Studies.

Hale, Edward Everett. 1945. *The Queen of California: The Origin of the Name of California with a Translation from* The Sergas of Esplandián. Colt.

Harvey, L. P. 2005. *Muslims in Spain: 1500–1615*. U of Chicago P.

Heliodorus. 2019. *An Ethiopian Story*, translated by J. R. Morgan. *Collected Ancient Greek Novels*, edited by B. P. Reardon, U of California P, pp. 407–686.

Heng, Geraldine. 2018. *The Invention of Race in the European Middle Ages*. Cambridge UP.

Hermenegildo, Alfredo. 2001. "Introducción." Rueda 2001, pp. 9–58.

Hernández Valcárcel, María del Carmen. 1983. "Cronología y apuntes biográficos." *Comedias*, by Andrés de Claramonte, edited by María del Carmen Hernández Valcárcel, Academia Alfonso X El Sabio, pp. 9–38.

Herrera Navarro, Jerónimo. N.d. "Manuel Vicente Guerrero." Real Academia de la Historia, *Diccionario Biográfico*, dbe.rah.es/biografias/73505/manuel-vicente-guerrero. Accessed 5 March 2023.

Herzog, Tamar. 2012. "How Did Early-Modern Slaves in Spain Disappear? The Antecedents." *Republics of Letters*, vol. 3, no. 1, pp. 1–7.

Huerta Calvo, Javier, et al. 2005. *Teatro español de la A a la Z*. Espasa.

Hutchinson, Steven. 2002. *Frontier Narratives: Liminal Lives in the Early Modern Mediterranean*. Manchester UP.

Irigoyen-García, Javier. 2005. "Ascensión social y enfrentamiento entre negros en *El valiente negro en Flandes* de Andrés de Claramonte: una aproximación postcolonial." *Afro-Hispanic Review*, vol. 24, no. 2, pp. 151–64.

Isidore of Seville. 2010. *The Etymologies*. Translated by Stephen A. Barney et al., Cambridge UP.

Ivory, Annette. 1979. "*Juan Latino*: The Struggle of Blacks, Jews, and Moors in Golden Age Spain." *Hispania*, vol. 62, no. 4, pp. 613–18.

Jason, Howard M. 1977. "The Negro in Spanish Literature to the End of the Siglo de Oro." DeCosta, pp. 29–35.

Jauralde Pou, Pablo, editor. 2010. *Diccionario filológico de literatura española (siglo XVII)*. 2 vols., Cátedra.

Jensen, John B. 1989. "On the Mutual Intelligibility of Spanish and Portuguese." *Hispania*, vol. 72, no. 4, pp. 848–52.

Jiménez de Enciso, Diego. 1652–1951. *Juan Latino*.

    [A] 1652. Segunda *parte de comedias escogidas de las mejores de España*, Madrid, Imprenta Real, fols. 33r–63v, bdh-rd.bne.es/viewer.vm?id=0000073306&page=1. Accessed 5 March 2023.

[B] 1951. *El encubierto y Juan Latino: comedias de Don Diego Ximénez de Enciso*, edited by Eduardo Juliá Martinez, Real Academia Española, pp. 143–356.

Jones, Nicholas R. 2019. *Staging Habla de Negros: Radical Performances of the African Diaspora in Early Modern Spain*. Pennsylvania State UP.

Juan Manuel. 1990. *El conde Lucanor*. Edited by Alfonso I. Sotelo, Cátedra.

Juliá Martínez, Eduardo. 1951. "Observaciones preliminares." Jiménez de Enciso 1652–1951 [B], pp. vii–lxxii.

Kamen, Henry. 1991. *Spain: 1469–1714*. 2nd ed., Longman.

———. 1997. *Philip of Spain*. Yale UP.

———. 1998. *The Spanish Inquisition: A Historical Revision*. Yale UP.

Kaplan, Paul H. D. 1985. *The Rise of the Black Magus in Western Art*. UMI Research P.

Kidd, Michael. 1998. "The Fairest of Them All: Racial and Sexual Signification in Vélez de Guevara's *Virtudes vencen señales*." *A Society on Stage: Essays on Spanish Golden Age Drama*, edited by Edward H. Friedman et al., UP of the South, pp. 117–32.

———. 2004. "Translator's Notes." *Life's a Dream*, by Pedro Calderón de la Barca, edited and translated by Michael Kidd, UP of Colorado, pp. 41–70.

Kirk, Charles Frederick. 1957. "Introduction." *Virtudes vencen señales*, by Luis Vélez de Guevara, edited by Charles Frederick Kirk, PhD Diss., Ohio State U, pp. vi–xcv.

Koerner, Joseph Leo. 2010. "The Epiphany of the Black Magus Circa 1500." Bindman and Gates, pp. 7–92.

Lacan, Jacques. 1977. "The Mirror Stage as Formative of the Function of the I as Revealed in Psychoanalytic Experience." *Écrits: A Selection*, translated by Alan Sheridan, Norton, pp. 1–7.

Lambert, A. F. 1980. "The Two Versions of Cervantes' *El celoso extremeño*: Ideology and Criticism." *Bulletin of Hispanic Studies*, vol. 57, pp. 219–31.

Lawrance, Jeremy. 2005. "Black Africans in Renaissance Spanish Literature." Earle and Lowe, pp. 70–93.

Lazarillo de Tormes. 1987. Edited by Francisco Rico, Cátedra.

Leavitt, Sturgis E. 1931. *The Estrella de Sevilla and Claramonte*. Harvard UP.

LeNotre, Gaston. 2018. "'In the Human Heart': A Premodern Philosophy of Race and Racism in Thomas Aquinas." *Proceedings of the American Catholic Philosophical Association*, vol. 92, pp. 301–20.

Libro del caballero Zifar. 1983. Edited by Cristina González, Cátedra.

Lipski, John. 1986. "'Black Spanish': Existence and Coexistence." *Afro-Hispanic Review*, vol. 5, no. 1/3, pp. 7–12.

———. 2005. *A History of Afro-Hispanic Language: Five Centuries, Five Continents*. Cambridge UP.

Livy. 1960. *The Early History of Rome*. Translated by Aubrey de Sélincourt, Penguin.

Lowe, Kate. 2005. "The Stereotyping of Black Africans in Renaissance Europe." Earle and Lowe, pp. 17–47.

Maravall, José Antonio. 1990. *Teatro y literatura en la sociedad barroca*. Rev. ed., Editorial Crítica.

Marín Ocete, Antonio. 1925. *El negro Juan Latino: ensayo biográfico y crítico*. Librería Guevara.

Mármol y Carvajal, Luis de. 1852. *Historia del [sic] rebelión y castigo de los moriscos del Reino de Granada*. M. Rivadeneyra.

Marquina, Rafael. 1938. "El negro en el teatro español antes de Lope de Vega." *Ultra*, vol. 4, no. 2, pp. 555–68.

Martín Casares, Aurelia. 2000a. "Cristianos, musulmanes y animistas en Granada: identidades religiosas y sincretismo cultural." Ares Queija and Stella, pp. 207–21.

———. 2000b. *La esclavitud en la Granada del siglo XVI: género, raza y religión*. U de Granada y Diputación Provincial de Granada.

———. 2005. "Free and Freed Black Africans in Granada in the Time of the Spanish Renaissance." Earle and Lowe, pp. 247–60.

———. 2014. "Evolution of the Origin of Slaves Sold in Spain from the Late Middle Ages till the 18th Century." *Schiavitù e servaggio nell'economia europea secc. XI–XVIII*. Firenze UP, pp. 409–30.

———. 2016. *Juan Latino: talento y destino. Un afrohispano en tiempos de Carlos V y de Felipe II*. Editorial U de Granada.

Masó, Calixto C. 1973. *Juan Latino: gloria de España y de su raza*. Northeastern Illinois U.

Menéndez Pelayo, Marcelino. 1894. "Observaciones preliminares." *Obras de Lope de Vega publicadas por la Real Academia Española*, vol. 4, Real Academia Española, pp. ix–cxxv.

———. 1907. *Orígenes de la novela*. Vol. 2, Bailly-Ballière.

Menéndez Pidal, Ramon. 1902. EL POEMA DE YÚÇUF: *materiales para su estudio*. Tipografía de la Revista de Archivos, Bibliotecas y Museos.

Meyer, Harvey K. 1972. *Historical Dictionary of Nicaragua*. Scarecrow.

Mira Seo, J. 2011. "Identifying Authority: Juan Latino, an African Ex-Slave, Professor, and Poet in Sixteenth-Century Granada." *African Athena: New Agendas*, edited by Daniel Orrells et al., Oxford UP, pp. 258–76.

Morabito, María Teresa. 2020. "Vaticinios y visiones en *Juan Latino* y *El Encubierto* de Diego Jiménez de Enciso." *Pictavia Aurea: Actas del IX Congreso de la Asociación Internacional "Siglo de Oro,"* edited by Alain Bègue and Emma Herrán Alonso, P U du Midi, pp. 1007–15.

Morel-Fatio, Alfred. 1900. *Ambrosio de Salazar et l'étude de l'espagnol en France sous Louis XIII*. Paris, A. Picard et fils.

Moreno, Isidoro. 1997. *La antigua hermandad de los negros de Sevilla: etnicidad, poder y sociedad en 600 años de historia*. U de Sevilla/Consejería de Cultura de la Junta de Andalucía.

Moreno Báez, Enrique. 1989. "Introducción." Diego de San Pedro, pp. 11–41.

Morley, S. Griswold, and Courtney Bruerton. 1936. "How Many *Comedias* Did Lope de Vega Write?" *Hispania*, vol. 19, no. 2, pp. 217–34.

———. 1968. *Cronología de las comedias de Lope de Vega*. Translated by María Rosa Cartes, Gredos.

Naveros Sánchez, Juan, and María Eugenia Santos Flores. 2000. "El negro Juan Latino: gloria de España y de su raza." *Angélica: Revista de Literatura*, vol. 10, pp. 95–117.

Ndiaye, Noémie. 2022. *Scripts of Blackness: Early Modern Performance Culture and the Making of Race*. U of Pennsylvania P.

Nirenberg, David. 2007. "Race and the Middle Ages: The Case of Spain and Its Jews." Greer et al., pp. 71–87.

———. 2009. "Was There Race before Modernity: The Example of 'Jewish' Blood in Late Medieval Spain." Eliav-Feldon et al., pp. 232–64.
Núñez Muley, Francisco. 2007. *A Memorandum for the President of the Royal Audiencia and Chancery Court of the City and Kingdom of Granada*. Edited and translated by Vincent Barletta, U of Chicago P.
Olmedo Gobante, Manuel. 2018. "El mucho número que hay dellos: *El valiente negro en Flandes* y los esgrimistas afrohispanos de *Grandezas de la espada*." *Bulletin of the Comediantes*, vol. 70, no. 2, pp. 67–91.
Panford, Moses E., Jr. 1993. La figura del negro en cuatro comedias barrocas: *Juan Latino* (Jiménez de Enciso), *El valiente negro en Flandes* (Claramonte), *El santo negro Rosambuco* (Lope de Vega), and *El negro del mejor amo* (Mira de Amescua). PhD Diss., Temple U.
———. 1999. "*La Comedia famosa de Juan Latino*: el discurso hegemónico como artefacto sociopolítico." *Afro-Hispanic Review*, vol. 18, no. 2, pp. 3–9.
———. 2001. "El tipo del negro religioso en el teatro siglodorista." *Hispanic Journal*, vol. 22, no. 1, pp. 237–49.
———. 2003. "Introducción." Guerrero, pp. 9–59.
Pastor, Juan. 1912. *Farsa de Lucrecia. Cinco obras dramáticas anteriores a Lope de Vega*, edited by Adolfo Bonilla y San Martín, Bulletin Hispanique, vol. 27, pp. 48–65.
———. 1914. *Farsa de Lucrecia: Tragedia de la castidad de Lucrecia. Obras dramáticas del siglo XVI*, primera serie, facsimile edition by Adolfo Bonilla y San Martín, no publisher.
Peale, C. George. 1983. "Ingenio y cortesanía en *El diablo cojuelo* (dos notas sobre el haz y envés de Vélez de Guevara)." *Antigüedad y actualidad de Luis Vélez de Guevara: estudios críticos*, edited by George C. Peale, John Benjamins, pp. 233–53.
———. 2003. "Estudio introductorio." *El águila del agua: representación española*, by Luis Vélez de Guevara, edited by William R. Manson and C. George Peale, Juan de la Cuesta, pp. 13–82.
———. 2004. "Luis Vélez de Guevara, casos de cortesanía histórica y de ingenio efímero." *Paraninfos, segundones y epígonos de la comedia del Siglo de Oro*, edited by Ignacio Arellano, Anthropos, pp. 77–87.
———. 2009. "Vélez de Guevara contextualizado: una vida singular y su ámbito ético." *Bulletin of the Comediantes*, vol. 61, no. 1, pp. 51–96.
———, and Héctor Urzáiz Tortajada. 2003. "Vélez de Guevara." *Historia del teatro español*, edited by Javier Huerta Calvo, vol. 1, Gredos, pp. 929–59.
Pérez Priego, Miguel Ángel. 1985. "Introducción." *Farsas*, by Diego Sánchez de Badajoz, edited by Miguel Ángel Pérez Priego, pp.13–71.
———, editor. 1997. *Teatro medieval: Castilla*. Crítica.
Perry, Mary Elizabeth. 1990. *Gender and Disorder in Early Modern Seville*. Princeton UP.
Phillips, William D., Jr. 2014. *Slavery in Medieval and Modern Iberia*. U of Pennsylvania P.
Pike, Ruth. 1972. *Aristocrats and Traders: Sevillian Society in the Sixteenth Century*. Cornell UP.
———. 1990. "The Converso Origins of the Sevillian Dramatist Diego Jiménez de Enciso." *Bulletin of Hispanic Studies*, vol. 67, pp. 129–35.

———. 1991. "Adding to the Biography of Diego Jiménez de Enciso." *Bulletin of the Comediantes*, vol. 43, no. 2, pp. 233–37.

———. 1993. "The Dramatist Diego Jiménez de Enciso and the Linajudos of Seville." *Bulletin of Hispanic Studies*, vol. 70, pp. 115–19.

Platt, Frank Thomas. 1956. *El Príncipe Don Carlos of Diego Ximénez de Enciso: A Critical Edition with Introduction and Notes*. PhD Diss., Ohio State U.

Pliny the Elder. 1991. *Natural History: A Selection*. Translated by John F. Healy, Penguin.

Plutarch. 1932. *The Lives of the Noble Grecians and Romans*. Translated by John Dryden, revised by Arthur Hugh Clough, Modern Library.

———. 1939. "On Tranquility of Mind." *Moralia*, translated by W. C. Helmbold, vol. 6, Harvard UP, pp. 161–241.

Poema de Mio Cid. 1990. Edited by Colin Smith, Cátedra.

Profeti, Maria Grazia. 1965. "Introduzione." Vélez de Guevara 1640–2010 [D], pp. 5–60.

———. 2005. "Il negro nella commedia aurea." *La maschera e l'altro*, edited by Maria Grazia Profeti, Alinea Editrice, pp. 223–38.

Real Academia Española. 1990. *Diccionario de Autoridades*. 3 vols, facsim. ed., Gredos.

Reinosa, Rodrigo de. 2020a. "Coplas a los negros y negras." Santos Morillo 2020, pp. 282–92.

———. 2020b. "Otras suyas a los mismos negros." Santos Morillo 2020, pp. 292–93.

Rennert, Hugo Albert. 1907. "Notes on the Chronology of the Spanish Drama." *Modern Language Review*, vol. 3, no. 1, pp. 43–55.

———. 1963. *The Spanish Stage in the Time of Lope de Vega*. Dover.

Restall, Matthew. 2000. "Black Conquistadors: Armed Africans in Early Spanish America." *The Americas*, vol. 57, no. 2, pp. 171–205.

Restori, Antonio. 1891. *Una collezione di commedie di Lope de Vega Carpio: CC.* V. 28032 della Palatina Parmense*. Francisco Vigo.

———. 1903. *Piezas de titulos de comedias. Saggi e documenti inediti o rari del teatro spagnuolo dei secoli XVII e XVIII*. V. Muglia.

Robbins, Jeremy. 1997. *Love Poetry of the Literary Academies in the Reigns of Philip IV and Charles II*. Tamesis.

Rodríguez Cepeda, Enrique. 1975. "Consideraciones sobre Luis Vélez de Guevara." *Mester*, vol. 5, no. 2, pp. 112–22.

Rodríguez López-Vázquez, Alfredo. 1997. "Prólogo." Claramonte y Corroy 1638–2016 [P], pp. 5–19.

———. 2010a. "Andrés de Claramonte y Corroy." Jauralde Pou, vol. 1, pp. 341–52.

———. 2010b. "Bibliografía comentada de Andrés de Claramonte." *La estrella de Sevilla; El gran rey de los desiertos*, by Andrés de Claramonte, edited by Alfredo Rodríguez López-Vázquez, Cátedra, pp. 128–36.

———. 2017. "*La vida es sueño, Virtudes vencen señales* y *El alba del sol*: las hipótesis divergentes." *Illuminazioni*, no. 39, pp. 3–43, www.rivistailluminazioni.it/2019/03/07/alfredo-rodriguez-lopez-vazquez/. Accessed 5 March 2023.

Rodríguez de Montalvo, Garci. 2003. *Sergas de Esplandián*. Edited by Carlos Sainz de la Maza, Clásicos Castalia.
Rojas Villandrando, Agustín de. 1972. *El viaje entretenido*. Clásicos Castalia.
Rosenbaum, Alvin. 2016. "By Our Will," ch. 6. *The Voice of Guanacaste*, vozdeguanacaste.com/en/by-our-will-chapter-6-nicaragua-y-costa-rica. Accessed 5 March 2023.
Rout, Leslie B., Jr. 1976. *The African Experience in Spanish America: 1502 to the Present Day*. Cambridge UP.
Ruano de la Haza, J. M. 1988. "Hacia una metodología para la reconstrucción de la puesta en escena de la comedia en los teatros comerciales del siglo XVII." *Criticón*, no. 42, pp. 81–102.
———. 2010. "Estudio introductorio." Vélez de Guevara 1640–2010 [E], pp. 13–43.
———, and John J. Allen. 1994. *Los teatros comerciales del siglo XVII y la escenificación de la comedia*. Editorial Castalia.
Rueda, Lope de. 1567. *Las quatro comedias y dos coloquios pastoriles del excellente poeta y gracioso representante Lope de Rueda*. Biblioteca Nacional de España, ms. R/12055.
———. 2001. *Las cuatro comedias*. Edited by Alfredo Hermenegildo, Cátedra.
———. 2006. *Gila. Tres colloquios pastoriles de Juan de Vergara y Lope de Rueda (Valencia, 1567)*, edited by Pedro M. Cátedra, Cilengua, pp. 123–92.
Russell, P. E. 1978. "La poesía negra de Rodrigo de Reinosa." *Temas de La Celestina*, Ariel, pp. 377–406.
Saavedra Fajardo, Diego de. 1942. *Idea de un príncipe político-cristiano, representada en cien empresas*. Vol. 1, edited by Vicente García de Diego, Espasa-Calpe.
Sainz de la Maza, Carlos. 2003. "Introducción." Rodríguez de Montalvo, pp. 7–92.
Salazar, Ambrosio de. 2015 [1615]. *Espejo general de la gramática en diálogos*. Facsimile edition, Consejería de Educación y Universidades de la Región de Murcia.
Sánchez, José. 1961. *Academias literarias del Siglo de Oro español*. Gredos.
Sánchez de Badajoz, Diego. 1968. *Recopilación en metro*. Edited by Frida Weber de Kurlat, Instituto de Filología y Literaturas Hispánicas, U de Buenos Aires.
Sánchez Jiménez, Antonio. 2018. *Lope de Vega: el verso y la vida*. Cátedra.
Sánchez Marín, José Antonio, and María Nieves Muñoz Martín. 2009. "El maestro Juan Latino en la Granada renacentista: su ciudad, su vida, sus protectores." *Florentia Iliberritana*, vol. 20, pp. 227–60.
———. 2018. "La obra poética de Juan Latino." *eHumanista*, vol. 39, pp. 261–96.
Sandoval, Alonso de. 1956. *De instauranda Aethiopum salute: el mundo de la esclavitud negra en América*. Edited by Ángel Valtierra, Empresa Nacional de Publicaciones de Colombia.
Santos Morillo, Antonio. 2011. "Caracterización del negro en la literatura española del XVI." *Lemir*, vol. 15, pp. 23–46.
———. 2020. *¿Quién te lo vező a decir? El habla de negro en la literatura del XVI, imitación de una realidad lingüística*. Iberoamericana.
Schevill [Schwill], Rudolph. 1903. "The Comedias of Diego Ximénez de Enciso." *PMLA*, vol. 18, no. 2, pp. 194–210.

———. 1933. "*Virtudes vencen señales* and *La vida es sueño.*" *Hispanic Review*, vol. 1, no. 3, pp. 181–95.

Serpi, Dimas. 1600. *Chronica de los santos de Sardeña, dividida en quatro libros*. Sebastián de Cormellas.

Shakespeare, William. 1997. *Othello. The Norton Shakespeare: Based on the Oxford Edition*, edited by Stephen Greenblatt et al., Norton, pp. 2091–2174.

Shergold, N. D. 1967. *A History of the Spanish Stage: From Medieval Times until the End of the Seventeenth Century*. Clarendon.

———, and J. E. Varey. 1963. "Some Palace Performances of Seventeenth-Century Plays." *Bulletin of Hispanic Studies*, vol. 40, no. 4, pp. 212–44.

Silva, Feliciano de. 1874. *Segunda comedia de Celestina*. Imprenta de Miguel Ginesta.

Solinus, Gaius Julius. 2011. *Polyhistor*. Translated by Arwen Apps, Topos Text, topostext.org/work/747. Accessed 5 March 2023.

Spencer, Forrest Eugene, and Rudolph Schevill. 1937. *The Dramatic Works of Luis Vélez de Guevara: Their Plots, Sources, and Bibliography*. U of California P.

Spratlin, V. B. 1934. "The Negro in Spanish Literature." *The Journal of Negro History*, vol. 19, no. 1, pp. 60–71. Reprinted in truncated form in DeCosta, pp. 47–52.

———. 1938. *Juan Latino: Slave and Humanist*. Spinner.

Stella, Alessandro. 2000. *Histoire d'esclaves dans la péninsule ibérique*. Editions de l'Ecole des Hautes Études en Sciences Sociales.

Stoichita, Victor. 2010. "The Image of the Black in Spanish Art: Sixteenth and Seventeenth Centuries." Bindman and Gates, pp. 191–234 and 367–74.

Strausbaugh, John. 2007. *Black Like You: Blackface, Whiteface, Insult and Imitation in American Popular Culture*. Penguin.

Teresa de Ávila. 1990. *Libro de la vida*. Edited by Dámaso Chicharro, Cátedra.

Ticknor, George. 1882. *History of Spanish Literature in Three Volumes*. 5th American ed., vol. 3, Houghton.

Todorov, Tzvetan. 1984. *The Conquest of America: The Question of the Other*. Translated by Richard Howard, Harper.

Urzáiz Tortajada, Héctor. 2002a. *Catálogo de autores teatrales del siglo XVII*. Fundación Universitaria Española.

———. 2002b. "Vida y obra de Vélez de Guevara." *Teatro breve*, by Luis Vélez de Guevara, edited by Héctor Urzáiz Tortajada, Iberoamericana/Vervuert, pp. 17–25.

Valdés Gázquez, Ramón. 2010. "Luis Vélez de Guevara." Jauralde Pou, vol. 2, pp. 580–616.

Varey, J. E. 1985. "Stages and Stage Directions." *Editing the Comedia*. Edited by Michael D. McGaha and Frank P. Casa, U of Michigan, pp. 146–61.

Vega Carpio, Lope Félix de. 1611. *Jerusalén conquistada*. Lisbon, no publisher.

———. 1965. *El santo negro Rosambuco de la ciudad de Palermo. Obras de Lope de Vega*, edited by Marcelino Menéndez Pelayo, vol. 10, Atlas, pp. 133–77.

———. 1985. *Cartas*. Edited by Nicolás Marín, Clásicos Castalia.

———. 1995. *El negro del mejor amo*. *Obras completas de Lope de Vega*, edited by J. Gómez and P. Cuenca, vol. 11, Turner, pp. 433–513.
———. 2002. *Arte nuevo de hacer comedias en este tiempo*. *Biblioteca Virtual Miguel de Cervantes*, cervantesvirtual.com/obra-visor/arte-nuevo-de-hacer-comedias-en-este-tiempo--0/html/ffb1e6c0-82b1-11df-acc7-002185ce6064_4.html. Accessed 5 March 2023.
———. 2005. *El prodigio de Etiopía*. Edited by John Beusterien, Mirabel Editorial.
Vega García-Luengos, Germán. 2008. "Sobre la trayectoria editorial de las comedias de santos." *La comedia de santos: coloquio internacional (Almagro, 1, 2 y 3 de diciembre de 2006)*, edited by Felipe B. Pedraza Jiménez and Almudena García González, U de Castilla–La Mancha, pp. 21–37.
———. 2021. "Las comedias de Lope de Vega: confirmaciones de autoría y nuevas atribuciones desde la estilometría." *Talía: Revista de Estudios Teatrales*, vol. 3, pp. 91–108.
Vélez de Guevara, Luis. 1640–2010. *Virtudes vencen señales*.
   [A] 1640. *Parte treinta y dos, con doze comedias de diferentes autores*. Zaragoza, Diego Dormer, pp. 91–128. 26596.T(3), British Library.
   [B] 1600s (no date). Single-play printing, no place or publisher. CC.IV.28033.23, Biblioteca Palatina di Parma.
   [C] 1957. Edited by Charles Frederick Kirk, PhD Diss., Ohio State U.
   [D] 1965. Edited by M. G. Profeti, U di Pisa.
   [E] 2010. Edited by William R. Manson and C. George Peale, Juan de la Cuesta. 1981.
———. 1981. *El diablo cojuelo*. 5th ed., Espasa-Calpe.
Verlinden, Charles. 1955. *L'esclavage dans l'Europe médiévale: Péninsule Ibérique, France*. De Tempel.
Vicente, Gil. 1912. *Fragoa d'amor*. *Obras de Gil Vicente*, edited by Mendes de Remedios, vol. 2, Franca Amado, pp. 151–72.
von Germeten, Nicole. 2006. "Routes to Respectability: Confraternities and Men of African Descent in New Spain." *Local Religion in Colonial Mexico*, edited by Martin Austin Nesvig, U of New Mexico, pp. 215–33.
———. 2008. "Introduction." *Treatise on Slavery: Selections from DE INSTAURANDA AETHIOPUM SALUTE* by Alonso de Sandoval, translated by Nicole von Germeten, Hackett, pp. ix–xxx.
Weber de Kurlat, Frida. 1962. "El tipo cómico del negro en el teatro prelopesco: fonética." *Filología*, vol. 8, pp. 139–68.
———. 1963. "Sobre el negro como tipo cómico en el teatro español del siglo XVI." *Romance Philology*, vol. 17, no. 2, pp. 380–91.
———. 1970. "El tipo del negro en el teatro de Lope de Vega: tradición y creación." *Nueva Revista de Filología Hispánica*, vol. 19, no. 2, pp. 337–59.
Weissbourd, Emily. 2013. "'I Have Done the State Some Service': Reading Slavery in *Othello* through *Juan Latino*." *Comparative Drama*, vol. 47, no. 4, pp. 529–51.
Williamsen, Vern G. 1981. "Women and Blacks Have Brains Too: A Play by Diego Ximénez de Enciso." *Studies in Honor of Everett W. Hesse*, edited by William C. McCrary and José A. Madrigal, pp. 199–206.

———. 1982. *The Minor Dramatists of Seventeenth-Century Spain.* Twayne.

Wiltrout, Ann. 1987. *A Patron and a Playwright in Renaissance Spain: The House of Feria and Diego Sánchez de Badajoz.* Tamesis.

Woodson, Carter G. 1935. "Attitudes of the Iberian Peninsula." *The Journal of Negro History*, vol. 20, no. 2, pp. 190–243. Reprinted in truncated form in DeCosta, pp. 36–46.

Wright, Elizabeth R. 2016. *The Epic of Juan Latino: Dilemmas of Race and Religion in Renaissance Spain.* U of Toronto P.

Wright, John. 2007. *The Trans-Saharan Slave Trade.* Routledge.

Wynter, Sylvia. 1977. "The Eye of the Other: Images of the Black in Spanish Literature." DeCosta, pp. 8–19.

Young, Karl. 1933. *The Drama of the Medieval Church.* Vol. 2, Clarendon.

Ziomek, Henryk. 1984. *A History of Spanish Golden Age Drama.* UP of Kentucky.

Zugasti, Miguel. 2017. "Luis Vélez de Guevara y la comedia palatina." *Criticón*, no. 129, pp. 41–68.

Zurara, Gomes Eanes de. 1841. *Chrónica do descobrimento e conquista de Guiné.* Edited by the Visconde de Santarem, J. P. Aillaud.

JUAN LATINO

(Juan Latino)

By Diego Jiménez de Enciso

Dramatis Personae *in order of appearance*

*Dr. Carlobal, learned cleric
*Doña Ana Carlobal, Dr. Carlobal's sister
Juana, Doña Ana's servant
*Magister Villanueva, learned cleric and teacher
*Don Gonzalo, student and son of the duke and duchess
Don Diego, student
Don Martín, student
Castle, impoverished and clownish student, lackey to Don Diego and Don Martín
Onlookers (nonspeaking)
*Juan Latino, black slave of the duke and duchess
*Don Fernando de Válor, Morisco nobleman and town councilor
Cañerí, black Moor, dressed in animal skins and a staff
Page to Don Fernando
*Duke of Sessa
*Duchess of Sessa, the duke's wife
Two guards
Two Morisco soldiers
Attendants to the duke and duchess (nonspeaking)
Page to the duke and duchess
*Aben Aboo, Don Fernando de Válor's uncle
Zaida, Moorish maiden
Diego, Morisco bailiff
Moriscos (nonspeaking)
Dancers (nonspeaking)
Archbishop of Granada
Head of school ceremonies
Supporters of Juan Latino and Villanueva
*Don Juan of Austria, half brother of King Philip II
*Luis Quijada, attendant to Don Juan of Austria
Page to Don Juan of Austria
Two soldiers
Painter (nonspeaking)
Coal merchant
Page to Juan Latino
Page to the Duke of Sessa
Two students
Rector and other officers of the university (nonspeaking)
Ensign

*Denotes a historical character included in the Glossary.
Setting: Granada, Spain, and the nearby Alpujarras region, 1569–1570.

ACT 1, Scene 1

([A room in the Carlobal home, overlooking the street.] Enter CARLOBAL, in a housecoat; his sister DOÑA ANA, stylishly dressed; and the servant JUANA. The women are veiled. DOÑA ANA wears a ribbon on her arm.)

CARLOBAL. Remove that veil, Doña Ana, or by God you're going to make me angry. Who gave you permission to wear it?

DOÑA ANA. Am I your sister or your wife? Is this not Saint John's Eve?

CARLOBAL. An insolent reply!

DOÑA ANA. You closed the curtains on me. I intend to see the festivities.

CARLOBAL. A maiden, leave her house at night? Whose pages and coach are those?

DOÑA ANA. *[To JUANA.]*

What's the owner's name?

JUANA. Don Fernando de Válor.

CARLOBAL. You don't even know his name, yet he parades down our street every day? Tell the driver, Juana, to return the coach.

DOÑA ANA. You make me so angry!

[To JUANA.]

Here, take the veil.

(DOÑA ANA removes the veil and hands it to JUANA, who exits with it.)

CARLOBAL. Do not be shocked, sister, that I fear your behavior will lead to my dishonor, for a man's honor is wrapped up in a woman. I have . . .

DOÑA ANA. What a bother you are.

CARLOBAL. . . . educated you poorly. Graceful of wit and fetching of figure, you are regaled, courted, and celebrated by wealthy, handsome, and clever suitors. Your face may limit your options, but a chaste woman who loves her honor should stand out for her reputation. Every well-born suitor in Granada prowls our street day and night, like a fierce bullfighter or a determined jouster. Love reigns on this promenade, where my honor is chased after. Someone is going to end up dead or dissatisfied, for dismay always lurks beneath pleasure.

DOÑA ANA. Enough, Doctor. I won't be lectured to by my brother. You know I wouldn't let my hand be kissed by anyone, no matter how dashing or discreet. Are you really going to harbor suspicions about that suitor? A man who's barely even a Christian? How can you suspect I'd be interested in Don Fernando, a Morisco? His grandfather was a Moor, his father a Berber!

CARLOBAL.   Does he not have the blood of kings?

DOÑA ANA.   I wouldn't care if he were the king of Cordova or Granada.

[The voices of an excited crowd are heard offstage.]

CARLOBAL.   *[Distastefully.]*

The revelers begin their mad competitions.

DOÑA ANA.   May they compete like captives of love.

CARLOBAL.   *(Sarcastically.)*

What an honorable maiden.

[VOICES].   *(Offstage.)*

Move, move! Clear the way!

DOÑA ANA.   Must we miss the fun?

CARLOBAL.   You grate on my nerves. Go to your chamber this instant.

DOÑA ANA.   Don Diego and Don Martín approach in their masks, sir. They are part of your household. On my life, will you not allow them in?

CARLOBAL.   That's another disaster in the making, and their shenanigans will end here and now. I know your honor does not cross the bounds of reason and courtesy, but they are *students*! I won't have them teaching you to sing.

DOÑA ANA.   You drive me mad.

CARLOBAL.   You would have Don Diego and Don Martín see your bedchamber?

[VOICES].   *(Offstage.)*

Move, move!

(Enter JUANA.)

JUANA.   Swifter than the wind, my lords just dashed by.

CARLOBAL.   Am I to tolerate this on my own street? You take it upon yourself to learn to sing without my permission! If I see you singing again, Heaven help me, I'll make you regret it.

DOÑA ANA.   Enough of your suspicions!

CARLOBAL.   Your anger will do you no good, for I will put an end to this matter. Take care, madam, where you lay your eyes, for, by God, I shall be the one to arrange your marriage. Of all those who court you with their gifts, choose the lucky man carefully or you may end up promising your hand to a peasant.

DOÑA ANA.   Do you dare suggest I would marry anyone who isn't a duke, a marquis, or a count? And why do you assume I want to marry at all? Doña Ana Carlobal, whom all the world wishes to serve and all Granada celebrates, would not offer even her servant to the grandest and noblest of her suitors. Stop talking to me, sir, of marriage and income and titles.

CARLOBAL.   Oh, you mad and vain woman, I pray God you exercise sound judgment in the matter of your marriage, or I shall have to send you to a convent to tame your ways. And stay away from this window!

(Exit CARLOBAL.)

JUANA.   The sermon has ended.

DOÑA ANA.   He is a storm of criticism, day and night!

JUANA.   Marry, and it will end.

DOÑA ANA.   Marry whom? None of them is serious about me.

JUANA.   You're so fussy.

DOÑA ANA.   So who ran by the window?

JUANA.   The junior duke, Don Gonzalo.

DOÑA ANA.   Do you jest? That little adolescent persists?

JUANA.   He ran circles around the others.

DOÑA ANA.   He's so childish. He deserves a good drubbing.

JUANA.   I have several messages for you.

DOÑA ANA.   On my life, do tell.

JUANA.   Don Fernando lives like an ailing prisoner: sad, dejected, scorned.

DOÑA ANA.   Losing his mind amid melancholy memories.

JUANA.   Don Juan moans. Don Alonso whimpers.

DOÑA ANA.   Let them whimper and moan.

JUANA. Don Simón promises enough gold to save you from all your cares. Don Martín waits expectantly. Don Diego brims with chaste love and bad sonnets, for poets love like the Portuguese and write like the Basques.

DOÑA ANA. What a delight to see them all in an uproar, from the wittiest to the most brutish; to solicit gifts and provoke anxiety in the poorest peasant as well as the blue-blooded gentleman; to treat lords like servants and be serenaded by numbskulls at the crack of dawn; to see my name on paper, tablets, even marble!

JUANA. So which one do you like the most?

DOÑA ANA. I'm attracted to wit and fond of words. Only intelligence is beautiful to me.

JUANA. The gossip around Granada is that you address famous men and noble ladies with an arrogant familiarity.

DOÑA ANA. They don't like my familiarity? I'd speak that way to the king himself.

JUANA. God help me! So who's the lucky man you'll choose from all these suitors?

DOÑA ANA. If our little junior duke were just a tad more gallant, I'd do him the favor of making him my husband.

JUANA. If I tell you who will be your husband, what will you give me?

DOÑA ANA. What are you talking about?

JUANA. Is it not Saint John's Eve? I'd love to hear you recite the charm between eleven and twelve.

DOÑA ANA. And then what?

JUANA. Stand at the window and listen.

DOÑA ANA. I wouldn't want to see you dragged before the Inquisition over this, Juana.

JUANA. I learned the prayer from my grandmother, who was a saint. It's as Christian as the Hail Mary, and it never fails.

DOÑA ANA. The Devil speaks in you!

(Aside.)

And how easily we women listen.

[Aloud.]

How accurate is it?

JUANA.　You wouldn't believe!

DOÑA ANA.　*(Aside.)*

What if I learn I'm to be married against my will!

JUANA.　I wouldn't stop reciting this charm for all the gold in the Alhambra.

DOÑA ANA.　Very well, I will do it.

JUANA.　You'll be married by the end of the year.

DOÑA ANA.　Open the window.

[JUANA opens the window. The chimes of a clock are heard in the distance.]

JUANA.　It's eleven.

DOÑA ANA.　I bet it tells me I'll wed a duke or a count.

ACT 1, Scene 2

([A street before the Carlobal home with a view of Doña Ana's window, immediately following the previous scene. The festivities and competitions of Saint John's Eve continue.] Shouting, singing, and boisterous music are heard offstage.)

[VOICES].　*(Singing.)*

¶Suitor, musician, poet, or soldier:
Don't give him your love, girl,
Throw him into the Darro.¶

(Shawms play as the competitions continue offstage.)

[VOICES].　*(Offstage.)*

Move, move, out of the way!

CASTLE.　*[Offstage.]*

You're drunk!

VILLANUEVA.　*[Offstage.]*

Liar!

DON MARTÍN.　*[Offstage.]*

Did someone fall?

DON DIEGO. *[Offstage.]*

Wait, it's his lordship!

> *(Enter DON GONZALO, son of the duke; DON MARTÍN; DON DIEGO; VILLANUEVA; and CASTLE, clownishly dressed; the rest wear splendid masks and unique carnival costumes. Enter as many others as possible, supporting DON GONZALO. Servants bear torches before carrying them offstage.)*

VILLANUEVA. Did you hurt yourself?

DON GONZALO. It's nothing, just a bruised shin, but we'll need to pause the games. Not to worry, Don Diego and Don Martín, we'll keep the party going!

DON DIEGO. This is not funny.

CASTLE. The horse is to blame.

DON MARTÍN. A classic student production!

DON GONZALO. I'm happy to have fallen where so many suitors have.

VILLANUEVA. Is that Doña Ana at the window?

DON DIEGO. Doña Ana? Unlikely. She's averse to the damp night air.

DON GONZALO. If only she'd peek out a moment!

(Music sounds offstage.)

CASTLE. *[To VILLANUEVA.]*

Sir magister, you're all three in quite the mood!

DON GONZALO. Listen, what's that music?

CASTLE. Music indeed.

[JUAN LATINO]. *(Offstage [singing].)*

> ¶A cup of water from the well,
> A biscuit for to hunger quell.¶

(Offstage [speaking].)

Marriage is not in your future.

DON GONZALO. What's going on over there?

CASTLE. A foolish superstition to predict marriage.

DON DIEGO. *[Shouting toward the offstage area.]*

Sing more, you drunkard.

JUAN LATINO. *(Offstage.)*

Here's one you'll like.

(Singing.)

❡Hail the orchard, hail the peak,
Hail the fountain, hail the creek.❡

CASTLE.

❡The creek, the creek . . .❡

(His voice cracks.)

[VOICE]. *(Offstage.)*

Cluck, cluck.

JUAN LATINO. *(Offstage.)*

Cluck, cluck goes the cuckold.

DON GONZALO. That's the voice of my slave, little Juan.

(DOÑA ANA and JUANA appear at the window. DOÑA ANA wears the ribbon from the beginning.)

JUANA. It's time for the prediction, madam.

DOÑA ANA. They say one fool is as bad as a hundred. I've recited the prayer. Now what?

JUANA. Listen for the answer. I hear people out there.

DOÑA ANA. I still think the prediction will be a duke or a count.

JUANA. Which would be a good answer.

DOÑA ANA. Does that mean I am to wed the little duke?

JUANA. Listen to the voices.

DOÑA ANA. Who will be my husband?

(Enter JUAN LATINO, laughing. He is neatly dressed in a clerical collar and a cape trimmed in cheap lace.)

ALL. Look, it's little Juan the *negro*!

DON GONZALO. By God, you're looking spiffy.

(JUANA jumps in fright. DOÑA ANA laughs.)

JUAN LATINO.   Is that my lord Don Gonzalo?

JUANA.   Little Juan the *negro*? This is terrible.

DOÑA ANA.   *Negro*, did they say?

JUANA.   So they did, Juan the *negro*, and I wish I'd never heard it.

DOÑA ANA.   Why does it concern you?

JUANA.   A *negro* for a fiancé?

DOÑA ANA.   Don't worry. It's not going to happen.

DON MARTÍN.   A famous *negro* he is.

DON GONZALO.   You win the prize for best-dressed.

JUANA.   He congratulates him and everything.

DON MARTÍN.   Brother, where did you get that lace?

JUAN LATINO.   From a mill in Milan.

CASTLE.   Did you now?

JUAN LATINO.   Ah, Castle, you're here too? Why didn't you say so?

CASTLE.   I mistook you for the lord Don Diego's shadow.

ALL.   Ha, ha.

(DOÑA ANA pulls JUANA aside with the arm adorned by the ribbon, which falls to the ground.)

DOÑA ANA.   Oh, the ribbon from Don Fernando de Válor! My good gentleman . . .

CASTLE.   You mean me?

DON GONZALO.   Is that Doña Ana? Everyone quiet down.

DOÑA ANA.   Can you please retrieve that ribbon for me?

JUAN LATINO.   *(Aside.)*

   It'll be mine if I spot it first!

(All race for the ribbon. JUAN LATINO finds it.)

DON GONZALO.   I'll give a thousand gold coins for it.

JUANA.   That's our little junior duke and Castle's lords, scrambling for the ribbon.

DOÑA ANA.   I'm going to regret this, all because of that madman Don Fernando.

CASTLE.   I can smell the money, but it's just beyond my reach!

DOÑA ANA.   Please throw the ribbon through the window, whoever finds it.

JUAN LATINO.   I shall do so!

[He tosses a ribbon through the window. Aside.]

I tossed her a different one, from my master the duke, Don Gonzalo's father.

DOÑA ANA.   Who is he, Juana, that forsakes coin to do my bidding?

JUANA.   It's the *negro*'s voice.

DOÑA ANA.   On my honor, he has placed me in his debt.

JUANA.   Close the window, quickly, for your brother calls. Come.

(Exit [JUANA and DOÑA ANA].)

DON GONZALO.   Doña Ana, my darling? Wait! This is the fault of this dog, who gave up the ribbon against my will.

DON MARTÍN.   The *negro* has excellent discretion, by God, for he rejected your money to do what Doña Ana asked.

DON GONZALO.   Goodbye, street.

DON DIEGO.   Goodbye, window.

JUAN LATINO.   Goodbye, divine woman.

[VOICES].   *(Shouting offstage.)*

Whoa, whoa!

JUAN LATINO.   The revelers are at it again.

CASTLE.   It's getting old.

DON MARTÍN.   Goodbye, my beloved idol.

CASTLE.   Goodbye, Juana, my beautiful sweeper girl.

DON MARTÍN.   Sing to us some more, little Juan.

DON DIEGO.   Where shall we go, Castle?

CASTLE.   To dance the night away!

(Exit [all].)

ACT 1, Scene 3

([A room in Don Fernando de Válor's home.] Enter DON FERNANDO, reading a letter aloud.)

DON FERNANDO.   "Dear nephew, all across the land and throughout the Alpujarras, it is rumored that the crown intends to squeeze us more tightly. New laws will require us to change our dress, our customs, our language: all allowed us by previous kings. Thus the bandit Cañerí, a black Moor—"

(Enter CAÑERÍ [dressed in animal skins and carrying a staff], causing DON FERNANDO to jump in fright.)

What am I seeing?

CAÑERÍ.   Do not fear. I am that black man of whom you read. Speak.

DON FERNANDO.   *[Calling to unseen attendants.]*

You there!

CAÑERÍ.   Silence!

DON FERNANDO.   Is there no page at my disposal? Kill this *negro* at once. Follow him!

(Exit CAÑERÍ. Enter VILLANUEVA and a PAGE.)

VILLANUEVA.   What's going on?

DON FERNANDO.   Did you happen to see a savage *negro* leaving just now? A giant monster with the hide of a lion, a pine branch for a staff, a long beard, and a fiendish countenance?

VILLANUEVA.   Are you mad?

PAGE.   No one has entered this house.

DON FERNANDO.   Never mind. No doubt the predetermined day of my death has arrived. No doubt the creature's colossal size represents my affliction, its blackness my bad luck.

VILLANUEVA.   Lord Don Fernando de Válor, have you lost your mind?

DON FERNANDO.   Is it coincidence that I saw him today, the first day of my house arrest, just as I was arriving home, my misfortunes swirling in my head?

VILLANUEVA.   It must have been some spasm of your imagination.

DON FERNANDO. No, it's the misfortune I was born to! A Morisco once foretold, in a thousand weighty words, that I would be stabbed to death on the battlefield by a *negro*.

VILLANUEVA. Stop.

DON FERNANDO. I don't know what to do. The town council has done me in, by God, by stripping me of my dagger.

VILLANUEVA. If I'd known I'd find you in this state, I'd never have come.

DON FERNANDO. What do you want with me?

VILLANUEVA. To lift your spirits with the news I bring: tonight the academy meets at the duke's house, and Doña Ana will be there.

DON FERNANDO. I'll send her the coach again, though it did not please her last time. Did you go to the festivities?

VILLANUEVA. Yes.

DON FERNANDO. Was she at her window?

VILLANUEVA. She was, though she was very aloof.

DON FERNANDO. She's beautiful, and she knows it. I've made a fool of myself for her, squandered my whole inheritance to impress her. I don't know what to do about this infernal love.

VILLANUEVA. Pliny prescribes a remedy, though extreme.

DON FERNANDO. What does he say?

VILLANUEVA. That the love fool who cannot conceal his affliction should smear himself with the musk of a mule. And according to Ovid and others, you shouldn't limit yourself to one woman.

DON FERNANDO. Those are the ravings of madmen.

VILLANUEVA. If you say so.

PAGE. The Duke of Sessa awaits in the vestibule.

DON FERNANDO. The duke? Such favor on this humble abode!

(Enter the DUKE of Sessa and his retinue.)

DUKE. It is fitting that he who professes to serve you come to your house and respond to your command.

DON FERNANDO. Your generosity goes too far, but I accept it like a sickly captive.

DUKE. *[To VILLANUEVA.]*

I shall consider it a great favor, sir magister, to enjoy your company this evening.

VILLANUEVA. I shall be there, at your excellency's service.

DUKE. Very well. I would speak alone with Don Fernando.

(*Exit [VILLANUEVA and the PAGE].*)

Give me leave to speak.

(*They sit.*)

As warden of the Alhambra and captain general of Granada, I am sent by his majesty to communicate certain measures, just agreed in Madrid, concerning assimilation of the Morisco population. His majesty orders that these provisions be announced immediately, under penalty of law.

DON FERNANDO. The measures will bring revolt to this land. King Philip is misled by his council: Archbishop Guerrero, the Duke of Alba, Cardinal Espinosa, Judges Menchaca and Velasco, Don Antonio Toledo, Don Pedro de Deza, Don Bernardo de Borea, and that crowing cock, Magister Gallo, who seeks to awaken all those sleeping in peace and calm. These men conspire to destroy Granada, and I pray God they don't take all Spain with it.

DUKE. With you on his majesty's side, there is nothing to fear.

DON FERNANDO. Duke, my blood comes from the kings of Cordova, whose memory is forever preserved by fame in the annals of time. I would appreciate your attention.

(*Aside.*)

Each word is a stake through my heart.

DUKE. (*Aside.*)

I see through to his soul. In the end he is a Moor.

DON FERNANDO. Speak the measures, your excellency, but let Spain tread carefully.

(*Aside.*)

The heavy yoke of servitude shall not return to our necks!

DUKE. The first order is that everyone cease speaking Arabic, with exceptions for the elderly, and that they learn Castilian within three years. Second, full-body tunics and any other clothing foreign to our customs are prohibited. You have two years to get rid of them. Your women may not cover their faces or adorn their heads with henna, nor dance the *zambra* or the *leila*. Doors may not be shut on Friday afternoons and shall remain open for Sundays, holidays, and weddings, which shall observe the ceremonies of our Roman Church. Names and surnames of your caste must be changed to Christian ones. Your bathhouses must be destroyed. You may not own black slaves, male or female, and you may not carry sharp weapons. Such is the edict, Don Fernando. Consider that it comes directly from his majesty the king.

DON FERNANDO.   Does your excellency not realize how poorly the Moriscos from across the Alpujarras will receive these measures? From the vermillion sierra to the snow-covered one, from the peaks to the stables, they will turn on you. It is an odious thing to order them to give up the language into which they were born. I will be happy to meet with your excellency later to expound at greater length on the reasons these provisions must be suspended.

DUKE.   You owe so much to the kings of Spain that I am shocked by your resistance.

DON FERNANDO.   *I* owe so much to the kings of Spain? What did they give us in exchange for the kingdom they took from us? A tiny piece of land around Válor Castle and a regiment in Granada. And that pathetic town council has stripped me of my arms and sent my father to the galleys. Is this what I owe to the kings of Spain?

DUKE.   *[Aside.]*

Such contempt!

[Aloud.]

No need to get upset. His majesty sends me here to satisfy your concerns. I am at your service. I shall await an answer from you in my palace.

(*He stands.*)

DON FERNANDO.   *[He stands.]*

My house arrest prevents me from coming.

DUKE.   Your presence will be allowed in the great room.

DON FERNANDO.   I kiss your excellency's hands.

DUKE.   *[Aside.]*

This fool is terrible at hiding his intentions.

(*Exit the DUKE.*)

DON FERNANDO.   Oh, my unfortunate people! But let's see, where was I . . .

[He takes the letter out again and continues reading aloud.]

"Thus the bandit Cañerí, a black Moor, with the biggest pack of thieves I've ever seen, rouses all the Alpujarras into rebellion. He promises me the throne, scepter, and crown of these people and this land, without realizing that my loyalty and my blood do not allow a crown to sit upon my humble brow, which belongs to his majesty. And thus I beg you, nephew, because it's important to me and because the journey is a short one, to come join me before the damage grows and it becomes too late. May God keep you and grant you prosperity. From the Alpujarras, on the twentieth of June in the year one thousand five hundred sixty-nine."

[He finishes reading and folds the letter.]

Such confusion these lines from my uncle stir in me! The Alpujarras are in revolt, he bids me come to him, yet he doesn't request backup or mention the outfitting of soldiers. What mad fancy is this? Can it be they wish to stand me up as their king?

(Enter CAÑERÍ. DON FERNANDO *is startled.*)

CAÑERÍ.   Calm down.

DON FERNANDO.   Shadow, demon, or vision: What do you want with me?

CAÑERÍ.   To help you.

DON FERNANDO.   Help me?

CAÑERÍ.   And to harrow you.

DON FERNANDO.   Why?

CAÑERÍ.   Because I must serve you in order to overthrow you.

DON FERNANDO.   Who are you?

CAÑERÍ.   He who shall give you a kingdom.

DON FERNANDO.   *[Aside.]*

   I tremble!

   [Aloud.]

   Tell me: Who are you?

CAÑERÍ.   I am he who shall kill you.

(*Exit* CAÑERÍ.)

DON FERNANDO. Wait, and I shall test your resolve! But if you intend to follow me, why do you flee from me? Where are my servants?

[Enter a PAGE.]

PAGE. Sir.

DON FERNANDO. Did you see a *negro* come through here? I must be going mad from all my misfortune. But what if it's death's shadow and the harsh grip of my star? I am saddened and confused. Ready my horse and summon my men, for I fear some rashness on the part of the duke.

PAGE. What about your house arrest?

DON FERNANDO. What house arrest? A king cannot be arrested.

PAGE. What king do you refer to?

DON FERNANDO. To myself: a mad king who cannot hide his heart.

(Exit [all].)

ACT 1, Scene 4

([A room in the Duke of Sessa's palace.] Enter, in student capes and tricorn hats, DON GONZALO, DON DIEGO, and DON MARTÍN; and CASTLE, in the pointed cap worn by impoverished students. JUAN LATINO enters in a cassock and clerical collar, no cape or hat, with Doña Ana's ribbon over his collar. He studies the pages of a book while the others jeer at him.)

DON GONZALO. The dirty *negro* will hand over the ribbon or I'll break his teeth.

JUAN LATINO. Enough with the schoolboy taunting. *Per Deum.*

ALL. Shut your mouth, you dirty dog.

JUAN LATINO. It's not Doña Ana's ribbon. My lord gave it to me.

DON MARTÍN. [To the others.]

Leave him be.

DON DIEGO. He's not in the mood.

CASTLE. He's playing with us.

JUAN LATINO. *[Reading aloud in Latin.]*

"Quotiescumque..."

DON DIEGO. I can't ignore him.

JUAN LATINO. *Vivat Dominus!*

DON MARTÍN. Does this mastiff speak Latin?

DON DIEGO. Speak.

DON MARTÍN. He falls silent.

JUAN LATINO. I speak, and I fall silent.

[Reading aloud.]

"... duo nomina..."

CASTLE. By God, the *negro* studies syntax!

JUAN LATINO. Better than you. Ten years wasting your father's income, and you know nothing more than my mother.

[Reading aloud.]

"... substantiva..."

CASTLE. Oh, you got your voice back?

JUAN LATINO. *[Reading aloud.]*

"... in oratione continuantur, alterum erit genitivi casus, ut supplicium est poena peccati."

DON MARTÍN. This doggie is something else with his Latin!

JUAN LATINO. Latin indeed, which says that punishment is the price of sin. For a man who scorns virtue laughs in youth and cries in old age.

(Reading aloud.)

"Accommodatus, appositus, aptus, idoneus..."

DON GONZALO. He spends all day in this, never leaving my tutor's apartment.

CASTLE. Hilarious!

DON GONZALO. And he sleeps in my father's library. No one can drag him from it.

DON DIEGO. Castle, jeer at little Juan.

CASTLE.   Add your boos.

[All jeer and boo at JUAN LATINO.]

JUAN LATINO.   *[Reading aloud.]*

"... habilis, utilis, et inutilis ..."

(All hiss at him.)

CASTLE.   I'll be the first to spit at him.

(All spit at him.)

JUAN LATINO.   My lords ...

DON MARTÍN.   Pelt that darkskin good.

CASTLE.   Turn him from black to white.

DON DIEGO.   No honey for you, horse.

DON GONZALO.   Quiet, that's enough.

CASTLE.   Hey, I've got a question for you in the vernacular.

(He strikes JUAN LATINO, who returns the blow.)

JUAN LATINO.   And I answer in Latin. *Hanc rem, ut hic liber.*

DON MARTÍN.   That's a good one.

DON GONZALO.   Indeed.

JUAN LATINO.   Jokes among the ill-bred start with fists and end with feet.

ALL.   Bravo, bravo!

CASTLE.   Let's stick to words then.

JUAN LATINO.   So be it, and may the Devil take the loser.

ALL.   Agreed, agreed!

CASTLE.   Why do they call you little Juan?

JUAN LATINO.   Ho, a sentence from the mouth of an ass!

DON DIEGO.   That's the best you can do, Castle?

JUAN LATINO.   Why do they call a clown a Castle?

CASTLE.   Stop. What are you laughing at, you donkey? It's a long story.

ALL.   Let's hear it!

CASTLE. I shall tell it then. I have a father who is so modest in his desires that he prefers to live in a tiny shack. So the whole village calls him Alfonso the Shack. But I turned out exactly the opposite: ridden with vices, always hungry and looking for food. So instead of the Shack they call me the Castle.

ALL. Bravo, bravo!

CASTLE. *[To JUAN LATINO.]*

Did you find that amusing?

JUAN LATINO. Delightful.

CASTLE. Well, sir, I think you deserve the reception you got here. You're like a bucket of ice water, despite your dark skin.

ALL. Dog!

JUAN LATINO. What happened to your oath?

DON GONZALO. My father the duke approaches with Doña Ana and my mother.

(Enter the DUKE, DUCHESS, CARLOBAL, and VILLANUEVA; DOÑA ANA and JUANA, in veils, with the ribbon thrown to Doña Ana by Juan Latino wrapped around her arm; and DON FERNANDO.)

JUAN LATINO. *[Aside.]*

Oh, love, show my joy.

DUCHESS. *[Aside.]*

I don't understand what I'm seeing, and I don't like it.

(JUAN LATINO gazes at DOÑA ANA, the DUCHESS at the latter's ribbon, and DON FERNANDO at Juan Latino's.)

DOÑA ANA. I am such a devotee of words that there is no one of refined taste in Granada who doesn't recognize me by sight. I attend all the learned debates I can, for my plain countenance allows me this freedom. If it were lawful, I would go to school every day.

(The DUCHESS and DOÑA ANA chat among themselves, as do the DUKE and VILLANUEVA.)

JUAN LATINO. *[Aside.]*

Doña Ana wears the ribbon I gave her.

JUANA. *[Aside, to DOÑA ANA.]*

The negro *wears the ribbon he found in the street.*

DOÑA ANA. *[Aside, to JUANA.]*

And to toy with him, Juana, I wear his.

JUAN LATINO. *[Aside.]*

My lady the duchess eyes the duke suspiciously. This will be interesting!

DUCHESS. *[Aside.]*

The duke adores Doña Ana. My suspicions are confirmed.

JUANA. *[Aside.]*

Don Fernando gazes at the *negro* with contempt. I fear some great evil.

DON FERNANDO. *[Aside.]*

My anger rages. The beautiful ingrate has given my ribbon to a *negro*.

DUCHESS. *[Aside.]*

I can't believe my eyes. I never thought I'd be jealous of this woman!

[Aloud, to DOÑA ANA.]

What a lovely ribbon.

DOÑA ANA. A favor from a man of your household.

DUCHESS. *[Aside.]*

What outrage I suffer! His love and my betrayal are clear.

DON FERNANDO. *[Aside.]*

O vengeful heavens, bring me black omens and black fortune, black life and black death, black love and black jealousy! I am pursued by one *negro*, intent on killing me, while another flaunts my ribbon. Enough of *negros*!

JUAN LATINO. *[Aside.]*

Lucky is the ribbon that girds her lovely arm.

DON FERNANDO. *[Aside.]*

But my concerns are ridiculous. A woman so callous that love cannot bend her would never show favor to a *negro*. It must be a different ribbon.

JUAN LATINO. *[Aside.]*

Oh, my love!

DUKE. Let the academy commence.

(All sit, DON MARTÍN at the head of the table and JUAN LATINO at the feet of his master the DUKE.)

DON MARTÍN. I ask the lord doctor: Whence comes the custom of removing one's hat as a greeting?

CASTLE. Capes are also removed.

CARLOBAL. Listen to my muse. In ancient times, he who sacrificed birds and beasts to fictitious gods did so with his head covered. So to differentiate between gods and men, people bared their heads before a judge, a prince, or whoever it might be, to avoid equating him with a god, for back then it was neither an honor nor an insult. Also when a man appeared in court, the judge would tell him to remove his hat to give him a certain confidence. As the practice took root among the rural nobility, courtiers began to think it was an honor to remove one's hat. It then came to be a silly custom among wealthy city residents, and from there it spread to all nobles, peasants, and bumpkins. Another reason is that the head is venerated as the seat of judgment, and thus its primary dressing is removed as a compliment and show of courtesy to powerful men. It was also a general custom in antiquity for mortal enemies to cover their heads in combat, and thus we keep our hats on before our adversaries while to the ally we say, in taking it off, I am your servant and your friend. This is all according to Plutarch, Varro, Galeotto, and Ludovico. I humbly await commendation or correction.

JUAN LATINO. Such erudition!

DUCHESS. And a silver tongue.

DOÑA ANA. That's my brother for you.

DUKE. He speaks in perfect poetry.

CASTLE. I'm an ass, so I would have tripped all over myself in my answer.

DON FERNANDO. Give it a try.

CASTLE. Would you like to hear a sonnet?

VILLANUEVA. Oh God, please no.

CASTLE. According to learned authorities like Poptart, Varicose, Macchiato, Judaica, and of course the great Castle, freeloading students have their talents as well. And you can bet that if I get my bagpipes and flute nice and tuned, you'll see my muse is nothing to sneeze at. Would you like to hear a saraband or a chaconne that'll have you dancing in your seats?

(He hums a catchy tune with nonsense lyrics.)

DON GONZALO.   Amusing.

CASTLE.   I'm capable of marvels when I feel . . .

(Looking at JUANA.)

. . . a tickle in my chest, like the swipe of a broom.

DON MARTÍN.   Enough.

CASTLE.   *[To JUANA.]*

I am at your service, and I am honorable.

DON MARTÍN.   Don't take such license, you prattling schoolboy.

CASTLE.   As a schoolboy, I am full of license.

DON DIEGO.   Full of something.

DON MARTÍN.   It's your excellency's turn. Tell us who discovered paper and words.

CASTLE.   What a boring topic.

DON MARTÍN.   Where does the word *letter* come from? And what counts as good style in a letter?

CASTLE.   This is worse than the origin of hats.

DON MARTÍN.   Who invented the machine with which we print? And before there was paper, what did they write on?

DUKE.   It's a long story. Listen well.

CASTLE.   We have no choice.

DUKE.   When in ancient times . . . I believe I've lost my notes. I apologize. Let someone else speak.

(JUAN LATINO stands.)

JUAN LATINO.   I shall speak.

DUKE.   Are you serious?

DOÑA ANA.   What a funny thought from a black man.

JUANA.   A good joke.

DON GONZALO.   I understand Juan is quite learned.

DUKE.   Little Juan?

DON GONZALO. Yes, sir. He's got an intellect worthy of Cicero.

DUKE. I'm astonished.

DON GONZALO. He studies with me so eagerly . . . never misses a lesson, not even when we pelt him with spittle and snot.

DUCHESS. What an amazing *negro*.

DON GONZALO. He learns with great pain and effort, because he never enters the classroom but waits in the doorway and audits the lesson from there. And he always learns it perfectly, for he spends day and night in his studies: awake, asleep, at home, away, fencing, singing, even courting.

DUKE. I admire that kind of ambition.

VILLANUEVA. I'm shocked your excellency believes a *negro* capable of advanced understanding.

JUAN LATINO. Am I not a man? A man with a desire for knowledge?

VILLANUEVA. There is no soul in that desire.

JUAN LATINO. The soul does not necessarily reflect the body.

VILLANUEVA. Do not engage in disputations with me.

JUAN LATINO. If I ever complete my studies, you will one day see proof of a beautiful soul in an ugly body. And I swear on my lord the duke's life, because it's my own as well, that your excellency will see the magister proved wrong. And I swear that I shall study the arts and sciences until I am fully able to demonstrate my knowledge and his ignorance.

DUKE. That's quite an oath.

VILLANUEVA. What arrogance!

DUKE. Come, kiss the magister's hand.

JUAN LATINO. *[Aside.]*

Oh, color, what I suffer because of you!

(*JUAN LATINO kneels and kisses the hand of VILLANUEVA, who bids him rise.*)

DOÑA ANA. *[Aside.]*

Such humility, grace, and courtesy. I should buy him to carry my litter. Or to be my brother's lackey.

DON FERNANDO.   *(Aside.)*

That ribbon drives me mad. I must kill the *negro*.

DON MARTÍN.   Speak, little Juan.

CASTLE.   God free me from this foolishness.

DUKE.   Speak, darkskin.

DOÑA ANA.   It will be a pleasure to hear you.

JUAN LATINO.   Jews and Gentiles claim writing came from the Greeks, Asians, and Egyptians, which makes it a modern invention, from after the flood, in the time of Abraham and Moses. But I maintain that it was invented by Adam or his children, for Pliny, in his seventh book, calls it eternal. In Josephus's *Jewish Antiquities*, I have read that the children of Seth and grandchildren of Adam built two columns of brick and stone, and that Josephus saw one in Syria adorned with many scripts and sculpted figures. Moreover Saint Jude, in his epistle, cites the ancient Book of Enoch, which was written long before the flood, and this point is abundantly confirmed by Josephus, Justin, and Saint Augustine. When the righteous flood arrived, washing away the sins and vices of man, Noah, in great wisdom and foresight, preserved the craft of writing aboard his ark, from which his children and grandchildren learned it. Later, when men built their swaggering tower of Babel, they were justly punished from birth with the loss of speech and writing, which remained solely with the tribe and family of Eber. From him the Jews have descended, preserving their language. Then Abraham learned the whole craft from the Assyrians, and Moses from the Egyptians. The Phoenician captain Cadmus taught it to Greece, and the Pelasgians to Italy. Strabo, in a discussion of Andalusia, says that scholarship, writing, law, and poetry are so ancient in Spain that there are words that have survived from Noah's children, who populated the country. And in John Annius I have read that writing first developed along the river known to us as the Guadalquivir and to the ancients as Betis. It now remains to determine what surfaces were used for writing in olden times, before paper and parchment came into existence. Everyone agrees that palm leaves were used, and thus the pages of books are still called leaves. After this they discovered a kind of fiber from myrtle, banana, ash, and elm, which they carefully extracted from between the bark and trunk, binding the sheets together to record their wisdom. And because Latin gives the name *liber* to these bound sheets, we call them *libros* in Spanish, though our books no longer come from bark. Other ancients wrote on lead tablets in various colors or on smooth canvas with reed pens. Still others used smooth tablets on which they scratched letters with a thin iron pick called a *stylus*. And from this word, we say today that those who write well write with style. Sheepskin was also found to be useful, and because it was invented in

Pergamon, we call it parchment. Then ingenuity led man to the bushes that grow in pools on the banks of the Nile. And in Syria, near the Euphrates, they cured the material and turned it into paper: white, smooth, pliant, and beautiful. This invention occurred during the reign of Numa Pompilius in Rome, according to Lactantius, Plutarch, and Livy. These bushes, or reeds more properly speaking, were called *papyrus* according to Pliny, and thus paper takes its name from that word. The noun *carta*, which was used for letters and other written documents, comes from a city near Tyre with that name. Thus did people write until, in our golden centuries, paper and the wondrous art of printing came into use. The latter was invented in the year 1465 by a German named Conrad, who first put it to use in Rome. The first book he printed was Saint Augustine's *City of God*. He also printed Lactantius's massive tome, *The Divine Institutes*, which fittingly made its author divine. This, sir, is what I know of the ancient origins of writing. I ask your excellency to forgive my poor delivery.

DUKE. That was astonishing.

DOÑA ANA. What a charming slave.

DUCHESS. Wondrous.

CARLOBAL. Impressive command of Latin!

DON MARTÍN. Astonishing.

DOÑA ANA. If your excellency professes friendship to me, you will sell me this slave.

DON DIEGO. He is without peer.

DUKE. Come here, Juan de Sessa. Tell me: Who taught you so much Latin, so much learning?

JUAN LATINO. I am self-taught, through much effort and practice.

CARLOBAL. The answer of a wise man.

DUKE. With more study, this black slave will be a prodigy.

JUAN LATINO. In a learned household, everyone is motivated to learn. I was born into your excellency's care, so how can you profess surprise? How could your knowledge not rub off on me? You raised me with such love that if my mother weren't black, I would think you my father in addition to my lord. I grew up like a tender sapling watered by your knowledge and discipline. I came to ask myself who I was, and the answer was always the same: a poor black slave, to be bought and sold. Realizing I had no chance at honor, I devoted myself to the pursuit of knowledge, given that color is no impediment to learning. I chose, as Pythagoras recommends, a life of labor, not of affliction. For the man who occupies himself in remarkable work, as Democritus tells us, will not feel the sting of slavery. Likewise the divine Virgil, in celebrated verses, notes that ceaseless labor triumphs over all. And in Proverbs, Solomon says that the industrious hand finds wealth while the lazy man flees poverty in vain. Likewise the famed lawmaker Draco established severe penalties for idle Athenians, and Solomon cites the industrious ant as a worthy model. The Gentiles built a temple to the virtues of labor, and they worshiped Jenovia and other goddesses because in hard work they found pleasure, wealth, and fame. And as my birth took place in the midst of such greatness, my proud thoughts look past their wretched origin. And thus, though I am a lowly man, I have carefully placed my hopes in your excellency, confident that my hard work will secure my reputation.

DUKE.   You are correct to think that, Juan. And since you have placed your hopes in me, I intend to reward you. What do you desire?

JUAN LATINO.   To learn.

DUKE.   An excellent request.

[To CARLOBAL.]

My lord doctor, it is my pleasure to place Juan in your keeping. Take him to your household.

DON FERNANDO.   *(Aside.)*

My soul rages!

DOÑA ANA.   *(Aside.)*

My desire has been fulfilled. I am overjoyed.

DUKE.   Because the lord doctor does me such favor, he shall take possession of this slave. And believe me when I say I think of him as a son. His education must be carefully attended to. I cannot overstate the courtesy and pleasure you do me in granting my request, doctor; you are a true friend to do so only because I wish it. Forgive me if I have become emotional.

CARLOBAL.   To such favor I can only respond, sir, that I am the most unworthy servant of this house. You do me great honor in entrusting Juan to my care. My desires have been fulfilled.

DUKE.   God keep you.

JUAN LATINO.   *(Aside.)*

Oh, love, after living through such scorn, am I really to look into the divine eyes of the sun that blinds me? Upon your altar I sacrifice my soul in exchange for such a strange miracle. If you remedy, as you are able, the suffering in which I live, I shall adorn your walls with a captive *negro*.

DUKE.   Juan, it is time for you to go off to study. You are black, and you are my slave. From one source a river is formed, and from many rivers, an ocean. Do not be deflated by your poverty, your color, or your servitude, for knowledge and virtue are the parents of wealth; and given the madness and inclemency of fate, a lack of knowledge brings about a lack of good fortune. Take heart, Juan, for I remain here and will never desert you. I cannot give you the knowledge you seek, but I can give you the means to acquire it. And because the lord Don Fernando awaits an audience with me, the academy is hereby suspended.

JUAN LATINO.   May fame report such favor for all the world to hear. Offer me your feet, your excellency.

[He kneels.]

In response to your generosity, I depart, a latter-day Horace, to study vast spheres of knowledge. I ask God to grant your excellency a long and prosperous life.

DUKE.   Be a most obedient slave to the lord doctor, and you will not be forgotten by posterity. Rise.

[JUAN LATINO rises.]

DON DIEGO.   A great favor he has won.

DON MARTÍN.   And a great act of kindness.

VILLANUEVA.   I praise his good fortune.

DUKE.   Goodbye, and farewell.

DON FERNANDO.   *[Aside.]*

I can't believe my eyes.

DUCHESS.   Come back to our company soon, my friends.

CASTLE.   Juan, I bet you'll end up as Canon of Guinea.

DOÑA ANA.   It is a pleasure to listen to you speak, darkskin.

DON FERNANDO.   *[Aside.]*

I can't take it anymore.

JUANA.   *[Aside, to DOÑA ANA.]*

My heart is pulsing in my throat!

DOÑA ANA.   *[Aside, to JUANA.]*

Oh, Juana, what a charming slave!

(The DUKE accompanies all but DON FERNANDO to the door, where they exit. The DUKE and DON FERNANDO sit.)

DUKE.   Is the lord Don Fernando convinced of the necessity of the new laws we discussed?

DON FERNANDO.   On the contrary, I am convinced that there is no reason for God or the king to do us this injustice and throw my people into such slavery. These measures are not a just reward for our service to a king who is known for rewarding service so well. To order us to abandon our native language within three years and to stop wearing our traditional clothing is inhumane in the extreme. How are we to learn a new language in three years when that's not even long enough to learn one's own language well? How are the poor supposed to buy new clothes? And what is the problem with what they wear now? Egyptians, Armenians, and Swabians wear similar clothing, and Arabic is spoken among them, yet they all worship Christ. What barbaric law would prohibit traditional dances? Only savage peoples lack them. What does dancing have to do with religion? The *zambra* is not danced in Africa or Turkey precisely because it lacks ceremonial significance. *Negros* are allowed to speak, dance, and sing all day, however they wish, yet our language and joyful customs are deemed offensive? Bathing and adorning the head with henna are not religious rites but cosmetic ones, just as with Christians who dye their hair blond. Ordering doors to remain open honors those with rich and sumptuous palaces, but what about those who live in poverty? The names you would strip from us are necessary for men to recognize one another, and they are legal and honorable; for Spain is exalted when its renown and great deeds remain alive, and may she live on forever in our names. Requiring women to go about town with their faces uncovered will give license to the unscrupulous and open the door to evil; for the beautiful maiden, pursued by all, will succumb more quickly while the unsightly one will have no chance of marrying at all. Furthermore, prohibiting us from owning blacks from Guinea because you suspect the masters will force the slaves to worship Muhammad is deeply offensive; I avoid calling it intentional malice because I respect the bounds of propriety. But such a measure is unheard of, and to take away our slaves under this pretense is to make greater slaves of us, for it allows the law to draw our blood to satisfy its thirst, for blood is the poor man's currency. I wish to serve my king, but I will not consent to these measures as long as this sword is within my reach. The Morisco forces are legion, as is the righteousness of our cause, and he who angers me shall pay the price with his life. As proof, I cite our past rebellions, and I pray your excellency treat us with honor and respect. A cowardly king may have surrendered our realm to Spain in the past, but a great Válor shall restore it.

DUKE.   Guards!

(Enter two GUARDS.)

Seize Don Fernando and throw him into the tower. I don't care if all Granada protests.

[To DON FERNANDO.]

You are a discredit to the word *gentleman*, and if it weren't for the fact that the king treats you better than you deserve, I would punish you myself. Take him away!

DON FERNANDO.   What humiliation is this! My rage boils over.

[Exit the DUKE.]

GUARD 1.   Let's go, sir.

DON FERNANDO.   *[Aside.]*

What shall I do? Should I not take my vengeance on the duke and his people? What other option is there for a nobleman to recover his honor?

(Reenter the DUKE along with DOÑA ANA, DON MARTÍN, VILLANUEVA, CARLOBAL, CASTLE, and JUAN LATINO.)

GUARD 2.   Will you not come?

DON FERNANDO.   Where is my brother?

[GUARD 1].   The judge has sent for him.

DON FERNANDO.   I shall move Heaven and Earth in my defense.

[Aside, noticing the new arrivals.]

But what new humiliation is this? The whole palace accompanies Doña Ana to witness my shame. And the *negro* goes home with her, my ribbon about his neck. I'll kill them all in my rage!

DUKE.   *[To the GUARDS.]*

I gave you an order. Why do you delay?

DON FERNANDO.   They await my vengeance, which shall shake the pillars of the sky with its ferocity. Speak, Doña Ana: Is this how you express your nobility and beauty? Through insults and taunting? Is this what you mean by discretion and refinement? You would share my favor with a *negro*? And with him pursue the pleasure and affection you have spurned in so many suitors? You are a vile woman!

JUAN LATINO. Vile, you call her? You lie!

DON FERNANDO. Dog!

DUKE. I can't believe what I'm witnessing.

(*DON FERNANDO and JUAN LATINO unsheathe their swords and lunge at each other.*)

Kill him!

DON FERNANDO. Where are my men?

[Enter armed MORISCOS.]

MORISCO 1. Right here.

DON FERNANDO. If your excellency wishes to live, you will turn the *negro* over to us.

JUAN LATINO. I will end your life as you've ended my patience.

DUKE. Death to them all!

DOÑA ANA. Kill him!

DON FERNANDO. You'll never do it, you hoodlums!

MORISCO 2. Granada's Moriscos are here to fight!

CASTLE. As are its Christians—and a slacker student or two!

(*Exit [all] fighting.*)

ACT 2, Scene 1

(*[A room in the Duke of Sessa's palace overlooking the street.] Enter the DUKE, DUCHESS, and attendants.*)

DUKE. I had the new measures announced, which so enraged the Moors that they attacked the king's guard, killed several of the heralds, and liberated the traitor Don Fernando from the tower. Pursued by numerous officers of the law, he has fled to the mountains, where they say he seeks the company of other bandits.

DUCHESS. I fear widespread damage across the land.

DUKE. His majesty is a great Christian and will expand the faith through both peace and war.

DUCHESS. Don Fernando behaved like a boor to Doña Ana, and now all Granada knows she has spurned many princes. To accuse such a proper lady of denying a thousand highborn suitors in favor of a *negro* was ridiculous and unthinkable.

DUKE. Such is the fury of a scorned suitor. Doña Ana's brother has not learned of the scandal.

DUCHESS. If I were you, I'd be jealous of all her suitors.

DUKE. I, duchess? What have I to be jealous of? I care about no love but yours.

(The clash of swords is heard offstage.)

JUAN LATINO. *(Offstage.)*

Get off me! I'll kill you!

DUKE. What's the meaning of this?

PAGE. *[Looking offstage.]*

A mob of students is trying to kill Juan de Sessa, or Juan Latino as he's now called.

DUKE. What! Take me there at once.

PAGE. No need. Here they come.

(Enter JUAN LATINO and CASTLE, defending themselves with broadswords or scimitars. JUAN LATINO wears a torn cassock.)

CASTLE. Thugs! Do you know who you're dealing with?

DUKE. Juan, what's going on?

CASTLE. Sir, a pack of smelly, drooling students laid into us as if he were a *negro* and I were his chump.

DUKE. But why?

JUAN LATINO. Because I applied . . .

CASTLE. He applied for a teaching chair, and that fool Villanueva paid his leeches to spit at him: six pennies per shot.

DUKE. He has them treat you badly because of his own aspirations?

JUAN LATINO. I have been humiliated.

CASTLE.   He's not exaggerating. They are a pack of cowards.

DUKE.   Calm yourself, Juan. Tell me: How goes the doctor's tutelage?

JUAN LATINO.   Very well as a matter of fact, except that I am exhausted and dispirited. No matter what I do, I cannot come to terms with these pranksters. They destroy me with their shouts and jeers while the teachers laugh. They mock everything I say. They pick apart my logic, for a poor man has no defender. As soon as I enter the school they start with their taunting. "Beware the dog!" one will say amid so much heckling and hissing it sounds like a hornets' nest. I desire knowledge, but I can find no way to apply my will to the task. From the very moment I took on Magister Villanueva in applying for the distinguished teaching chair, I lost all my friendships. The other students hold him in such esteem that they turned on me immediately, openly insulting me and calling me arrogant, rabid, and frightful. And though the magister is very learned and I am a black man who has only begun to learn, I have honor from your excellency. They say that I am bought and sold and that it is not right to admit a slave and a *negro* to any gathering of nobles. It is malicious the way they call me *negro*, for blacks are noble. It is slavery that will impede my success.

(He kneels.)

Sir, sir, my life and honor will end here if your excellency does not favor me by rebranding the rebus of fate. I understand what a preeminent honor it is to be slave of slaves in this household, but my competition is none other than the magister. They refuse to accept my candidacy, and if I miss the deadline to apply, the flame that consumes me will kill me. I beg your excellency's help in this: grant me my sweet and longed-for freedom. Lift your humble slave to a high station, for it is unworthy of a renowned and noble hand to leave this work undone, which has been in progress since my birth. And though my body seeks liberty, my soul desires sweet captivity, for with such an owner, shackles cannot be cruel. I would like to improve myself, God willing, for he who dies just as he was born will not count himself among the blessed. Books and chronicles are filled with the honors of the House of Aguilar. Today is the day. I am worth little, my service even less. My duke—my king I should say—and my lady: honor Juan de Sessa and set this poor black man free, for he desires to be so much more.

DUKE.   Rise. On my life, it disturbs me that Villanueva mistreats you when he knows what I think of you.

DUCHESS.   *[To the DUKE.]*

Keep your promise. Let's give my black friend his teaching position. Honor him, on my life.

JUAN LATINO. Such a felicitous boost will raise me high.

[He rises.]

DUKE. Have you excelled in your studies?

CASTLE. He is most learned.

DUKE. Who else seeks the position?

JUAN LATINO. Apart from Villanueva, no one. Only I was bold enough.

CASTLE. They fear having their throats slit one by one.

DUKE. And you dare take on Villanueva?

JUAN LATINO. Anything is worth the risk when it comes to honor.

DUCHESS. To think a student would take on the magister!

JUAN LATINO. I have studied extensively and feel confident I can prove my knowledge.

DUKE. Who has endowed the position you seek?

JUAN LATINO. The archbishop.

DUKE. It must come with a handsome allowance.

JUAN LATINO. And a seat of honor in the choir. And thus Villanueva insists my slave status makes me ineligible.

DUKE. I shall speak with his lordship the archbishop and whoever may be advising him against you. I'll ensure you're allowed to apply for the position and will back you with my life, reputation, and estate. Your ambition is honorable, Juan, but make sure you're up to the task. If you lose this teaching chair, I swear on my life, instead of celebrating you I'll never speak to you again, for it's my name we're talking about. Rest assured that if Villanueva is your enemy, the House of Aguilar is your defense.

JUAN LATINO. I kiss those feet a thousand times.

[He kneels again.]

If your excellency sets me free, I promise to accept all consequences, good and bad. Am I free, great lord?

DUKE. Cheer up. Your competition is not all that fearsome.

JUAN LATINO. He really has it in for me.

DUKE. My presence will smooth the way for you.

JUAN LATINO.   Am I free?

DUKE.   It's time to be on your way. I'll send four pages with you so you'll not be harassed again. Rise, student.

   [JUAN LATINO rises.]

JUAN LATINO.   You do not respond? No one will receive me in the choir because I am a slave. I am poor and thus deemed indecorous. Free me, your excellency, and as you do me so many favors, do me this one more today.

DUKE.   You have nothing to fear as long as I live. I give you . . .

JUAN LATINO.   My freedom?

DUCHESS.   *[Aside, to the DUKE.]*

   He's an insistent one!

DUKE.   . . . four thousand ducats for this endeavor. My whole estate is at your disposal: horses, coaches, and servants. Earn your honor, student.

JUAN LATINO.   I'm so grateful for your favor.

   (Aside.)

   Oh, unhappy fate!

DUKE.   Take care you don't lose my goodwill along with the teaching chair.

JUAN LATINO.   Am I free?

DUKE.   That remains to be seen. Focus on your application.

DUCHESS.   And let me know what I may do for you, my black friend.

JUAN LATINO.   I humbly beg your excellency to solicit my freedom before more time passes.

DUCHESS.   It shall be done, friend.

JUAN LATINO.   Thus would your excellency do me much honor.

   (Exit [all].)

ACT 2, Scene 2

([The Alpujarras region of southern Spain.] Enter DIEGO, ZAIDA, ABEN ABOO, CAÑERÍ, and other Moriscos carrying a basket with several iconic items of Moorish dress, a turban with a crown, a long gown, and a scepter. A group of dancers perform the zambra to guitars. Four flags with crescents are planted in the ground.)

ABEN ABOO. Strip off those animal skins and dress yourself in lawful and honorable clothing. Cast aside the crooked staff and take up the scepter. Lay this crown upon your haughty brow. Long live the king!

CAÑERÍ. Aben Aboo, I do not intend to usurp the crown of this kingdom. Your nephew, Don Fernando de Válor, is the rightful heir to the throne. Only his brow is worthy of the crown, for he is descended from the great Caliph. Allah has ordered Don Fernando to be king and indicated his divine will through omens that are now being fulfilled. Do not ignore the stars. Remember the mistakes for which you now live in harsh exile. Recall the holy revelations and horoscopes that predict victory, including the prophecy of Castares Cave, which in Arabic meter reads thus:

(He takes out a parchment and reads aloud.)

"We most illustrious Arab prophets, observing how the paths of the constellations, the powers of the stars, and the poles of the planets make themselves felt here in our world, conclude that our people will be oppressed and subject to Christian rule in Spain, but that they will free themselves through war and become free lords of all the earth. They will be in servitude for eighty years when, tired of pain and punishment, they take matters into their own hands and revolt, killing and destroying their oppressors. Strange marvels will be seen as the time approaches, led by a young man of royal blood, his forehead anointed in holy oil. Outwardly Christian, he will turn apostate on his law, for on the inside, in both ancestry and faith, he will be a true believer in Muhammad. O ye friends who happen upon this prophecy, worship it and you will see that it refers—alas, poor Spain!—to the year one thousand five hundred and seventy."

DIEGO. Such strange prophecies!

ABEN ABOO. Straight from our great prophet Muhammad.

CAÑERÍ. Take heed, Moors: in recent nights a comet has been observed hurtling toward Spain, a great fireball streaking through the sky. You lost your lands, as the prophecy predicted. You have suffered through pain and punishment. And now you wage war on Spain as the eight decades predicted in the prophecy approach fulfillment in the year 1570. Don Fernando is a Christian, a young man anointed in holy oil, descended of royal ancestry and true to Muhammad's law. He embodies everything the parchment predicts. There can be no doubt, my friends; let us draw our swords on our enemies. One Ferdinand took Granada from us, and Heaven decrees that another will restore it to us.

(*To ABEN ABOO.*)

If he hasn't replied to your letter, what are you waiting for? Go to Granada and find him. I was born only to rule my own weary life. The crown would sit unsteadily upon my frail head.

ABEN ABOO.   Don Fernando delays too long.

CAÑERÍ.   He alone will rule if I have any say in it.

ABEN ABOO.   *[Aside.]*

Envy devours me. Ah, to be king myself!

[VOICES].   (*Offstage.*)

Up here, this way! He's over here!

ZAIDA.   What's going on?

(*A tumult sounds offstage.*)

CAÑERÍ.   Get rid of these clothes and guitars, now!

[VOICES].   (*Offstage.*)

Chase him down, kill him! . . . Fire the harquebus!

(*A gunshot is heard [offstage].*)

ZAIDA.   God help us!

CAÑERÍ.   *[Looking offstage.]*

Swifter than a deer, a hounded man flees across the craggy mountain. Soldiers, arm yourselves. Aben Aboo, I charge you with this mission!

ABEN ABOO.   *[Aside.]*

Oh, unlucky assignment!

DIEGO.   It must be officers of the Brotherhood, pursuing some bandit.

CAÑERÍ.   Then they shall die. Free the criminal! No officers of the state shall go unpunished. Pursue them!

ABEN ABOO.   At once!

(Exit ABEN ABOO.)

CAÑERÍ.   May your courage show itself, general. Kill those villains. Don't let them escape!

(Exit [all]. Drums and shouts are heard. Enter DON FERNANDO, out of breath from running.)

DON FERNANDO.   Where am I? Am I a beast, hunted down by man? The shouts of "Kill him, kill him!" ring in my ear, for a wretch hears things that aren't there and see trees transformed into men in the denseness of this grove. Hide me, O mountain, in your caves, where, despite the wild solitude, your branches burst with new leaves and your springs swell into rivers. Do not give me away: calm your winds and trees. But what is this? A turban, tunic, scepter, and crown? The heavens conjure the unhappy memory of my grandparents before my eyes. What fantasies are these? Where do they come from? "I am he who shall give you a kingdom," that sad shadow told me. "I am he who shall murder you," you added, O shadow, with a hideous expression. No doubt my fortune offers me a kingdom at the same time it plots my death. But my sword shall put an end to my enemies, and I shall die avenged. I am the king of Granada, O mountain dwellers. I have arrived.

(Raising his voice.)

Come forth, for it has pleased Heaven that you shake the heavy yoke from your neck. Come forth, for your king has arrived. Come forth to see the sad and downtrodden Don Fernando. But what am I doing? I flee at the same time I summon my supporters, fitting the crown to my forehead. I am king. I am king! Am I not?

(He stands as if in a daze. Enter CAÑERÍ, startling DON FERNANDO.)

CAÑERÍ.   Who is king?

DON FERNANDO.   What luck! O shadow, if today is the day of my death about which you predicted so many evils, then fulfill the path of my fate. Come, shadow: strike me dead, finish me off. But wait, phantom, and tell me first: Who are you?

CAÑERÍ.   *(Aside.)*

Am I so hideous looking that I give him fright?

DON FERNANDO.   Tell me what you want. Finish off Don Fernando. Are you a man? A mute? A fleshless spirit?

(CAÑERÍ throws himself at Don Fernando's feet.)

CAÑERÍ.   What, Don Fernando?

DON FERNANDO. Wait.

CAÑERÍ. Unvanquished Don Fernando, what fear afflicts you? From what do you flee, cowardly and trembling? I am a man, not a beast or a shadow.

[Shouting.]

O Moriscos of the highlands, come down and kiss the hand of our king, scorcher and flogger of Christians. Come down, come down!

(The Moriscos come down and kneel.)

Long live Don Fernando!

ALL. Long live Don Fernando!

DON FERNANDO. Rise, my friends. I owe my life to your warm welcome. It's time to bring death to our enemies.

(Aside [observing CAÑERÍ].)

Have I not seen this monster in my home?

[Aloud.]

Where is my uncle?

(ABEN ABOO steps forward.)

ABEN ABOO. I am here, great lord.

DON FERNANDO. *(Aside.)*

This is the face and body of the *negro* I saw earlier. I have overcome my fate. As king, I can kill him and ensure my life with his death. Thus does the man who rebuffs fate take charge of his fortune. In short, I am king. Uncle, kill that *negro* when I leave for Granada, for he will be defenseless. His death is important to me; let it come unsuspecting. Don't try to dissuade me.

ABEN ABOO. *[Aside, to DON FERNANDO.]*

Take heed that you order the death of he who delivered you a kingdom.

DON FERNANDO. *[Aside, to ABEN ABOO.]*

You'll lose your own head if you refuse me.

ABEN ABOO. Your pleasure is law, sir.

(Aside.)

Such vile treachery! I must rule now, O unjust king! As soon as he leaves I shall warn Cañerí of his plot.

CAÑERÍ. Let's go.

DON FERNANDO. O cruel Doña Ana, I am ensnared by my own fate, not your charms. But just wait, my ungrateful lady, for I shall slaughter the duke and his *negro* and play Tarpeia to Granada. All hail King Aben Humeya!

(Exit [all] amid hails and shouts.)

ACT 2, Scene 3

([A room in the Carlobal home.] Drums sound. Enter DOÑA ANA, CARLOBAL, CASTLE, DON DIEGO with a guitar, and DON MARTÍN with writing materials, which he places on a table.)

CARLOBAL. Get out, by God! You do not have permission to be in my living room. Go back where you came from!

CASTLE. Calm down.

DON DIEGO. If my friend Doña Ana requests a lesson, am I to refuse?

CARLOBAL. Don't be ridiculous. I'll not have my sister singing, ciphering, reading, or writing. She does so against my will. Out, I say, all of you!

DON MARTÍN. As you wish.

(Exit all but CARLOBAL and DOÑA ANA.)

DOÑA ANA. My homely appearance does not warrant such suspicions.

CARLOBAL. Indecent sister, you are the source of all my trouble.

DOÑA ANA. You are a very strange man.

CARLOBAL. You were born to stoke my ruin and raised to offend me. Your madness and depravity lead you to disobey my wishes, singing with Don Diego and ciphering with Don Martín. You will please neither me nor the world nor God with this plan, for in learning to count, you only give a poor account of yourself. Are reading and writing not enough for a noblewoman? What good will numbers do you? But if you insist, there are other teachers in Granada I would approve of.

DOÑA ANA. I am perfectly capable of maintaining my honor while singing and ciphering. I aspire to much higher ends and much nobler names than those men can offer. They are unfit to polish my slippers. It is foolish to guard me the way you do. But to make you happy, they shall not enter my bedchamber if you provide for my instruction. Find me a tutor, lord doctor, and I will conform to your will.

CARLOBAL. I am content with that solution and will find you a thousand tutors. The duke's slave is sharp, witty, and sings like the Portuguese. He will teach you better than anyone.

DOÑA ANA. The slave?

CARLOBAL. Yes. What does it matter?

DOÑA ANA. A black tutor?

CARLOBAL. He doesn't teach with his skin color. He is skilled at the vihuela and the harp, an excellent poet, and the greatest of wits in the classroom. He is so wondrous at his skill that, though his name is Juan de Sessa, they now call him Juan Latino. He will be a force to reckon with if he beats out Magister Villanueva for this teaching chair, for the duke has offered him a salary of a thousand ducats a year.

DOÑA ANA. Incredible!

CARLOBAL. It looks promising. The archbishop has admitted him as a candidate. They are preparing for the competition.

DOÑA ANA. Can a black slave be so learned?

CARLOBAL. Why not? Is he not a man? Is his soul less pure or less rational because his skin is black? A man is shaped only by his soul. Color is an accident that does not change it. It is insulting to compare a wise, discreet, virtuous, and devoutly Christian black man to a white man ruled by vice. Our higher faculties are rational, not corporal, and color is an insubstantial thing.

DOÑA ANA. I'm still in awe of his speech at the academy. Tell him I await him here.

CARLOBAL. I believe he is studying what he plans to read at the competition tomorrow, so I don't want to interrupt him right now.

DOÑA ANA. He can come later. Oh, what a good slave!

CARLOBAL. By God, I feel such calm now, knowing your tutor will be a black man. It really eases my mind, for I know he won't attempt anything rash and you won't take a fancy to him. I shall summon him now.

DOÑA ANA. I'll be very grateful.

(Exit CARLOBAL.)

DOÑA ANA. O fearless love, I am the one who refused to subject myself to your care; for of all the arrows you shot at me, none has passed through my clothing. My heart, armor-clad in fire and ice, has resisted your heat and cold; your storied temple has never clothed itself in my robes. Happily do I watch the storm from a place where the ravages of the sea neither reach me nor cause me fright. And happily do you, O love, now that your shots have failed against those who understand your aim, turn to more cowardly targets.

(Enter JUAN LATINO in a robe and felt cap, carrying a book. He pauses in the doorway.)

JUAN LATINO. *[Aside.]*

This has the disaster of Troy written all over it. My feet are frozen in place.

DOÑA ANA. Welcome, darkskin.

JUAN LATINO. Darkskin, yes. Clown, no. The lord doctor has bid me take good care to instruct you . . .

(Aside.)

The words catch in my throat. "In the art of love" is what I should like to say. Shall I bare my soul to her, since the die is cast, and hope for the best?

DOÑA ANA. What gives you pause? Are you upset?

JUAN LATINO. How did you notice, my lady? For though I be upset, my face cannot flush.

DOÑA ANA. Compose yourself.

JUAN LATINO. *(Aside.)*

So serious she is! This does not bode well for my intentions.

DOÑA ANA. Juan, are you a Morisco?

JUAN LATINO. I am black.

DOÑA ANA. You could pass for a bloodletter.

JUAN LATINO. I would gladly be one if I had Cupid's arrows to bleed you with.

DOÑA ANA. You would maim us all. And who would I fall in love with, darkskin, if I were to be bled by one of those arrows?

JUAN LATINO.   With the bloodletter, madam.

DOÑA ANA.   You are amusing. What's in that book?

JUAN LATINO.   Poetry.

DOÑA ANA.   Whose poetry, tutor?

JUAN LATINO.   Mine. For blacks are people too.

DOÑA ANA.   You are a poet?

JUAN LATINO.   Yes, madam.

    (Aside.)

  I can scarcely speak.

DOÑA ANA.   Is there a lady you celebrate in your verse?

JUAN LATINO.   All poets have their muse.

DOÑA ANA.   *[Aside.]*

  So elegantly he speaks!

    [Aloud.]

  Is she very beautiful?

JUAN LATINO.   May my health be as beautiful as she, amen.

DOÑA ANA.   *(Aside.)*

  He woos me: not surprising. A dog tugging at the lady's skirt.

JUAN LATINO.   *(Aside.)*

  She shows no reaction to my wooing. Be steady, my heart.

DOÑA ANA.   *(Aside.)*

  I shall wait and see how this turns out.

    [Aloud.]

  Read something, on my life, for I adore poetry.

JUAN LATINO.   It's not worth anything.

DOÑA ANA.   Don't be silly! Read, unless there be some secret to hide.

JUAN LATINO.   I fear disappointing you, but I shall obey.

    (Reading aloud.)

"Sonnet to a ribbon."

DOÑA ANA.   That's good.

JUAN LATINO.   *(Reading aloud.)*

"Once on Saint John's Eve,
There was a gallant black man—"

DOÑA ANA.   Enough of that. Read something else, darkskin.

JUAN LATINO.   *(Reading aloud.)*

"Song to the knife wounds I received for my lady."

DOÑA ANA.   Did they hurt?

JUAN LATINO.   They did not, nor were they prized by her.

DOÑA ANA.   You must be very valiant.

JUAN LATINO.   Without a doubt, and I fought well, so help me God.

DOÑA ANA.   Not surprising, darkskin, since you have a built-in dog on your side.

JUAN LATINO.   When I bare my teeth, they'll find out if I'm all bark.

DOÑA ANA.   Continue.

JUAN LATINO.   *[Reading aloud.]*

"A dream of love."

DOÑA ANA.   Let's hear that dream, tutor.

JUAN LATINO.   *(Reading aloud.)*

"The cold night bathed me in sad darkness,
The dream in sweet oblivion.
Yet I was not forgetful of you,
Nor did I see the clear light of day.
I dreamt, my Anarda, that I held you close.
Who would doubt it was a dream?
But how quickly I awoke!
For even in dreams you would not be mine.
Yet it thrills me to have known such pleasure,
For though it was but fleeting,
What pleasures in love are permanent?
And thus, as long as the deception lasted,
You were mine, my Anarda: a dream, perhaps,
But what past pleasures were not so?"

DOÑA ANA.   Are you mad? That's what you choose to read to me? What gall! Out of my bedchamber. I don't want you for my tutor. Be thankful I don't have you scalded. Out! I can't believe you read that to me!

JUAN LATINO.   It's what's in the book, madam.

DOÑA ANA.   I've never heard such poetry! But you are right: you shouldn't believe in dreams. Read.

JUAN LATINO.   No need for alarm. Dreams are but dreams.

(Reading aloud.)

"Lyrical musings on fear."

DOÑA ANA.   Why didn't you start with that? Let me see it, and I'll read.

(Reading aloud.)

"Shrunken fear, cowardly fear,
You do well to give fright to the soul
While I boast tearfully of my pain.
He who refuses to admit his illness
Rightfully faces death."

[She points to the page.]

What does this symbol mean?

JUAN LATINO.   That's a musical notation I added to the verses.

DOÑA ANA.   *(Aside.)*

How poorly love hides!

[Aloud.]

I wish to hear you sing.

JUAN LATINO.   I inherited my father's voice. Listen to me bark and you'll judge me a new Orpheus.

DOÑA ANA.   Sing.

JUAN LATINO.   What shall I sing?

DOÑA ANA.   Sing those lyrical musings on fear.

(Aside.)

I must guard my honor carefully, for this is a *negro*.

JUAN LATINO. *(Aside.)*

> Her eyes speak what her lips do not.
>
> *(He strums the vihuela and sings.)*
>
> > ¶Sacred muses of Parnassus,
> > If ever you care to favor me,
> > Let your assistance come today,
> > For I require the gift of sweet poetry.
> > Let me drink from your lofty fount
> > And render my torment into verse.
> > And you, sonorous instrument,
> > Steeped in eternal torment,
> > Turn the muses' indifference into joy.
> > Accompany my sad voice and become
> > The instrument of my happiness.¶

DOÑA ANA.   Step past the doorway and sing.

JUAN LATINO.   That's a fair request, so that I may be heard without being seen.

DOÑA ANA.   Your voice will sound better from far off.

JUAN LATINO.   Juan is obedient.

> *(Exit JUAN LATINO.)*

DOÑA ANA.   How discreetly he woos! Thus does love avenge my disdain.

JUAN LATINO.   *(Singing offstage.)*

> > ¶A meager prize for song
> > Will to Juan Latino go,
> > For though my love be true
> > My voice ringeth faux.¶

DOÑA ANA.   Faux?

JUAN LATINO.   Faux. False. Falsetto. But may love never reward me if there's anything in me that's off besides my voice and color.

DOÑA ANA.   *(She looks at the book and reads aloud.)*

> > "Shrunken fear, tyrannical fear,
> > What purpose does it serve
> > To give fright to the soul
> > While I tearfully boast of pain?

> For since the body dies out,
> It behooves the soul to speak its desire."

[She stops reading. Aside.]

He has adapted all the lyrics to reveal his passion to me. Such ingenuity!

(JUAN LATINO peeks in on DOÑA ANA.)

JUAN LATINO.   Good news: she is not angry.

(He withdraws and sings from an inner stage or offstage.)

> ¶If my ugliness is nature's law,
> My wit can overcome this flaw,
> For the soul erases the body's lack
> And Perseus loved Andromeda black.¶

DOÑA ANA.   The words are aimed at me, to excuse his color. What shall I do? My honor must win out.

JUAN LATINO.   *(He peeks in again.)*

I've made her angry, but I shall continue.

(He withdraws again and sings.)

> ¶Behold the snow-white dove
> That couples with a mate of blue,
> While the bird that glistens black
> Is loved by one of different hue.
> And now, my lady, as for you . . .¶

DOÑA ANA.   That's enough, stop singing. It's no more than silly growling.

(Enter JUAN LATINO.)

JUAN LATINO.   I sang because you bid me sing.

DOÑA ANA.   I asked you, bigmouth, to sing your lyrical musings on fear, not the brazen verses I just heard.

(Aside.)

I'm finished!

JUAN LATINO.   Your offense is misplaced. It is Ovid's work, a letter from Sappho to Phaon.

DOÑA ANA.   So you're telling me Ovid wrote it that way, and you're just translating it for me?

JUAN LATINO. Yes, madam, and by God, it goes like this in Latin:

> Si mihi difficilis formam natura negavit,
> Ingenio formae damna rependo meo.

DOÑA ANA. Fine. Now get out.

JUAN LATINO. I'm going.

DOÑA ANA. Wait, tutor.

JUAN LATINO. What do you bid of me?

DOÑA ANA. Did I call you back?

JUAN LATINO. You did, madam.

DOÑA ANA. I would like a math lesson.

> *(Aside.)*

> What strange attraction is this?

JUAN LATINO. Oh? Another lesson?

> *(Aside.)*

> It's time, then, to talk of love. If she understands my intention, why would she ask me to stay if not to listen to me? A woman is always flattered by someone who loves her, as Martial explains in an epigram: "I wrote to Naevia and she did not respond, therefore she is not interested. Yet I know she read what I wrote, therefore she is interested." Similarly, I spoke to my lady, and though she showed anger, she gives me another opportunity. Therefore she wishes to hear me, which I shall use to my advantage.

(DOÑA ANA sits at a desk with a quill pen in hand, JUAN LATINO right at her side.)

DOÑA ANA. Tell me what to count.

JUAN LATINO. Count my woes, madam, for they are more numerous than the sands.

DOÑA ANA. You must be well-versed in counting them.

JUAN LATINO. On the contrary: such is the suffering in my breast that my heart loves without number, my soul without reason. And because I have always loved thus, I lose count of my affections along with my senses.

DOÑA ANA. Tutor, are you going to teach me?

JUAN LATINO.   Yes, my lady.

DOÑA ANA.   I'm ready.

JUAN LATINO.   *(Aside.)*

She wishes to learn accounting so she can pay me properly.

DOÑA ANA.   I can't understand you, tutor.

[She scribbles.]

Are my numbers good?

JUAN LATINO.   No, I'll show you how to make them better.

(Aside.)

Oh, to touch that hand!

(JUAN LATINO takes Doña Ana's hand and writes on it. [Aside.])

Oh, cruel hand! Oh, beautiful hand!

DOÑA ANA.   What are you doing?

JUAN LATINO.   Writing.

DOÑA ANA.   On my hand?

JUAN LATINO.   It's so fair I took it for paper.

(JUAN LATINO takes Doña Ana's hand, she pushes him away, and he takes it again and places the quill in it.)

This is how you hold the quill.

DOÑA ANA.   You do it well, but I fear you'll stain my hand.

JUAN LATINO.   It's necessary if I am to teach you addition. Six plus three plus five plus four plus nine plus nine equals thirty-six.

DOÑA ANA.   Thirty-six.

[Writing.]

Three . . . six.

(JUAN LATINO takes Doña Ana's hand and places it next to his.)

JUAN LATINO.   Like coal and snow.

DOÑA ANA.   One plus six equals seven, plus three equals ten, plus five equals fifteen.

JUAN LATINO.   This should be a zero.

(JUAN LATINO raises Doña Ana's hand as if to kiss it, but stops and returns it to the paper.)

Add the zero and five, then bring down the one. Fifteen.

BOTH. *(In unison.)*

One plus two equals three, plus four equals seven . . .

(JUAN LATINO kisses Doña Ana's hand.)

. . . plus five equals twelve.

DOÑA ANA. [*Recoiling in shock.*]

What are you doing?

JUAN LATINO. Speeding the count along.

DOÑA ANA. *(Jumping from her seat.)*

Do you want me to throw this desk at you? You cunning dog! You have the gall to kiss my hand? You're a dog.

JUAN LATINO. For God's sake, it was a kiss, not a bite. I am a dog, but blind love, which is responsible for my error, made me a water retriever, not a fiery bloodhound. I am a dog and I am rabid with love, and you are wise enough to know that a rabid dog might attack its owner. But as you understand the nature of my ailment, please forgive my indiscretion. Love this dog, madam, and he will give you loyalty in return.

DOÑA ANA. I should have you beaten! A *negro*, declaring his love to me? It's insufferable! Courtesies and courtship from *you*? Gifts and favors? From this day forward, I'll have you know . . .

(Aside.)

Oh, love, what am I doing?

[*Aloud.*]

. . . that although there are women made of air, I am not one of them. And because it is a mistake to expect a change of heart from me, tell your hope that I am marble, fire, and iron.

(Exit DOÑA ANA.)

JUAN LATINO. You are not marble, for my blemished life leaves no mark on you. Nor are you iron, for the fire you've awakened in my chest does not soften you. Nor are you fire, for the fount of my tears does not extinguish you. Nor are you water, for the breath of my laments does not stir you. Much less are you wind, for your firmness finds no root in such a flighty element. The origin of my torment, instead, is a monster of nature: not wind, but woman.

(Exit JUAN LATINO.)

ACT 2, Scene 4

([Interior of Granada Cathedral.] Enter the ARCHBISHOP; the DUKE; and the HEAD OF CEREMONIES, who carries an hourglass and a staff.)

ARCHBISHOP. What news, sir?

DUKE. A mob of Morisco outlaws, led by the brazen *negro* Cañerí, has brutally tortured and killed all the Christians it could find. They have liberated the traitor Don Fernando from the tower, according to two men who escaped with their lives. On the king's life, I intend to avenge these deaths on the Moriscos I caught the night Don Fernando disrupted my academy.

ARCHBISHOP. It would be wise to arrest the other members of the Válor clan as well: Don Antonio and his son, Don Francisco.

DUKE. They are in custody.

ARCHBISHOP. And what does Secretary Torrijos report?

DUKE. That there is rebellion all across the Alpujarras.

ARCHBISHOP. How does he know?

DUKE. You would have to be blind to miss the signs. The roads are littered with the bodies of those massacred by the Morisco outlaws: faces flayed, noses cut off, their sad hearts ripped out through the back.

ARCHBISHOP. Appalling! Does the Council know about this?

DUKE. His majesty knows, and I believe the Marquis of Mondéjar and his son are on their way to Granada as we speak. And if there is a war, we can count on Don Juan of Austria, who is a great prince even at his young age.

ARCHBISHOP. He takes after his father in valor.

DUKE. The candidates are here.

ARCHBISHOP. Let us sit.

DUKE. I implore your lordship to recognize the justice of my side, for Juan Latino finds a fierce opponent in Villanueva.

ARCHBISHOP. Just as he finds a great sponsor in your excellency.

(Enter, on one side, VILLANUEVA, to cheers from his partisans; and on the other, JUAN LATINO, cheered on by his supporters including CASTLE, DON GONZALO, and CARLOBAL. VILLANUEVA ascends the platform to the teacher's chair and JUAN LATINO sits below. The DUKE and the ARCHBISHOP watch from elevated positions. The HEAD OF CEREMONIES turns over the hourglass.)

[VOICES]. Victory to Magister Villanueva!

[VOICES]. Victory to Magister Juan Latino!

CASTLE. *[To the HEAD OF CEREMONIES.]*

He gave a great speech.

HEAD OF CEREMONIES. Divine. In all my years as Head of Ceremonies, Castle, I've never seen a candidate prepare a speech so quickly.

CASTLE. His intellect is amazing.

HEAD OF CEREMONIES. Now comes the real test: the debate.

CASTLE. My money is on Juan Latino.

HEAD OF CEREMONIES. Anyone with his command of words will hold an advantage in the debate.

CASTLE. His fortune will improve today.

HEAD OF CEREMONIES. His color will not, however.

[VOICES]. Hoorah for Villanueva!

DUKE. Villanueva suffers from arrogance.

HEAD OF CEREMONIES. It's time for the arguments.

VILLANUEVA. It's beyond me how a dog has been admitted to this competition.

HEAD OF CEREMONIES. His lordship the archbishop has ordered that for each word uttered outside the bounds of propriety and courtesy, the speaker shall be fined one gold coin. You have incurred the first penalty.

VILLANUEVA. I shall pay. But this mad dog—

HEAD OF CEREMONIES. That's another gold coin.

VILLANUEVA.   Fine, but an ill-born *negro*—

HEAD OF CEREMONIES.   Another.

VILLANUEVA.   Must we remain mute before such an animal?

HEAD OF CEREMONIES.   Another. You would be wise to silence yourself.

VILLANUEVA.   Fine! I'll advance thirty gold coins in order to speak freely.

(He takes a coin purse from his pocket and gives it to the HEAD OF CEREMONIES.)

Here you are, sir. May I call him a dirty dog now? Keep track of my insults.

[VOICES].   Hoorah for Villanueva!

DUKE.   *[Aside, to the HEAD OF CEREMONIES.]*

Say something. This is ridiculous.

HEAD OF CEREMONIES.   *[Aside, to the DUKE.]*

Let him spend eighty for all I care.

VILLANUEVA.   Setting out to hunt letters, this hound came upon the summit of the mountain where the winged horse called forth the spring that gives light to the blind. Arriving at the waters of Parnassus, rabid with thirst, he saw his own image in them, startling himself at the sight of the dog. This teaching chair is mine by right, today more than ever, and everyone knows that no one is better prepared for it than I. Slaves are not men. They are nothing but inert bodies whose names, works, and dealings have no value. They may not hold public office nor carry out honorable actions. This principle is everything, and therefore it is clear that he may not hold a teaching position. But even if he were allowed to apply, I should be preferred on account of my reputation, knowledge, poverty, and nobility of birth. So denying this slave the appointment does him no injury. His only injury is the envious rage that eats away at him as I name my accomplishments. The Church has endowed this chair, and it is wrong to give it to a slave. He has plenty with what his excellency the duke provides for him. It also offends all sense of decency that a man bought and sold by other men, spawn of a slave mother, should hold a seat of honor in the cathedral's choir. I cite the fable of the man who taught his cat to hold a candle while he prayed: to test what the animal had learned against its instinct, he set a mouse loose on the table, which the cat promptly pounced upon. I submit that this slave falsely wraps himself in clerical garb and will cast aside his holy vestments as soon as he spots a hare in the choir. And though I have much more to say, I've lost track of my arguments and do not wish to start over. If I've exceeded my quota of thirty insults, I'll pay the additional fine.

(VILLANUEVA *descends from the chair, and* JUAN LATINO *takes his place after kissing the duke's hand.*)

JUAN LATINO. *Incipit in nomine Domini sanctissimi.* In God's name.

A VILLANUEVA SUPPORTER. Boo!

JUAN LATINO. God help you.

CASTLE. The jeers at my jet-faced friend are not as bad as I thought they'd be.

JUAN LATINO. I would remind you—

(*Jeers from the crowd. JUAN LATINO is handed a sheet of paper.*)

[VOICES]. Read it! Read it!

JUAN LATINO. (*Reading aloud.*)

"Tell us, if you do not object, what region of the world breeds a people whose men measure a yard apart from eye to eye?"

(*Repeating.*)

A yard apart from eye to eye?

CASTLE. Come on, you can do it!

JUAN LATINO. If judgment doesn't fail me, Granada is home to such men, but they are measured from forehead to behind.

ALL. Bravo, Juan Latino!

JUAN LATINO. My application for this position has been declared preposterous, some sort of madness. Hear now my response. Villanueva is free, and I am a slave, and I am happy to be one. But excluding me is unjust, for it was Heaven that stained my skin with this scorched color. If it was Heaven's wish that I be a slave, I do not rage, for Heaven does not punish he who covets wisdom. Yet I do not envy you,

[*Looking at VILLANUEVA.*]

for I cannot envy one who spurns my God-given wisdom only to take advantage of it. You purchased the right to insult me at will for thirty coins, but surely you recall that Christ, too, was betrayed that way. You call me a hound in the hunt for letters, but God has given me such talent that, in the hunt for those of your breed, I needed no letters to find you. Yes, I saw the spring atop the mount and wet my lips in its liquid element, and it's true I saw the reflection of a dog, but what you saw was an ass. I drank like a hound from that sacred stream, but its waters mixed poorly in your gut, stuffed with the barley that is your natural diet. I seek the stipend offered by the archbishop, which I believe is entirely reasonable, and despite being a slave, I am confident I shall win it. And though a teacher holds a public and highly honorable office, I am worthy of it because it will redound to the public good. How many Roman slaves taught great citizens, noblemen, doctors, teachers, judges, and emperors? And if that is the case, it follows necessarily that I can hold this position, for I am worthy of the honor. There are laws that allow my people to serve as bishops, so I trust that the archbishop, in deciding this case justly, will find no objection to my holding the position. You cite the case of the cat that shows its true nature when a mouse appears. I assure you that my inclinations are incorruptible, even while yours are in doubt. If I were free, I would pounce on the hare like a loyal hound, whereas with a bit of training I'm sure you'd be worshipping the golden calf.

ALL. Bravo, Juan Latino!

(*JUAN LATINO is handed another sheet of paper, amid boos from Villanueva's side.*)

ALL. Read, read!

JUAN LATINO. (*Reading aloud.*)

"If we overstep, forgive our curiosity, but please reply without anger: Why does the dog enter the church?"

[*He reflects before answering.*]

If I enter church, you childish name-callers, as a dog with a public office, I shall fear only the whip of the dogcatcher. Yet you wretches fear the blood of your ancestors, whom God cast from the temple. In conclusion, I am confident that when this competition is justly decided, Juan Latino shall wear the winner's laurel upon his brow.

(*JUAN LATINO steps down from the teacher's chair. Exit [all] amid continued shouts in support of both candidates.*)

ACT 2, Scene 5

(*[A street before the Carlobal home.] Flourish of shawms and drums. Enter DOÑA ANA and JUANA at the window.*)

JUANA. Your brother has thrown Don Martín and Don Diego out of his household.

DOÑA ANA.   *[Aside.]*

What strange fire seizes hold of my frigid breast! O mad jealousy, so vain and cowardly, your malice means you are either foolish or uncouth. You've blinded my brother, who in trying to guard the kitchen, has welcomed the very charcoal that started the fire. Who would believe the harsh truth: That I profess love to a black man? What thing is woman? Woe unto me for thinking that love was not in my fate, for love always wins. And now that it has conquered me, I see it was my fate after all.

[Aloud.]

So they're leaving?

JUANA.   Your brother orders it, so resign yourself to it.

DOÑA ANA.   What about Castle?

JUANA.   What Castle? Destroyed along with the ramparts.

DOÑA ANA.   What will he do?

JUANA.   I imagine he'll serve Juan Latino if he wins the teaching chair. The duke has given him a house where he can tutor students and live at leisure.

DOÑA ANA.   *[Surveying the street.]*

The streets are so empty. There's no one to ask how the competition turned out.

[VOICES].   *(Offstage.)*

Victory to Villanueva!

DOÑA ANA.   Oh, no! That doesn't sound promising.

[VOICES].   *(Offstage.)*

Juan Latino has lost! Victory to Villanueva!

(Enter CASTLE.)

CASTLE.   What more could be expected of a *negro*?

[VOICES].   *(Offstage.)*

Victory, victory! The secretary heads to the cathedral to make the announcement.

CASTLE.   Disastrous.

DOÑA ANA.   What happened?

CASTLE. Juan Latino lost. It was ridiculous to think a dog could stop wagging its tail.

DOÑA ANA. Is the outcome confirmed?

CASTLE. Almost. The secretary is about to certify Villanueva.

JUANA. Funny, the *negro* paled in comparison.

DOÑA ANA. So where is he?

CASTLE. In the Plaza del Carmen, all by himself.

DOÑA ANA. And what about the duke?

CASTLE. Back in his palace, I assume.

DOÑA ANA. And he can't fix it?

CASTLE. How? It was madness to take on a man of such renown.

[VOICES]. *(Offstage.)*

> Victory, victory to Juan Latino!

> *(Offstage, the sound of shawms, excited voices, and celebration.)*

DOÑA ANA. What's going on, Castle?

CASTLE. I have no idea. Don't they say sometimes the secretary tricks the contestants?

> *[Pause.]*

> That must be it! The secretary is headed toward the Plaza del Carmen now!

[VOICES]. *(Offstage.)*

> Victory, victory!

CASTLE. *[Straining to see offstage.]*

> Oh my God! They're carrying him around on their shoulders, crowned in laurel! Goodbye, I'm off to celebrate!

DOÑA ANA. I'm so relieved!

> *(The DUKE and DUCHESS appear at another window.)*

> So does he still belong to our household?

JUANA. The duke and duchess are at their window.

DUCHESS. Did he pass by already?

DUKE. I think he's coming now.

(Enter a group of students carrying JUAN LATINO on their shoulders, crowned in laurel leaves. Others wave swords and bucklers. A crowd forms in the street while flowers rain down from balconies.)

DOÑA ANA. Has there ever been such a black man?

JUANA. Never. He has no peer.

ALL. Victory, victory!

JUAN LATINO. I am embarrassed by such pomp.

CASTLE. Not me! It's time to party!

(Exit [all].)

ACT 3, Scene 1

([A room in the Carlobal home during Don Juan of Austria's entry into Granada. Enter DOÑA ANA and JUANA.] Offstage, sounds of shawms, fireworks, and musket salutes.)

DOÑA ANA. They're giving Don Juan the full military salute.

JUANA. Spectacular.

DOÑA ANA. He's so young.

JUANA. And gallant. A very eligible bachelor.

DOÑA ANA. His entry was something to see.

JUANA. And how serious Juan Latino has become!

DOÑA ANA. Not surprising. He's admired around the world and honored for his wondrous intellect.

JUANA. And guess who's become his page? Yep, Castle.

DOÑA ANA. It's a great honor for him.

JUANA. There's no son of a lord who doesn't go to him now for tutoring. He's surrounded by a thousand students when he leaves the house.

DOÑA ANA. Tell me more. My soul burns with love's sweet fire. Oh, my *negro*!

JUANA. What's wrong?

DOÑA ANA.   My brother has me upset. I'd rather not speak about it.

JUANA.   Cheer up. I want to see the sparkle back in your eyes. Tell me: Why did you ask me to sew up the pocket in your gown yesterday?

DOÑA ANA.   Because, my dear friend, I am resolved to triumph or die. I had you sew it up because love attempts to gain entry to the castle of my honor through that opening.

JUANA.   Explain.

DOÑA ANA.   With great gall Juan Latino attempts to force his hand through it.

JUANA.   He gropes like a blind man.

DOÑA ANA.   He attempts that folly while teaching me numbers.

JUANA.   What won't Juan Latino attempt?

DOÑA ANA.   He's a devil.

JUANA.   Full of temptation, that's for sure. And the doctor thought a black man would resolve his worries! Did all those precautions end up spawning love?

DOÑA ANA.   I'll say. I've almost given in completely.

JUANA.   You won't be able to say "almost" much longer. You speak to him every day. That will break down anyone's resistance.

DOÑA ANA.   That's why I had you sew the pocket shut. Go call him to give me my lesson. I don't care if he's busy.

JUANA.   You want him to come now?

DOÑA ANA.   I want to finish my math lesson.

JUANA.   I bet you'll be unsewing that pocket soon.

(Enter JUAN LATINO in a cape and cassock.)

JUAN LATINO.   They gave me quite the reception!

JUANA.   Look, he saved me the trip.

DOÑA ANA.   (Aside.)

Love, I am resolved to find a way out of this torment.

JUAN LATINO.   My lady Doña Ana, you remain at home on a day like today?

DOÑA ANA.   There's no space left in the crowd to watch the entry.

JUANA.   I leave you, my lady.

(Exit JUANA.)

DOÑA ANA. Did you participate in the festivities, Mr. Tutor?

JUAN LATINO. Does my soul's happiness not show in my eyes?

DOÑA ANA. And how did you find the lord Don Juan?

JUAN LATINO. Very regal. I kissed his hand, and he showed me great favor and courtesy. He has asked me to visit him later this afternoon.

DOÑA ANA. He shows you great honor. God keep him.

JUAN LATINO. He appreciates lettered men in addition to soldiers.

DOÑA ANA. As is fitting.

(Aside.)

What have I gotten myself into?

JUAN LATINO. (Aside.)

How tenderly she looks at me! Either she's gone mad, or she's on fire for me, for love's fever seeks an outlet through trembling lips.

DOÑA ANA. You have been neglectful of my company, tutor.

JUAN LATINO. I have been busy, but I'll be honored to serve you even when I assume my position.

DOÑA ANA. It is greatly appreciated.

JUAN LATINO. (Aside, staring [at Doña Ana's gown].)

What happened to the pocket?

DOÑA ANA. The day is getting away from us. Let's return to the math lesson.

JUAN LATINO. I'm sorry, I should go.

DOÑA ANA. Please don't.

JUAN LATINO. The boys await my tutelage.

DOÑA ANA. You can go to them later, tutor. Let's finish the lesson.

JUAN LATINO. [Aside.]

I can't believe she sewed up the pocket! By God, I can't let this go unpunished.

DOÑA ANA. Teach me to tally.

JUAN LATINO. It's too difficult.

DOÑA ANA.   How so? Do I not learn easily?

JUAN LATINO.   I don't know . . .

DOÑA ANA.   When did I ever make a mistake? Do you think me an imbecile?

JUAN LATINO.   I know what I'm saying. You lack the basic thing needed to learn.

DOÑA ANA.   And what's that?

JUAN LATINO.   An open . . . mind. There's no way you'll learn numbers.

DOÑA ANA.   But why, Mr. Tutor?

JUAN LATINO.   I could teach a rock better than you.

DOÑA ANA.   I will study with great care.

JUAN LATINO.   Impossible. Your mind is . . . sewn shut.

DOÑA ANA.   Sewn shut? What do you mean?

JUAN LATINO.   A mind is a receptacle . . . like a pocket. How can I teach to a pocket that's sewn shut? There's no way in. You'll need to find someone else for your lessons.

   (JUAN LATINO makes a move to leave, but DOÑA ANA grabs him.)

DOÑA ANA.   Wait, tutor!

JUAN LATINO.   I must go.

DOÑA ANA.   Please don't. Come back.

JUAN LATINO.   Release my gown. You'll never see me again.

DOÑA ANA.   *[Crestfallen.]*

You would do that?

JUAN LATINO.   It is my desire. Let me go. You're causing a scene.

   (Enter CARLOBAL.)

CARLOBAL.   What's going on here?

JUAN LATINO.   *[Aside.]*

God help me. The cause is almost lost.

   [To CARLOBAL.]

Sir doctor, my lady Doña Ana is so stubborn that she's embarrassed by her own ignorance. I've come to give her a lesson, and it's as though I never came, for her mind is as closed to learning as a pocket that's been sewn shut. When I pointed this out, she grew so angry that I'm all flustered now. I cannot teach multiplication to a sealed pocket!

CARLOBAL.   I knew my sister would cause a scene like this in order to ask for a new tutor. But by God, I will not allow her to have her way this time. Only you will teach her and enter her bedchamber, at any time you wish. No one else may speak to her. This is my decision, and she will have to abide by it. Her pocket will be open to you and only you.

(Exit CARLOBAL.)

DOÑA ANA.   You have spoken wisely, turning a vice into a virtue.

JUAN LATINO.   If I were truly wise, I would have squelched these feelings and might be free by now. I would not continue to trust in the wings of a blind god only to fall prey to fire and dissolve in tears. Nor would I have been mad enough to aspire to this lofty love, for Juan Latino and his fortune are black indeed.

DOÑA ANA.   Blacker still is my luck! Oh, tutor!

(She gives her hand to JUAN LATINO.)

JUAN LATINO.   Oh, lovely hand!

DOÑA ANA.   Not so loud! My brother will hear!

JUAN LATINO.   Joy is never mute. It bids me shout. Oh, my love! Oh, lovely hand!

DOÑA ANA.   Tutor, my star has triumphed. I will be your wife if you can win your freedom from the duke.

JUAN LATINO.   Do I hear correctly?

DOÑA ANA.   My love should not surprise you, for love is blind.

JUAN LATINO.   How can I respond to such divine favor? Only love could have wrought this miracle. But unlucky fate places a great sadness at the heart of my joy.

DOÑA ANA.   What is it?

JUAN LATINO.   One worse than death. I'm afraid I will not win my freedom.

DOÑA ANA.   Why?

JUAN LATINO.   As my ill fortune would have it, I already asked the duke, and he refused.

DOÑA ANA.   Be more resourceful and you might succeed.

JUAN LATINO.   I will ask the lord Don Juan to intervene on my behalf with his excellency. That is all I can do. Does white snow really wish to be touched by soot?

DOÑA ANA.   Why wouldn't it? Love has bitten my soul.

JUAN LATINO.   You no longer fear my stain?

(JUAN LATINO and DOÑA ANA embrace. Enter CARLOBAL.)

CARLOBAL.   *[To JUAN LATINO.]*

Don Diego awaits you.

JUAN LATINO.   I'm off.

[Exit JUAN LATINO.]

CARLOBAL.   What's going on, sister?

DOÑA ANA.   *(She curtsies to CARLOBAL.)*

I found a way to open the pocket, sir.

(Aside.)

Oh heavens, if he saw us embrace, that's it for me!

CARLOBAL.   *[Aside.]*

Juan Latino in her arms, embracing her tenderly! I can't believe it even though I saw it! That's what I get for staking my honor on the whimsies of a woman! I must cover this up, on account of the duke as well as my honor.

DOÑA ANA.   The doctor is angry?

CARLOBAL.   By God, I shall have to send you to a convent first thing tomorrow. Confound you, sister, and all your talk of pockets!

DOÑA ANA.   Oh, my Juan!

[Exit DOÑA ANA.]

CARLOBAL.   Vile sister!

(Exit CARLOBAL.)

ACT 3, Scene 2

([A room in Don Juan of Austria's lodgings.] Enter DON JUAN OF AUSTRIA, LUIS QUIJADA, and two SOLDIERS.)

QUIJADA.   You were right, your highness, to reject Don Fernando's embassy.

DON JUAN OF AUSTRIA.   What does he write?

QUIJADA.   A thousand haughty threats, demanding the release of his brother and father.

DON JUAN OF AUSTRIA.   What response was made to him?

QUIJADA.   None.

DON JUAN OF AUSTRIA.   Good.

QUIJADA.   Intelligence reports that Ronda and the Alpujarras have joined forces with the black Moor.

DON JUAN OF AUSTRIA.   And Cañerí turns against Don Fernando?

QUIJADA.   Yes, and the reports suggest he will defeat him.

DON JUAN OF AUSTRIA.   How astonishing that there are, at the same time, two renowned black men in Spain: one in letters and another in arms. Tell Captain Mondéjar to lead a thousand troops to the mountains.

QUIJADA.   As you command, your highness.

(Enter a PAGE.)

PAGE.   Sir, the painter is here.

DON JUAN OF AUSTRIA.   Does he bring the portrait?

PAGE.   Painted skillfully onto wood, my lord.

DON JUAN OF AUSTRIA.   Excellent.

PAGE.   Magister Juan Latino also awaits an audience.

DON JUAN OF AUSTRIA.   Luis Quijada, show him in.

(QUIJADA exits to receive JUAN LATINO. [DON JUAN OF AUSTRIA sits, unmindful of the soldiers' conversation.])

SOLDIER 1.   This is quite an honor for a black man.

SOLDIER 2.   He's now a favorite of the prince, who addresses him as an intimate.

SOLDIER 1. As a brother perhaps? Does he offer him a seat?

SOLDIER 2. A back seat.

[SOLDIER 1]. He's in the vestibule now.

SOLDIER 2. By God, he's got an army of attendants! How his fame has grown.

[DON JUAN OF AUSTRIA rises.]

SOLDIER 1. Don Juan rises to greet him. A great honor!

SOLDIER 2. He has earned it.

PAGE. Make way.

(Enter JUAN LATINO [hat in hand], escorted by LUIS QUIJADA.)

JUAN LATINO. Give me your feet to kiss, your highness.

[He kneels.]

DON JUAN OF AUSTRIA. You would ask permission to enter my house, magister? The guards' services won't be needed with such a great friend. You shall have your own key so that you may come and go as you please.

JUAN LATINO. A thousand kisses for your feet, my lord.

DON JUAN OF AUSTRIA. Rise.

JUAN LATINO. *[Rising.]*

Your highness always lifts my lowliness.

DON JUAN OF AUSTRIA. You may return your hat to your head.

JUAN LATINO. Sir?

DON JUAN OF AUSTRIA. You heard me. Return your hat to its place.

JUAN LATINO. Such honor for a black man, sir?

DON JUAN OF AUSTRIA. Yes, for it is the soul that I worship. Pompey the Great visited the philosopher Posidonius in his house; the tyrant Dionysius honored Plato; and Alexander, in his destruction of Thebes, ordered his soldiers to spare Pindar's home and family. So you shouldn't be shocked, magister, that I show appropriate respect to you, for you are the pride of your homeland. Cover your head.

(JUAN LATINO returns his hat to his head.)

PAGE. Remarkable!

DON JUAN OF AUSTRIA.   Call the painter in.

PAGE.   Enter.

[Enter a PAINTER with a portrait cloaked in canvas.]

DON JUAN OF AUSTRIA.   Magister?

JUAN LATINO.   Sir?

DON JUAN OF AUSTRIA.   Your fame will be eternal from this day forward, despite the ravages of time. You may know that my lord the king has a room in his palace filled with portraits of Spain's most illustrious men. In just recognition of your virtue and learning, he requests a portrait of you to hang in the chamber among the great nobles. I had an artist go to your house and paint one.

[To the PAINTER.]

Reveal your work.

[The PAINTER begins to draw back the canvas.]

JUAN LATINO.   That's why your highness had my portrait painted?

DON JUAN OF AUSTRIA.   Yes, magister.

JUAN LATINO.   It astonishes me to imagine his majesty requesting my portrait. Such honor for a lowly black man!

DON JUAN OF AUSTRIA.   You are worthy of a thousand statues. Let's compare the copy with the original.

[They observe the portrait.]

QUIJADA.   Excellent workmanship!

JUAN LATINO.   It's clear the painter has a fondness for shadow.

DON JUAN OF AUSTRIA.   Very clear. And a very good likeness of you. Magister, I'd like your critique of a poem composed in your honor.

JUAN LATINO.   Composed by whom?

DON JUAN OF AUSTRIA.   I wrote it in praise of you.

JUAN LATINO.   Your highness, great lord? What books did this humble slave write to deserve your celebrated quill? In appreciation, I promise your highness I shall borrow fame's pen to record your memorable deeds. In the manner of famous poems of the past, it will bear a title that reflects its illustrious subject. I shall call it *The Austriad* and fill it with just praises of Don Juan of Austria, thus repaying those that your highness composes on the subject of my wretched life.

DON JUAN OF AUSTRIA.   Can Alexander weep again?

JUAN LATINO.   Yes, but he would weep in envy of your highness.

DON JUAN OF AUSTRIA.   Shall I recite the poem?

JUAN LATINO.   Please.

DON JUAN OF AUSTRIA.   *[Reading aloud.]*

> "Son of a slave, I was born in Baena,
> Where I first learned the alphabet.
> I grew up seeking the depths of truth:
> A prize that Heaven bestows on virtue.
> As a result of my labors of love
> I have become Granada's public servant:
> Its Orpheus, Mars, Cicero, and Homer
> In song, in arms, in Latin, in poetry.
> I became a prized professor of Greek,
> An illustrious man by all rights,
> Worthy of a stipend from this town.
> And just as ancient Rome
> Called Emperor Hadrian *the Greek*,
> Noble Spain has dubbed me *the Latin*."

JUAN LATINO.   Silence is all I can manage in reply.

DON JUAN OF AUSTRIA.   My dear Quijada, send the painter away with the portrait, and clear this chamber. Leave us to ourselves.

QUIJADA.   As you wish.

(Exit all but DON JUAN OF AUSTRIA and JUAN LATINO.)

DON JUAN OF AUSTRIA.   Juan Latino?

JUAN LATINO.   How may I serve your highness?

DON JUAN OF AUSTRIA.   Be seated, magister. Be seated.

JUAN LATINO.   The courtesies your highness extends to me go far beyond custom.

DON JUAN OF AUSTRIA.   Nonsense. Virtue and letters are the grandees in my home. Be seated. Do you need anything?

(JUAN LATINO sits.)

Don't hesitate to ask. What are you waiting for? On my brother's life, I came to Granada only to gain your friendship.

JUAN LATINO.   Your highness's words are remarkable. They encourage me to bare my soul.

DON JUAN OF AUSTRIA.   I am an educated man, a Bachelor of Arts. No need to be timid.

JUAN LATINO.   I aspire to be a teacher. Money is not the obstacle. It is liberty: sweet, precious, and beloved.

DON JUAN OF AUSTRIA.   Being a slave keeps you from your goal?

JUAN LATINO.   Yes, sir, for it is shameful and my enemy is powerful.

DON JUAN OF AUSTRIA.   But your virtue is enviable. Who is your enemy?

JUAN LATINO.   Magister Villanueva, whom I just defeated for my teaching chair.

DON JUAN OF AUSTRIA.   Continue.

JUAN LATINO.   Apart from that, a certain lady—noble, modest, and beautiful—has promised herself to me in marriage on the condition that my lord the duke . . .

DON JUAN OF AUSTRIA.   Yes? Why do you tremble?

JUAN LATINO.   . . . grant me my freedom. I beg your highness to . . .

DON JUAN OF AUSTRIA.   Enough, I understand. The point is, you would like to marry?

JUAN LATINO.   Yes, sir.

DON JUAN OF AUSTRIA.   May I know, magister, the name of the lucky lady? Who is she? Do I know her?

JUAN LATINO.   Doña Ana Carlobal.

DON JUAN OF AUSTRIA.   Well do I know of her: a modest and graceful lady. And a relative, I believe, of the Honorable Carlobal, who is a magistrate in this town?

JUAN LATINO.   His sister.

DON JUAN OF AUSTRIA.   His sister?

JUAN LATINO.   Correct. She is also sister to Dr. Carlobal, founder of the famous University of Osuna.

DON JUAN OF AUSTRIA.   And how has it come to marriage?

JUAN LATINO.   In one way or another, sir, love finds a way. I fell in love in Baena, I courted her here in Granada, and my efforts have finally paid off.

DON JUAN OF AUSTRIA.   I will undertake this cause and speak with the duke. But I fear he will not do it.

JUAN LATINO.   Is it not enough for your highness to request it?

DON JUAN OF AUSTRIA.   I don't know, but I can tell you: if I were lucky enough to have you for my slave, and my lord the king . . .

(At the mention of the king, both men remove their hats.)

. . . and the pope were to ask for your freedom, I wouldn't grant it.

JUAN LATINO.   Please do this for me, your highness.

(He kneels.)

DON JUAN OF AUSTRIA.   For God's sake, magister! On your feet. On my soul and my life, if I am unsuccessful with the duke, I will seek an exception for you from the university.

(Marching drums sound. Enter the DUKE and his retinue.)

DUKE.   The drums announce a contingent of Sevillian soldiers headed to the front.

DON JUAN OF AUSTRIA.   Oh, duke, your excellency's arrival is timely.

DUKE.   How may I serve your highness?

DON JUAN OF AUSTRIA.   By giving eternal fame to your house. Juan Latino's freedom is important to him, and as he has requested my support, I would be very pleased if my intervention moved your excellency. Farewell.

(Exit DON JUAN OF AUSTRIA.)

DUKE.   In not awaiting my answer, his highness has shown more wisdom than you have in testing my patience.

JUAN LATINO.   I have angered you?

DUKE.   You have grown tiresome, magister. What need have you for freedom? Did you not win the teaching chair? Are you not respected by all? Are you not in charge of your house, your property, your servants? Have I not given you my word that I will facilitate the conferral of your degree?

JUAN LATINO.   Sir . . .

DUKE.   Not another word. My titles of Duke of Sessa and Count of Cabra are less important to me than having you as my slave. What prince or monarch can claim what I can? My fame will live in you more eternally than in the ancient and awesome deeds of my illustrious grandparents. Do not bring this matter up again. All you need to know is that I do not wish it.

(Exit the DUKE.)

JUAN LATINO.   Oh, my beloved Doña Ana!

(Exit JUAN LATINO.)

ACT 3, Scene 3

([A street before Juan Latino's house.] Enter a rustic coal MERCHANT [blackened with soot].)

MERCHANT.   This must be where he lives, according to the directions I got from the letter writer. But will anyone open at this early hour? I'll have to knock and see.

(He knocks on the door.)

Is anyone there? By God, they must be sound asleep. Whoa!

(Each time he says "Whoa!" he looks offstage where his donkey is understood to be tied up.)

I should just forget about Juan Latino and the person who sent me here. Whoa! I know you're mad. This waiting around is getting to me too. I don't care who this Juan Latino or Juan Porkino is. Whoa, you crazy ass! He could be lord of the Latin language for all I care. Whoa! I'm losing my patience, and I hope to God he speaks to me in my own tongue and not in gobbledy-gook. Whoa! Hey, people! What's going on in there?

(He knocks again.)

They're ignoring me. Whoa! May wolves swallow them whole! Is this whole house empty? Maybe I should knock louder.

(He beats on the door.)

Are you all deaf in there or what the hell? You swimming in so much money it's plugged up your ears?

JUAN LATINO.   *(Offstage.)*

Someone get the door! Castle, do you hear me? What's going on? Who's at the door?

(He pokes his head out of a second-story window, wearing a nightcap.)

MERCHANT.   It's me! Ho ho, look at the little *negro*! Tell me, brother, does the lord Juan Latino live here? Whoa, you blasted ass!

JUAN LATINO.   *(Laughing.)*

This peasant is something else!

MERCHANT.   Does he live here, I say.

JUAN LATINO.   Yes, brother, he lives here.

MERCHANT.   Brother? Good to know! If you're calling me that because of Adam, Mr. *Negro*, remember that Adam was white.

JUAN LATINO.   That's obvious.

MERCHANT.   Is Juan Latino home I say.

JUAN LATINO.   He is.

MERCHANT.   Tell him I wish to speak with him. Go, call him, and bring him here to me.

JUAN LATINO.   What do you wish to say to him? Speak softly.

MERCHANT.   Curse you, just bring him to me!

JUAN LATINO.   Calm down and tell me what matter you wish to discuss with him. Speak, pal.

MERCHANT.   *Pal?* Are you that unmannered? That's how you choose to address me? *Pal?*

JUAN LATINO.   My friend . . .

MERCHANT.   *Pal* from a *negro*! I can't believe this!

JUAN LATINO.   What do you seek?

MERCHANT.   Courtesy, you dog.

JUAN LATINO.   Are you looking for Juan Latino, my good gentleman?

MERCHANT.   That's better.

JUAN LATINO.   Sorry for the offense.

MERCHANT.   Forget about it. Just go call him.

JUAN LATINO.   I'm going.

   (Aside [laughing].)

   My sides are splitting!

MERCHANT.   Hey! Is someone gonna tie up the dog?

   (JUAN LATINO leaves the window. CASTLE and a PAGE appear at the doorway before the MERCHANT.)

CASTLE.   *[Aside, to the PAGE.]*

   This promises to be funny.

PAGE.   *[Aside, to CASTLE.]*

   Hilarious.

CASTLE.   What have we here? An argumentative messenger? *Vis argumentare mecum?*

   (He slaps the MERCHANT.)

PAGE.   Good morning, companion.

   (He slaps the MERCHANT.)

MERCHANT.   Why such harsh treatment for me, my lords?

CASTLE.   Figure it out.

   (He slaps the MERCHANT.)

MERCHANT.   Do you think me Christ that you slap me thus, you Jews? Do you hanker to beat him the way you did on the cross? Still?

PAGE.   *[Aside, to CASTLE, laughing.]*

   That was a good one!

MERCHANT.   Call your lord, brother. Tell him a coal merchant wishes to speak with him and doesn't want to be here all day.

CASTLE.   Are you off your rocker?

MERCHANT.   I'm Beelzebub, Satan, the demon, and the Devil. Are you happy now? For the love of Saint Paul, go call him!

CASTLE.   I'm going, you'll see.

MERCHANT.   Tell him who I am, for God's sake. I can't wait any longer!

   (CASTLE turns to leave, then turns back around.)

CASTLE. I'm going.

MERCHANT. May Barabbas accompany you!

CASTLE. Tell me first, though: How do you understand the words you just used? *Beelzebub, Satan, demon.* Define them for me.

MERCHANT. You're going to need the help of all the demons who tempted Saint Anthony. My patience is running out! Call your lord!

CASTLE. Yep, I'm on it. Oh, shoot, I forgot the best part of what I wanted to say . . .

MERCHANT. For the life of the blessed Apostle, it can wait!

CASTLE. Righto, I'm going.

PAGE. Just one more thing though . . .

MERCHANT. No, not just one more thing!

CASTLE. Hear me out just a second.

MERCHANT. I'm losing my mind here.

PAGE. Let's toss him in a blanket to jiggle his mind back into place.

CASTLE. Good idea! Where's the blanket?

MERCHANT. No, please . . .

(Enter JUAN LATINO, *in a housecoat.*)

JUAN LATINO. What's going on here? Out with it.

MERCHANT. Are you not the *negro* who spoke to me from the window? This is all part of the joke, isn't it, my lords? I get it now. You've dressed this bloke up to play the part and make fun of me. But you won't fool me!

JUAN LATINO. What do you want, my good man? Are you looking for me, friend?

MERCHANT. Haha, your poker faces don't fool me.

JUAN LATINO. What do you want, pal?

MERCHANT. Are we back to *pal* again?

JUAN LATINO. Calm down.

MERCHANT. What a crock of nonsense this is.

CASTLE. Speak politely, or so help me God . . .

JUAN LATINO. Everything's fine, lad.

MERCHANT. Oh, I'm a lad now? A lad? Didn't I warn you, you dirty dog, not to speak to me with such familiarity?

CASTLE. Be advised that you're talking to my lord, Magister Juan Latino.

MERCHANT. Magister Juan Latino? Don't you mean Muppet Juan Latino? Take off that disguise. Your tricks don't fool me. Why so serious? Who are you, anyway? Enough of your joking around, darkskin.

JUAN LATINO. *[To CASTLE.]*

He's in quite the mood.

MERCHANT. How far do you plan to take this, brothers?

(Enter a second PAGE, from the duke.)

PAGE 2. *[To JUAN LATINO.]*

Allow me to kiss your hands.

JUAN LATINO. What news?

PAGE 2. My lord the duke wishes to know when the recognition of your degree will take place.

MERCHANT. *[Dumbfounded.]*

What?

JUAN LATINO. I kiss his excellency's feet . . .

MERCHANT. *[Aside.]*

No way, this must really be the guy.

JUAN LATINO. . . . for his interest. I'm afraid the ceremony can't be today. I will let his excellency know when.

(Exit the second PAGE.)

MERCHANT. *[Aside, trembling in fear.]*

He's going to crucify me. I'm such a jackass.

JUAN LATINO. What do you want, my honorable man?

MERCHANT. I'm as ignorant as my donkey. Forgive me, my lord.

(He kneels.)

JUAN LATINO. Rise and tell me what you came here for.

MERCHANT.   *[Rising.]*

Are you really Juan Latino?

JUAN LATINO.   I am he.

MERCHANT.   I have overstepped. I beg your mercy.

JUAN LATINO.   What can I do for you?

MERCHANT.   My lord, please read this letter.

CASTLE.   Are you a matchmaker, brother? What's all this about letters?

JUAN LATINO.   *(Reading aloud.)*

"Sir, my brother insists that I become a nun, despite my disinclination. Come see me today, at any time. If you have gained your liberty, you can remedy this situation by becoming my husband. This merchant, who furnishes the convent with coal, will show you the way. Disguised as him and his partner, you and Castle can gain entry and see me today. Otherwise, I'm in such a state that you may never see me."

[Aside.]

Oh, Doña Ana, such unhappy fate! Such lost hope! What shall I do if she who gives me life finds herself in the arms of death? The thought tyrannizes me. O odious slavery, what a miraculous opportunity you have stolen from me. My beloved wishes me a free man, not a slave, in order to wed me. I applaud her resolve, but it doesn't mean I can't see her in the meantime.

[To the MERCHANT.]

I need to enter that convent, my friend.

MERCHANT.   Yep, I get it now, and I know the way in. I've taken a liking to you, so I'll help.

JUAN LATINO.   I'll sneak in as a coal merchant.

MERCHANT.   You could pass for the coal.

JUAN LATINO.   Let's go.

CASTLE.   What wondrous twists this story takes. This is my chance to see Juana!

JUAN LATINO.   Oh, my love, my Doña Ana!

MERCHANT.   So this is Juan Latino!

(Exit [all].)

ACT 3, Scene 4

([The courtyard of a convent.] Enter DOÑA ANA and JUANA, modestly dressed.)

JUANA.   So you're going through with this madness?

DOÑA ANA.   I love Juan Latino, and I cannot suffer my brother's mood.

JUANA.   What will the world say about you? Married to a *negro*? A slave?

DOÑA ANA.   Yes, for love is beautiful and unconstrained. If love cared only about bodies and wanted no place in souls, I've no doubt it would choose the king over his lowly oxherd. But because love takes its seat in souls and the latter are equal in essence, love, and quantity, it's quite possible for love to abandon the lord for his slave given that both, in terms of their souls, have the same value.

JUANA.   Oh, madam, this is a grave mistake!

DOÑA ANA.   Mistake? You insult love.

JUANA.   I fear you suffer from the bite of a rabid dog.

DOÑA ANA.   You judge by skin color, ignoring proportion and reason and the effects of love. If Heaven has inclined my will to this object, the more I bend, the more perfect it will be. Because he held me in his arms, everyone denigrates me, tarnishing my reputation on account of his black embraces. But God does not make mistakes to be corrected, Juana, and reason counsels reserving judgment on whether it was love or the vice of my own inclination. For me it was all love: I unleashed it, my trust drives its effects, and my honor stands guard. Love pushes me to offer my hand to this man, for though he is black, he is a man, and in his arms I shall recover all I have lost.

JUANA.   You wouldn't prefer to offer your hand to one of your many other suitors? They've been courting you for so long.

DOÑA ANA.   They've all lost interest. The flame went out in the little duke, who is but a child. Don Diego and Don Martín loved like students. My black lover is the most loyal of all.

JUANA.   True: a mastiff is very loyal. You see how the prayer we recited on Saint John's Eve worked?

DOÑA ANA.   Do you really believe such madness, you silly girl?

JUANA.   Madness you call it?

DOÑA ANA.   Stop this foolishness, Juana. Oh, how my soul aches for the black man!

(Enter JUAN LATINO and CASTLE, disguised as coal merchants.)

JUANA.   The fox has entered the henhouse.

CASTLE.   *(Singing.)*
>¶Black my face, black my heart,
>The fire of love with coal doth start.¶

JUAN LATINO.   Is anyone here?

DOÑA ANA.   Oh, God! Is that my Juan Latino?

JUAN LATINO.   It is I.

DOÑA ANA.   Is the merchant with you?

JUAN LATINO.   He awaits us outside.

(CASTLE begins to chat with JUANA.)

DOÑA ANA.   It is an angel, not a merchant, that has delivered you to my presence. How have you been in my absence?

JUAN LATINO.   Like a man absent from the one he loves, from the glory of his soul, his senses suspended. And fearing you'd forget me, for memory has the frailty of woman.

DOÑA ANA.   Is that what you tell all the girls?

JUAN LATINO.   Of course that's not what I tell them.

DOÑA ANA.   Aha! Traitor! Dog!

JUAN LATINO.   You know that's not what I meant.

DOÑA ANA.   What fortune this moment brings!

(She takes Juan Latino's hand.)

JUAN LATINO.   My love!

CASTLE.   Well, isn't this cozy.

DOÑA ANA.   So you're a coal merchant now, are you?

JUAN LATINO.   Apparently.

DOÑA ANA.   At least the coal won't show on your skin.

JUANA.   And how are you?

CASTLE.   A bit smelly.

JUANA.   That worries you?

CASTLE.   This merchant thing is killing me, Juana. I smell like tar.

DOÑA ANA.   Did you bring the coal?

JUAN LATINO.   Just as you instructed. Though the coal in my heart is already aflame.

DOÑA ANA.   Coals blaze between us, the effects of a blind god. But you put them out.

JUAN LATINO.   Put them out? I don't understand.

DOÑA ANA.   Your slavery puts them out and kills everything.

JUAN LATINO.   Is that my fault?

DOÑA ANA.   Whose would it be otherwise?

JUAN LATINO.   It is Heaven's will.

DOÑA ANA.   Isn't the remedy here on Earth?

JUAN LATINO.   I apologize. I have been unable to find it.

DOÑA ANA.   Why?

JUAN LATINO.   My lord the duke does not wish to free me.

DOÑA ANA.   Then I can't give you what love bids.

JUAN LATINO.   Don't you love me?

DOÑA ANA.   I do.

JUAN LATINO.   How much?

DOÑA ANA.   So much, it borders on adoration.

JUAN LATINO.   Do you feel my pain?

DOÑA ANA.   It drives me to tears and death.

JUAN LATINO.   Tell me: Can the soul be a slave?

DOÑA ANA.   No.

JUAN LATINO.   And the body?

DOÑA ANA.   Yes.

JUAN LATINO.   So if I'm unable to free my body, doesn't my soul still deserve something?

DOÑA ANA.   I want to be mistress of both.

JUAN LATINO.   My body is another's property, but you shall have my soul.

DOÑA ANA.   Your soul is a treasure I adore, which is why it's so troubling to have it locked away in a vault that belongs to another. But I see no other way. Either I die as a nun or I live as your wife. Hear me, friends: I give my hand to Juan Latino as his lawful spouse.

JUAN LATINO.   You are all witnesses that I give her mine as well.

DOÑA ANA.   We just need a judge to confirm our union.

JUAN LATINO.   The day of my happiness has arrived. It is done.

CASTLE.   By God, Juana, since my lord has married Doña Ana, why don't we get hitched as well?

(CASTLE and JUANA take each other's hands.)

JUANA.   You have my hand. And my heart.

CASTLE.   This coal has set everything ablaze.

JUAN LATINO.   It's not pixie dust, that's for sure.

(Exit [all], with CASTLE singing.)

❡Black my face, black my heart,
The fire of love with coal doth start.❡

ACT 3, Scene 5

([A street in the university district.] Enter two STUDENTS.)

STUDENT 1.   Though the uprisings have postponed the conferral of Juan Latino's degree, there is word that the rebellion is now being suppressed, as quickly as *veni, vidi, vici*.

STUDENT 2.   Anything's possible from this new Christian Achilles, Spain's own Scipio, the Marquis of Mondéjar. He'll soon have the Moriscos beneath his boot. Let's be off, then, for the great Spaniard Latino's degree will be awarded now, and we'll witness his wondrous, eclipsed sun come out to shine.

STUDENT 1.   An event well worth witnessing, for he honors us all.

STUDENT 2.   If a black habit can confer honor, Spain is indeed honored.

STUDENT 1. Let's go claim our share of it. We'll watch the starling squawk in cap and gown.

STUDENT 2. Today regal Granada shall recognize that the writings that make it famous originate from a desk of dark wood. Rumor has it that Juan Latino broke Doña Ana out of the convent and a judge signed off on their marriage this morning. Peace will come between him and Dr. Carlobal, who will end up accepting what he cannot change. Don Juan will see to it, for in this he has been counseled by both the duke and the archbishop.

STUDENT 1. An amazing story!

STUDENT 2. Let's be off to watch the magister, then, and make sure we get a good seat.

STUDENT 1. What a fun afternoon we have in store!

(Exit [all].)

ACT 3, Scene 6

([A public square or university quadrangle.] A platform stage and bleachers have been set up, with a special seat for the graduate. Enter the DUCHESS, DOÑA ANA, and JUANA.)

DUCHESS. *(Taking a seat. [To DOÑA ANA.])*

This is going to take a while. You should sit.

DOÑA ANA. It is not proper for your excellency's slave to sit in her presence.

DUCHESS. Though I always abhorred your presumption, my noble heart cannot bear a grudge. So I shall not seek vengeance for your rash conduct, Doña Ana, but rather consider you a sister. I knew about your game with the ribbon, but because you're now the wife of my black friend, and because of who he is, I respect you.

DOÑA ANA. I shall do as your excellency commands.

(She sits.)

DUCHESS. Is your brother angry with you? Does he still speak to you?

DOÑA ANA. Yes, but he is greatly saddened.

DUCHESS.   If he speaks to you, it is because the lord Don Juan and I have both encouraged it.

DOÑA ANA.   God keep your excellency and his highness for me.

DUCHESS.   Patience can calm even the angriest soul.

DOÑA ANA.   Despite everything, my brother is participating in the ceremony. He is Magister Juan Latino's sponsor.

DUCHESS.   Of course he is, for he is most courteous. And I believe this event will be worth watching.

DOÑA ANA.   Indeed. There is to be a lampoon, conducted by Castle.

DUCHESS.   It promises great hilarity. Castle has a caustic wit.

DOÑA ANA.   And to top it off, we are honored by the presence of his highness Don Juan along with my lord the duke and the archbishop.

DUCHESS.   The fame and honest life of the graduate are enough to honor the occasion.

JUANA.   It's starting!

(Enter two mace-bearers; followed by as many doctors as possible as well as lay friars and clerics, all with hoods and tassels; followed by DR. CARLOBAL in a white hood and JUAN LATINO in a blue one, drawn back; followed by the DUKE, the ARCHBISHOP, DON JUAN OF AUSTRIA, and the RECTOR of the university, who wears a gray cassock and red sash; followed by a PAGE with a tray bearing a book and another PAGE with a tray bearing a cap and blue tassel. The procession members enter through a passageway, on either horseback or foot, playing shawms and kettledrums.)

CASTLE.   *(From the pulpit, in histrionic style.)*

O invincible lord, glory of the House of Austria, great defender of the faith, terror of Flanders and France; O most illustrious archbishop, light and splendor of the homeland; O great Duke of Sessa; O knights of Granada; O citizens and townspeople; O beautiful and discreet ladies; O judges of the Audiencia and Chancery Court; O weapons, books, quills, and staffs; O critical busybodies in your stockings and bonnets, and all ye rabble and soulless people in general. Isten-lay to my eech-spay and shut your traps: that means no laughter, joking, or chatter. *Hodie*, i.e., *today* if you don't know your Latin, we are gathered to honor a man . . . but I misspeak: he's more like Aristotle's great shadow, or maybe Plato's shade, or Cicero's cloak of mourning, or that charred statue of Demosthenes that made its way to Spain. Get my drift? I refer of course to Juan Latino, ladies and gentlemen, a man worthy of such high praise that he will no doubt be an inkwell to the pen of fame.

JUAN LATINO. The inkwell begs to be of silver or lead and not of horn, which is black.

(Cheers and applause for JUAN LATINO.)

CASTLE.   *[To the audience.]*

Be silent and listen to me.

[To JUAN LATINO.]

And you, listen to me as well, O *protonegro*, so unique among your kind; O flask of dark wine; O overripe fig; O pinch of stocking dye; O shriveled prune; O Benedictine slipper. Listen to my harangue, for its pearls of wisdom will shine against your chestnut complexion. The Capuchin Scholar, in his wise *Miscellany*, writes that one day Nature entertained several goddesses who were passing through that region. It was a Saturday, and feeling sad that she could not entertain them properly, she began making a tripe, some say even with meat. Thus learned Nature took a long string of intestine and stuffed it with letters, symbols, and all sorts of knowledge: nominatives, gerunds, in short, the sum total of all grammar, theology, and the arts. But she added too much black pepper, and the sausage came out like a dirty tunic. Minerva, goddess of war, seeing that the Duke of Sessa is clearly the king of arms, sent it to his house, where it has hung in the smoker all these years, never receiving its freedom, for some sausages remain slaves. Yet the lord duke, recognizing Juan's talents, provided for his studies, thus transforming a raven into a magnificent eagle. And thus, O great rector of the dashing red sash—though I hear that in Italy the sashes are nicer—I implore you, given all the black caps that adorn white faces, to let Juan place a white cap on his black face. Black over black is neither attractive nor elegant, so a white cap is best.

JUAN LATINO.   You beast! Wait ten years and you'll see how time graces me with a naturally white cap.

(Cheers and applause for JUAN LATINO.)

CASTLE.   Go ahead and applaud—or offer plaudits, if you understand more proper Latin—and listen to all the charming stories that led the Duke of Sessa to seek advanced instruction for Mr. Potato, who, though black, Goddess knows has a little whitey-brighty *animam* (that's Latin, accusative singular, for soul). And indeed, Mr. Juan Latino has a soul like a sword, all sharp and shiny-white, though he keeps it in too dark a sheath. But it bites like a good sword and like the good doggie he is. Anyway, to get back to the charming stories, one day the duke's majordomo held an open table at which a Dominican friar was present. He winked and wiggled his chin at Juan Latino, indicating that he wanted to be served a drink. Juan went to the kitchen and brought back a glass of dark wine, whispering to the friar: "Here it is, my lord." The perplexed friar turned and said, "Here what is?" "The wine," Juan said, pointing to the glass in his hand and adding, "Your reverence winked at me in secret, so I brought the wine in secret. Drink, and I'll hide it again." The second story is that, fleeing from his house on one occasion, he entered the service of an organist as a bellows-blower. He returned to Baena after learning the trade and, in the town square, told many gentlemen that he was an organist of great honor in Cordova. They believed him, and the whole town gathered together on Easter Eve. Juan took a seat at the organ and pronounced loudly, while everyone waited for him to play, "Where's the fellow who plays the keyboard? For I only bellow." In terms of his studies, who can enumerate all his practical jokes, tricks, mockeries, tall tales, and misfortunes? Once a judge appeared in our court, summoned to rectify certain wrongs, and it is said that Juan Latino went to his house one morning and said, "You come to Granada to remedy all that is ugly and poorly crafted. If you'd like to make a name for yourself, start with me, sir, for there is nothing in the whole city uglier or more poorly fashioned than my form, figure, and face." They say that the duke's majordomo wrote a letter to the preceptor of grammar in which he bound Juan to serve him for six years to study sentence parsing. The preceptor was so strict that he beat Juan for the smallest error, turning him even blacker than normal from all the bruises. Juan was angry at his treatment and desirous of vengeance, and as God would have it, one winter they were on their way to the square when the preceptor fell into a ditch and called to Juan for help. At which Juan answered, "I've parsed all the sentences of my contract and don't think they say anything about pulling you out of ditches, so I'll see you back at home." But a few misfortunes also befell Juan, all of which you might like to hear if it weren't getting so late. Once a lady brought him to court arguing he'd stolen her dog, a puny little creature the size of a fist. As the judge was hearing the case, the magister said, "Your Honor, this lady claims I stole a miniature dog from her, but the only dog you'll find in my house is me. Cut a fist-sized slice from me to replace it." And though he seems modest, he is a man who has dealt in love and aspired to the likes of Cleopatra, for he is full of airs and humors and love. Once he was in love with a certain cunning woman, who tricked him into entering her house through a secret door. And when he was inside, he heard the woman's husband speaking, so the poor magister crawled into the fireplace to hide. The husband asked for fire, and a maid brought a candle and match to the hearth. The poor *negro* was still crammed inside, and the maid, seeing his eyes shining like a cat's, thought they were embers. She lit the match and threw it in, and, well, let's just say our gallant *negro* wasn't of any use in his house for weeks. O sausage stuffed with Latin! O wine jug full of dregs! O guard dog of

Apollo and mastiff to the muses. O faithful Labrador who retrieves all the pretty birds shot down by Love. You who equal Diogenes in the subtlety of your replies; you who once told a lady who'd called you night, "Sister, if you'd like a really good night, take me to your house"; you who were once walking between two other men when someone at a window said, "Look, there go the three magi," and when you saw a beautiful lady sitting there, you replied, "Look, there's the beautiful star that guides them"; you who honor Guinea with the laurel you are about to wear . . . may Zape present you with figs, Cape Verde with capers, Mandinga with black pepper, and Timbuktu with yams. No one shall insult you with sneezes, O raven. And not the raven of Noah's ark, for your dark brow comes back crowned in green laurel. O you who earned dinner with our lord Don Juan of Austria and, when he handed you the breast of a fattened chicken, grabbed it between two slices of bread and said, "Black fingers may not touch white flesh"; O you who have made a chessboard of this school and of the holy Church, advancing your black pawn among so many white ones; O you who are known as the Latin *par excellence* and who, because of your fame, enjoy exemption from normal restrictions; O *negro* whitened by learning; O *negro* to whom knowledge has become a slave: may God grant you long life so that you may bring honor to Spain and to all of us: *mihi et vobis et caeteris*. That's Latin for "all of us," you dolts.

(CASTLE steps down from the pulpit.)

DON JUAN OF AUSTRIA.   *[To the ARCHBISHOP.]*

Confer the diploma, your lordship.

ARCHBISHOP.   Sir, your royal presence honors this occasion, not mine.

[To JUAN LATINO.]

By the royal and pontifical authority vested in me, I confer upon you this diploma and, with it, the faculty to teach Aristotle from the chair you have won. In the name of the Father, the Son, and the Holy Spirit, amen.

(Enter an ENSIGN.)

ENSIGN.   *[To DON JUAN OF AUSTRIA.]*

On this happy occasion, which recognizes such a celebrated man, it is fitting that I deliver this news to you, O great offspring of Charles the Fifth. Cañerí has been defeated by the Marquis of Mondéjar. After killing Don Fernando, the barbarian fled to a tower, where his African heart told him there was no escaping our Christian Achilles. He hurled himself onto the rocky cliffs below, where his body was smashed into a thousand bits.

DON JUAN OF AUSTRIA.   For delivering this excellent news, I promote you to the rank of captain and award you this medal.

ENSIGN.   I kiss your royal hands.

DON JUAN OF AUSTRIA.   *[To CARLOBAL.]*

Sir doctor, on my life, let's make peace today with Juan Latino, for he is worthy of being your brother. He is not black but rather a man whom the sun has struck more vigorously than everyone else, for he has spent much time staring at it.

[To the ARCHBISHOP.]

Assist me in this, your lordship.

ARCHBISHOP.   The doctor is surely wise and honorable enough to recognize Juan's merits.

CARLOBAL.   So honorable is the magister that I am unfit to be his slave. Give him your hand, sister, and I shall offer him my embrace.

JUAN LATINO.   Grant me permission, good Duke of Sessa, to embrace him.

DUKE.   I grant you that permission, Juan Latino, along with six thousand ducats.

CARLOBAL.   Here we end this play without the promise of a sequel, for the black man who astonished the world had no second.

The Brave Black Soldier

(El valiente negro en Flandes)

By Andrés de Claramonte y Corroy

Dramatis Personae *in order of appearance*

Juan de Mérida, black servant
Don Agustín de Estrada, Spanish captain
Spanish ensign
Barrientos, Spanish sergeant
Spanish soldiers (nonspeaking)
Doña Leonor de Vargas, Spanish lady
Doña Juana de Vera, a lady, cousin to Doña Leonor
Elvira, servant to Doña Juana
Isabel, servant to Doña Juana
Male servant to Doña Juana
Don Pedro Osorio, Spanish captain
Don Juan, Spanish captain
*The Duke of Alba
Antón, clownish black slave to Doña Leonor
Two Flemish soldiers, captives of Juan de Mérida
Monsieur de Vivanblec ⎫
*Prince William of Orange ⎬ Flemish commanders
Monsieur de Vila ⎪
Monsieur Lanstrec ⎭
Musicians
Don Gómez ⎫
Don Pedro ⎬ Spanish noblemen
Don Martín ⎪
Don Francisco ⎭
Palace guards
*King Philip II
Don Juan de Estrada, elderly father of Don Agustín
Two gentlemen
Servant

*Denotes a historical character included in the Glossary.
Setting: Spain (Mérida and Madrid) and Spanish Flanders, 1569–1570.

ACT 1, Scene 1

([The main square in Mérida. Upstage, Doña Leonor's residence.] Enter the captain DON AGUSTÍN de Estrada, an ENSIGN, the sergeant BARRIENTOS, JUAN DE MÉRIDA [and other soldiers].)

DON AGUSTÍN.   Beware the dog!

JUAN DE MÉRIDA.   Defect does not reside in blood, nor does courage.

ENSIGN.   But it does reside in skin color.

JUAN DE MÉRIDA.   Dark skin does not make one a dog. That word is reserved for Arabs and Turks.

BARRIENTOS.   Tell me then: What is a darkskin? Let's hear it from the source.

JUAN DE MÉRIDA.   What is a darkskin? He is fortune's inkblot, cruelly spilt onto the pages of the world. Yet there is no fault in color itself, for nature is universal and variety makes her beauty greater. Blacks and whites are both children of men, animated by the same essence. Only geography and climate differentiate them. If whites excel over blacks and rule over them, it is the result of misfortune. Whites would be equally lowly and incomplete if they lived subject to the will of blacks. Thus, since we differ only in color and share the same essence, well do we say that, although black, we leave no stain.

BARRIENTOS.   Such philosophical arguments from the black face of a kettle!

JUAN DE MÉRIDA.   The beating sun is the origin of our color.

ENSIGN.   You are all living lumps of coal.

JUAN DE MÉRIDA.   Coal that, when heated properly, produces sparks like lightning. Juan de Mérida is my name, and though I may be a darkskin, I carry the valor of Mérida in me, for it is here I was born. Yes, I am black, but my valor and my martial disposition render my blood of the highest nobility, which accredits my color. It is a cape that delights the soul cloaked in it, for those of highest rank always wear black. Jet adorns the fairest neck, while the ink with which the world communicates is also black. Pitch fashions feet that flee the advances of the sea. Black gunpowder is the soul of empires. Beautiful porphyry is black, as is ebony, which is enriched by the sun. Black is the pantarbe jewel, which protects against the destruction of fire. Even the whale has a glossy black beard that brings honor to the ocean.

BARRIENTOS.   Now let the dirty dog squeeze in its moral: "Such are the virtues of darkness."

JUAN DE MÉRIDA. Such are they.

ENSIGN. Let it speak also of the virtues of soot, which is black.

JUAN DE MÉRIDA. In short, I am black, and my blackness is of such high character that I wish to prove it by serving his majesty on the battlefields of Flanders.

DON AGUSTÍN. That would be unheard of!

ENSIGN. We all know the virtues of black: a vile color in the presence of ivory. Thus in Mérida is this man known as vile. For though it is claimed he is the son of a Spanish nobleman, that is a fiction contradicted by his color.

DON AGUSTÍN. If you desire to be a soldier, why not go to Guinea? If Flanders were Guinea, I would give you the position you desire. And take not another step toward this guardhouse or I'll pummel you with the hilt of this jineta sword.

JUAN DE MÉRIDA. This black man has never suffered a drubbing from anyone, for unless it were the king himself doing the beating, I'd kill him.

BARRIENTOS. You dog!

JUAN DE MÉRIDA. I am a black man of honorable intentions, and you lie if you imagine otherwise. Don't you know chickens are plumed in white as well?

(He draws his sword and lunges at them.)

A few good slashes from the sword of this black man are worth more than an army of white men, if this is how white men fight.

DON AGUSTÍN. The guardhouse will not be disturbed by a dog of such ilk! Seize him and garrote him!

JUAN DE MÉRIDA. I shall retreat into this house and leave you and your company to serve the king, though if this is how you fight I should just dispatch you now.

(Exit JUAN DE MÉRIDA.)

DON AGUSTÍN. Follow him.

BARRIENTOS. Sir, this home belongs to the finest of your land.

DON AGUSTÍN. I don't care if it belongs to the king himself. Follow him!

([Exit BARRIENTOS, the ENSIGN, and soldiers.] Enter DOÑA LEONOR.)

DOÑA LEONOR. Who dares pierce the peace and quiet of my home with clanging swords, bringing his weapons to my doorstep like a god of war?

DON AGUSTÍN. He who came chasing after night to find, in the arms of dawn, a sun that blinds me, a planet that scorches me. My soldiers chase after a shadow that will be impossible to find amid all the snow and pearly white. A reckless *negro* has injured several soldiers of the guardhouse, an outrage and offense to his holy majesty, whose flag proclaims his supremacy. The fugitive has escaped into your heaven.

DOÑA LEONOR.   If my house is akin to Heaven, how is it that Heaven is so defiled? Heaven's entrance is gained through good works, not evil ones, for it is all peace and glory, just as Hell is all war and weapons. Stay your hand and recall your soldiers immediately, or my honor, which guards my house like an archangel, will cast them into the abyss.

DON AGUSTÍN.   I praise the uncouth black man a thousand times, for his night has delivered me to such a brilliant day. With beautiful and flattering words have the people often praised the fame of this sun, chased by lilies of the dawn, but until seeing you with my own eyes, my soul was unconvinced.

DOÑA LEONOR.   Such lies from a uniformed soldier?

DON AGUSTÍN.   My words are proved by their obvious truth. The angels that praise your beauty are more numerous than the stars.

(Enter BARRIENTOS, the ENSIGN, and soldiers with JUAN DE MÉRIDA, disarmed.)

ENSIGN.   Beware the dog.

JUAN DE MÉRIDA.   Had I not been stripped of my sword, no one would have caught me.

DON AGUSTÍN.   Enough. Have him garroted immediately.

JUAN DE MÉRIDA.   Thus do my honorable intentions come to an end.

DON AGUSTÍN.   Take him away.

JUAN DE MÉRIDA.   Madam!

DOÑA LEONOR.   Wait! Are you not little Juan, son of the slave Catalina who belongs to my cousin Doña Juana de Vera?

JUAN DE MÉRIDA.   Madam, my mother is known as Catalina Darkskin.

ENSIGN.   That pretty black face, celebrated throughout Extremadura, belongs to his mother?

DOÑA LEONOR.   Well, if feminine privileges are worth anything, let mine argue for mercy on this man's behalf since he appeals to my clemency, and I shall remain eternally grateful for your kindness.

DON AGUSTÍN.   If this is the path to the favor I hope to gain from you, I would be foolish to ignore it. The *negro* shall have his life on your account.

BARRIENTOS.   But he injured four of your soldiers!

DON AGUSTÍN.   Even if he'd killed them, the beauty that bids him go free must be obeyed.

DOÑA LEONOR.   I am grateful for the favor.

BARRIENTOS.   Is the dog to be set free just like that? By God!

JUAN DE MÉRIDA.   That's enough, Mr. Sergeant.

BARRIENTOS.   If I ever catch you on the battlefield, you dog . . .

JUAN DE MÉRIDA.   I've seen a few soldiers turn tail in terror from a black man on the battlefield.

BARRIENTOS.   You should thank the one who has rescued you from death.

JUAN DE MÉRIDA.   I shall always be a loyal canine at her feet.

BARRIENTOS.   Many canines bark, then bite their owners.

JUAN DE MÉRIDA.   A canine bites when it is rabid.

DOÑA LEONOR.   Juan, you owe me your life.

JUAN DE MÉRIDA.   How am I to repay you when I am but a poor black man? But if good works can pay the debt of gratitude, I shall use this life you have given me toward whatever cause you desire, for some day this black man aspires to be a beauty mark on the white cheek of Spain.

DON AGUSTÍN.   *[To the ENSIGN.]*

Go settle the onlookers down.

[Exit the ENSIGN.]

DOÑA LEONOR.   *[To JUAN DE MÉRIDA.]*

And you may leave through the back gate of that garden.

JUAN DE MÉRIDA.   Through it I shall exit, not for fear of soldiers but in obedience to you.

BARRIENTOS.   Such strange arrogance from a darkskin!

JUAN DE MÉRIDA.   Call it bravery, not arrogance.

(*Exit [all but DOÑA LEONOR and DON AGUSTÍN].*)

DOÑA LEONOR.   I've heard amazing things about this black man from my cousin Doña Juana.

DON AGUSTÍN.   He came to ask for a place in my army.

DOÑA LEONOR.   He's certainly sure of himself.

DON AGUSTÍN.   He lacks only the right color to be a knight.

DOÑA LEONOR.   Since in restoring his life you leave me indebted to you, please allow me to go and I shall remain so.

DON AGUSTÍN.   In your absence I would be like the world without the sun, stuck in dismal shadow. And since love has given me this opportunity, wasting it would offend his arrows and insult his wings. Ever since the emerald spring of manhood etched my chin in blond, my inclination to war has kept me away from my country. I have marched to the drums of war in Naples and Milan, and now I have the honor of following the Duke of Alba to Flanders. Preparing to embark, he is now in Lisbon, to which my company marches in careful step and where I go like a man without a soul, for in a matter of minutes love has made irrelevant the glory of my deeds. Yet if you will promise to reward my hope, I will trade the harsh discipline I have followed for love's supple delights, for there are no bloodier battles than the war waged in those eyes. Only you can bend my will; only your splendor can change the course of my life and play phoenix to my soul. My divine Doña Leonor, I am Don Agustín de Estrada . . .

DOÑA LEONOR.   Your name rings familiar in my memory.

DON AGUSTÍN.   . . . to whom you were promised in marriage by your father and my lord, Don Juan de Vargas, who now rests in a better place. My father was delighted at the arrangement, but I did not pay his letters proper heed at the time, for I imagined you more noble than beautiful, much to my misfortune. And now that my eyes, madam, reveal the truth in your presence, they weep over my punishment and their deprivation. I am he who rejected you without meeting you, and now my insult awaits your rebuff, my love your vengeance. I offer myself to your harshest judgment, if harshness can reside in such beauty, though it's true that beauty has always been ungrateful. What absence once destroyed, let love now restore: let war turn to peace, if love rests in peace. I offer you six thousand ducats of income once our houses are joined, in addition to the two thousand you stand to inherit. I renounce my commission and place its insignia at your feet.

   [DON AGUSTÍN places his jineta sword at Doña Leonor's feet.]

Honor my gesture, Leonor, for you are now captain of my soul.

DOÑA LEONOR. Love is phlegmatic and does not aspire to the urgency of Mars, especially when he departs for Flanders so flush with aggression. Love demands a slow pace, even more so when requited.

DON AGUSTÍN. Love is my general as long as you inspire and command me. Flanders has been replaced by the celestial vision in front of me, its rebellious land by Mérida. I am a soldier of love.

DOÑA LEONOR. Courtship is required, for honor's fortress must be impregnable.

DON AGUSTÍN. All my intentions are honorable.

DOÑA LEONOR. When was love ever chaste? It is violent.

DON AGUSTÍN. Today violence is honor, for I aspire to marriage. This has been an unexpected turn of events, but love will make it lucky if I win you as my wife.

DOÑA LEONOR. I will agree to that, sir, if I can be assured that you will remain in Mérida. But if you march off to Flanders, how could it ever come to pass?

DON AGUSTÍN. So you'll believe me, if you agree to be my wife, bring me a sheet of paper right now and I'll happily grant whatever love requires.

DOÑA LEONOR. What a cruel choice I face!

DON AGUSTÍN. I aim to recover what I lost through absence. I will not leave your side unless you promise me your hand in marriage.

DOÑA LEONOR. You have my hand, my soul, and my consent as long as you remain in Mérida.

DON AGUSTÍN. I am a rock.

DOÑA LEONOR. *(Aside.)*

Oh, love, how quickly I am conquered!

[To DON AGUSTÍN.]

You may visit me tonight if you promise on paper what you have said.

DON AGUSTÍN. Your beauty ensures my loyalty.

DOÑA LEONOR. My servants call. Farewell.

DON AGUSTÍN. And all this I owe to a *negro*.

DOÑA LEONOR. My luck has taken a fortunate turn.

(Exit [all].)

ACT 1, Scene 2

([Doña Juana's residence in Mérida.] Enter DOÑA JUANA and JUAN DE MÉRIDA.)

DOÑA JUANA.   These quarrels and excesses of yours can no longer be tolerated, you crazy *negro*.

JUAN DE MÉRIDA.   Nor can I live in Mérida any longer, given who I am.

DOÑA JUANA.   Stop your silly growling.

JUAN DE MÉRIDA.   To choler and rage am I provoked when I contemplate, in my lowliness, thoughts worthy of eternal fame despite the color that defames me. To live in a world where blackness is infamy! Are blacks not men by chance? Is their soul more base, clumsy, or ugly? Is that the reason for their poor renown? What makes Spain any better than Guinea? And by what right, when blacks acquire honor and fame, do whites wish to knock them down?

DOÑA JUANA.   Instead of stirring up soldiers and citizens, a dog should content itself with carrying water all day.

JUAN DE MÉRIDA.   Such menial labor? Am I nothing more than a water boy? I'd rather endure the vilest humiliations.

DOÑA JUANA.   Such flights of fancy you have.

JUAN DE MÉRIDA.   Consider that my valor is yours, for I am a dog of your house, madam, and I wish to go forth to conquer the globe.

DOÑA JUANA.   And go forth you may, for my father grows weary of your mischief.

JUAN DE MÉRIDA.   Heaven has a hand in my behavior; do not fret if it seems madness to you. It behooves me to take quick leave of this land, where I live at the mercy of fools. Give me license to turn the coal discarded from your house into a torch.

   [Pause.]

Content and prosperous I depart with this letter, for it attests to my freedom. I shall use it to rebrand the vile rebus of fate and bring an end to the infamy of color. My valor I shall represent to the world, for though I am black, I have not known slavery, and the sun in the sky is a liar if it thinks otherwise. Madam, please continue to show kindness to my mother, Catalina, and I beg your father and my lord to forgive me, for my presence in his house brought him no advantage. And when I return wealthy and satisfied by fortune, I shall repay the favor that I do not speak of today, and he shall find in me a loyal slave.

DOÑA JUANA. Such eloquent madness!

(Exit DOÑA JUANA.)

JUAN DE MÉRIDA. If I can't change my color, I shall change my fortune. I'll journey to Lisbon and stow away with the Duke of Alba, hoping to illumine myself in his glorious dawn. If I am frightful, if I am night, the color that disgraces me today shall make me resplendent tomorrow, for triumphant virtue is a heavenly liquor that pays no heed to the material of the vessel.

(Exit JUAN DE MÉRIDA.)

ACT 1, Scene 3

([Doña Leonor's residence in Mérida.] Enter ELVIRA and ISABEL along with a male SERVANT.)

ELVIRA. What's the story?

SERVANT. I saw him leaving with his troops just as the sun was rising, ruby red in the arms of dawn.

ISABEL. It must've been his ensign.

SERVANT. I'm telling you: I saw him, and he spoke to me.

ELVIRA. So much for the faithful suitor. For love, in order to trample appetite, hardens the heart when the soul wells in the eyes.

SERVANT. My lady approaches.

ISABEL. Go.

[Exit the SERVANT.]

ELVIRA. Who will give her the news?

ISABEL. He will, for she will note his absence in her heart.

ELVIRA. How well he fulfills what he promised in writing.

ISABEL. If the letter was the foundation of his love, Elvira, it is gone with the wind, for his commitment has evaporated. But let's withdraw, and I'll find an artful way to reveal this news to her.

(Exit ELVIRA and ISABEL. Enter DOÑA LEONOR.)

DOÑA LEONOR. I gather the troops have left Mérida, for I just heard the grating echoes of their departure, enough to wake the sun as it slumbered among roses and lilies. Now I shall have Don Agustín's full attention, for those he entrusted to his ensign have marched off, and I shall be the harsh captain. Sudden love is always glorious in a defeated soldier. I'm still treasuring the tenderness and favors I enjoyed last night.

ELVIRA. *(Singing [offstage].)*

¶A soldier's love
Is ever fleeting.
At the sound of drums
He'll be retreating.¶

DOÑA LEONOR. Good heavens! What a fright those lyrics stir in me, for it's true that a soldier's love is never constant. He falls in love in an hour, his affection lasts an hour, and thus the security of his love lasts no more than an hour. And though he betters himself through love, its brief duration means the passion ends at the sound of the drums. But these are silly thoughts, for it's delusional to think my love would have departed without so much as a "Farewell, madam." But this grating song has not been sung by coincidence. I shall get to the bottom of the mystery.

[Enter ELVIRA.]

What's the meaning of this, Elvira?

ELVIRA. It was a way of telling you in song what I can't in speech.

DOÑA LEONOR. I can't listen anymore, for the mad lyrics speak my madness, now punished with betrayal. You are a harbinger of misfortune, revealing through song that Don Agustín is but a soldier after all.

ELVIRA. The ungrateful owner of your love has slipped away into dawn's canvas, aided by the shadows of a poorly sketched day. As the drums fell silent he was seen holding a garter, surrounded by his troops, beating a chaotic retreat.

DOÑA LEONOR. Say no more; leave me. For in such horrible misfortune, imagination is enough and the truth is too much.

[Exit ELVIRA.]

What madness is this? I can't think straight. Shall I shout to the stars, since they match my griefs in number? Oh, treacherous captain, soldier of my dishonor! But *sol-dier* is the wrong word for you. You are the opposite of anything *sol-ar*, for you flee like a coward into darkest night. Let this offense be made public, not only in Mérida but throughout Spain, so that ingrates everywhere may see themselves in it. I shall inform his father as well as my relatives, so that by my death they may put an end to this affront and restore their honor. Oh, *negro*, vile cause of this frightful tragedy, you are a stain on my purity, a shadow on my virtue!

(*DOÑA LEONOR takes out a letter [from DON AGUSTÍN].*)

Oh, treacherous epistle and boundless sea of flatteries, full of lies and scant on truth! You deserve to be torn to shreds, with vipers and asps spitting on your flowered words.

[*Pause.*]

Yet you are key to the vengeance my offenses compel me to seek, so I must keep you close to my breast. I shall follow him from Lisbon, braving the ocean's churning abyss and sapphire crests. My purity shall pursue its lost honor, though it runs the risk of besmirching my name and ruining my reputation. Without anyone knowing, I shall change my clothes and form. Driven by my foolish hopes, I shall become a man. The jewels I thought would be the foundation of my marriage shall accompany me as funeral pomp. Flanders, I come to your icy land, which I hope will save me from this conflagration, if injustice can be remedied with ice. Heavens, supply me with lightning; serpents, lend me your poison; wild beasts, fill me with your cruelty. A man has taken advantage of me, yet rather than complain I recognize my guilt, for I gave my heart to a soldier with little forethought. Let it be proclaimed in plaques, books, chronicles, and a thousand tragic tales to be lamented worldwide:

> A soldier's love
> Is ever fleeting.
> At the sound of drums
> He'll be retreating.

(*Exit.*)

ACT 1, Scene 4

([The Spanish encampment in Flanders.] Drums sound. Enter the captains [DON PEDRO OSORIO and DON JUAN].)

DON PEDRO OSORIO.   A successful voyage.

DON JUAN.   The ships sailed like comets.

DON PEDRO OSORIO.   The duke is responsible for the calm passage, for he keeps the furies of the sea in check.

DON JUAN.   With the wind at our back, the fortunate crew reached the icy coast of Flanders in a week.

DON PEDRO OSORIO.   He's a second Caesar.

DON JUAN.   A second Alexander if the earth were bigger.

DON PEDRO OSORIO.   The country has welcomed him with open arms.

DON JUAN.   The silver of his venerable beard causes fear in some and respect in others.

DON PEDRO OSORIO.   He is relentless.

DON JUAN.   A true lord.

DON PEDRO OSORIO.   Worthy of love.

DON JUAN.   The Prince of Orange, learning of the duke's arrival, curses his miserable fate. But what's this?

DON PEDRO OSORIO.   The duke's guard escort him into camp.

DON JUAN.   His virtues promise us great glory.

(Drums sound. Enter soldiers and the sergeant BARRIENTOS, pushing JUAN DE MÉRIDA ahead of him.)

BARRIENTOS.   I warned you once that this is a company of free white soldiers, not a place for *negros* or slaves. Be gone, and don't try to slip your way into the ranks when we start marching or you'll pay dearly.

JUAN DE MÉRIDA.   Is it so base to be black? Does my face's unfortunate color rub off on you?

BARRIENTOS.   Like smoke.

JUAN DE MÉRIDA.   Well, it rises to my nostrils now, and I swear—

BARRIENTOS. Does the dirty dog wish me to break my halberd across its back?

JUAN DE MÉRIDA. Easy, Mr. Sergeant.

BARRIENTOS. If I raise this halberd . . .

JUAN DE MÉRIDA. You'll be forced to lower it again.

BARRIENTOS. Does the dog know this is the parade ground before the duke's palace?

JUAN DE MÉRIDA. And if instead of here we were in Mérida right now, you'd be two steps from Hell.

BARRIENTOS. Easy, *negro*.

JUAN DE MÉRIDA. Easy, paleface.

DON PEDRO OSORIO. Darkskin, show some respect to the man you're speaking with. He commands these regiments.

JUAN DE MÉRIDA. I do respect him, and I show him the decorum his halberd deserves. It is he who has determined to be my enemy, and I make a bad enemy.

DON JUAN. Listen to the gall of this *negro*!

DON PEDRO OSORIO. I grow tired of hearing him. Beware the dog.

DON JUAN. Beware the *negro*.

JUAN DE MÉRIDA. It would be worse to be whiter.

DON JUAN. If you say so. Soldiers . . .

(Drums sound.)

Formation!

(Exit [all but JUAN DE MÉRIDA].)

JUAN DE MÉRIDA. So this is what it means to be black? These are the consequences of color? I hold all who made me black responsible for this injustice: fortune, time, Heaven itself. Oh, what a burden color is when no one pays attention to souls. I'm losing my mind. What shall I do in my desperation? Serve the king by myself, a one-man company, rash and unbreakable? But I see the Duke of Alba approaching in a gallant squadron. I should withdraw. Oh, heavens, that blackness should be so shameful! But wait: If I have come to Flanders to serve, what am I waiting for? I shall speak with him and share my honorable intentions, which he may appreciate even if he shows contempt for my color. It looks like he's reading a letter. I'll need to step in front of him.

(Enter the entire company along with the DUKE of Alba, armed and reading a letter.)

    May I speak with your excellency?

DON AGUSTÍN.   Keep your distance.

JUAN DE MÉRIDA.   I do so.

DON AGUSTÍN.   This *negro* stalks me.

JUAN DE MÉRIDA.   Great duke, most honorable bulwark of the army!

    (He kneels.)

DON JUAN.   Shut your mouth, darkskin.

JUAN DE MÉRIDA.   I'm not speaking to you.

    [To the DUKE.]

Alba: dawn. Such a fitting name, for your sun dawns gloriously over two hemispheres.

DON PEDRO OSORIO.   Go away.

JUAN DE MÉRIDA.   Duke, sir, I seize your arm, great lord, so you'll hear me out.

DON AGUSTÍN.   Away with you, dog.

DUKE.   Let him speak.

JUAN DE MÉRIDA.   Pardon my boldness.

DUKE.   Courteous boldness grants its own pardon. What seek you?

JUAN DE MÉRIDA.   I shake not out of fear but respect, for my black night finds itself in the presence of Alba's dawn, which it venerates with pale shadows.

DUKE.   The black man's confidence astonishes and astounds.

BARRIENTOS.   The Council awaits.

DUKE.   *[To JUAN DE MÉRIDA.]*

You may speak to me at greater length later.

JUAN DE MÉRIDA.   I shall not depart your side or they will slice me to bits.

DON JUAN.   You are without shame!

DON PEDRO OSORIO.   Away with you.

DON AGUSTÍN.   You heard him, dog.

DUKE. Let him speak.

JUAN DE MÉRIDA. I have come to these lands, sir, with a desire to serve his majesty of Spain, but when I seek a position I am rejected for being black and lowly. And thus, to prove the worth of my color, I come to beg your excellency to allow me to capture an enemy soldier and provision myself with his weapons and gear, for I wish to earn it by my own hand and not at royal expense. To the king I shall prove my blackness with deeds, not flattering words. And if my color be seen as an impediment, then let the magi vouch for me, for one of them was black.

DUKE. Color comes from Earth, courage from Heaven: honor it, for a mole on a beautiful face tends to enhance it. Bring me a spy from the enemy ranks, and be advised that our honor depends on the mission I charge you with.

JUAN DE MÉRIDA. I throw myself at your feet.

DON JUAN. Great lord, this is an insult to the rest of us.

DON PEDRO OSORIO. With so many able captains to spare, you would entrust a task of such importance to a *negro*?

DON AGUSTÍN. Consider that it requires greater care, courage, and character.

DUKE. Then I charge it to you, Don Agustín. Bring me back an enemy spy.

DON AGUSTÍN. I'll raze the entire enemy camp if necessary.

DUKE. *[To JUAN DE MÉRIDA.]*

Find something to distinguish yourself at if you wish to prove the worth of your color. For then, as I am dawn, I shall pull you from your shadows.

(Exit all but JUAN DE MÉRIDA.)

JUAN DE MÉRIDA. What terrible luck! To come so close, like Tantalus with food and drink before his lips! All because of this enemy who torments me, this ungrateful Don Agustín! By God, I'm ready to murder him. But wait: What better opportunity to have my vengeance than the one in front of me? I'll follow him on his mission and see that he returns kicking and screaming, without the spy and deprived of his honor. I'll wear a mask as a precaution. I'm off then. O night, as we are brothers in color and shadow, I offer you my jet so that whites may understand: though we are black, we leave no stain.

(Exit JUAN DE MÉRIDA.)

ACT 1, Scene 5

([A battlefield in Flanders.] Enter the captain DON AGUSTÍN, dressed in the Teutonic style, a ribbon about his collar.)

DON AGUSTÍN. In enemy dress do I carry out this rash mission: a perverse promise and result of the envy that eats away at my breast. Envy of a *negro*! The night is gloomy, the bogs and ditches limitless, the errand fearsome. And to punish my wrongs, Heaven unleashes torrents of crystalline snow across the fields. But since my Flemish disguise protects me, I'll walk along this levee. May fortune send me some spy or sentinel who, to shelter himself from the snow, seeks shadowy refuge beneath a pearl-white tree.

(Enter JUAN DE MÉRIDA, wearing his mask.)

JUAN DE MÉRIDA. Despite my rush, I was unable to overtake him. Just my luck!

DON AGUSTÍN. I hear a soldier. Whether spy or sentinel, it's a fortunate turn of events.

JUAN DE MÉRIDA. I hear steps. Who goes there?

DON AGUSTÍN. A friend.

JUAN DE MÉRIDA. You shall die if you don't give me your name.

(Aside.)

It's Don Agustín. I can't believe my luck!

[Aloud.]

Speak without fear.

DON AGUSTÍN. Fear? I?

JUAN DE MÉRIDA. State your name or you'll not be safe from death.

DON AGUSTÍN. Saint Maurice!

JUAN DE MÉRIDA. Nonsense. Death to the liar.

DON AGUSTÍN. I am a soldier of the Prince of Orange.

JUAN DE MÉRIDA. Another lie. You are an effeminate coward and a barbaric Spaniard. Keep your hands off me, for I am a spy who has wandered from camp.

DON AGUSTÍN. I'm here to kill you or take you prisoner.

JUAN DE MÉRIDA. You can do both, but be advised that my spirit is immortal.

DON AGUSTÍN.   Your boldness is proof of that. Are you a man?

JUAN DE MÉRIDA.   A man and a demon. And more demonic if I take off my primary face.

(They fight.)

DON AGUSTÍN.   Stop! I give up.

JUAN DE MÉRIDA.   Who are you?

DON AGUSTÍN.   A Spanish captain.

JUAN DE MÉRIDA.   Gallant and brave?

DON AGUSTÍN.   At times.

JUAN DE MÉRIDA.   I'm delighted to see you at my feet, vile captain.

DON AGUSTÍN.   Who are you?

JUAN DE MÉRIDA.   A German who two hours ago was black . . . because this mission was black: an uncertain and aimless endeavor. Yet inkblots tend to sully the whitest of paper, and now one has sullied you. In such a short span of time, I have become whiter than snow and you, blacker than pitch. I could kill you here and now, but I decline, seeing how your fate has blackened while my luck has whitened.

DON AGUSTÍN.   Such is war.

JUAN DE MÉRIDA.   And I shall wage mine without capturing or killing you. But I need something from you as a spoil. What can you give me?

DON AGUSTÍN.   This ribbon.

JUAN DE MÉRIDA.   That's what I want.

(He takes Don Agustín's ribbon.)

Go in peace.

DON AGUSTÍN.   You are a gentleman.

JUAN DE MÉRIDA.   Courage animates my flesh. Because you beg for mercy, I set you free. But watch out, for I am a man of two faces.

DON AGUSTÍN.   You do me honor with the face you wear now.

JUAN DE MÉRIDA.   *[Aside.]*

I know you will lose yours when you see my other one.

DON AGUSTÍN. *(Aside.)*
I am humiliated and without honor. What excuse shall I give the duke?

JUAN DE MÉRIDA. Yours was all arrogance.

DON AGUSTÍN. I am your slave.

(Exit DON AGUSTÍN.)

JUAN DE MÉRIDA. Fortune has begun to favor me, fear to abandon me. I no longer need my mask. Away with you, mask, for immortality beckons.

(He removes his mask.)

Black I shall be from fame, which gives me this opportunity. Divine dawn approaches in purple and pink, giggling as it imagines my plan. I shall wreak havoc on the enemy camp and bring its sentinels with me to the duke. Allow me, fortune, to restore my honor with this maneuver. Having made me black, you must correct the imperfection.

(Exit JUAN DE MÉRIDA.)

ACT 1, Scene 6

([The Spanish encampment.] Enter DOÑA LEONOR, disguised as a male page, and her black slave ANTÓN.)

ANTÓN. All ma'am twere commanding, Antón twere doing. Slaves twere good at quiet keeping.

DOÑA LEONOR. I will grant you freedom if you keep the secret I've entrusted to you.

ANTÓN. Swarthy skin, honorable heart, quiet keeping.

DOÑA LEONOR. My plan is working out beautifully.

ANTÓN. Here twere revenge taking on the paleface. Fie!

DOÑA LEONOR. This is the duke's palace.

ANTÓN. Perchance inside twere the falsehearted dung.

DOÑA LEONOR. You mean *don*, Antón, not *dung*.

(Shots sound offstage. Enter the DUKE and the captains DON PEDRO OSORIO and DON JUAN.)

DON PEDRO OSORIO.   The enemy camp is up in arms.

DON JUAN.   Three artillery pieces have been fired.

DUKE.   They react to Don Agustín, who has kept his word.

DOÑA LEONOR.   That must be the duke, judging from the deference they give him.

ANTÓN.   An if that twere our duke, Spain twere fear striking in the wide world.

DUKE.   The spy or sentinel has roused his squad.

(Enter the captain DON AGUSTÍN.)

DON AGUSTÍN.   *(Aside.)*

Who ever heard of such humiliation so early in the day!

DOÑA LEONOR.   Antón, that's the scoundrel there.

ANTÓN.   Lesson time twere for teaching to the crafty dong.

DOÑA LEONOR.   It's *don*, Antón!

DON AGUSTÍN.   *(Aside.)*

My rashness may cost me my life.

[To the DUKE.]

If I am worthy of those feet, I ask your excellency for them.

[He kneels.]

DUKE.   What's the meaning of this, captain?

DON AGUSTÍN.   The mistakes of war. I promised to return from the enemy camp with a spy or sentinel, confident of my valor and diligence. But even the best-laid plans depend on fate, and only the lucky achieve what they desire. Since war is always about tricks and stratagems, for greater security I donned a Teutonic disguise. In carrying out my plan I wandered along swampy pathways and poorly constructed levees. Near a tiny cluster of houses I was accosted by two captains escorting twenty or thirty soldiers. With the defiance of a Spanish knight I made a glorious escape across bogs and fields, fired at on three occasions by those imagining an ambush, though I took a few lives with me in my withdrawal.

DUKE.   Courage is best illustrated in adversity, for difficulty makes glory more certain.

(Enter JUAN DE MÉRIDA with two FLEMING soldiers and their harquebuses.)

FLEMING 1. Nee-tay!

FLEMING 2. Nee-tay!

JUAN DE MÉRIDA. Nee-tay, schmee-tay. Even Beelzebub is at a loss to understand your gibberish!

DON PEDRO OSORIO. Who goes there?

JUAN DE MÉRIDA. A black bear with two beehives for snacks.

ANTÓN. What? Here too twere swarthy soldiers?

DOÑA LEONOR. It's Juan de Mérida!

ANTÓN. Twere Juan forsooth: flower of Mérida, stink of *merda*.

JUAN DE MÉRIDA. And now, most distinguished lord, I repeat my request for a position.

DON AGUSTÍN. *(Aside.)*

I'm finished! It's the *negro*, and he's got my ribbon! All my shame is written on his face.

JUAN DE MÉRIDA. I promised to bring back a soldier who would give me his harquebus so I could be a soldier myself. Well, I've brought two in case one explodes. So I've got two harquebuses along with gunpowder, powder horns, and straps: the position is all I lack. Honor the darkskin people by creating a position for me. I'll prove myself again by bringing back the halberd, pennant, and jineta sword from Orange's camp, and I'll even bring back the tents. The time has come, sir captains, for this darkskin to walk about with his face uncovered and punish presumption. He who was defeated by my other face will now fear this one. Before I ran into these two soldiers, I vanquished an enemy captain and robbed him of this ribbon. I beg your excellency receive it as the spoils of my first mission.

[JUAN DE MÉRIDA tosses the ribbon at the duke's feet, where DON AGUSTÍN cowers.]

There it is at your feet, blushing with shame.

DON AGUSTÍN. *(Aside.)*

I'll kill the dog!

DUKE. I accept the ribbon as if it were yours, for it is fitting that a duke be honored with the spoils of a black soldier.

JUAN DE MÉRIDA.   It belonged to a captain, full of envy and all mouth: an arrogant white man.

DON AGUSTÍN.   *(Aside.)*

Who ever suffered such insults?

DUKE.   Don Agustín, you'll have the honor of wearing this ribbon.

JUAN DE MÉRIDA.   You do offense to so valiant a soldier, great lord, for the ribbon comes from a black man and will stain him.

DON AGUSTÍN.   I shall improve the quality of its lowly condition.

JUAN DE MÉRIDA.   I believe you will. Keep it safe and don't lose it, for there are soldiers with two faces who show no respect to a captain.

DUKE.   What a remarkable black man.

DON JUAN.   Astonishing.

DUKE.   I shall give you a position in my own company.

JUAN DE MÉRIDA.   A fitting reward from a prince.

DUKE.   What is your name?

JUAN DE MÉRIDA.   Juan de Mérida, for in that province I was born a free man. And so that no one may insult me further, here is my letter of freedom, which I carry about my neck like an indulgence.

DUKE.   Then today, Juan, you are reborn into the army, and your name shall be Juan de Alba.

JUAN DE MÉRIDA.   You desire, sir, that your dawn light up this night?

DUKE.   Alba shall you call yourself.

JUAN DE MÉRIDA.   I content myself, great lord, with being the barest glimmer in your dawn.

DUKE.   In so black a dawn, the world shall worship the sun, which just begins to illumine you.

JUAN DE MÉRIDA.   For a black man to call himself Juan de Alba . . . John of Dawn . . . it's like calling himself John White. I promise to make your dawn eternal in these lands, for I shall respond to their ferocious people with the ample bark and bite of a hound.

DUKE.   Find out from these two spies what the rebels are planning.

DON AGUSTÍN.   *[Aside.]*

   My humiliation is complete.

DUKE.   Juan de Alba, your life begins today.

JUAN DE MÉRIDA.   With the second nature you give me, I am rosy dawn in addition to black night. With your pearls around my neck, I shall be Alba's dog to the Flemish squadrons.

DUKE.   Since you have two harquebuses, you shall have two positions.

JUAN DE MÉRIDA.   Great lord, I swear to God I will fight like two hundred.

   (Exit [all but JUAN DE MÉRIDA, ANTÓN, and DOÑA LEONOR].)

DOÑA LEONOR.   Let's go speak with him.

ANTÓN.   Buddy! Little Antón de Vera twere hugs wanting.

JUAN DE MÉRIDA.   Antón, friend.

ANTÓN.   Me too twere into Spain's wars crashing.

DOÑA LEONOR.   Give me hug as well, though you probably don't remember me.

JUAN DE MÉRIDA.   I do not.

DOÑA LEONOR.   I am Esteban.

JUAN DE MÉRIDA.   Esteban who?

DOÑA LEONOR.   Former page boy to Don Juan the prior.

JUAN DE MÉRIDA.   You look familiar, but I don't remember you.

DOÑA LEONOR.   The point is, we are from the same land.

JUAN DE MÉRIDA.   And what brings you to the Low Countries?

DOÑA LEONOR.   The stars, which have been harsh with me.

JUAN DE MÉRIDA.   What do you seek?

DOÑA LEONOR.   To serve a captain, friend, until I come of age, for I make a great page and am eager to carry my lord's jineta sword. And I think you're going to be a great friend of mine.

JUAN DE MÉRIDA.   *(Aside.)*

   Something's not right about this page boy. He grips my hand too eagerly! I don't trust him.

DOÑA LEONOR. Where do you lodge?

JUAN DE MÉRIDA. Wherever night finds me. I have no fixed lodging.

DOÑA LEONOR. Well, come with us and choose one, where we may be pampered. I have money.

JUAN DE MÉRIDA. *[Aside.]*

He grips my hand too eagerly!

DOÑA LEONOR. We shall share a bed.

JUAN DE MÉRIDA. I'm afraid I smell bad, my friend, so I sleep alone.

DOÑA LEONOR. I cannot sleep without company.

JUAN DE MÉRIDA. Antón can sleep with you.

ANTÓN. Twere Antón in a fairy white bed? Avaunt!

DOÑA LEONOR. *(Aside, to ANTÓN.)*

This is the path to my vengeance. Play along, Antón.

ANTÓN. *(Aside, to DOÑA LEONOR.)*

Twere playing along.

DOÑA LEONOR. *(Aside, to ANTÓN.)*

He doesn't recognize me.

[To JUAN DE MÉRIDA.]

Is there an inn nearby?

JUAN DE MÉRIDA. I don't know.

DOÑA LEONOR. Why so aloof with me? We are countrymen. Take my hand.

JUAN DE MÉRIDA. It's very soft and white. I'll stain it.

DOÑA LEONOR. It'll make a lovely contrast.

JUAN DE MÉRIDA. *[Aside.]*

He grips my hands too eagerly!

DOÑA LEONOR. Come, and I shall toast to your health.

JUAN DE MÉRIDA. My health is fine.

DOÑA LEONOR. So unapproachable you are!

JUAN DE MÉRIDA.   I am a demon.

DOÑA LEONOR.   I will put you in an amorous mood with my tender attention and sweet words.

JUAN DE MÉRIDA.   *[Aside.]*

Why hasn't this fairy been burned alive?

DOÑA LEONOR.   Come. My coins itch to be spent.

JUAN DE MÉRIDA.   The Devil take you, page, and whoever brought you to this land!

(*Exit [all].*)

ACT 2, Scene 1

([The Spanish encampment in Flanders.] Enter JUAN DE MÉRIDA, alone.)

JUAN DE MÉRIDA.   I'm mad with joy, and I owe the favor to my boldness: the duke has promoted me to sergeant despite my color. Fortune approves great rewards for me. A black sergeant in Flanders: who would've imagined it! I'm a little ashamed I haven't carried out any noteworthy missions against the enemy. I want to bring back two or three halberds along with their sergeants chattering away: *gran bot, moltuyn, butir, estricot, zerbeza, flin flan*. Their language sounds worse than my own, assuming I spoke like a newly arrived black slave. It's as if Guinea started breeding white people. But here comes Barrientos with my enemies. I shall withdraw.

(He hides. Enter the captain DON AGUSTÍN, the sergeant BARRIENTOS, and the captains [DON PEDRO OSORIO and DON JUAN].)

DON AGUSTÍN.   A most cruel action!

BARRIENTOS.   I repeat: it's an insult to all sergeants when a vile *negro* assumes their rank.

JUAN DE MÉRIDA.   *[Aside.]*

Oh, envy, ignoble monster that stalks the most generous intention!

DON PEDRO OSORIO.   The duke decided to honor him because he's a *negro*.

DON JUAN.   And because he's lucky: more lucky than daring.

JUAN DE MÉRIDA.   *[Aside.]*

I can't believe what I'm hearing! I can barely contain myself.

DON PEDRO OSORIO.   He's accomplished some noteworthy deeds.

DON AGUSTÍN.   He's a brash one.

DON JUAN.   The enemy already fears his boldness.

DON AGUSTÍN.   He's a soldier but, in the end, just a *negro*.

BARRIENTOS.   I'm going to resign my post as of today.

DON AGUSTÍN.   What a bold resolution. The three of us should encourage a revolt among all the sergeants.

JUAN DE MÉRIDA.   *[Aside.]*

Such evil plots from gentlemen! By God, I'll have to discredit them in front of the general. Evil must be answered with evil.

DON JUAN.   Let's go: stirring up the sergeants is the solution. Only thus will the duke strip the *negro* of his jineta sword.

(*Exit DON JUAN, DON PEDRO OSORIO, and DON AGUSTÍN.*)

JUAN DE MÉRIDA.   *[Aside.]*

Envy gnaws away at them like a termite. Virtue is the remedy. All this just clarifies my purpose.

BARRIENTOS.   *[Aside.]*

I'll track him down on my own and have my vengeance, for I'm the one wronged.

JUAN DE MÉRIDA.   *[Aside.]*

This is an excellent opportunity. Time to cross paths.

BARRIENTOS.   *[Aside.]*

Here comes the dog itself. It corners me.

[Aloud.]

Good morning.

JUAN DE MÉRIDA.   Good night, you mean.

BARRIENTOS.   Why good night?

JUAN DE MÉRIDA. Because I always carry night with me, so mornings for me are like evenings. White people are good mornings and the swarthy are good evenings. And thus, since we're always walking around in the dark, we must feel our way. But since I know you'll be delighted to hear my happy news, I'll tell you, Mr. Sergeant: we're all sergeants now.

BARRIENTOS. I heard and was delighted.

JUAN DE MÉRIDA. *(Aside.)*

Right!

[Aloud.]

I'm a sergeant because, even though I'm unworthy, the duke decided to give me that honor. Yet I lack a halberd and am too poor to purchase one: not surprising since I'm black. And thus, attentive to my poverty and to what I deserve, you will do me the honor of giving me yours, for I desire to elevate my blackness with others' distinctions.

BARRIENTOS. I wish I had another to give you.

JUAN DE MÉRIDA. I'll take the only one you have. Hand it over immediately, or by God, you'll meet your death at my hands. For time has made us equals, though I'm not content with being equal.

BARRIENTOS. Only the king can be my equal.

JUAN DE MÉRIDA. Well, I'm no king of Manicongo, just a wretched darkskin, so I do not wish to be your equal. I take your halberd from you because I know you've already determined to relinquish it. And so that you'll see I deserve it more than you even though I'm black, let us fight for it. I'll set it here on the ground. Come, unsheathe your sword and reclaim it.

BARRIENTOS. You offend not me but the duke and the king.

JUAN DE MÉRIDA. Well, go call them if you like, but I do no dishonor to your office. I take your halberd only because it's clear you do not deserve it. If this offends you and you don't dare face me alone, go round up all the sergeants and bring them back with their halberds. For without ceding ground or even unsheathing my sword, I'll do the same with all of them.

BARRIENTOS. I'm going.

JUAN DE MÉRIDA. Godspeed, and sheathe the sword you've used so well.

BARRIENTOS. By God!

JUAN DE MÉRIDA. By God is right, for if I get angry and unleash the dog in me, I'll make the white sergeant labor more and talk less.

(Exit BARRIENTOS.)

Given the smell I just detected, I'd say he's rushing off to find perfume. He'll serve as a lesson to the rest. This halberd suits me. I already seem to be a different man, filled with soul and a new spirit. I aspire to more, with generous military honors. Hark, fortune, for I have reached the third step. If Mars is the fifth planet, two steps remain for me to reach its glory.

([JUAN DE MÉRIDA withdraws.] Enter DOÑA LEONOR [disguised as a page], with a military baton, and ANTÓN.)

DOÑA LEONOR. *[Out of earshot of JUAN DE MÉRIDA.]*

Antón, I can hardly describe my delight.

JUAN DE MÉRIDA. *[Aside, unseen.]*

I fear no one on the battlefield, yet I fear this page boy. He deserves to smell of charred flesh rather than perfume and musk.

DOÑA LEONOR. Embrace me as I celebrate my happiness.

ANTÓN. Everybody twere happy for ma'am.

DOÑA LEONOR. The captain acknowledged me.

ANTÓN. What twere said?

DOÑA LEONOR. The truth. With tears and flatteries and a thousand tender sighs, he asks my forgiveness.

ANTÓN. Little Antón twere losing our head with joy. Willst to kiss her hand?

[He kisses Doña Leonor's hand.]

JUAN DE MÉRIDA. *[Aside.]*

What perversion is this!

ANTÓN. A fine dung forsooth.

DOÑA LEONOR. He tells me we'll depart as soon as the duke completes the withdrawal. He asks me to remain in disguise until then.

ANTÓN. Pray God twere returning anon to Spain.

DOÑA LEONOR. Where you'll witness my joyful wedding.

ANTÓN. Weddings twere signifying sweetmeat and fairy rumps kissing.

JUAN DE MÉRIDA. *[Aside.]*

> It's not the page boy who bothers me. He's clearly vice-ridden. My problem is with my little Antón. It galls me that the dog has stooped to this level and comes to Flanders to give a bad name to the color I give nobility to. I must put out this fire or I'll lose my mind.

> *[He approaches the others.]*

DOÑA LEONOR. Here comes our friend.

ANTÓN. Meesieur?

DOÑA LEONOR. I hope to fulfill my pleasure in your arms.

JUAN DE MÉRIDA. Stop.

DOÑA LEONOR. It's insulting that you would put a stop to the love I show you.

JUAN DE MÉRIDA. I embrace men from afar.

DOÑA LEONOR. You must be made of stone.

JUAN DE MÉRIDA. A stone to suffering.

DOÑA LEONOR. Men with your features make me want to love, esteem, and pamper them. I seat them at my table, for both the table and the bed stimulate desire.

JUAN DE MÉRIDA. Go to Italy if that's what you want.

DOÑA LEONOR. Changing subjects, I have met the perfect captain, from whom I hope never to part. He is gallant, beautiful, and discreet, and he comforts me and holds me in great esteem. He is, in short, a gentleman of Mérida.

JUAN DE MÉRIDA. Is it Don Agustín by any chance?

DOÑA LEONOR. The one and only. My lord and sir.

JUAN DE MÉRIDA. An excellent lord.

DOÑA LEONOR. And I owe it all to you.

JUAN DE MÉRIDA. To me?

DOÑA LEONOR. Yes, friend, to you.

JUAN DE MÉRIDA. How so?

DOÑA LEONOR. You delivered him to me.

JUAN DE MÉRIDA. By God, I don't remember.

(*Aside.*)

The Devil take this page boy! The demons have brought him here to stalk me, and I'm ready to send him back to Hell with a good swift kick.

DOÑA LEONOR. Goodbye, friend. I must follow the captain, but I'll see you tonight. Where do you sleep?

JUAN DE MÉRIDA. Where do I sleep? In the swamp, with the mud up to here.

DOÑA LEONOR. Antón and I will look for you and bring a snack and a bit of beer.

JUAN DE MÉRIDA. I don't drink at night.

DOÑA LEONOR. I've never met such an austere black man. Arrivederci.

(*Aside, to ANTÓN.*)

In this way I'll keep him confused and distracted. Play along, Antón.

ANTÓN. (*Aside.*)

Twere playing along.

DOÑA LEONOR. (*Aside.*)

Your freedom hangs in the balance.

ANTÓN. Where now twere going to?

DOÑA LEONOR. Following after my lord, for I'm beside myself at his striking figure and graciousness. Isn't he handsome? Beautiful even? Do I not have excellent taste?

ANTÓN. Yes ma'am.

(*Exit DOÑA LEONOR.*)

JUAN DE MÉRIDA. What a dishonest and lascivious demon! Don Agustín has sealed his infamy, but what more could be expected of such a pretty boy? And you, vile *negro* . . .

ANTÓN. Twere vile *negro*, me?

JUAN DE MÉRIDA. By God, I'll kill you.

ANTÓN. Why in Juan twere killing little Antón?

JUAN DE MÉRIDA. You reprobate, if I see you with that page boy again, in public or in private, I'll burn you alive.

ANTÓN. And food for Antón twere coming from where?

JUAN DE MÉRIDA. I will feed you.

ANTÓN. Antón eating twere forgetting the page and serving the lord Juan. Halberd twere carrying.

JUAN DE MÉRIDA. You promise loyalty?

ANTÓN. Twere promising.

JUAN DE MÉRIDA. Then take it and follow me.

[He hands ANTÓN his halberd.]

ANTÓN. Time twere to get going.

JUAN DE MÉRIDA. More slowly and imperiously.

ANTÓN. Twere slow and perious moving.

JUAN DE MÉRIDA. My little Antón, what do I look like to you?

ANTÓN. Twere a magus king and his lackey.

JUAN DE MÉRIDA. Antón?

ANTÓN. Meesieur?

JUAN DE MÉRIDA. Show more respect, for I am a sergeant of Flanders.

ANTÓN. All of us twere knowing that.

JUAN DE MÉRIDA. Antón?

ANTÓN. Meesieur?

JUAN DE MÉRIDA. Walk.

ANTÓN. Twere silly *negros* walking.

(Exit [JUAN DE MÉRIDA and ANTÓN].)

ACT 2, Scene 2

([Headquarters of the Spanish encampment.] Enter the DUKE and the captains DON AGUSTÍN, DON PEDRO OSORIO, and DON JUAN.)

DUKE. The withdrawal is proving disastrous to our honor and to Spain's reputation.

DON PEDRO OSORIO. Then let's go down fighting, my lord, since living has become impossible. The winter has turned brutal with the snow's assault, which the sky unleashes in copious quantities. It's all a frozen chaos.

DON AGUSTÍN. The barracks sink into the bog; the troops are up to their necks in water and muck. The bulwarks do nothing against this muddy fate. Every day we bury soldiers the dawn finds frozen in their beds.

DUKE. Winter comes after us in a thousand different ways, but Spain will not surrender to its strange fury. We must resist the snow and ice and the harsh watery bogs. The rebels shall see how the heavens fortify us against the cruel climate while we clothe their mad and arrogant squadrons in fear and distress. They shall know that the sun's sweet, eternal balm is born here, for here rises the dawn.

DON JUAN. A withdrawal, sir, would be disgraceful under the injurious terms that Orange demands. But it would be even more disgraceful and dreadful to resist in such harsh circumstances, for we are outnumbered sword to sword. Cruel arithmetic prevents any offensive on our part, and Spain's fate remains in enemy hands, submerged in muck and mire.

DON AGUSTÍN. The rebels, offspring of the snow, have the advantage of home turf. The water does not bother them, no matter how much it rains. Nor does the ice, to which they have inbred resistance. Their position drinks in the elements and does not give way, defended by craggy hills, whereas we, sir, find our backs up against four unrelenting lagoons. Our only choice is to take the exit the prince has offered, for winter has closed in on us and water fills our trenches.

DUKE. Black is the Christmas that Heaven offers us.

(Shots are fired offstage. Enter JUAN DE MÉRIDA, carrying a flag.)

But what's this?

JUAN DE MÉRIDA. Do not succumb, your excellency, to the gloomy mood of your men, for behold the enemy flag I bring you. Drape it over your feet while I go off to capture the rest, and let the captains join me if a black man can persuade them to such an infamous task. I am black, and my words and actions instill fear in white souls that lack the actions to back up their words, made as they are of sugar and icing.

DUKE. Enough, Ensign Juan de Alba.

JUAN DE MÉRIDA. *Ensign?* I kiss your feet for the honor.

DUKE. Raise your flag like a proper ensign, and contain your fury.

JUAN DE MÉRIDA. I did not mean to be excessive. I was responding to the cruel envy that stalks me.

DUKE.   I confess, Juan de Alba, that if I weren't who I am, I would envy you too. But you needn't worry about envy, for he who is not envied for his virtue is a miserable wretch.

JUAN DE MÉRIDA.   I am Alba's dog. Bring on the Jews!

DUKE.   That's fine, ensign.

JUAN DE MÉRIDA.   I am a dog, great lord, and my bite is rabid.

(Enter the sergeant BARRIENTOS.)

BARRIENTOS.   We are approached by a Frisian horse: whiter than the hills, sweating rivers of snow and chafing at an iron bit, its mouth filling with cold flakes of silver spittle. Atop sits a Teuton captain, demanding a challenge at the top of his voice.

JUAN DE MÉRIDA.   He's here for punches and kicks.

DUKE.   For the flag, more likely.

JUAN DE MÉRIDA.   Oh, sir, let him come and I will give it to him.

BARRIENTOS.   He's right outside in the parade ground.

JUAN DE MÉRIDA.   Let every soldier ready himself with choler, though he threatens only captains.

DUKE.   Show him to my tent. Let no one stop him.

JUAN DE MÉRIDA.   He has a ferocious bearing, as if he would devour us all. I'm delighted that my blackness may work to my advantage this time.

(Enter Monsieur de VIVANBLEC et Raballac, a Teuton.)

VIVANBLEC.   God keep you, Duke of Alba, terror of our lands and cause of so many wars following the disastrous designs of Counts Egmont and Horne.

DUKE.   Get to the point, Fleming, and state the reason for your visit, for nothing demands punishment like idle talk.

VIVANBLEC.   Only Heaven can punish me, and furthermore—

DUKE.   Get to the point.

VIVANBLEC.   I am Monsieur de Vivanblec et Raballac.

JUAN DE MÉRIDA.   A name as dreadful as your appearance.

VIVANBLEC.   I am a captain in the army of Orange, whose discipline is to be envied by the sovereign Caesars.

DUKE. You are correct, and I give you license to equate him with the sun, for he has proved a valorous and invincible opponent. He is Prince of Orange, and nothing more need be said.

VIVANBLEC. These are the conditions, general, for your ill-fated withdrawal.

(He hands the DUKE a sheet of paper.)

DUKE. The time and place demand it.

VIVANBLEC. You will retreat by the first day of Christmas, or we will open all the dikes on you.

DUKE. I shall see to it. Do you come charged with a specific task?

VIVANBLEC. I seek a duel with your captains.

DUKE. Choose one, then.

VIVANBLEC. One, you say? I demand fourteen or fifteen.

JUAN DE MÉRIDA. Such choler. Do you think them flies or ticks?

VIVANBLEC. I think them Spaniards.

JUAN DE MÉRIDA. That they are. But I'll have you know that the humblest soldier in the Spanish army is sufficient to kill you. No captain need stoop to the petty task. If the duke will permit me, a black man and a slave to my captains, I shall force you, arrogant German, to vomit up with your soul all the beer you've drunk, assuming you didn't gulp down Rhine.

(He seizes VIVANBLEC.)

DUKE. Ensign?

JUAN DE MÉRIDA. Sir, I'll be right back. I just need a second to tear him apart.

[Exit JUAN DE MÉRIDA, dragging VIVANBLEC.]

VIVANBLEC. *(Offstage [shouting].)*

He murders me!

JUAN DE MÉRIDA. *[Offstage.]*

You've got that right.

(Reenter JUAN DE MÉRIDA.)

Vivanblec Barabbas has gone to dine with Beelzebub, so he'll no longer be demanding duels with us. And since I just annihilated a captain, it's fitting that your excellency make me one.

DUKE. Such a deed shouts for a great reward.

JUAN DE MÉRIDA. All my deeds bear the stamp of my color.

DUKE. A color worthy of fame's envy. Right, my captains? What say you?

DON PEDRO OSORIO. Such a glorious deed demands your excellency give him a jineta sword.

DUKE. The squadron elects you its captain. Give the men your thanks.

JUAN DE MÉRIDA. Sir, I promise to repay this honor.

DON JUAN. It's time to salute him.

DON PEDRO OSORIO. From today on, my captain, consider me your servant.

DON JUAN. And me your comrade.

DON AGUSTÍN. May our embrace affirm our friendship.

JUAN DE MÉRIDA. *[To DON AGUSTÍN.]*

If ever you get rid of your lackey, you'll find an eternal slave in me.

DON AGUSTÍN. I give you my word I'll get rid of him, though I know you'll ask me to take him back.

JUAN DE MÉRIDA. I? That page boy stalks me more than my own color. I on his behalf? Do I hear you correctly? Call me a coward and a left-handed *negro* or whatever insult you wish if I ever ask such a thing of you.

DUKE. Vivanblec's death will not pass unnoticed by the prince.

JUAN DE MÉRIDA. Vivanblec came here to kill us, sir, so our self-defense is justified. But if the prince sends white lions out for vengeance, I shall be a black dog and your captains, tigers.

DUKE. I wish to see the conditions of the withdrawal.

DON JUAN. Heaven oppresses our squadron.

JUAN DE MÉRIDA. If the demands for retreat are injurious, your excellency, do not cede ground.

DUKE. What, then?

JUAN DE MÉRIDA. Go down fighting. Courage to the end.

DUKE. Our encampment sinks into the bog, the winter is brutal, the soldiers cannot resist the elements . . . The lieutenant general shall announce our withdrawal for the day after tomorrow.

DON AGUSTÍN. That's Christmas Day.

JUAN DE MÉRIDA. A sad and black Christmas it will be for Spain.

DUKE. It's all due to the weather and the circumstances. Spain will understand that it was the harshness of the elements that did me in, for the Duke of Alba is invincible to men.

JUAN DE MÉRIDA. By God, this cackling raven agrees with you, O brave and venerable swan.

DUKE. Captain, summer will come round again.

JUAN DE MÉRIDA. And then this ground will turn firm, and it will sink as soon as your foot touches it.

DUKE. Honor the captain with a jineta sword.

DON AGUSTÍN. Which one would you like?

JUAN DE MÉRIDA. Yours would do me the greatest honor.

DON AGUSTÍN. It takes its honor from you.

(Exit DON AGUSTÍN.)

DUKE. The sword looks good in your hands.

JUAN DE MÉRIDA. I think, rather, it mocks me and laughs in my hands.

DUKE. Alba, your color proves itself by merging with the dawn.

JUAN DE MÉRIDA. If I am Alba, let my dawn immortalize itself in you, and let peerless Philip's sun rise in it.

(Exit the DUKE [and all but JUAN DE MÉRIDA].)

I find myself on fortune's final step, but I am not content with it. My ambition aims higher. Another heroic deed is necessary, one that brings greater honor to my jineta sword and that is worthy to call itself Spanish. A deed that will transform the dawn into the sun and make me one of its rays. O sword, you shall temper this harsh withdrawal despite, by God, the inclement weather. And if I am to survive, I promise to accredit you before this country sees the last of me, so that your glory will become eternal.

(JUAN DE MÉRIDA withdraws. Enter the captain DON AGUSTÍN and DOÑA LEONOR [disguised as a boy].)

DON AGUSTÍN. The hours I have spent without seeing myself in your eyes have been all hell and death.

DOÑA LEONOR.   Imagine what it's like for me, the one who admires and adores you.

JUAN DE MÉRIDA.   *(Aside, unseen.)*

I swear this page boy is possessed!

DON AGUSTÍN.   Give me beauty, my Leonor, in your loving arms, like ivy to the elm.

[They embrace.]

DOÑA LEONOR.   Oh, if only this could last forever!

JUAN DE MÉRIDA.   *[Aside.]*

Unfortunate wretch! I must advise Don Pedro Osorio and his comrades so they can punish this vile behavior. They embrace again. I can't watch!

(Exit JUAN DE MÉRIDA.)

DON AGUSTÍN.   Someone's coming.

DOÑA LEONOR.   Just when I steal a moment of hope, it gets trampled by a thousand obstacles.

DON AGUSTÍN.   You may return later.

DOÑA LEONOR.   Oh, love, so fleeting are all your delights!

(Exit DOÑA LEONOR. Enter DON PEDRO OSORIO with a letter.)

DON PEDRO OSORIO.   In the latest correspondence from Spain, in which his majesty absolves the duke of responsibility for the enemy's endurance, this letter comes for you. The secretary just gave it to me.

DON AGUSTÍN.   That's my father's seal. Just what I was hoping for.

(Reading aloud.)

"Return at once to marry Doña Juana de Vera, who is the sole heir of her house. While her nobility alone is to your advantage, she also claims an income of ten thousand ducats, complemented by her beauty and the Vera name. Ask the duke for his sponsorship, for love demands quick action. I'm sure you can understand the urgency, Agustín, of returning swiftly."

[To DON PEDRO OSORIO.]

God help me!

DON PEDRO OSORIO.   What's the matter? Why does the news bring tears?

DON AGUSTÍN. Oh, Don Pedro! You're not in love, so I'm not sure you'll understand my predicament. But you are prudent and discreet, and I shall not hide my secret from you. Between the two of us, this page boy who carries my jineta sword is a fine and graceful lady, of noble lineage and fame. I have a secret obligation to her, for she is a woman of reputation to whom I owe my word. Yet the arrangement my father proposes promises greater glory, for Doña Juana is richer and more powerful, yet even her wealth is eclipsed by her beauty. And now you see the no-win situation love puts me in, for I feel tenderness toward Leonor but joy at the thought of Doña Juana.

DON PEDRO OSORIO. Do you love Leonor truly?

DON AGUSTÍN. I love her the way one loves a conquered woman: once possessed, she grows tiresome, even though love may linger.

DON PEDRO OSORIO. Did you give her your word?

DON AGUSTÍN. Yes, and in writing, though I think she'll keep quiet about it when she sees my change of heart, if I'm already married to Doña Juana.

DON PEDRO OSORIO. A fine plan.

DON AGUSTÍN. If we complete the withdrawal today, I plan to leave tomorrow.

DON PEDRO OSORIO. What about Leonor?

DON AGUSTÍN. Forgotten already, for my love is a phoenix, reborn in Doña Juana.

(*Exit [all].*)

ACT 2, Scene 3

(*[The Flemish encampment.] Enter JUAN DE MÉRIDA, brandishing a dagger.*)

JUAN DE MÉRIDA. Seeing the duke afflicted with desperation and madness, I find little value in my life, so I've decided to follow my fate wherever it leads. Fortune, if you dyed the face that disgraces me, let it not be an inkblot on my fame. This is the night that outshines the day, sovereign in God's divine hierarchy, for with his resplendent and beautiful star, he guides me like a magus. I am the black man in the nativity scene, and on this holy night, as the angel chants of glory, I respond with my instrument: a hoarse and unsteady voice that celebrates the night with songs from Guinea. Into enemy territory I have strayed, and what a fun and cheerful scene I've stumbled upon, full of celebratory toasting. Amid the clatter of the festivity I shall survey the drunken troops. Fortunately, I have my mask with me.

([JUAN DE MÉRIDA puts on his mask and withdraws.] Enter as many Flemings as possible, with vihuelas and masks, carrying an effigy of the duke. Among them are the Prince of ORANGE and the generals, Monsieur de LANSTREC and Monsieur de VILA.)

VILA. Does your excellency enjoy the festivities?

ORANGE. My heart will not rest until I witness the Spanish army's withdrawal tomorrow.

LANSTREC. What a Christmas Eve for Spain!

ORANGE. A black one on account of my valor.

VILA. Your excellency should retire to his tent.

ORANGE. You two go. I want to stay here alone.

JUAN DE MÉRIDA. *(Aside, unseen.)*

If he remains alone, by God, what an opportunity for this darkskin.

ORANGE. I'm going to take a stroll along this levee. As we're safe from the Spaniards, send everyone to rest.

VILA. Be mindful, excellent lord, how far you stray from camp.

LANSTREC. The guard has turned in.

(Exit LANSTREC.)

ORANGE. Time to change the watchword.

VILA. I'll go do it.

(Exit VILA.)

ORANGE. What a state the enemy is in! I'm happy to witness it. Oh, Duke of Alba, this time your arrogance was laid low.

JUAN DE MÉRIDA. *[Revealing himself, he points his dagger at Orange's throat.]*

Not while there's color left in this darkskin.

ORANGE. What treachery is this, heavens!

JUAN DE MÉRIDA. You've strayed from your people, and I'm going to take you to mine. Let's go.

ORANGE.   Treachery! Soldiers, Monsieur de Vila, friends!

(JUAN DE MÉRIDA seizes ORANGE and forces him offstage. Exit both.)

ACT 2, Scene 4

[The Spanish encampment, immediately following the previous scene. Enter JUAN DE MÉRIDA, still in his mask, forcing ORANGE.]

JUAN DE MÉRIDA.   Quiet! Or by God, I'll quiet you with this dagger. This is the duke's tent. Sir?

(Enter the DUKE and BARRIENTOS.)

BARRIENTOS.   Who calls the duke?

JUAN DE MÉRIDA.   Juan de Alba.

DUKE.   I recognized the voice.

JUAN DE MÉRIDA.   I come to deliver the Prince of Orange.

DUKE.   Heavens, what are you saying!

JUAN DE MÉRIDA.   Only for you, great lord, would I have attempted this. I'm going to go change clothes and wash up, for I am muddied from this operation.

(Exit JUAN DE MÉRIDA.)

DUKE.   Give me your excellency's hand to kiss.

ORANGE.   If your excellency counts such men on his side, who could possibly prevail against them?

DUKE.   Though Juan de Alba prepared me for this moment, I am so astonished by your presence I can scarcely believe it.

ORANGE.   A solemn Christmas evening this has become for me.

DUKE.   To vanquish such an enemy is an eternal glory. Where did he find your excellency?

ORANGE.   It drives me mad to think about it. He dragged me from my tent. I'll say no more so as not to offend the heavens. Such an amazing soldier should be rewarded by the king. And I, though his bravery has brought me low, shall reward him as well, for I am privileged to have been defeated by such a soldier. Who is he? A captain?

DUKE.   He is a captain, but I dare not say more.

ORANGE.   Is he not a man?

DUKE.   His fate stamped his courage onto his skin so that with his color he could astonish the world.

ORANGE.   Do you mean to say he's black?

DUKE.   Black he is.

ORANGE.   When fortune humbles me before a black man of such renown, I am happy and glorious in my adversity. What I'd give to be him!

(Enter the captains DON AGUSTÍN, DON PEDRO OSORIO, and DON JUAN.)

DON AGUSTÍN.   Orange's army is in an uproar and preparing for battle. Even its lowest ranks charge toward us. What's happening?

DUKE.   The answer lies in front of you.

ORANGE.   *[To DON AGUSTÍN.]*

I am the cause of the uproar, though for you it means only peace.

[To the DUKE.]

To quiet my troops down, have a captain deliver this ring to Lanstrec and explain that I am with your excellency. Tell him and Monsieur de Vila to come as hostages immediately.

DUKE.   Don Pedro Osorio, I charge you with this mission.

(Exit DON PEDRO OSORIO.)

ORANGE.   I surrender myself at your feet, prisoner to your clemency, with whatever conditions you impose. For fortune, mad and unrelenting, has turned my Christmas black.

[VOICES].   *(Offstage.)*

The Prince of Orange has been captured!

DON AGUSTÍN.   The troops are nervous about the consequences of this action.

DUKE.   The lieutenant general will calm them down.

DON AGUSTÍN.   How did this capture happen?

BARRIENTOS.   I can't fathom it.

DUKE. Let's share a repast.

ORANGE. I shall obey. What about the black man?

DUKE. *[To BARRIENTOS.]* Go fetch him.

BARRIENTOS. We don't know where he quarters.

DON AGUSTÍN. In the manger I'm sure, for tonight black men and shepherds are singing their carols to God.

DUKE. So far from the honors he deserves.

ORANGE. Such elegant place settings and goblets!

DUKE. You flatter me. They are unfit for your person. Here is your place.

ORANGE. Sir . . .

DUKE. Patience, for your excellency is my prisoner.

(All sit. Enter JUAN DE MÉRIDA [without his mask].)

JUAN DE MÉRIDA. I went through three loads of firewood in my bath. I'm warm and clean now, though I couldn't wash off my face. It's stamped into my flesh.

DUKE. This is Juan de Alba.

ORANGE. The most remarkable soldier a prince has ever met.

[ORANGE stands.]

JUAN DE MÉRIDA. Great lord, do not rise to honor a black man.

ORANGE. It is fitting that I lower myself before he who lifted me up on his shoulders.

DUKE. Sit, your excellency.

ORANGE. Great lord, I will not sit if the captain does not.

JUAN DE MÉRIDA. You mean me, sir?

ORANGE. He who triumphs over Orange may sit with Orange.

DUKE. Juan de Alba eats with the domestics.

JUAN DE MÉRIDA. I am the duke's canine, happy to eat the bones from his table.

ORANGE. Such a grand soldier may sit with grandees.

DUKE. Don't make the prince ask you a second time, captain.

JUAN DE MÉRIDA. What? Am I really to sit, sirs? How about I kneel?

ORANGE. This is growing tedious.

DUKE. Don't keep the prince on his feet.

JUAN DE MÉRIDA. Out of obedience I sit, black jet surrounded by shining crystal.

ORANGE. I would much prefer your jet, captain, to my noble ivory.

DON AGUSTÍN. *[Aside.]*

   Are these the rewards of virtue? Such shame I feel!

DUKE. Tonight I wish all the captains to serve the prince.

JUAN DE MÉRIDA. A black man makes Christmas black for everyone.

DUKE. Let me never be without such black festivities, captain.

   [Enter MUSICIANS.]

MUSICIAN. *(Singing.)*

   ¶The Prince of Orange hankers
   To accompany at the banquet
   The amazing Duke of Alba
   And the black terror of Flanders.¶

JUAN. Music already?

MUSICIAN. Aye, for in composing tunes I am swifter than justice from God. I can compose a hundred in an afternoon, all flawless in wit and rhyme.

JUAN DE MÉRIDA. You gush poetry like the bloody flux. Here, take this plate . . . the contents, I mean. Sorry, the scraps aren't mine.

DUKE. What's cast from my table is not to return.

MUSICIAN. Heaven keep you.

   (Singing.)

   ¶Attending the tables
   Went soldiers and captains,
   Like good little waiters
   Serving liquor and viands.¶

   (Enter DOÑA LEONOR [disguised as a boy] and ANTÓN.)

ANTÓN. Meesieur?

JUAN DE MÉRIDA. My little Antón! You're just in time. Grab a slice of meat for yourself and for that page boy.

(Enter DON PEDRO OSORIO.)

DON PEDRO OSORIO.   I have returned with Generals Lanstrec and Vila.

DUKE.   Clear the table so we may discuss the terms of the prince's freedom.

(Enter LANSTREC and VILA [carrying coffers].)

LANSTREC.   *[Kneeling before the DUKE.]*

Let us embrace you, your excellency.

DUKE.   Rise to my arms.

VILA.   *[To ORANGE.]*

Sir, what happened?

ORANGE.   The mad caprices of fortune.

LANSTREC.   The withdrawal is turning out backwards for us.

ORANGE.   *[To the DUKE.]*

I will accept peace under any conditions your excellency imposes.

DUKE.   They will be the same ones that were imposed on me.

LANSTREC.   Your excellency's exploits have been remarkable. Much do you owe to your fortune.

DUKE.   I owe more to my blood.

VILA.   Who was responsible for such a bold feat?

JUAN DE MÉRIDA.   I, for only a black man would risk such a thing because only a black man is nothing.

VILA.   This wasn't the deed of a black man but of a prince.

JUAN DE MÉRIDA.   All that matters is that my king be served at such a difficult moment.

DUKE.   The conditions are that Orange shall withdraw his flags from the Low Countries and swear loyalty and obedience to the king for six years. His soldiers shall march out with their harquebuses pointed at the ground, their pikes dragging behind them, and their flags rolled up.

ORANGE.   Those are shameful conditions!

DUKE.   Complain to yourself, then, for they are the ones you ordered.

ORANGE.   The king owes all this to a black man.

DUKE.   The hostages must be turned over before you leave my tent.

LANSTREC.   The hostages and the ransom are both ready.

VILA.   The ransom comes in gold and jewels.

ORANGE.   *[To JUAN DE MÉRIDA.]*

   Open those coffers. Take from them whatever you wish.

JUAN DE MÉRIDA.   *[He opens the coffers.]*

   For my lord the duke, this diamond necklet and this gold medallion.

DUKE.   I accept.

JUAN DE MÉRIDA.   For the lord Don Pedro, this glossy chain, and these jeweled hatbands for Don Juan and Don Agustín. The gold coins shall be divided equally among the soldiers.

ORANGE.   Remarkable! The black man seeks to outdo me in everything.

DUKE.   May his valor be a lesson to these lands.

ANTÓN.   And twere Antón to get what?

JUAN DE MÉRIDA.   I shall pay you well, *negro*. Since you serve me, do not ask for a reward from anyone else.

ORANGE.   Now that you've divided up the spoils, what do you claim for yourself?

JUAN DE MÉRIDA.   I wish to honor myself with your sword alone. It is the most valuable prize to me because it comes from the belt of Orange.

ORANGE.   I shall give it to you with the condition that you give me yours.

JUAN DE MÉRIDA.   Mine is a trinket fit for a dog. It cost me nine silver coins.

ORANGE.   I value it above my whole country simply because it's yours.

DUKE.   It's getting late. Let's retire so your excellency may rest, for such are the demands of fortune.

ORANGE.   Tomorrow my people will vacate the Low Countries.

LANSTREC.   What a miserable turn of fortune in the space of an hour!

DUKE.   *[To JUAN DE MÉRIDA.]*

   Captain, I shall be embarking soon. I wish to take you with me so that your valor may be recognized by his majesty, whom I am to serve as majordomo.

JUAN DE MÉRIDA. Such a great prince as yourself should be God's majordomo, not just anybody's.

DUKE. Our king is not just anybody. He is a majesty of majesties.

JUAN DE MÉRIDA. Well, what will he name me if he makes Alba his majordomo? I am not fit to be his kitchen boy.

DUKE. You may expect a handsome reward from the king, as befits one who has made his Christmas so joyful.

(Exit all but JUAN DE MÉRIDA, DOÑA LEONOR, and ANTÓN.)

DOÑA LEONOR. Sir captain?

JUAN DE MÉRIDA. Who calls me?

DOÑA LEONOR. It is I.

JUAN DE MÉRIDA. What do you want with me, page boy of Beelzebub? Be gone immediately or I swear to God I'll kill you.

DOÑA LEONOR. Kill me? Why?

JUAN DE MÉRIDA. You ask why? You know very well why.

DOÑA LEONOR. I would have a word with you in private.

JUAN DE MÉRIDA. May a tiger attend you in private.

DOÑA LEONOR. I know you will attend me, captain, once you understand . . .

JUAN DE MÉRIDA. Understand what?

DOÑA LEONOR. That I am the one who, at a difficult moment, saved your life.

JUAN DE MÉRIDA. Saved my life? You?

DOÑA LEONOR. You yourself admitted it.

JUAN DE MÉRIDA. Who are you?

DOÑA LEONOR. I am Leonor.

JUAN DE MÉRIDA. You, Leonor? What are you talking about?

DOÑA LEONOR. Let my eyes do the talking.

JUAN. Good God! Why didn't you say so before? Give me that hand to kiss.

DOÑA LEONOR. You owe me your life, and I have come all the way from Mérida for my payment.

JUAN DE MÉRIDA.   By the shining heavens, I would give my life for you. Tell me how I can help.

DOÑA LEONOR.   By preventing the vile Don Agustín, who has deceived me, from marrying anyone else.

JUAN DE MÉRIDA.   Has he dishonored you?

DOÑA LEONOR.   I've come after him for that reason.

JUAN DE MÉRIDA.   And how do you know, madam, that he intends not to marry you?

DOÑA LEONOR.   From this letter, which I picked from the coward's pocket.

   [She hands JUAN DE MÉRIDA a letter.]

JUAN DE MÉRIDA.   *[Reading the letter to himself.]*

   I see. I will have him on his knees, begging to marry you. Let's wait until the duke sets sail, for Heaven desires that I repay you for my life in the same place you gave it to me.

ANTÓN.   Meesieur twere revenge taking upon the paleface dung. All the way from Mérida twere I come with ma'am to help.

JUAN DE MÉRIDA.   You knew she was a woman?

ANTÓN.   Aye aye, meesieur.

JUAN DE MÉRIDA.   You tricked me, you dog! I'm mortified.

ANTÓN.   Twere suckered Juan, Antón's joke!

JUAN DE MÉRIDA.   *[To DOÑA LEONOR.]*

   How dare Don Agustín dishonor such an angel! If only he were a Caesar, for then, in forcing a Caesar to marry you, my vengeance would be all the greater.

LEONOR.   With you by my side, I shall be fortunate.

JUAN DE MÉRIDA.   My hand is here to back up my word.

LEONOR.   Your hand gives me the assurances I need.

JUAN DE MÉRIDA.   Rest assured.

LEONOR.   Go with God then, my brave black soldier.

JUAN DE MÉRIDA.   May he keep you, lovely Leonor.

ACT 3, Scene 1

([An antechamber in the royal palace in Madrid.] Enter JUAN DE MÉRIDA, finely dressed; ANTÓN, in a page's outfit; and DOÑA LEONOR, as a lackey [disguised as a boy].)

JUAN DE MÉRIDA.   God help me, I'm already tiring of this court. Armies of stylish courtiers do nothing but point at me and whisper among themselves.

ANTÓN.   Sundry and very pale faces twere mocking and jeering. Tush tush, sneezing and farting.

DOÑA LEONOR.   If they spent one freezing night in the Low Countries, Antón, they'd learn to work more and jeer less.

JUAN DE MÉRIDA.   I swear I've been counting the flagstones in this floor for three days now. I'd rather be back in the bog, with the water up to here, than suffer this unending wait.

DOÑA LEONOR.   I'm ready to leave as well.

JUAN DE MÉRIDA.   No need to worry. We shall both leave soon.

[He takes a letter from a pocket.]

This letter from the duke will keep the captain from further mischief until I'm able to make him honor his written word to you.

DOÑA LEONOR.   My deliverance depends on you.

JUAN DE MÉRIDA.   You will depart with the letter and, after having it delivered to the captain, discreetly sequester yourself in the Convent of Saint Eulalia, from which you'll emerge to punish the disrespect of so vile a knight.

DOÑA LEONOR.   I entrust my vengeance to your hands.

JUAN DE MÉRIDA.   I am yours, for yours is the life I possess. You saved it when he would have taken it, and now I repay the favor by avenging you. Until I arrive, the duke's letter will delay the captain's marriage to Doña Juana. When I get to Mérida and cross paths with him, I'll settle the matter with swords and fists if necessary.

(Exit DOÑA LEONOR.)

ANTÓN.   Twere time for finding the duke.

JUAN DE MÉRIDA.   By God, my little Antón, these chambers are an arena of flatterers and fill me with more fear than the enemy battlefield. Straighten your cape and do not leave my side.

ANTÓN.   Best twere making signs of the cross.

JUAN DE MÉRIDA.   Don't embarrass us when we go in.

([JUAN DE MÉRIDA and ANTÓN pace nervously.] Enter DON GÓMEZ and DON PEDRO on one side, and DON MARTÍN and DON FRANCISCO on the other, with petitions for the king.)

DON GÓMEZ.   We may wait for his majesty here.

DON FRANCISCO.   He's on his way to the chapel. I'll give him the petition I've been waiting months to deliver.

DON MARTÍN.   I've spoken with the Duke of Alba twice.

DON FRANCISCO.   That's the path to life everlasting.

DON PEDRO.   Look at those remarkable *negros*.

DON FRANCISCO.   I've seen them in the antechamber for two days now.

DON MARTÍN.   The dog struts with such gravity!

DON FRANCISCO.   And the page hangs at his footsteps.

DON PEDRO.   They would fetch a good three thousand silver coins.

DON GÓMEZ.   Achoo!

JUAN DE MÉRIDA.   What was that?

ANTÓN.   Palefaces twere sneezing to make jest of swarthies.

DON FRANCISCO.   Achoo!

DON PEDRO.   Hey you, Mandinga!

DON MARTÍN.   Achoo!

JUAN DE MÉRIDA.   Pay them no attention.

ANTÓN.   No attention paying? How now, twere I drawing my sword!

DON PEDRO.   The dirty dog is so stiff and solemn.

DON FRANCISCO.   The feathers in his hat are hilarious.

DON MARTÍN.   Feathers from Saint Anthony's raven as far as I'm concerned.

(DON GÓMEZ farts.)

DON PEDRO.   Look how grandly he turns his face to us!

JUAN DE MÉRIDA.   Did someone just fart?

ANTÓN.   Fart.

JUAN DE MÉRIDA.   At whom?

(ANTÓN holds his nose and points at JUAN DE MÉRIDA.)

JUAN DE MÉRIDA.   No, *negro*, I think it was at you.

ANTÓN.   At Antón?

JUAN DE MÉRIDA.   Yes.

(More farting sounds.)

ANTÓN.   Whom twere farting at now?

JUAN DE MÉRIDA.   Yes, I think that one was for me. God, it stinks. I'll teach these cowards better manners. Such shameful behavior calls for cracking skulls.

[He attacks them.]

DON FRANCISCO.   He murders me!

DON PEDRO.   Help us!

JUAN DE MÉRIDA.   Fart at me now, you idiot.

(Enter palace GUARDS with halberds.)

GUARD 1.   What's going on here?

JUAN DE MÉRIDA.   A black man teaching white men manners, that's all.

GUARD 2.   Oh, negro!

DON MARTÍN.   You vile man!

DON FRANCISCO.   You attacked us!

DON GÓMEZ.   Kill him or take him prisoner.

JUAN DE MÉRIDA.   Me, prisoner?

DON PEDRO.   Seize him!

JUAN DE MÉRIDA.   Cowards, see if I let myself be seized.

DON FRANCISCO.   *[To the GUARDS.]*

This way! Get him!

JUAN DE MÉRIDA.   Cowards! You attack me from behind?

DON PEDRO.   Kill this dog.

ANTÓN.   Alas, poor Antón twill die too.

DON GÓMEZ.   The duke is here.

GUARD 1.   I bet he'll have him hanged from the rafters.

(Enter the DUKE, with a majordomo's staff.)

DUKE.   Guards, hang the ruffian who dared such a barbaric deed.

GUARD 2.   It's this dog, sir.

DUKE.   Hold that order, soldiers. What's going on here, Captain Juan de Alba?

JUAN DE MÉRIDA.   Your excellency can see for himself. Consequences of my color. Some gentlemen made me lose my temper. If I deserve punishment or prison, I am at your excellency's mercy.

DUKE.   The prison shall be the tight embrace of my arms.

DON MARTÍN.   This is an insult!

DON PEDRO.   I'm dumbstruck.

DON FRANCISCO.   So this is the famous *negro* of Flanders? More like a *negro* from Hell, for he cracks skulls like a demon.

JUAN DE MÉRIDA.   Defects of my color.

DON GÓMEZ.   You dare to strut around in your color?

DUKE.   Gentlemen, this man you see is the lord Captain Juan de Alba, whose color has earned him eternal fame. And because of his night, I am dawn and his majesty is sun of the Flemish pole. We owe untold glory to his color.

ANTÓN.   And moi twere Little Antón.

JUAN DE MÉRIDA.   Shush.

ANTÓN.   Twere shushing now, anon to speak.

[Exit the four GENTLEMEN.]

JUAN DE MÉRIDA.   I am the one who owes all my being to your excellency, for though I am vile night, I am dawn in your light. I beg your excellency, for God's sake, to forgive me for the embarrassing situation my color has caused in the palace.

DUKE. His majesty has considered the issue of your reward.

JUAN DE MÉRIDA. I fear I am not fit for this court, by God.

DUKE. You will depart soon: tomorrow or the next day.

JUAN DE MÉRIDA. I kiss your excellency's hand for the favor.

DUKE. His majesty desires to meet you, and now is the perfect opportunity, for he comes to the chapel. Stand here. I hear the sound of his guard approaching. I'll go tell him you're here.

(Exit the DUKE.)

JUAN DE MÉRIDA. My little Antón, I'm fearful of meeting the king.

ANTÓN. Twere not a man, him?

JUAN DE MÉRIDA. He's a man, but it's said that Heaven has carefully imbued him with such majesty and conviction that it astonishes everyone who looks upon him. And as I consider myself a vile being compared to an eagle that rules tropical fiefdoms and remote empires, I'm beginning to feel cowardly for the first time in my life.

(Enter the DUKE with KING Philip, collecting petitions. [The DUKE points to JUAN DE MÉRIDA.])

DUKE. That man over there, holy majesty . . .

JUAN DE MÉRIDA. Antón?

ANTÓN. Meesieur?

JUAN DE MÉRIDA. I tremble.

DUKE. . . . is Captain Juan de Alba.

KING. Have him approach, duke. I wish to admire such an extraordinary black man from up close.

DUKE. Captain, you may approach. Approach.

JUAN DE MÉRIDA. Can a king be so powerful he causes one to tremble?

DUKE. Humble yourself at his majesty's feet.

JUAN DE MÉRIDA. Sir, I . . .

DUKE. Approach.

KING. Remarkable ... astonishing ...

JUAN DE MÉRIDA. ... am a black man, a *negro* ...

DUKE. Relax, captain.

JUAN DE MÉRIDA. So wretched that I embarrassed your holy majesty in Flanders with my color.

DUKE. *[To the KING.]*

Last Christmas he was the glory and honor of Spain, which delights at his return.

JUAN DE MÉRIDA. *[To the KING.]*

I gave Flanders, sir, a black Christmas. The duke honors me with his light, which would be, without his purity, as black as my fortune. On Christmas I was a shadow in his shining rays.

KING. Captain Alba, God shines favor on my kingdoms because of you. May he reward you on my account.

(Exit [the KING and DUKE].)

ANTÓN. Swearing to God, the king twere turning swarthies white. Such a mighty dong twere making me tremble. Meesieur?

JUAN DE MÉRIDA. I've lost track of myself.

ANTÓN. Twere possible to say now: blacks are people too.

JUAN DE MÉRIDA. Does the majesty that sets two hemispheres to tremble speak to me and honor me thus? Black men everywhere owe me thanks for giving their color this promotion and privilege.

ANTÓN. Twere finished speaking to the majesty and turning swarthy again.

JUAN DE MÉRIDA. Your work on my behalf is done, fortune, for in terms of honors, you have nothing left to give me nor I to ask of you. The king has honored me and I have looked upon his majesty. I cannot ask for anything more. I have accredited my color, fortune, more than I ever imagined.

(Enter the DUKE.)

DUKE. Your lordship now has an office here.

JUAN DE MÉRIDA. Lor ... what?

DUKE. Lordship.

JUAN DE MÉRIDA. Your excellency must have meant to say *dogship*. Surely it was a mistake. A lordship? For me . . .

DUKE. He who, through honorable actions, shows the ability to rule over great lords has earned a lordship. His majesty offers you a seat in the Order of Santiago.

JUAN DE MÉRIDA. *[Stunned.]*

But how do I qualify for the order with Guinean blood?

DUKE. Your deeds here in Flanders qualify you, for such an outstanding captain needs no qualification other than his valor. You are the product of your accomplishments, through which fortune accredits your color. The cross of the order proclaims your valor, regardless of your color, for it establishes a lineage that qualifies you. For the moment your income will be six thousand ducats.

JUAN DE MÉRIDA. What!

DUKE. Virtue has promoted you thus.

JUAN DE MÉRIDA. May blacks everywhere exchange their outrage for honor. Six thousand ducats!

DUKE. Tremendous.

JUAN DE MÉRIDA. Such a lowly dog could never imagine that kind of wealth.

DUKE. His majesty has also named you lieutenant general.

JUAN DE MÉRIDA. There must be, great lord, some kind of bet between fortune and the king, to see who can do more. This is unheard of. If fate once bucked me, it now walks beside me. Thanks to your excellency, I achieve great honor and favor, though my merits be few.

DUKE. Fortune favors the bold, and such a great soldier deserves no less than the rank of lieutenant general. Thus does courtesy reward your lordship with the fruits of bravery.

JUAN DE MÉRIDA. I believe, sir, that just as Spain has given us Juan the Scholar, it now names me Juan the Soldier. Juan Latino and Juan Soldado: our dark costumes give credit to our color and show that blacks are capable of distinction in both arms and letters. But if I am a ray of that beautiful dawn, then color has saved me. I am white, the son of Alba, which is the star of the Spanish sun.

DUKE. Your light will shine eternally white in the dawn.

ANTÓN. Buddy, twere a fancy *negro* lord now!

DUKE.   Let's go, for the king wishes to confer the title on you today.

JUAN DE MÉRIDA.   Little Antón?

ANTÓN.   Meesieur?

JUAN DE MÉRIDA.   Prepare the horses, for we shall journey to Mérida before the break of day.

ANTÓN.   Twere going.

JUAN DE MÉRIDA.   And there we shall force Don Agustín to the altar.

(Exit [all].)

ACT 3, Scene 2

([The main square in Mérida, as in act 1, scene 1.] Enter MUSICIANS, the captain DON AGUSTÍN, and DOÑA JUANA in fine dress.)

MUSICIANS.   (Singing.)

¶May glory sound Mars's siren
Though it interrupt Cupid's peace.
Lucky is the soldier who
In cruel war finds love so sweet.¶

DOÑA JUANA.   Love misspeaks, for his peace is all war.

DON AGUSTÍN.   From the icy fields of Flanders, love has brought me to such splendid rewards.

DOÑA JUANA.   I'm fortunate to have earned them in Mérida.

DON AGUSTÍN.   Everything works out with time.

DOÑA JUANA.   And with hope. For though goosefleshed winter, pale and frostbit, may sit entrenched in the shadows of eternal chill, its damp sun mocking the summer, and though it be smothered in horizonless snow and untouched by the warmth of April and May, yet soon its cruel ice thaws into crystalline streams that snake through flower-strewn banks in the green of spring: symbol of he who hopes.

DON AGUSTÍN.   Fortunate is he who has such hope.

DOÑA JUANA.   And a thousand times fortunate is my love.

DON AGUSTÍN. Tomorrow our bond will be eternal, in a sovereign and sacred union of the stars.

DOÑA JUANA. When love breathes, how can the stars not be involved?

(Enter DON JUAN DE ESTRADA.)

DON JUAN DE ESTRADA. Son, a messenger boy just gave me this letter.

DON AGUSTÍN. I'll bet it's an order calling me to war, though I want peace more than glory.

(Aside.)

If it's from Leonor, it could ruin everything! But my fear is misplaced, for I left her with Don Pedro Osorio in Antwerp.

DON JUAN DE ESTRADA. Whose signature is it?

DON AGUSTÍN. The duke's.

DON JUAN DE ESTRADA. It must be important.

DON AGUSTÍN. *(Reading aloud.)*

"His majesty desires that I wait out the stubbornness of the rebel countries in his palace for now, where I shall serve him as head majordomo. Thus it has been necessary to name a lieutenant general in my absence. He will be passing through Mérida on his way to port in Lisbon, and I wish him to attend the captain's wedding. I ask that the marriage be delayed until he arrives so he may serve as my proxy. In this way do I show the love I bear the captain. May God keep you. Signed in March, in Madrid, by the Duke of Alba."

DON JUAN DE ESTRADA. He shows you great favor!

DON AGUSTÍN. I would prefer he not show it at so pressing a moment. For desire is hell when hope runs thin. And many times, my lord, delayed glories turn to misfortune.

DON JUAN DE ESTRADA. When the wait is so short and the duke looks out for you as is proper, the delay is just.

DON AGUSTÍN. Love is dismayed by delay. I will postpone my affairs no longer, my father and lord, for love dies in desire, and desire is hell. Marrying is not like assaulting a fortress or jumping a trench, which require a general's command. Love recruits its own glories, and I plant my feet on the ground of peace. The lieutenant general's presence is superfluous in so sweet a victory.

DOÑA JUANA. All of Mérida's nobility is ready, sir: its beauty summoned, its servants in a fuss. A delay makes no sense.

DON AGUSTÍN.   Today, sir, I shall reap the fruits of my love.

DON JUAN DE ESTRADA.   I do not mean to stop it. I shall work to facilitate the marriage as best as possible.

(Enter two GENTLEMEN, elegantly dressed.)

GENTLEMAN 1.   What are you doing here? A wedding sponsor worthy of your father and my lord now arrives at your house.

DOÑA JUANA.   Love and honor today make me eternal.

GENTLEMAN 2.   A host of elegantly dressed men, soldiers, and decorated captains march in with the green spring, as vast as the firmament in the golden light.

DON JUAN DE ESTRADA.   Who saw them?

GENTLEMAN 1.   Many have seen them, including us.

DON AGUSTÍN.   *[To the GENTLEMEN.]*

I have a thousand tasks to attend to. Go give them my regrets.

[Exit the GENTLEMEN.]

DON JUAN DE ESTRADA.   May you linger on the flower-strewn bridal bed, giving life to eternity with glorious offspring, greener than the tender hearts of palm. May your loving bond be one of constant peace and joy. May Mérida find a phoenix of elegance in the splendid groom and a well of joy and distinction in his divine bride.

DOÑA JUANA.   I cannot ask of fortune any greater gift than the husband it gives me today.

DON AGUSTÍN.   Nor I for any greater happiness than the love I see in your eyes.

DOÑA JUANA.   Who has ever been so lucky?

DON AGUSTÍN.   Who has ever deserved such rewards?

(Enter a SERVANT.)

SERVANT.   The lieutenant general is here.

DON JUAN DE ESTRADA.   What are you saying? We must attend him at once.

DON AGUSTÍN.   *(Aside.)*

For the sake of my love, may Doña Leonor not be with him.

SERVANT.   This is going to be bad.

(Enter JUAN DE MÉRIDA with full accompaniment.)

DON AGUSTÍN.   May your lordship consider me your servant. But whose hands do I have the pleasure of kissing?

JUAN DE MÉRIDA.   It is I.

DON AGUSTÍN.   May your lordship live a thousand years.

DOÑA JUANA.   God help me, is that not my *negro*, little Juan?

JUAN DE MÉRIDA.   Why are you all so astonished?

DON AGUSTÍN.   But how?

JUAN DE MÉRIDA.   Such extraordinary changes, sir captain, are the workings of fortune and her inconstant wheel, which levels all obstacles. Thus is virtue rewarded. His majesty has honored my color with a seat in the Order of Santiago and an income of six thousand ducats, and he wishes to exalt me with the position of lieutenant general, delighting in the black man whose sword, valor, and fortitude have earned him the merits of a white man. Thus shall whites learn an important lesson: courage comes from Heaven, color from Earth. In this very place, if you remember, incited by my lowliness, you refused to grant me a position in the army; and in the same spot you now recognize me—who would have believed it!—as your general. For thus does time transform fortune. And while I could take black vengeance on you here for your offenses, I wish to honor your person so you'll see me as a black man who both acts white and targets whites . . . for promotion! And thus I name you to my regiment as a three-star colonel, though it's insufficient for so great a soldier.

DON AGUSTÍN.   Allow me to shake your lordship's hand.

JUAN DE MÉRIDA.   A full embrace would earn you more glory. And now, with her permission, I wish to kiss my lady's feet.

DOÑA JUANA.   I am frozen in confusion.

JUAN DE MÉRIDA.   I have always prided myself, my lady, on being your servant. For vile is he who denies the origin of his fortune, and ungrateful is he who is ashamed of his past. I promised to return to your presence made wealthy by fortune, and I now ask for your favor and honor.

DOÑA JUANA.   Our entire house, from this day forward, is honored by your lordship.

JUAN DE MÉRIDA.   Who would ever have imagined you would one day address me with the word *lordship*?

DOÑA JUANA.   Merit increases virtue, and arms and letters have always been the two poles of the world's nobility. All noble lines have their beginnings in them.

JUAN DE MÉRIDA.   And in me, blacks have the beginnings of their nobility. Please allow me to see my mother, the slave Catalina.

DON AGUSTÍN.   A fortunate slave is she whose son holds a lordship.

DOÑA JUANA.   Catalina is back in the village. Later we'll all go together to give her the good news.

JUAN DE MÉRIDA.   She'll be so rewarded to see me with my lordship and my great wealth.

DON AGUSTÍN.   *[Aside, to DON PEDRO OSORIO.]*

So you lost track of Leonor?

DON PEDRO OSORIO.   *[Aside, to DON AGUSTÍN.]*

I did, though I heard she was ailing in Brussels. As there is no recent news of her, we must assume she has died.

DON AGUSTÍN.   *[Aside, to DON PEDRO OSORIO.]*

May God confirm this good news.

JUAN DE MÉRIDA.   Don Agustín could never have imagined such a black wedding.

(Enter ANTÓN.)

ANTÓN.   *(Aside, to JUAN DE MÉRIDA.)*

Leonor twere waiting at the door.

JUAN DE MÉRIDA.   *[Aside, to ANTÓN.]*

Tell her to come in.

DON AGUSTÍN.   You mean I could never have imagined such a happy one, for your lordship's presence is sufficient to brighten it. With your permission, I shall offer my hand to my wife.

JUAN DE MÉRIDA.   Stay that hand, sir, for if you mean to offer it to your wife, this is she.

(JUAN DE MÉRIDA reveals DOÑA LEONOR.)

ANTÓN.   Into the trap twere falling, a mouse man forsooth!

DOÑA JUANA.   Oh, I feel faint!

DON AGUSTÍN.   My wife! What! How?

JUAN DE MÉRIDA.   What do you mean how? By your own word. And by the workings of justice.

DON AGUSTÍN.   Sir . . .

JUAN DE MÉRIDA.   Marry her immediately, or by the life of the king I shall cut your throat.

DON JUAN DE ESTRADA.   Lieutenant general, sir, you cannot force him to marry.

JUAN DE MÉRIDA.   His own commitment forces him.

DOÑA JUANA.   My hopes have been clouded with uncertainty.

DON JUAN DE ESTRADA.   What commitment?

JUAN DE MÉRIDA.   This will explain it.

(He hands Don Agustín's letter to DON JUAN DE ESTRADA.)

DON JUAN DE ESTRADA.   *[To DON AGUSTÍN.]*

Is this true?

DON AGUSTÍN.   Sir . . .

DON JUAN DE ESTRADA.   Enough. He who commits himself must honor his word. That means you.

JUAN DE MÉRIDA.   Doña Leonor's beauty, purity, and goodness should have been enough to obligate you. Because I received my life from her in this spot, despite your anger and cruelty, it is fitting that I restore her life and honor to her here. You granted me my life because of her, and thus the two of you, because of me, shall have one life, one being, and one soul with a new nature.

DON AGUSTÍN.   Let it be thus, since you command it.

JUAN DE MÉRIDA.   I implore it, and the love and commitment that you promised in this letter demand it.

DON AGUSTÍN.   *[To DOÑA LEONOR.]*

I offer you my hand and my life.

DOÑA JUANA.   This is humiliating!

DOÑA LEONOR.   *[To DON AGUSTÍN.]*

Sir, allow me to surrender my soul at your feet.

DOÑA JUANA.   *[To JUAN DE MÉRIDA.]*

You betray me.

JUAN DE MÉRIDA. On the contrary, madam: I look out for your good name. For if Don Agustín had given you his hand in deception, you would have looked foolish and lost all honor. And if I have stripped you of your husband—though your complaint is without justification—choose another from Mérida to your liking, and I shall, through my position and my income, offer him to you.

DOÑA JUANA. Well, since I am to be married under your sponsorship, and Heaven has bestowed upon you an honor that equals my nobility, I wish to promote you from servant to husband.

JUAN DE MÉRIDA. What are you saying?

DOÑA JUANA. That this is what I wish.

JUAN DE MÉRIDA. Who would have believed such a thing!

DON AGUSTÍN. Such are the turns of fortune.

JUAN DE MÉRIDA. Consider me, my ladyship, your slave.

DOÑA JUANA. And from this day forward, I shall be yours.

JUAN DE MÉRIDA. Since the matter has ended so joyfully, let the weddings take place tonight.

DON JUAN DE ESTRADA. And the merriment and celebrations shall commence tomorrow.

JUAN DE MÉRIDA. The exploits of this black man will continue in another play, which will tell the whole true story in all its detail.

VIRTUES OVERCOME APPEARANCES

(Virtudes vencen señales)

By Luis Vélez de Guevara

Dramatis Personae *in order of appearance*

Admiral of Albania
Dionisio, Sicilian ambassador to Albania
Leda, princess of Albania
Ladies-in-waiting to the princess (nonspeaking)
King Lisandro of Albania
Attendants to the king (nonspeaking)
Alberto ⎱
Artenio ⎬ courtiers
Roberto ⎪
Ricardo ⎰
Tebandro, Filipo's warden
Filipo, prince of Albania
Bugle, clownish lackey
Sergesto ⎱
Lidonio ⎬ robbers
Timbreo ⎪
Liseno ⎰
Tirrena, peasant girl
Servant
King Enrico of Sicily
Alfreda, Enrico's sister
Celio, herald
Courtiers (nonspeaking)
Grandees of Albania (nonspeaking)

Setting: The Albanian court and countryside, unspecified era.

ACT 1, Scene 1

([A chamber in the royal palace of Albania.] Enter through one door DIONISIO and the ADMIRAL; and through another door, simultaneously, LEDA, in a hunting outfit, and her ladies-in-waiting.)

ADMIRAL.   Her highness crosses our path. I believe she is bound for the countryside.

DIONISIO.   No light is equal to the sun her beauty radiates.

ADMIRAL.   *[To LEDA.]*

This is the ambassador.

DIONISIO.   *(Aside.)*

Never have I seen such beauty, which deserves sole ownership of the world.

[He kneels.]

LEDA.   What did you say?

DIONISIO.   Madam, your divine presence causes anxiety, admiration, and love.

LEDA.   Rise.

(DIONISIO [rises and] hands LEDA a letter.)

DIONISIO.   This is from Alfreda, sister to King Enrico of Sicily.

LEDA.   Fare they well?

DIONISIO.   Each of them, madam, is prepared to show much gratitude for your highness's sweet affection.

[LEDA reads the letter to herself.]

LEDA.   I do not wish to marry at the moment, ambassador. In this matter my father will have already given you my reply, for I represent Albania's male line, and Albania, to prevent its throne from passing to a foreigner, does not wish me to marry beyond its borders. Though the crown would find its clout greatly enhanced through union with the monarchy of Sicily, reason of state, ambassador, dictates that it remain with a legitimate and natural-born owner.

DIONISIO.   Thus does the crown expose itself to an unfortunate predicament, for Enrico, who aspires to this union, is hardly a foreigner. His claim to the throne is indeed greater, in the absence of a male heir, than anyone else's. For it is well-known and widely demonstrated that the crown may not be inherited by a woman.

LEDA. If that were the case, and if Enrico were to insist on pressing his claim, Albania has the power to make me queen so that . . . Let's leave the matter there, ambassador, for I needn't go into detail about the kingdom's clout when it is proved by the blade of its sword: the true guarantor of the king's law in court. May my father live many years as guardian of Albania, amen, for he is quite capable of guiding us through this predicament until the day he falters. At that point, in choosing the owner of my heart, I shall rely on the vassals whose honor and equanimity I trust. And in such cases, Albania's admirals, unswerving in their loyalty to the royal family, will support my rejection of Sicily's offer. This is my answer to Enrico, and may God keep you, for I'm off to kill a boar.

(Exit LEDA with her ladies-in-waiting.)

DIONISIO. That's quite the answer, sir admiral.

ADMIRAL. The princess has responded with the firmness of her vassals. She is a credit to her father's watchful eye.

DIONISIO. She clearly holds you in great esteem.

ADMIRAL. May Heaven keep her a thousand years, for she appreciates my service and the nobility of my blood.

DIONISIO. That must be the primary reason that moves you, admiral, to rebuff the offer I bring from Enrico, even when in doing so you make Albania the enemy of Sicily and provoke Naples. For Alfreda, who promotes this mission, is engaged to Carlos of Naples, and when their two crowns are united on land and sea, Albania will find little defense in you, admiral. A single admiral of Albania cannot compete against the power of two kings.

ADMIRAL. Ambassador, he whom you address holds in his breast a valor that does not shrink from the world. Enrico and Carlos are my path to ruling the globe once I become lord of Albania, for they shall give me, when I defeat them, the motive, the means, the opportunity, the manpower, and the desire to see the world at my feet.

DIONISIO. Enough, Albanian!

ADMIRAL. Because I know you are unworthy of defenestration, I shall not attempt it.

DIONISIO. By God in Heaven, on all of Albanian soil there is no breast with the courage to resist me, even if all hearts were to beat as one!

ADMIRAL. You speak, ambassador, with the confidence of diplomatic immunity, but so help me God . . .

DIONISIO.   Careful, Albanian, for there is greater courage in me than you think.

ADMIRAL.   Not so much, Sicilian, and you'd better hope this hand does not withdraw the sword it rests upon or, on her highness's life, you'll have no head for the sun to shine on.

DIONISIO.   Your bluster and pretense do not fool me.

ADMIRAL.   Such is my pretense that I must depart in order not to kill you!

DIONISIO.   If it leads to your departure, I shall not be a little grateful.

ADMIRAL.   This matter is not closed, but for now, the king is here.

(Exit the ADMIRAL, and enter as many attendants as possible in the company of KING Lisandro, who boasts a long white beard, along with ROBERTO, ALBERTO, ARTENIO, and RICARDO.)

KING.   *[To ALBERTO.]*

I recognize the admiral's voice in those shouts. Does he argue with the Sicilian ambassador?

DIONISIO.   *[Aside.]*

I am beside myself with rage at that damned braggart! Upon the life of Enrico, I shall avenge such an appalling breach of decorum!

ALBERTO.   *[To the KING.]*

The admiral left just as you were entering.

KING.   They have had some kind of disagreement, for Dionisio is angry.

DIONISIO.   I have carried out my mission, sir, in a manner worthy of Enrico, who wishes to reach an alliance with Albania, having learned from his first attempt to broker this marriage for the emperor's sake. This crown is his by birthright, despite Princess Leda's antagonizing comments about Albania's admirals. When she tries to marry or to become queen, she will find out if anyone defends the crown that belongs to Enrico, who is the male heir with the greatest claim to this throne. For there will be no one to save it even if Albania, which today rejects Enrico's offer, summons an entire fleet of admirals.

KING.   Enough, Dionisio.

DIONISIO.   Sir . . .

KING.   Leda has responded to your offer with my own thoughts, which animate her courage, and there is no need for you to await additional replies. Tell your king you have observed in me all the valor of Pyrrhus, Achilles, Caesar, and Alexander combined, and that King Lisandro the Albanian does not fear vile threats. Leda alone represents the male line of my country, and Leda alone is the heir to my courage. The Albanian people will not submit, through either marriage or inheritance, to a foreign king. Nor will they agree to anything other than what I've just stated, for they deny any foreign rights to the kingdom. This is my final word on the matter. Go with God.

DIONISIO.   May Heaven keep you.

(Exit DIONISIO.)

ARTENIO.   Such insistence!

KING.   He must think that old age fills my breast with fear since frigid time crowns my head with snow.

ROBERTO.   Never does a heart freeze over that beats with the blood of courage.

ALBERTO.   Though Leda's capability is reassuring to all, Heaven was cruel to Albania in denying us a male heir who could represent your worth and inherit such an invincible nation. For I see the same drawback in marrying her to a vassal like the admiral as to a foreigner: the people would not want to be governed by him.

RICARDO.   Albania's lack of a male heir may bring mortal ruin upon its crown.

ARTENIO.   If only there were such an heir—even if he were a malformed monster—the people would revere him for carrying your blood and valor.

ROBERTO.   Even if the mother were the strangest barbarian ever bred of Libyan heat or Scythian cold, as long as you were the father of such an aberration, it would be a happy occasion for Albania. For then you would need not risk the peace of your kingdom by giving it to a foreigner or a vassal.

KING.   Intrepid Albanians, may Heaven defend you for many centuries, with long periods of happiness. You do have a male heir, born of my own blood and nobility, brother to Leda and son to the same saintly mother. Though he did not spring from some barbarian bride of Libya or Scythia, he is nonetheless an astonishing freak of nature, among her greatest aberrations. And while you may marvel at this sudden revelation, its extraordinary subject needn't cause you alarm. Listen carefully. You already know, through stories from your parents or from each other—for there are several generations among you—how I was married in Hungary to Margarita, who reclines eternally in my memory as if preserved in jasper. Heaven, in the green years of our union, refused to give me children, for reasons only it knows. In my more mature years, I fathered Leda, an image of the sun who brought joy to both me and Albania. You celebrated her birth, and Heaven lit up the sky in a dazzling tribute of stars and comets. The happy birth gave hope that Albania might expect a male heir, a noble Atlas to support its crown. Many times desire sought to engender its likeness, a natural inclination in all animals. On one such night, I happened to have before my eyes, in a gold and silk tapestry, the astonishing figure of Queen Saba of Ethiopia: she who, to satisfy her curiosity, journeyed from the scorched climate of the phoenix to visit the Hebrew king. So intently were my eyes cast upon the jet-black skin, brought to pulsing life by the white hand of some Belgian Timanthes, that the visual cues triggered my imagination to engender what was being seen. For in such cases all natural historians confirm that what is seen is reproduced through communication with the imaginative faculty of the soul. And it is true, as proved in many instances that are called *exempla* when they concern God. The rods that Jacob placed before Laban's sheep with such heavenly ingenuity are proof of these truths, not to mention many similar cases, recounted in the ancient annals of both Christians and Gentiles, that lay all doubts to rest. Thus, when nine months had passed—oh, heavens!—the queen gave birth, and from my imagination sprouted such a garish copy of myself that, though beautiful Margarita was its dawn, it looked to us more like Queen Saba than its mother: so dark black that those present suspected something disgraceful. To understand the extraordinary violation that had produced such an abominable birth in Margarita, I thought about where my concentration had been the night of the conception. I reasoned that either I'd looked at Saba at the key moment or that Heaven had refused to allow Margarita's innocence to suffer injury. With these explanations of the aberration, I satisfied the doubts of those present so they wouldn't spread unfounded rumors. As for myself, astonished and confused by such a turn of events, I cast blame on my sad fortune and, in a mix of optimism and cowardice, turned the happy birth into a wretched miscarriage: after baptizing him, I locked him away forever, charging a nurse with his care and telling no one else of the matter, instead announcing that the child was a stillborn. In the prison of a palace tower, which rises above the woods like a mute sentinel, he languishes like a soulless giant. I arranged for him to be raised in isolation, and to this day the only man he has laid eyes on is the one who has educated him and kept him company. Tebandro comes and goes from the tower to take him food and sometimes to inform me, when he leaves the prince in slumber, of how he speaks and reasons and of the remarkable inclination toward greatness that he shows, without knowing who he is. For he is of royal lineage and, despite his color, of graceful appearance and disposition. He is quiet, honest, serious, truthful, generous, discreet, valiant, affable, cheerful, temperate, tidy, grateful without being false, swift to action, attentive, resolute, reasonable, patient, free of the coward's cruelty, and never inclined to idleness: all qualities that speak to his generous blood. Though he is twenty years old I have not seen his face, for I am moved by fatherly love but ashamed to have fathered a monster. Until now. Your strong resolve, Albanians, has inspired my own, which will speak to you through Filipo, for that is the prince's name. From the black clouds of his color, after so many nights of prison, the sun shall shine forth on Albania with the shimmer of his crown, just as it sets on me and my own rays turn to long shadows. Filipo is Albania's legitimate heir: swear loyalty to him, Albanians, for he is the male offspring of my blood and the barbarian son you have wished for. Beneath the dark black varnish lies a moon that runs seamlessly into the diamond sky, for he is Margarita's and my son: perhaps more regal than those Caesarean majesties, born of sacred laurel, whose immortal deeds exalt the two empires of the rising and setting sun. And in his offspring, as is natural and inevitable, the white color will return to offer restitution for the injury suffered by the father for the grandfather's error, if *error* be the correct term for a powerful imaginative faculty, the source of this remarkable aberration. Heaven, responding to your entreaties, piously reveals itself in Albania today, giving you the crown prince you desire so that no non-Albanian may inherit this throne, for it would be a calamity for it to pass to foreigners through birth or marriage. And while Filipo may stand out for his color and come across as different, unfamiliar, abnormal, extraordinary, monstrous, horrifying, astonishing, ugly, and bizarre, it must be remembered that virtues overcome appearances.

RICARDO.   Lord of the planet Filipo deserves to be, for Albania alone is not spacious enough for his great worth.

ALBERTO.   Delay no longer in bringing us the prince of Albania, that we may swear loyalty to him. And you needn't offer any further admonitions about his appearance. As long as he has your blood, as you claim he does, even if his body were bereft of the rational workings of a man's soul, we would rightly show him the same reverence we show you.

ROBERTO.   Give us Prince Filipo, and may the hope that once seemed impossible free Albania from its captivity. For though Leda, like a new Evadne or Semiramis, deserves to be the sun of two planets, the future of Albania rests more securely in Filipo.

ALBERTO.   We desire a fully lawful male heir. Delay no longer. Bring forth Filipo!

KING.   With such laudable resolve and heroic ambition backing him, O Mars-like Albanians, Filipo promises to be lord of a thousand worlds. Come forth to show the prince your obedience.

RICARDO.   So we shall. And with greater applause than Albania has ever showered on its natural-born rulers, let us shout: long live Filipo!

ALL.   Long live Filipo!

(Enter TEBANDRO with a letter in his hand.)

TEBANDRO. Take no farther step, sir, if by these shouts you mean to bring forth Filipo, for I'm afraid the intention you have revealed to Albania today misses the opportunity available to you for so long.

KING. Your words fill me with dread, Tebandro.

TEBANDRO. It does me no good to hide what you will find out eventually.

KING. If Filipo has died, may my hopes perish with him, along with Albania's last means of legitimate succession.

TEBANDRO. The misfortune is not quite so grave. Read this letter.

[He hands the KING the letter.]

KING. I'm lost in confusion!

(Reading aloud.)

"Tebandro, by virtue of my reason, I was born free of this cell in which I've been held prisoner for crimes that my baffling fortune refuses to reveal. Today I break free to become my own owner; twenty years in captivity are enough. Forgive me for deciding to abandon your company. I hope one day I can repay you for your care and instruction, for apart from you I know no father to whom I owe either my knowledge or my existence. You understand my ambition, so don't be shocked that I should wish to break free of my cramped cell to stretch my limbs and glimpse the sky, for such broad realms of thought as mine cannot be contained in such a tiny world."

TEBANDRO. I found the letter this morning when I went in to wake him. He'd managed, before the break of dawn, to hurl himself, like a miscarried infant, from his cell window into the woods below, cleverly tying his sheets into a rope to reach the ground in safety. I offer you my head. Punish me however you like, if you feel I'm to blame for an incident I never could have foreseen or prevented.

[He kneels.]

KING. Rise, Tebandro. I do not blame you, for I know your loyalty.

TEBANDRO. *[Rising.]*

God bless you.

KING. We must organize a search party for Filipo all across Albania. Let no one who comes face-to-face with him be frightened by his extraordinary color. Let criers spread the word through cities and villages across the country, if my own desire does not find him first, carrying my heart toward him on the wings of fatherly love.

(Exit [all].)

ACT 1, Scene 2

([A wilderness area.] Enter FILIPO, dressed in colorful clothes and a ruffled collar, and carrying a large branch for a staff.)

[Translator's note: The Spanish stage directions indicate that the actor, assumed to be white, is to appear in blackface.]

FILIPO. O liberty, I thank you for this sun that I see, this blue dome that I admire, these green fields that I observe. On your account I am made human, on your account I am reborn, on your account I come to understand God's awesome power when I contemplate the heavens, the sun, the fields, and the sea. I see their author in all of them, as they chant in sweet harmony that they are an example of his omnipotence. The whole world is his temple. Everything adores and worships him, and everything beneath the sun—animal, vegetable, mineral—seems to say: "God is my primary cause." From that mountain, neighbor to the sun, I have observed the deep sea, and in it, more than in anything else in the world, I am awed by God's power, for I understand how that wild, salty, watery Pegasus, bucking up on its hind legs against the sun, is reined in by God with a thin strip of sand. I am tired and thirsty, and in the distance I hear the trickle of a fount, a silvery queen that graces the meadow with her shimmer. Give shelter and succor to this wayward pilgrim with shade and water, O beautiful diamond liquid. Such is your power because you also know God, to whom everything is akin.

[He observes himself in the water.]

But good heavens! Am I this ugly monster in the water, equal in appearance to the night? It is indeed myself that I see! Even as I stare at the copy of myself that you show me, O silvery fount, I can't believe it, for it would seem impossible for such a proud soul to inhabit such a crude and clumsy casing.

(Enter LEDA from above, carrying a javelin [and addressing the animal she chases].)

LEDA. Winged brute, you outrun the wind in your flight, but my wings are swifter, for I fly on the wind of thought. Stop! What am I saying? This precipice, which cuts through the meadow, impedes my advance. What shall I do?

FILIPO. Either my soul is deceived, or it perceives another form copied here in the pool. What new deity shines its rosy light upon the water? Next to my shadow stands the sun; next to my night, the day. Could it be my own soul, desiring to show me its immortal essence?

(LEDA begins to descend.)

LEDA. I'll follow this path down to the meadow.

FILIPO. It's gone, but what was it? If it was divine, it must have returned to Heaven. If it was my soul, I fear it has rejected my body as hideous and clumsy. But what is this fire or ice that runs through me, now that I stare at the original whose copy I watched burn and shine in the water? What phantasm is this, this divine beauty in human form that holds the world at its feet? I have seen the sky and the sun, the earth and the sea, which all surpassed my expectations, but I've never seen anything as strange and beautiful as this miracle.

[*To LEDA.*]

What deity are you who flatter the meadow with your presence, climbing down that mountain as if descending from Heaven?

LEDA. [*Startled.*]

Oh!

FILIPO. Have I frightened you?

LEDA. Who are you? Speak, you hideous and fantastical monster!

(*She tilts the javelin at FILIPO.*)

FILIPO. No need for steel, O sun whom I adore. Your rays of gold are sufficient to bring me to surrender to your feet.

[*He kneels.*]

LEDA. Who are you?

FILIPO. A man who has lived in ignorance of your beautiful existence. I surrender myself to you, so cast aside your fear. Yours is a power over death, for the spell you cast tyrannizes body and soul.

LEDA. What a remarkable turn of events. Rise.

FILIPO. [*Rising.*]

Tell me: Who are you? You make me forget myself at the same time that you show fear.

LEDA. A woman.

FILIPO. A woman!

LEDA. And heroic of heart.

FILIPO. Heaven help me! Is this what is meant by woman?

LEDA. Have you never seen a woman? Speak.

FILIPO. I seem a monster to you because you're the first woman I've seen since my birth.

LEDA. Where have you been living?

FILIPO. I have been a prisoner my entire life, my guilt decided by the harshness of fate.

LEDA. Incredible!

FILIPO. Today is the first day I've ventured out to see the sun, and before meeting you, woman, I thought the sun was the sun: the day that crowns these beautiful meadows with its rays, the soul that Heaven gave to the world. The sun that, appearing between sea green and celestial sapphire, admires its beauty in opposing mirrors and fills my soul with remarkable joy. But now that I've laid my eyes on you, I call the sun and the day liars. In you alone is human beauty represented, in you alone sovereign Heaven, in you alone love and desire. Such is your power over me in the short time I've known you that if I didn't know God, I'd mistake him for you.

LEDA. *[Aside.]*

What a beautiful soul this ugly body houses! What inclination is this, upon hearing him bear his soul to me, that draws me to his ferocity? What mysterious force disposes me to this monster? I know not what blood runs through him, but his person pleases me.

FILIPO. O beautiful deity, made human in the shape of a woman, what secret force do you possess that bends my will to you? When I was a prisoner I belonged to myself, but my love for you has changed that. Fill my mouth or eyes with your snow, for I am blinded, and ease the fire that drives my soul to madness.

LEDA. Stop!

FILIPO. I shall do so, for you hold more power over me than I do over myself.

LEDA. *[Aside.]*

Never have I seen a greater soul!

FILIPO. Are you leaving?

LEDA. Yes.

FILIPO. What do you command of me?

LEDA. That you stay.

FILIPO. How am I to stay when you carry me with you?

LEDA. If your soul comes with me, your body shall stay.

FILIPO. Impossible, for that would give the soul all the glory and leave the body stranded here with none.

LEDA. Halt your step. Do not follow me.

FILIPO. I am yours and shall obey, but will I see you again?

LEDA. I give you my word.

FILIPO. When?

LEDA. When Heaven wills it.

FILIPO. Heaven will surely take its time in satisfying my desire, for I am unfortunate. But I misspeak: the earth has known no man more fortunate than me after laying my eyes on you.

LEDA. Goodbye.

FILIPO. May I know your name, woman, to give my life some encouragement in such a sad absence?

LEDA. My name is Leda.

FILIPO. A name as beautiful as your ruddy gold complexion, my Leda. Oh, how the sun sets on me now, how the day darkens! Leda . . .

ADMIRAL. *(Offstage.)*

Stop that horse!

FILIPO. *[Peering offstage.]*

A man who appears to wish to speak with you, Leda, dismounts from a beautiful brute.

[Enter the ADMIRAL in a rush.]

ADMIRAL. I've come at the sound of your highness's name, for it is my north star.

LEDA. Welcome, admiral.

FILIPO. *[Aside.]*

"Admiral," she calls him. And he calls her "Highness." So her name is not Leda. She has deceived me!

ADMIRAL. Hardly did I hear the echo of your name, Leda, when I stepped onto the grass of this green meadow.

FILIPO. *[Aside.]*

I don't think she has deceived me. Her name is both Leda and Highness. Men must employ several methods to celebrate her beauty.

(Enter the [admiral's] lackey BUGLE, adorned in white felt.)

BUGLE. This time I get to see her highness too. Or did you forget me with the horse?

ADMIRAL. *[Ignoring BUGLE.]*

My good fortune overwhelms me.

LEDA. To what purpose do you arrive, admiral?

ADMIRAL. To thank you for the favors you have done me.

FILIPO. It seems that everyone worships this woman as a goddess.

ADMIRAL. What monster is this?

LEDA. I crossed paths with him, admiral, in my boar hunt. Observing my valor, and without recognizing who I am, he has kept me company with chivalrous and amorous flattery.

ADMIRAL. Give me license to dispense with him.

FILIPO. *[Aside.]*

O celestial beauty, what envy you provoke in me with the arrival of this man! I feel as though I've been poisoned. It must be jealousy: the offspring of love and rejection, as I've read. A second death do you give me, woman, with your beauty! Such great good and evil there are in you!

ADMIRAL. Ahoy, why do you wait around where you're not wanted?

FILIPO. *[Aside.]*

He calls me a hoy. That must be what men call each other around here.

ADMIRAL. Away with you, I say!

FILIPO. What makes you think you can speak to me that way?

BUGLE. He's got sass, this little *negro*. I bet he'll be in the doghouse before long.

ADMIRAL. Is it not sufficient that I'm the one commanding you?

FILIPO. No, why should it be?

ADMIRAL.   I'll kill you!

FILIPO.   *[Glancing at LEDA.]*

I'm already dying.

BUGLE.   Get out of here then.

ADMIRAL.   I'll finish you off.

FILIPO.   No you won't. Not while I carry this willow branch.

BUGLE.   Just wait till I get my hands on you.

FILIPO.   Let's see you try, you stupid oaf.

BUGLE.   In a second.

ADMIRAL.   Out of my sight!

BUGLE.   So you've got a little switch, do you? You gonna whip me or what? On her highness's life, I'll show you who you're dealing with!

FILIPO.   A bully with no fight in him. I see right through you.

ADMIRAL.   It's embarrassing to watch you speak! Leave this instant or I'll kill you. Your brutishness will not save you from the hands of death.

FILIPO.   On Leda's life, if you anger me, you'll no longer worship her sun.

LEDA.   Don't hurt him.

ADMIRAL.   I'm mad with rage! I can't resist the urge to kill him!

FILIPO.   They won't hurt me, Leda, for they see the black man's courage.

LEDA.   Go.

FILIPO.   I shall, for my love is obedient, but listen carefully.

LEDA.   I'm listening. Speak.

FILIPO.   Do you see this mountain, Leda, this latter-day Atlas? Observe how constant is its courtship of the wind, how steady its gaze toward the sun, greatest of the stars. Yet firmer in the face of time, more unflinching before the mutable course of fortune or the furious sea is my love, which admits no equal in sincerity or resilience. A mountain with a soul am I. If you find shelter in it, Leda, then your hesitation will eventually crumble, for a soul that withstands time can compete eternally against Heaven.

(Exit FILIPO.)

LEDA. Wondrous creature!

ADMIRAL. Strange indeed!

BUGLE. Let me go after him and kill him. I didn't want to do it in front of you.

LEDA. You are most valiant, Bugle.

BUGLE. Quite so, madam.

LEDA. So you've come, admiral, to thank me for my reply to Dionisio?

ADMIRAL. I was so honored. It gave new life to my soul, which is constant in its thoughts of you.

LEDA. Don't misinterpret my affection, admiral.

ADMIRAL. *[Aside.]*

Heavens, is my joy to be spoiled already?

LEDA. Let's go, for the afternoon bathes the mountains in shadow, and across the emerald fields the sun sets and the day dies. And in that valley the boar hunt begins.

ADMIRAL. *[Aside.]*

Doubt gnaws at me. I don't know what to think!

LEDA. I confess, admiral, that the strange creature who just left our presence could hold a privileged position in my court if his appearance weren't so terrifying, for his prudence and valor are great. I don't know what Heaven hides in him that finds such favor in me.

ADMIRAL. *[Aside.]*

Oh, womanly condition, always disposed to desire and choose the worst!

LEDA. Let's be off.

ADMIRAL. *[Aside.]*

My brief joy has been tempered by misfortune!

LEDA. *[Aside.]*

I shall order my men to seek him out, for the woman most disdainful of caution desires to be loved even by a monster.

BUGLE. *[Aside.]*

This time I faked my anger on the princess's account, you dirty dog, but next time I'll beat you silly!

ACT 2, Scene 1

([A mountainside in the wilderness.] Enter the highway robbers SERGESTO, LIDONIO, TIMBREO, and LISENO, stealthily, one by one, slowly scaling the mountain.)

SERGESTO. To the mountain!

LIDONIO. To the mountain!

TIMBREO. We'll be safer up there.

LISENO. And we'll be able to look out over two highways from one position.

SERGESTO. Upwards, Lidonio!

LIDONIO. Upwards, Timbreo!

TIMBREO. Upwards, Liseno!

LISENO. Upwards!

ALL. Upwards!

[The ROBBERS continue climbing until they are out of view.]

TIRRENA. *[Offstage.]*

Giddy-up, donkey! Stop dallying in the grass like you're being tickled!

[Enter FILIPO.]

FILIPO. From afar I saw men scaling the mountain. They must live there. I am in great need of human company.

TIRRENA. *[Offstage.]*

Giddy-up, donkey!

FILIPO. It sounds like someone's coming through the valley as well. I am in need of food, for in two days' time I've found no fruit, even bitter, among these mountain shrubs and trees. Oh, human frailty, subject in the end to all the body's encumbrances!

TIRRENA. I said giddy-up, donkey!

FILIPO. Someone's coming. And unless my desire deceives me, it's a woman.

TIRRENA. *[Offstage.]*

To keep meself company, Miss Donkey, let's go a-singing from here all the way to the village.

FILIPO. If it's a woman, she can be no match for the divine Leda, in whom Heaven has enshrined all human good.

TIRRENA. *(Singing, offstage.)*

> ¶Over the mount goes the girl
> Hair blowing in the wind.
> How lovely does she sing,
> How lovely does she weep,
> From jealousy and love so ill.¶

FILIPO. What sweet harmony from the tongue of this human siren! She has me madly hanging on her words.

TIRRENA. *(Singing [offstage].)*

> ¶Lost in private thoughts,
> Over the mount she goes.
> The shepherd who brings her hurt
> Shall reap a handful of woes.¶

(TIRRENA begins her entrance.)

> ¶She flees to the quiet
> High atop the mount,
> Hoping for a cure
> To the malady she's found—¶

[Noticing FILIPO.]

Oh, heavens! What savage or monster is this, so terrifying and hideous?

FILIPO. Don't be alarmed, woman, and restore that divine harmony to the sweet instrument of your voice. You have hurt me greatly in halting it, for I am human, and my soul is so noble that the novel melody from your lips had me in suspense.

TIRRENA. I can't. My voice is frozen in fear.

FILIPO. What is your name?

TIRRENA. Tirrena. At your service, naturally.

[Aside.]

I'll never see my donkey or my village again! May God rest your soul, Tirrena.

FILIPO. Come here, woman.

TIRRENA. I'm coming, though I wish I'd never set foot in this place.

FILIPO. Cast aside your fear, for I don't intend to offend or anger you, but tell me . . .

TIRRENA. Ask quickly.

FILIPO. Do you know Leda?

TIRRENA. Leda? The one from the poem who turned into a swan?

FILIPO. You know fables?

TIRRENA. I don't think anyone knows them better than women.

FILIPO. I suspect that's because women's wits are predisposed to fabrication.

TIRRENA. I don't know what's with our wits. All I can say about me is that I've never told the truth my whole life.

FILIPO. It is a great flaw in such beautiful creatures.

TIRRENA. We have others, even greater.

FILIPO. Greater than lying?

TIRRENA. Yeah, stuff like going crazy for men who make us forget the ones who really love us; changing our minds on a dime; choosing the worst option; and being extra smug, arrogant, and vengeful.

FILIPO. Despite all the flaws that you credit to your nature, I'll be damned if I'm not dying for a woman. I doubt you can show me anything of equal beauty in all of God's creation.

TIRRENA. Right. I just said all that to see if it'd make you stop liking us and leave me alone.

FILIPO. I won't hurt you, for your sex carries special privilege with me. And also because I adore Leda, who first captured my will, and I remain faithful to her. Do you have any food you can give me?

TIRRENA. I'm carting bread and onions from this village to the next on my donkey.

FILIPO. I don't want any onions. Give me the bread.

TIRRENA. He who rejects onions when he's hungry can't be of bad blood.

FILIPO. I don't know what kind of blood I have, but I sense a noble heart in my breast.

TIRRENA. I've never seen so white a soul in so black a body.

FILIPO. May Heaven keep you, woman.

TIRRENA. I'll go get the bread.

FILIPO. Go then.

TIRRENA. Whoa, donkey!

(Exit TIRRENA.)

FILIPO. Even animals obey women! But that's only natural, for if Heaven, in its divine providence, has made animals subject to man, and a man in love recognizes the rule of woman, then they are right to obey her before him.

(Enter TIRRENA.)

TIRRENA. Here's the bread.

[She hands him a roll.]

FILIPO. *[Taking the bread.]*

May Heaven reward you for the sustenance you offer me so dutifully. Perhaps someday I'll be in a position to reward you myself, woman.

TIRRENA. The only reward I want is permission to go.

FILIPO. I can't stop you.

TIRRENA. God keep you.

FILIPO. Go with him.

TIRRENA. We'll ride like the wind, my donkey and me.

FILIPO. If by any chance you come across Leda, to whom I've surrendered my soul, tell her, Tirrena, that I'm dying for her. Remind her to keep her promise to return to me in these mountains, one glorious day, so that on this same spot I might once again worship the two suns that shine from her. Tell her that a black man, breached by . . . bleached by her heavenly shafts, is being driven mad by the sight of her. And tell her—

TIRRENA. I promise, and the sooner you let me go, the more I'll be able to tell her.

FILIPO. Go forth in peace, Tirrena.

TIRRENA. Finally!

(Exit TIRRENA.)

FILIPO. O vast maker of so many heavenly orbs, caretaker of the earth's tiniest worm, to whom the four elements, the stars, the heavens, the sun, and the moon render eternal homage as their king, I give thee thanks for coming to my aid with nourishment, though I am unworthy of it, amidst these pitiless mountains and wastelands.

(Enter BUGLE, trapped in a burlap sack that rolls down the mountain and onto the stage.)

But what's this! A formless mass with no head or feet rolls down from the crest of the mountain. It must be some species of animal I've never seen. I shall approach to find out. It moves! A sack, with something trapped inside! I'll split it down the middle.

(FILIPO rips open the sack and BUGLE emerges immediately [half naked].)

God help me!

BUGLE. And me, for I've jumped from the frying pan into the fire.

FILIPO. Are you not a man?

BUGLE. An undeniable fact.

FILIPO. And your name is Bugle.

BUGLE. Call me Sack-butt.

FILIPO. I warn you not to lie, for I react very poorly to liars.

BUGLE. Good thing you don't work at court!

FILIPO. Of course not. Is anyone in the world worthy of being my lord other than God?

BUGLE. I'll stick with any lord who provides our daily bread in exchange for reciting the Our Father.

FILIPO. Tell me: What has brought you to me in this strange manner?

BUGLE. After I escaped your wrath yesterday, fortune stripped me of my clothes and brought me here.

FILIPO. I may appear cruel, my good fellow, but I don't take vengeance on the defenseless. I forgive you.

BUGLE. Eighty times I kiss your feet.

[He kneels.]

FILIPO. I am not fond of ceremony. Rise and explain the origin of this adventure.

BUGLE. *[Rising.]*

Listen then. When we parted ways where you left us yesterday afternoon, at the foot of these mountains, I headed for the court behind the admiral's horse. I followed it as I usually do, half on foot and half on my old nag, that bastard spawn of wind and comet fire. And given that I am but a man in the end, I tired myself out and was unable to keep up, and as the shadows of night approached, my fatigue turned to exhaustion. Whether from courage or fear, I walked for two leagues half asleep and strayed from the path, running into a band of highway robbers who roam these parts wreaking havoc. You can imagine how I feared for my life when they pointed their swords at my chest and ordered me to empty my purse if I wanted to live. As if I was carrying a kingdom in my britches! So, finding nothing on me of any worth, they roughed me up real good: what a nice welcome for a sleepy guest! Then, tearing off most of my clothes, they threw me into that hellish sack and sent me rolling down the mountain like a useless piece of garbage. But Heaven took pity on my misfortune in the turn of events you've seen, for thinking that I was dropping straight into the abyss, I've landed at your feet. This is my story, and here are the bruises to prove it.

FILIPO. Men of such condition exist? An animal so cruel it attacks its likeness?

BUGLE. They are worse than animals.

FILIPO. By God, if I cross paths with them on the mountain, I'll rip them to shreds.

BUGLE. There are many of them.

FILIPO. What does that matter when my courage dwarfs them all?

BUGLE. And my fear dwarfs them all.

FILIPO. Come here and tell me something.

BUGLE. As I am able.

FILIPO. That monster of superior beauty, that living sparkle, that gorgeous enigma, that heavenly harpoon directed against human hearts, she who is called Leda and Highness after the highness the world observes in such a miracle of charm and wit: Who is she?

BUGLE. Who is she? What a funny question! The princess of at least Albania, she who is legally sworn to inherit the kingdom.

FILIPO. That's it?

BUGLE. Does that strike you as little?

FILIPO. For her it does. She deserves to be queen of many worlds.

BUGLE. I suspect the admiral aspires to marry her, though he is her vassal.

FILIPO.   Over my dead body.

BUGLE.   The admiral would find that amusing.

FILIPO.   Leda will obey no lord other than me, though she search the world over.

BUGLE.   Righto.

FILIPO.   I wish you to keep me company in these mountains, for I am a social animal and desire camaraderie until the time is ripe for the joy I seek.

BUGLE.   At your service. Do you have any money?

FILIPO.   Money? What's that?

BUGLE.   The most amazing thing ever invented.

FILIPO.   Better than women?

BUGLE.   There's nothing greater on the face of the earth.

FILIPO.   If it surpasses the beautiful miracle of woman, it must be something else.

BUGLE.   It surpasses everything, by far.

FILIPO.   Tell me, Bugle, where we may find some to worship and adore it.

BUGLE.   I think I have one of the creatures stored away here, where it found safe haven from the robbers. I keep it for times of necessity, but as payment for the mercy you've shown me in giving me my life, I'll let you see it.

   (He takes a silver coin from a hidden pocket.)

FILIPO.   Can such a tiny thing hold such greatness?

BUGLE.   I believe so. Its greatness is godlike, for money is lord of all the world.

FILIPO.   There is no god other than God.

BUGLE.   And this.

   [He holds up the coin.]

FILIPO.   I'm looking at it closely, and it strikes me as the most miserable thing I've ever seen.

BUGLE.   It's clear you don't grasp the value of this mystery of human government. It holds the key to all that we see.

FILIPO.   How so?

BUGLE.   Behold here honor, life's first breath, beauty, friends, kinsmen, blood, lords, courage, wit, women, love, fun, poetry, music, bodies, dresses, collars, stockings, shoes, bread, water, wine, cake, stew, radishes, cheese, the whole wide world. And without it, the world is worth less than any of the things I've mentioned.

FILIPO.   God help me if everyone is like you! Here's what I think of this hoax!

(*He throws the coin to the ground.*)

Are men to worship idols of silver simply because it's a precious metal, when Heaven and Earth give them abundant proof that there is one eternal creator who alone deserves worship and respect? He lives forever, and everything else is worthless.

TIRRENA.   (*In a distant voice, offstage.*)

Heaven help me!

FILIPO.   Someone shouts, and if I'm not mistaken, it's a woman.

TIRRENA.   *[Offstage.]*

Heaven help me!

FILIPO.   They've done her some injury. Follow me, Bugle, and grab another stick from these trees, for I intend to come to her rescue.

BUGLE.   *[Aside.]*

What hands I've fallen into!

FILIPO.   Go first, Bugle. You'll lead the charge, as a bugle should.

BUGLE.   *[Aside.]*

The perfect way to end my fast!

FILIPO.   Come on, we mustn't lose time. It's a woman we're talking about!

BUGLE.   *[Aside.]*

What spectacular luck I have!

(*Exit FILIPO and BUGLE.*)

ACT 2, Scene 2

(*[The mountain hideout of the robbers.] Enter the ROBBERS, with SERGESTO pushing TIRRENA forward.*)

SERGESTO. No point in screaming or begging to Heaven for help, for it is far from earth and unable to hear you.

TIRRENA. That doesn't matter, for God's ears reach the whole way.

SERGESTO. Your tears are lost on me. Into this cave, which houses our beds, you will enter with me.

TIRRENA. You'll have to tear me to pieces first.

SERGESTO. Resistance and stubbornness will do you no good. This is going to happen.

TIRRENA. Not while I'm alive!

TIMBREO. You would tempt death to escape your misfortune, woman? Stop it, for the captain means to honor you.

TIRRENA. I'm better off without such a vile honor.

SERGESTO. Aren't I a better suitor to you than the ruffian you'll end up with for a husband? Stop your whining.

TIRRENA. I appeal to Heaven for help.

SERGESTO. You appeal in vain.

TIRRENA. Then I will keep trying.

SERGESTO. Either I enjoy your body or you die.

(Enter FILIPO and BUGLE with clubs.)

FILIPO. Take your vile hands off that woman, you thugs!

SERGESTO. Hideous monster, you think you have enough hands to stop us all?

FILIPO. Is reason not enough?

SERGESTO. Reason is insufficient here.

FILIPO. I'm not here to talk.

TIMBREO. Then defend yourself, monster!

FILIPO. And I shall defend Tirrena!

BUGLE. Don't bother addressing me, you stinking thieves, for I intend to have my vengeance for the sack and the bruises.

(FILIPO and BUGLE force the ROBBERS offstage.)

TIRRENA. Heaven has answered my prayers. How quickly the black man repaid me for the bread I gave him! But there goes my donkey, bolting off through the wheat field like there's a horsefly biting her rump! I'll follow her to the village since it's safe to cross the mountains again. My virginity has narrowly escaped this threat!

(As TIRRENA exits, the ROBBERS reenter, retreating before FILIPO and BUGLE.)

SERGESTO. Stay your freakish arm, you extraordinary man, if my surrender alone will satisfy you. For in heroic actions, the greatest victory comes in triumph without bloodshed.

[The ROBBERS kneel before FILIPO.]

BUGLE. Too late, you thugs! I still have six bruises to avenge!

FILIPO. Enough, Bugle. They have surrendered, and I will not fight defeated men.

BUGLE. What about the beating and bruises they gave me, and the sack they threw me in? Am I supposed to let all that go?

FILIPO. Bugle, natural clemency says yes. So speaks the nobility of my blood, for taking vengeance on the defeated is an act of cowardice.

[To the ROBBERS.]

Rise.

BUGLE. *[Aside, as the ROBBERS rise.]*

To think I'd end up with someone who gives speeches in the middle of a fight! He sweeps the injury done to me under the rug.

TIMBREO. In pardoning us, you show no less of your heroic vigor than you did in defeating us.

SERGESTO. Tell us: Who are you? And if you wish to be captain of us all, since your valor has earned you such an honor, I will give you that title.

FILIPO. The origin of my birth is unclear, but my lofty thoughts, though lacking in fortune, are endowed by Heaven with such a heroic drive for honor that I am moved to accept the title you offer. My valiant heart inclines me toward leadership, but I warn you that I accept only on the condition that you swear obedience to me.

LIDONIO. We will obey you unswervingly.

FILIPO. As proof of that statement, friends, I ask that you call me not captain but rather king of this countryside, for you will see that my courage warrants such a title more than any other. Though my black face may mark me as a hideous and extraordinary monster, virtues overcome appearances. With lesser physical endowments and lesser courage, Tamerlane became king of Asia and carried out plans full of ample ambition, though he started out as a field hand.

LIDONIO. The meadows swear vassalage to you, kingdoms of emerald at your feet.

SERGESTO. With this we swear you in as our king. Allow us to kiss your hand.

BUGLE. *[Aside.]*

By God, this is for real, for he allows them to kiss his hand! 'Tis done, he's king now alright. How seriously and calmly he accepts the swearing-in from these thieves!

[To FILIPO.]

I request compensation for my bruises, now that I see your majesty in this position.

FILIPO. Bugle, I desire to show you favor.

BUGLE. *[Aside.]*

The *negro*'s noggin swells with presumption!

FILIPO. From this day forward, friends, you will know my worth, and in my invincible courage you will see that I deserve to be your king and nothing more, for that is enough.

BUGLE. You're dreaming.

FILIPO. All human power, Bugle, is a dream.

BUGLE. That is a fact, but now that Heaven has put you in such a powerful position all of a sudden, it's reasonable to act upon your good fortune with grants and favors.

FILIPO. I'm not forgetting you, pal.

BUGLE. *Pal?* That's the best you can do?

FILIPO. I intend to grant greater favors to you than to everyone else.

BUGLE. I am your servant.

FILIPO. Not only my servant, Bugle, but my favorite.

BUGLE. I offer you my blood and my life in gratitude.

FILIPO. God keep you.

BUGLE. If I may ask without offending you, and just between you and me, when do servants to kings of meadows get to eat? For I'm fainting from hunger, and if my food is to be grass, then I am no better than a horse-favorite.

FILIPO. You have nothing to fear in my company, Bugle.

BUGLE. Caesar said the same thing to Amyclas as they crossed the storm-tossed sea, but at least the fisherman had food in his stomach.

FILIPO. I am greater than Caesar, for I am the product of my courage alone. And now that I'm king, I shall win Leda as my queen.

TIMBREO. A large crowd gathers at the green skirt of the mountain.

FILIPO. It must be my followers, captain, raised as tough as tree trunks in that thick forest, then fashioned into human beings. Forming a nimble squadron, they march up this slope to swear loyalty at my feet, knowing they will soon eternalize my union with Leda. For such is the glory Leda bestows upon the countryside that she appears to endow the plants with souls and life.

SERGESTO. They're getting closer, coming at us with weapons.

FILIPO. No better way to put my arm to the test.

BUGLE. We're all going to perish! What a fix I've got myself into. Misfortunes can be quite remarkable, and this one no less so, for I'm about to die on an empty stomach!

TIMBREO. War strategy demands that when the enemy looms powerful, it's time to fortify.

FILIPO. Is that not considered fleeing?

SERGESTO. No, it's called waiting for the right moment.

FILIPO. If there's so little risk to honor in it, we should climb to the craggiest part of the mountain.

LIDONIO. Reason of state demands it, for once entrenched there, you can hold off the most powerful of enemies with nothing but rocks.

FILIPO. Let's climb it, then, and defend our lives against the grip of death.

   [To LIDONIO.]

After you. I shall remain in the rear, for I am your king and wish in this way to be held accountable for the lives Heaven has placed in my care.

LIDONIO. Such courage!

BUGLE.   I'd prefer he be held accountable for drinks in a tavern!

(They begin climbing the mountain.)

Alas, poor Bugle, with Gestas to his left and a thieving boar to his right. If these robbers try to hang me, I'll scream to God while they're doing it.

FILIPO.   Upwards, brave soldiers, and take heart in the good fortune I bring you. No power in the two hemispheres should cause you fear.

([FILIPO, BUGLE, and the ROBBERS continue their ascent.] Enter ARTENIO, RICARDO, TEBANDRO, the KING, and TIRRENA.)

KING.   There are people up there.

TIRRENA.   It must be them, sir, fleeing from the monster you seek. For after he saved me, I'll bet they decided to seek refuge on this mountaintop.

KING.   May Heaven save him from mortal danger. And all of us.

TIRRENA.   There's no need to fear for the black man. Just recall his worth. He's capable of great skill when necessary. An example is the staff he wields so fearlessly, as proved by a few ribs he beat to a pulp.

KING.   We did well to leave the coaches and litters behind, as this rugged mountainside can only be traveled on foot.

ARTENIO.   We'll find out soon if Filipo is in this craggy pass.

RICARDO.   I believe it's best to raise a truce flag and talk to these people from here. They are afraid of him, and we can appeal to their fears. That way we'll find out if they've seen the prince or if he's with them.

KING.   Well said. Raise a flag, Ricardo, and go request a parley.

(RICARDO raises a truce flag.)

TIRRENA.   There's no flag like my donkey, for as soon as she showed herself they came from miles away to attack me.

SERGESTO.   *(From above.)*

The enemy calls for a truce by raising a white flag.

FILIPO.   *(From above.)*

I shall respond to it with my black flag.

RICARDO.   There are men huddled in those crags, which defend them like a castle wall.

KING. Hail them, Ricardo.

RICARDO. O you up there!

FILIPO. What say you down there?

RICARDO. The king desires to know, in exchange for amnesty, if there is among you a brave young man with the look of an Ethiopian and the name Filipo.

FILIPO. With that very person do you speak. What is the king's intention in coming to look for me? If he wishes to make war on me, let him be content to be king of the populated areas, leaving me the countryside and mountains. He has no greater claim to the inheritance of Adam than I do, for kingships were claimed through tyranny in the beginning.

KING. Ricardo, let me speak with him. For though his terrifying presence might astonish me, his blood speaks so clearly to my own that it seems to want to mix itself in my very veins. Filipo, what are you waiting for? Come down, come down, for I await you with open arms!

TEBANDRO. Filipo, come down!

FILIPO. Tebandro, Heaven knows you're a sight for sore eyes. I'm sorry I offended you by running away, but the call of liberty is strong. Who is that venerable old man who has spoken to me with such remarkable sympathy?

TEBANDRO. Filipo, it's your own father.

FILIPO. Don't deceive me!

TEBANDRO. Do his words not convince you if the blood in your veins does not?

FILIPO. You are right, Tebandro. I shall speed to his feet on outspread wings.

(FILIPO and BUGLE climb down the mountain.)

KING. My arms await you, Filipo, that you may find your center in them. May they be the oak to your ivy.

BUGLE. Bugle is on the way too, though I suspect I'm dreaming.

FILIPO. Oh, beloved father! I thank Heaven that I finally know him to whom, by law of nature, I owe all my being! Forgive me, Tebandro, for the natural inclination that drives me toward he who gave me my being and left me with the first debt of my life.

KING. I'm too overwhelmed to speak.

TEBANDRO. They both weep.

RICARDO. A tender scene!

ARTENIO. Such courage Filipo shows. Such wit, grace, and confidence.

FILIPO. Allow me, father, to ask you: What mysterious cause could have made us so different from each other? For you engendered me, and as the science Tebandro taught me shows, every living thing engenders its likeness.

KING. There's a natural explanation, Filipo. Later you will learn the circumstances of your extraordinary birth. For now, come and accept the inheritance Albania offers you, for you are its prince.

FILIPO. Wait. You are Albania's king?

KING. Yes, Filipo, and I wish Albania were the world so I could give you the world.

TIRRENA. He's gone stiff with kingliness!

KING. Come forth, Albanians, and kiss the heroic hand of your prince.

(All begin kissing Filipo's hand.)

ARTENIO. Albania rejoices at the expectation of your highness's valor.

FILIPO. God keep you.

RICARDO. What majesty!

TEBANDRO. The rare excellence you show today is a credit to my tutoring.

FILIPO. I shall not forget you, Tebandro.

TIRRENA. And don't forget the bread poor Tirrena gave you.

FILIPO. I shall not.

BUGLE. And to he who served you as favorite in your meadow kingdom, what will you grant? I mean, what will your highness grant?

FILIPO. Many favors, Bugle.

KING. Let's go, Filipo, so you can meet your sister and the whole court, which happily awaits your presence, preparing a great celebration for your swearing-in. The entire kingdom applauds you.

FILIPO. The first favor I wish to ask of you, sir, is to pardon the offenses and crimes of the men whom I have served as captain in these mountains. They were the first to give me a hint that I was your successor.

KING. The favor you ask shall be fully granted, Filipo. From this day forward you are Albania's crown prince.

FILIPO. God keep you.

(Enter a SERVANT.)

SERVANT. Her highness approaches with the admiral. She comes straight from court, full of joy at the news of the prince's arrival. She dismounts now with the admiral and her ladies.

(Enter the ADMIRAL with LEDA and her ladies-in-waiting.)

KING. Filipo, this is your sister. Come and greet her.

FILIPO. I am indebted to my sister's courtesy and shall reply in kind—

[*Aside.*]

But heavens! Is that not Leda? Do I suffer the deception of desire? An illusion of love?

[*Aloud.*]

Sir . . .

KING. What do you wish to say?

FILIPO. Which one is my sister?

KING. The most beautiful of them, the sun among the stars. The one whom the admiral leads by the hand.

FILIPO. But isn't that Leda?

KING. Yes, Leda: your sister.

FILIPO. My sister?

KING. Your sister Leda. What's the matter?

FILIPO. [*Aside.*]

Oh, heavens, what misfortune! Why do you spoil glory with such grief, happiness with such misery? Is this the burden I must bear as prince of Albania? So heavy is my misfortune that it outweighs my love! I'm losing my mind!

LEDA. [*Aside.*]

His soul reels, no doubt from the discovery that I am his sister.

FILIPO. [*Aside.*]

If only, Leda, you were the moon's sister rather than mine, for you are daughter to the dawn and shining sun to the earth. Oh, Albania, so much have you cost me today!

KING. What gives you such pause, Filipo?

FILIPO. A paradox, for Leda arouses all my joys and shackles all my abilities.

KING. *[Aside.]*

He is disillusioned because he fell in love with her on the mountain and now realizes she's his sister.

LEDA. Give me your hand, Filipo, and allow me to confirm the bond of our blood.

FILIPO. Stop, Leda, for my soul reels from the poison that my eyes drink from yours. Don't turn a lofty flame into a conflagration.

LEDA. It is only proper that I embrace you.

(*LEDA and FILIPO embrace.*)

FILIPO. Be advised that I am a man, Leda.

LEDA. It matters not, for I know who I am.

FILIPO. *[Aside.]*

A fiery bolt of lightning your beauty could be, or a comet shooting through the sky, for it has singed the feathers of my wings.

LEDA. *[Aside.]*

What a force love is!

ADMIRAL. Allow me to kiss your highness's hand, and may Albania enjoy many happy springs of your life.

[He kneels before FILIPO.]

FILIPO. Rise to my arms.

ADMIRAL. *[Rising, aside.]*

That cruel fortune should strike this blow against my hope! I shall turn the world upside down or encircle my brow with Albania's crown. It isn't right that it should be worn by an aberration, a monster, a brute!

FILIPO. Admiral.

ADMIRAL. Sir?

FILIPO. Leda is my sister.

ADMIRAL. Who would doubt the relationship?

FILIPO. So look upon her as a supreme deity, even more than when she was Albania's legitimate successor, though today she has become my successor. And measure prudently the distance from yourself, a mere vassal, to the ranks of Leda, my sister and princess of Albania.

ADMIRAL. *(Aside.)*

I suffocate from rage! Is Albania's admiral to be dressed down by this beast, this minotaur, this Orcus that Heaven punishes us with? Oh, a curse upon fortune, upon the king, upon the world! Yet it behooves me to conceal my reaction, for I may yet be able to work these strange happenings to my advantage.

KING. To the litters and coaches. It's time to depart.

LEDA. *[Aside.]*

I came to the countryside a crown princess, and I return crownless. Such are the vagaries of fortune and the privilege of men over women, for though Filipo is a monster, as a male he deprives me of my country's throne. Oh, heavens, give me valor or give me patience!

TIRRENA. I'm struck silly by all these twists and turns and claims of royalty. I'll follow the court on my donkey all the way back to my li'l village.

KING. Trust that I shall reward you, Tirrena, for the fortunate news you delivered to us.

FILIPO. The debt to Tirrena is mine to pay.

ADMIRAL. *[Aside, to BUGLE.]*

My little Bugle . . .

BUGLE. *[Aside, to the ADMIRAL.]*

Sir admiral, I shall endeavor to help your excellency in every way possible, and I shall keep his highness informed of you in a way that reflects well on your person. Let it not be thought that Mr. Bugle forgets his obligations.

ADMIRAL. *[Aside, to BUGLE.]*

Fortune has not pulled any punches on me this time!

FILIPO. Lovely Leda, I was yours, but now I am your brother. I was mad for your beauty, but now I've come to my senses and recognize its peril. Resisting the intensity of your flashing eyes, I summon my willpower and turn my back on the charms that call to me. Only thus do I avoid the shipwreck of your beauty. I flee in freedom and return as captive, but in the contradiction between fear and bravery, between hesitation and affection, virtues overcome appearances. Through reason or force, blood must conquer desire and courage must win out over love.

ACT 3, Scene 1

([A chamber in the royal palace.] Enter the highest-ranking Albanian nobles, among them TEBANDRO and the ADMIRAL, all formally dressed, followed by FILIPO, who takes a seat on his throne, and BUGLE.)

FILIPO.   Intrepid Albanians, noble and faithful vassals, whose shoulders form the pillars on which I rest the weight of so great a kingdom: I have convened you here today to inform you of my lofty intentions. You already know that, after I was sworn in as prince, my father passed away and now treads the sapphire floors of Heaven. He had barely the time to train me to govern the country and charge me with the burden of this crown, which, as a wise man once said, if people understood all its solemn duties, none would want to touch it or even to kick it with their foot. For though this is the greatest of offices, greater still are its many encumbrances and concerns. My father's death occasioned all the grief owed to paternal love and all that such a beloved king deserved. The kingdom mourned him with lengthy and widespread sorrow that obscured the light of day. As for me, the most burdened of all by the weight of such feeling, Heaven needed to do nothing to mark my face with grief, for it had already predisposed me to that sentiment when it defamed me with blackness. I attended the funeral, an Olympus of mourning and candles fit for a king. Several days later, to lift the people's spirits—for grief engenders fear in matters of state—I ordered an end to the period of mourning and appeared before the court many times on horseback. It is fitting for a king to thus delight his subjects with visions of himself, for like trees that worship the sun, they perish when deprived of his rays. And in fulfillment of all I promised my father as I kissed his dying hand, I intend to be a loyal executor of his will as well as an obedient son, keeping his image alive in my soul at all times. And thus I commence my imitation of so lofty a king and, in the name of God, call you here to command you as lord and request assistance as brother and friend. I ask you all, considering the weight of the task Heaven has charged me with, to assist me with your courage, your years of experience, and your care for the common good. Help and advise me so that I may always govern you in justice and peace. Tell me the truth at all times, for the best flattery is none at all with sovereign rulers who care for the commonwealth, and miserable are the kings who ignore the truth their subjects speak. I don't want advice from a single man or from a favorite trying to play king. What use are they to me? My palace doors will always be open to the rich, to the poor, to justice, to injury, to favor, to complaint, to advice, to truth, to administration, and to celebration, in slumber and in rest. This, O Albanians, is what it means to be king and to fulfill the role, necessary to all, of a human god who walks the earth. And this I intend to be, my friends: your help will make it possible, for without you I am but a man, subject to error. You can all be kings with me if, guided by the public good, you offer me your best counsel and make me a good king in turn. And thus shall other nations watch in awe as I overcome, through virtue, the outward signs of this peculiar appearance.

ADMIRAL.   May Heaven keep your majesty many long and happy years so that Albania, reaping the benefits that your greatness promises at such a tender age, may become lord of the world: a humble spoil of your peerless valor. Encouraged by your example, we shall all do our best to serve you, as we are required, for he who requests advice with such a wise spirit of collaboration needs none.

FILIPO.   Admiral, your lofty pedigree and impeccable blood, sprung from so many noble ancestors, cannot but ensure that you will serve me with loyalty. And I anticipate the same from the others summoned here today with the purposes I've stated. I name you royal chamberlain and chief of staff, as well as governor of Albania in my absence.

ADMIRAL.   I fall to your feet in gratitude!

[He kneels.]

FILIPO.   Rise. Great vassals, admiral, never seem to be sufficiently rewarded.

([The ADMIRAL rises.] Aside.)

In this way I'll reassure him, for in court politics the best way for a king to ease suspicious hearts is to indebt them through favors.

[Aloud, to TEBANDRO.]

I know how much I owe you, Tebandro, for your character and for all your service as my tutor, father, and companion over the years. And now that I'm king, I shall show my gratitude. I name you chief constable, and I charge you with assisting me at all times.

TEBANDRO.   I kiss your feet.

[He kneels.]

FILIPO.   You are worthy of my arms, Tebandro.

TEBANDRO. *[Rising.]*

I pray God that your majesty eclipse the memory of Alexander and that heroic monuments to your name be raised around the world.

FILIPO. I cannot repay all that I owe you. Artenio, you shall enjoy the title of first lieutenant of Albania.

ARTENIO. Heaven keep you.

FILIPO. Ricardo shall be royal ensign.

RICARDO. May Heaven lead you to prosper in Albania.

BUGLE. And for poor Bugle, what? Alas, left to choke on splinters!

FILIPO. Oh, Bugle!

BUGLE. If I'm not mistaken, you're no longer listening to me, despite the validity of my arguments. The high office of king has turned you deaf, Filipo. What a change time has wrought. When you were prince, I was your favorite, on a path to becoming your secretary. But as soon as you become king, the devil with Bugle! All those days and nights I attended you, my king, bending over backwards for you! Back then it was mutually beneficial, for we had a silent pact between us, like a pair of card sharks. But now, with a king in my hand and favors to be accrued, I fear I'm getting a-screwed.

FILIPO. That's just the way things have to be, Bugle.

BUGLE. Unfortunate Bugle: all his visions of titles and favors come to naught.

FILIPO. What is it you want?

BUGLE. A bugle should be the instrument of a favorite.

FILIPO. Bugle, your example shall serve as an important lesson to all my subjects. Nobody, through either pleasure or suffering, shall move up in rank unworthily. It is a violation to expect otherwise, for dispensing royal offices among those of unequal merit discredits the king. You were born to a humble station, Bugle. Content yourself with dressing and eating in the company of a king.

BUGLE. *[Aside.]*

The king's stinginess has turned today into Ash Wednesday and Friday of Sorrows combined.

(Enter LEDA, dressed in a hoop skirt and shawl.)

LEDA. Filipo, king of Albania—to Albania's good fortune if not to mine, for I was born unfortunate—do not be surprised that I air my grievances at your feet before the entire court, for I want the nobles to witness the cause of my complaints and to understand how your pitiless judgment has prompted my misfortune. You call yourself a just king, but is it just to hide behind reasons of state to do me such great injustice? One that robs me of choice? Normal offenses can be overlooked, Filipo, but those that undermine choice cut to the core. Up till now I've had the freedom of a slave, my tongue bound in chains, my words silenced behind walls. But now, overcoming hesitation and breaking shackles, fiery words pour from my mouth and dewy tears from my eyes: their message is that misfortune looms, and probably worse than I can imagine. Hope rises to my defense, complaints to my injury, weapons to my alarm. You seek to marry me to twice-widowed Rodulfo, king of Hungary, a foreigner unequally matched to my young years, because he offers you his daughter and successor Ninfa. Thus do you gain the Hungarian throne and perhaps even the tiara of the empire, if I bear him children, for he has the power to have Germany declare you Holy Roman Emperor. While King Enrico of Sicily and his sister Alfreda would be much better matches for Albania, you reject them in favor of Rodulfo and Ninfa because it's to your own benefit, though clearly to my detriment. Your ambitions are an insult to me and an offense to Heaven: they go beyond determination to cruelty, past injustice to tyranny. And I will not obey them, no matter how many worlds, empires, or Albanias they bring you. Mortal rulers cannot force the will, Filipo, for the soul is born free of human law, and mine, as sovereign, recognizes no lord outside the highest spheres. Heaven alone is its lord, and to Heaven alone does it show deference. In second place is the name and sacred memory of my father, of whom I know myself to be a living likeness, for my color does not contradict the truth of his stamp. My father is my only king; he rules over me after Heaven; and I obey him as king and father in my heart and in my soul. What's more, I was crown princess of Albania before you were ever prince or king. And by God, you'll witness the sun reverse its golden course across the sky before you ever compel me to violate the intention I've stated to you here. And along with the sun's reversal, the ocean will halt its waters, time will stop its march, death will grow weary of killing, and souls will lose their immortality: all before a woman, stinging from scorn, will surrender in defeat.

FILIPO. *[Aside.]*

What astonishing gall! A soft touch will be necessary to correct such an obstinate woman.

[Aloud, to the rest of the court.]

Leave us. Everyone out.

BUGLE.   *(Aside.)*

Such a furious display! By God, this is a woman capable of spawning serpents!

(Exit all but FILIPO and LEDA.)

FILIPO.   Now that we're alone, Leda, with a desire to calm your rage, and with the just temperance and reason owed to a noblewoman and a sister, I will address your concerns. And you will see how you are treated differently by a man, a brother, and a king in terms of bold resolution, for each speaks to you without witnesses in order to hold this advantage over you. To begin with, Leda, I would never try to marry you off without consulting you first, for nothing in the world is more destructive than the frequency with which highborn women are married against their will. This marriage occurred to me when the negotiations between King Enrico of Sicily and my ambassador got bogged down. But the matter is now happily settled, and, as I understand it, a pair of Sicilian galleys carrying Enrico and Alfreda is already parting the silver waves of the Tyrrhenian Sea as it makes its way here. For thus does Sicily, in its flattery, offer its princess to forge ties to our family, and any minute I am expecting news of the safe landing of their ships on Albanian shores. This is the truth, Leda, and now that I've revealed it to you and satisfied your doubts, I have a friendly warning for you. Listen very carefully. I alone am king and absolute lord of Albania, if not of its souls then of its lives, which is enough to make me lord of everything, for though I adore my deceased father just as much as you, his absence makes me king of Albania, Leda. It makes no difference that you were his sworn successor first, for a male successor's privilege displaces a woman's claims, even if he is born a thousand centuries after her. And even if I hadn't been born in the king's house, my valor redeems the blood he has given me, though my color contradicts the royal stamp. Even if I'd been born with this appearance in fiery Libya or frozen Scythia, I would deserve to be king of Albania and of all the world. And don't seek shelter in the fact that you're a woman or my sister or that I was once mad enough with blind love to adore your divine beauty: if you ever come at me again with that disrespectful tone, so help me God I'll . . .

LEDA.   King, sir, brother . . .

FILIPO.   Leda, the holy office of king, such a close imitation of God, is to be worshipped even in one's thoughts, for a king transcends the boundary between man and God, and your position as the king's sister—until and unless you become queen—does not mean you're not his subject.

LEDA.   Your majesty, sir . . . forgive me. I deposit my regretful boldness, my now-tamed rage at your feet. My humility, loyalty, and love have gained your antipathy because of the admiral: he misinformed me, and, being a woman with such feeble resistance, I fell for it . . .

FILIPO.   The admiral does me great offense and betrays his noble blood in his unprompted actions against me.

LEDA. I was rash and foolish with you in my accusations. I understand very well that you are my king, my sir, my lord.

FILIPO. That's enough, Leda. Just learn to be more prudent, and remember your duty to a king who is both your brother and your friend. For on the life of my soon-to-be queen Alfreda, the next time this happens, your head will be considered expendable.

(Exit FILIPO.)

LEDA. Filipo is right, for I have responded with ingratitude to the affection and esteem in which he has always held me, and my rashness has violated the decorum owed to the Caesarean majesty of a king. All because of falsehoods from the admiral, whose premature plans of kingship are stamped in his soul like a secret alphabet. I confess that I've never been as scared as when seeing Filipo reveal his rage just now. Such a different face an angered king assumes, such mysterious divinity hiding in human form! I am embarrassed to have given such easy credit to the words of so insecure a man. Alas, lack of caution and gullibility are universal flaws in women. I have offended the king. I shall have to scheme with Tebandro to return to his good graces, for the king respects him above all others and profits from his excellent advice, calling him *father* in private. Indeed, Albania should call him father of the country, for the success of his tutelage has become clear. But why does Bugle enter with such joy?

(Enter BUGLE.)

BUGLE. *[Aside.]*

The princess is here!

[Aloud.]

Give me my reward, your highness, for the good news I bring.

LEDA. What news is that, Bugle?

BUGLE. His majesty has received letters telling him that Enrico and Alfreda have disembarked in Albania.

LEDA. What are you talking about?

BUGLE. About what's happening, Leda. I heard it from the king's mouth, who sends me to request my reward. Reporting the happy occasion of your wedding—and may it last many years—provides the rationale for my tip. I hope it's the first of many.

LEDA. I take note of your request, Bugle.

BUGLE. You take note? That's it? A tip from a princess should consist of more than notetaking. That's no better than almonds or raisins! Why can't I be the lackey who on his first matchmaking mission earns a gold chain from the suitor and a ring from the lady, and to top it off the playwright comes up with a way to give him two thousand ducats in the third act and marries him off to Lady Celia's servant Dominga and he lives happily ever after? But noooo, I'm stuck with a princess of Albania, all empty promises.

[Aside.]

If the Sicilians don't show soon, by God, my bugle will be silenced forever!

(Enter TEBANDRO.)

TEBANDRO. Allow me to kiss your feet, your highness.

[He kneels.]

LEDA. Oh, Tebandro, rise to your feet. In valor, age, wit, and nobility you are the equal of kings, for your tutelage has delivered a remarkable prince to Albania and earned you immortal fame.

TEBANDRO. *[Rising.]*

Your praise of me is too generous, Leda.

LEDA. You deserve this praise many times over.

TEBANDRO. I bring a decree from his royal majesty.

LEDA. To what end, Tebandro?

TEBANDRO. I am to advise you that Enrico's fleet has landed in Albania and, at the same time, to prepare you for the return journey. I shall be in charge of you, and I look forward to being your humble servant.

LEDA. God keep his majesty, for this is a great favor he does me.

TEBANDRO. Believe me when I say I'll give my life to serve you true.

LEDA. Will my brother not accompany me on the return journey?

TEBANDRO. He's gone ahead with his noble friend, the admiral, and will await you at Valdelucero, I believe. As an amorous suitor, he wishes to disguise himself and observe Alfreda, even though it meant leaving you behind.

LEDA. I confess, Tebandro, that I would feel jealous over his amorous excesses if I didn't remind myself that I'm his sister.

TEBANDRO. He gives me a hundred thousand ducats for you to give to Enrico's servants, for he wishes you to show, through your generosity, that you are Lisandro's daughter. He doesn't want the kingdom's debts to obscure the richness of your nobility.

LEDA. I kiss his majesty's hand a thousand times for the favor he does me. His heart is more akin to that of a father than a brother. I wish to become queen to call myself his slave, for though I feared his anger toward me would never subside, I see not only that it has but that he treats me with the sympathy of a father, a brother, and a friend.

BUGLE. Now there's a man, by God, who knows how to reward servants! No almonds and raisins from him!

LEDA. Your share will be two thousand.

BUGLE. Say what? You mean two thousand *ducats*?

LEDA. Yes, Bugle.

BUGLE. Heaven keep you, Princess Velvet, star of stars, flower of the valley, aurora of thirty suns, north star of a thousand auroras. You are a warm stove in January and a cool canteen in August. You are a protowoman who dwarfs the men around her. You are a walking purse, a heavenly shawm to Bugle, a high priestess of love, and, finally, the greatest princess in all of princessdom. Let me kiss your feet and, next to them—if possible—the IOU. I'll pass on kissing your lovely hands, white like abundant jasmine in April, for the only abundance I care about is the number two thousand.

LEDA. Your wishes shall be fulfilled today, Bugle.

BUGLE. And from here on out, this Bugle's mouthpiece will be the sole to your slippers.

LEDA. I always trusted your heart, Tebandro.

TEBANDRO. In serving you I shall be who I've always been. It is my devotion that has earned this reward.

LEDA. Let's prepare for our voyage.

BUGLE. O princess, most honorable of all princesses, you've given me a much greater reward than I expected, that's for sure. I won't accept one ducat less than two thousand from any other princess!

(Exit [all].)

ACT 3, Scene 2

([A pleasant spot overlooking the sea.] Enter FILIPO and the ADMIRAL, dressed for the road.)

FILIPO. Let's wait, admiral, in this inviting spot of emerald and jasmine until the sun, requesting passage across the sea, sinks below the golden Spanish horizon.

ADMIRAL. The horses are well bridled at the foot of those willows.

FILIPO. *[Aside.]*

If only my concerns could be bridled that way.

ADMIRAL. *(Aside.)*

Heavens, you must wish me to fulfill my desire, for you put the means within reach. In this way we shall also rid ourselves of a monster king!

FILIPO. We are alone, admiral.

ADMIRAL. So much so that the horizon is barely visible to us, for the copious canopy of these willows forms a well-defended tent around the lush field, allowing gallant spring to slumber peacefully on a bed of green grass.

FILIPO. Admiral, does this letter look familiar to you?

[He hands the ADMIRAL a letter.]

ADMIRAL. This one, sir?

[He examines the letter.]

FILIPO. Is this how you return the favors and courtesies I always show you? Speak.

ADMIRAL. Sir, your majesty, I—

FILIPO. Silence, admiral. It's time for me to expose you for who you are. And to impress on you who *I* am, for I clearly cannot win you over with courtesies and favors and familiarity, given that the hearts of traitors are filled with ingratitude. You had the gall to write this letter, which I intercepted, even after all the courtesies I showered on you. In it you inform King Enrico of the measures you are taking to assassinate me, in coordination with his arrival. Yet Enrico, once enriched by you, will turn on you as a traitor, for in political matters where treason is advantageous, the traitor becomes expendable in the aftermath. For this reason I have had you come ahead of the others with me, just the two of us. We are alone, and your treasonous intent will end here. I shall now discover if you have in you what you see in me, for I'm confident you'll understand my valor, which cares for your reputation more than you care for mine. Unsheathe your sword, admiral, and be prepared to say, when our dispute has ended, that the courage in my breast has no equal and that, even if I weren't the king's son, my physical endowments have earned me this sovereign monarchy. For my charred black color, which crowns my soul in laurel, is but a shadow of the soul's sun, not an eclipse of its valor. And since I infer from this situation how little acquainted you are with my valor, you will now see it speak through the tongue of this sword. I speak here not as a king but merely as a man who wishes to punish an insolent enemy. Why do you delay? Unsheathe your sword, for we are alone, and you too are a man. We shall see, since nothing has moved you to respect me, if through this scheme you've concocted your valor proves you a better king than I. For even if Albania were to betray me and deny me the vassalage and homage I am owed, and even if I were to find myself alone on the battlefield, facing the country's entire army, I'm capable of turning all the soldiers into vassals at sword point.

ADMIRAL.   Sir, I confess that I have acted ungratefully toward your majesty, but I—

FILIPO.   Unsheathe your sword!

ADMIRAL.   I prefer to die at those feet without resistance, and my sword, so eager to defeat you, will lead to my own surrender, for no sword is of use against that peerless valor of yours. May the blade that shines in your royal hand kill me, with only these hearty green willows as witnesses to such a just punishment: so well deserved that your angry majesty conjures some new deity—I know not which—in the flash of your sword. You are a wholly different man when angry, so much so that I think the trees that line this meadow fear your wrath even though they are innocent, for it seems as though they ask the wind to be still in the king's anger. What then shall the *guilty* man do, dishonored at his king's feet?

[He kneels.]

FILIPO.   Live a better life.

ADMIRAL.   My lord, I do not deserve to live any life.

FILIPO.   Rise, admiral.

(He sheathes his sword. [The ADMIRAL rises.])

I'm ashamed my anger has led me to this.

(He hands the ADMIRAL the letter.)

Tear up that letter, and along with its shreds, cast to the wind the thoughts that turned you against me. Consider today your rebirth, and be careful not to stray again or you shall die, so help me God, for I'll not show the same restraint I've shown today. Now let's be off.

ADMIRAL.   I'm coming: edified, astonished, and indebted.

(Exit [all].)

ACT 3, Scene 3

([A riverside grove near the sea.] A bugle sounds. Enter a group of courtiers, brightly dressed, followed by King ENRICO of Sicily and [his sister] ALFREDA, dressed for the road. ALFREDA is despondent.)

ENRICO.   This pleasant canopy of trees is the best spot in which to await Filipo and Leda. Look, Alfreda, at this riverbank, flowery veneer to the water, which it seems the valley offers you, in the name of Albania, as a mirror.

ALFREDA.   My tears flow heavily and allow me little joy. Ill-fated was my star, for it forces me into marriage with a freakish human, a savage Ethiopian. Though his noble bearing is praised throughout Europe, how can desire be nourished in the absence of a beautiful object? Even if admirable virtues inhabit the soul, what the eyes fail to see can't be loved by anyone. For love enters through the eyes to communicate with the soul and is denied entry if what is seen is undesirable. But because it serves your own ends, Enrico, you want me to sacrifice my choice in marriage for a gloomy eternity. I prefer to die, though death does not come easily in misfortune, for life shows resistance in the face of great evil. And now that the evil I fear draws near, don't be shocked by my nonsensical babble.

ENRICO.   Do not fret, Alfreda. I shall share my intentions and thus restore the bright beauty to your sad countenance. I have not done so before now because I didn't dare speak my secret plans out loud. I aim to become, with the admiral's help, king of Albania, if you promise to murder Filipo the night you become his wife, in bed, with a flask of poison I shall give you. Then, Alfreda, in exchange for this favor, I will promise you to the admiral. But a traitor tends to be betrayed by his accomplices—if kings may be called accomplices to treason—and thus King Carlos of Naples, Heaven keep him, is in on my plan and will guard my back, with an armada spanning the Adriatic and Tyrrhenian Seas, in exchange for possessing your beauty. And when I have ensured my accession to Albania's throne and murdered the admiral, you will return to Naples as Carlos's wife, a siren in that beautiful Narcissus of cities.

ALFREDA.   Allow me to kiss your feet a thousand times for salvaging my happiness, for saving my life.

[She kneels.]

ENRICO.   Rise, Alfreda. What are you thinking? I am your brother. You may trust that I will never fail you.

([ALFREDA rises.] A cornet sounds, announcing a herald. Enter CELIO.)

Is that the sound of a herald?

CELIO.   A remarkable gentleman dismounts from his horse and appears to wish to speak with you, Enrico.

(Enter BUGLE, dressed for the road in an amusing outfit.)

BUGLE.   Give me your feet, your highnesses, if you don't want to give me your hands, and then give me my tip.

ENRICO.   Who the devil are you?

BUGLE.   Can't you see from my outfit? I am the Gentleman of the Tips, sir: a name that Filipo has honored me with, since I'm all about tips.

ALFREDA.   What a curious figure he cuts.

ENRICO.   You shall have your tip, have no doubt.

BUGLE.   In that case, fire away with your questions.

ENRICO.   When do their majesties arrive?

BUGLE.   This evening. Your highness will find in Leda the peerless image of a sunny April in slippers, an angel in a petticoat. In Filipo you'll find polite language cloaked in moonlight and a fully vested king, though one who might be sneezed at in the streets. He is goodnight in the flesh, a magus majesty who follows the star that leads him to you, darkening nobility and thundering grandeur as he goes. In short, a darkened husband who brings a kingdom to your feet, a soul of shining crystal buried in a body of jet. And now my description will take shape before your eyes, for here come Filipo and Leda, ready to be married.

(Flourish of shawms. The grandees of Albania begin their entrance, in formal dress, along with TEBANDRO, the ADMIRAL, FILIPO, and LEDA. ENRICO and ALFREDA cross the stage to meet them.)

FILIPO.   On behalf of my kingdom, I extend your majesties a warm welcome. Your visit does us great honor, as anticipated. How fare you?

ENRICO.   Our disposition will show that better than our words, which are unequal to yours.

FILIPO.   Heaven keep you.

ENRICO.   Fame has spoken of you with great praise, beautiful Leda, and I see it does not exaggerate.

LEDA.   Such flattery.

FILIPO.   Lovely Alfreda . . .

ALFREDA.   *[Aside.]*

Such graceful form, such kingly majesty!

FILIPO.   . . . such beauty and brilliance are too much for the soul to take in.

ALFREDA.   *[Aside.]*

So wise, kingly, polite, solemn . . .

FILIPO.   If your soul, seeing the sun in mine, could disperse the black cloud that obscures its virtues and beauties, you would see yourself in it like Narcissus at the fount.

ALFREDA.   *[Aside.]*

The extraordinary marks of color are overcome by the remarkable virtues of the soul. Never have I seen such a beautiful one revealed through speech.

FILIPO.   Don't let this shadow frighten you, for it will become a sun in the light of your day.

ALFREDA.   *(Aside.)*

I feel the pull of love . . . Enrico will have to forgive me, for not only am I unable to murder this man, but I will act to defend him. For his soul, so akin to God's beautiful image, makes his whole body beautiful.

ENRICO.   *[Aside.]*

Alfreda freezes in terror at the sight of him.

FILIPO.   *[To TEBANDRO.]*

Constable of Albania, arrest Enrico, king of Sicily, and leave him in custody in Valdelucero.

ENRICO.   What!

FILIPO.   Do not question me. I have twenty thousand men guarding my back, enough to take on not only Sicily but the whole world. And it matters not if Carlos of Naples threatens Albania from the sea or backs you up on land with all Europe in his power. For Albania has me, and I will defend Albania with all my strength and blood. The admiral stands behind me on this, for it's only logical that he abandon a foreign king for his natural-born lord.

ENRICO.   I cannot deny the truth, Filipo. But now that you're here, manifesting your great nobility, and now that I've had the opportunity to see you and to speak with you, you have overcome my resistance with the sovereign bearing that has become so renowned around the world. And I confess, in surrendering to your remarkable valor, Filipo, that you deserve to be called king not only of Albania but of all the lands that Daphne's shining lover bathes in golden light.

FILIPO.   Since you recognize my worthiness to be king, Enrico, I wish to call myself your brother as well as your friend.

ENRICO.   So great is your worthiness that it crowns you king of kings, overcoming your extraordinary appearance with your virtues.

FILIPO.   I shall give Carlos a wife equal to him in Ninfa, princess of Hungary, thus relieving you of your debt to him.

ENRICO.   May Heaven keep you many centuries!

BUGLE.   And don't forget my tips! For with them, and with forgiveness for its flaws, *Virtues Overcome Appearances* shall come to a better close.

GLOSSARY

This Glossary annotates names of people and places (both historical and legendary), key concepts and phrases, and other items of interest from the plays. Key cross-references are underscored. Bibliographical references may be found in the Works Cited at the end of the Introduction.

Aben Aboo (d. 1571). Uncle to Don Fernando de Válor and king of the Moriscos upon the latter's assassination in 1569, until his own murder two years later.

Aben Humeya. See Válor, Don Fernando de.

Abraham. A patriarch of the Hebrew Bible, to whom Judaism, Christianity, and Islam trace their roots.

Academy. A gathering of writers or scholars, often under the sponsorship of a nobleman and especially popular in early modern Spain.

Achilles. Greatest of the legendary Greek heroes who fought in the Trojan War, immortalized in Homer's *Iliad*.

Adam. First man in the Hebrew Bible (Genesis 1–5), husband to Eve and father to Cain and Abel. The human race is traditionally referred to as the family of Adam.

Admiral. Commander in chief of a navy.

Adriatic Sea. An arm of the Mediterranean that separates mainland Italy from the Balkans, including Albania.

Africa (African). At the time of the Triad, *Africa* sometimes retained the classical sense of "North Africa," while Guinea and Ethiopia were often synonymous with the sub-Saharan region. There was a great deal of imprecision in all three terms.

Aguilar, House of. A Spanish noble line that included the following members (see also Carlobal):

- Gonzalo Fernández de Córdoba y Enríquez de Aguilar (1453–1515), first Duke of Sessa, known as the Great Captain for his role in the Christian conquest of Granada.

- Elvira Fernández de Córdoba (d. 1524), daughter of the Great Captain and second Duchess of Sessa. She married her cousin Luis Fernández de Córdoba

(d. 1526), fourth Count of Cabra, and with him was the slave owner of Juan Latino. In *JL* Elvira and Luis are referred to simply as the duke and duchess.

- Gonzalo Fernández de Córdoba II (1520–1578), son of Elvira and Luis and third Duke of Sessa. He was close in age to Juan Latino, who reportedly carried his books to school for him. Known mainly as Don Gonzalo in the play, he is also referred to as the "junior duke" or the "little duke" to distinguish him from his father. *JL*'s altered chronology makes Don Gonzalo's youth coincide with the second Morisco revolt (1568), when in reality he was an adult at the time and had an important role, along with Don Juan of Austria, in suppressing the rebellion.

Alba. Spanish word meaning "dawn." In Spain near Salamanca, the town known as Alba de Tormes is home to the Duke of Alba. The third Duke of Alba, Fernando Álvarez de Toledo y Pimentel (1507–1582), had an important role in suppressing the revolt in the Low Countries and is a major character in *BBS*, lending his name to the Black protagonist. Additionally, "Alba's dog" was a popular antisemitic poem at the time of the Triad, known for insinuating that the blood of Jews could be smelled by animals (Gillet 1926 and 1928).

Albania (Albanian). A country of southeastern Europe, setting of *VOA* primarily for the symbolic value of its name (whiteness).

Alexander ("the Great," 356–323 BCE). King of ancient Macedon who conquered much of the known world. Plutarch (1939, 177) suggests he wept over his own insignificance.

Alhambra. A Moorish fortress and landmark in Granada that passed into Christian hands upon the conquest of 1492.

Allah. The Arabic word for God.

Alpujarras. A region of the Sierra Nevada mountains in southern Spain, setting of the Morisco revolt dramatized in *JL*.

Amyclas. An impoverished fisherman who, according to Lucan's *Pharsalia* (5.504–677), attempted to ferry Julius Caesar across a stormy sea.

Ana Carlobal, Doña. See Carlobal.

Andalusia. A large region of southern Spain, home to Seville, Granada, and Cordova.

Andromeda. An Ethiopian princess of Greco-Roman mythology, chained to a rock for sacrifice and rescued by Perseus. Though represented in most classical sources as white, she is referred to in *JL* as Black.

Annius, John (1432–1502). A Dominican friar and scholar whose historical writings, now known to be deeply flawed where not fraudulent, were popular in the early modern period.

Anthony, Saint (c. 251–356). A Christian monk who became a hermit in the Egyptian desert, famous for the temptations he faced from the Devil. Also said to have met the hermit Paul of Thebes, both of whom were supplied bread by a raven.

Antwerp. A major city in Flanders.

Apollo. A major Greco-Roman deity who presided over a range of domains including archery, music, poetry, prophecy, truth, light, and medicine. See also Daphne.

Apostle. One of the twelve original followers of Jesus in the New Testament.

Arab (Arabic, Arabian). Originally an inhabitant of the Arabian peninsula and a speaker of Arabic. In the medieval period, Arabs migrated across North Africa and invaded Spain, where they became known as Moors.

Aristotle (384–322 BCE). Together with Plato, one of the two great philosophers of the ancient world, whose works became central to the curriculum of medieval and early modern universities.

Armenia (Armenian). A country in the Caucasus region of Eurasia.

Ash Wednesday. The first day of Lent, marked by austerity and deprivation in contrast to the excesses of Shrove Tuesday, which precedes it.

Asia (Asian). At the time of the Triad, this word sometimes indicated Asia Minor (modern-day Turkey) and sometimes a much wider expanse, generally lacking the precision with which we use it today.

Assyria (Assyrian). A powerful empire of the ancient Near East beginning in the second millennium BCE.

Athens (Athenian). Capital of modern Greece and most famous city state of ancient Greece, which reached its cultural peak in the fifth century BCE.

Atlas. A Titan of Greco-Roman mythology who held up the heavens and was turned into a mountain by Perseus.

Audiencia and Chancery Court. The highest branch of Spain's royal judiciary at the time of the Triad, with a seat in Granada that held jurisdiction over all of Andalusia.

Augustine, Saint (354–430). A Christian theologian from the late period of ancient Rome whose writings were central to the development of the early Church.

Austria, House of. Family of the Habsburg line of kings including Charles V and Philip II. See also Juan of Austria, Don and *Austriad, The*.

Austriad, The. An epic poem in Latin hexameters, written by the real-life Juan Latino to honor Don Juan of Austria's victory at the Battle of Lepanto in 1571.

Babel. A city in the Book of Genesis, site of a tower that represented an affront to God, who scrambled the languages of the builders to keep them from completing it.

Baena. A city near Cordova in southern Spain.

Barabbas. In the New Testament, a prisoner chosen by the crowd to be pardoned instead of Jesus. Frequently used as insult or curse in early modern Spain.

Basques. A people native to the Basque region of northern Spain and southern France, often caricatured as speaking garbled Spanish.

Beelzebub. An ancient Near Eastern demon, associated in Christianity with the Devil and irrational speech and behavior.

Belgium (Belgian). A country in northwest Europe that was under Spanish control at the time of the Triad. See also Flanders and Low Countries.

Benedictine. Pertaining to a religious congregation that follows the rule of Saint Benedict, known for its austerity and black robes.

Berber. A member of an ancient North African tribe that converted to Islam in the eighth century and aided in the Arab invasion of Spain.

Betis. The ancient Roman name for the Guadalquivir.

Bloodletter. A person who extracted blood for medicinal purposes. One of the four humors of the body in premodern medicine, blood was associated with a cheerful temperament, but draining small amounts was believed to rid the body of impurities and thus prevent or cure disease.

Borea, Don Bernardo de (fl. sixteenth century). According to Mármol y Carvajal (1852, 161), vice-chancellor of Aragon and advisor to Philip II on his Morisco policy.

Brotherhood (also Holy Brotherhood). An association formed in medieval Spain to patrol highways and defend municipalities from bandits.

Brussels. A major city in Flanders, today the capital of Belgium.

Bugle. A valveless brass instrument, similar to a trumpet and used especially for military calls. As the lackey's name in *VOA*, it gives rise to various puns.

Cadmus. A legendary Phoenician prince credited with founding the ancient Greek city of Thebes.

Caesar (Caesarean). Title of the rulers of ancient Rome beginning with Gaius Julius Caesar (100–44 BCE), to whom the word usually refers in the early modern period.

Caliph. The supreme leader of an Islamic polity known as a caliphate.

Canon. A clergyman belonging to the chapter or staff of a cathedral or collegiate church.

Cape Verde. An island nation off the coast of West Africa, important in the Atlantic slave trade at the time of the Triad.

Capuchin. Member of an order of friars formed in 1529, known for their bulky capes and hoods. The Capuchin Scholar and his wise *Miscellany* are unclear references.

Carlobal. A Spanish family name that included the following members (see also Aguilar, House of):

- Dr. Carlobal, governor of the second Duke of Sessa's estate. Father to Doña Ana, he is her brother in *JL*, which also identifies him as founder of the University of Osuna.
- Doña Ana Carlobal. Wife of Juan Latino, both historically and in the play.

Castares Cave. According to Mármol y Carvajal (1852, 172–74), a cave in the Alpujarras containing books of false prophecies that the Moriscos interpreted as predictions of their liberation.

Castile (Castilian). The central region of Spain, whose language, Castilian, is often synonymous with Spanish.

Chaconne. A type of musical composition that emerged in Spain in the late sixteenth century, possibly of New World origin.

Chair. See teaching chair.

Chamberlain. An attendant to a sovereign or lord in his bedchamber. The royal chamberlain was a chief officer of the king.

Chancery Court. See Audiencia and Chancery Court.

Charles V (1500–1558). A Holy Roman Emperor, also known as Charles I of Spain (ruled 1516–1556). Father of both Philip II and the illegitimate Don Juan of Austria.

Choler. Also known as yellow bile, one of the four humors of the body in premodern medicine, associated with an angry or impatient temperament.

Christ (Christian). A title used with Jesus, the central figure of Christianity whom believers hold to be the son of God. According to the New Testament gospels, he was betrayed by his disciple Judas, crucified, and resurrected after three days.

Cicero (106–43 BCE). An ancient Roman orator, much admired for his Latin.

Cleopatra (69–30 BCE). The last queen of Ptolemaic Egypt, famous for her romantic entanglements with Julius Caesar and Marc Antony.

Cleric (clerical). A clergyman or ranking member of a church.

Conrad (fl. fifteenth century). A German printer who published a copy of Augustine's *City of God* in Rome in 1470. Erroneously claimed as the inventor of printing in *JL*.

Constable. A high officer of the law.

Convent. A Christian community, especially of nuns, and the associated building.

Cordova. A city in southern Spain, seat of a powerful Muslim kingdom in the Middle Ages.

Count. A title of nobility below a marquis, equivalent to a British earl.

Count of Cabra. See Aguilar, House of.

Count of Egmont. See Egmont, Count of.

Count of Horne. See Horne, Count of.

Courtier. An attendant at a royal court.

Cupid. The Greco-Roman god of love, child of Venus and Mars, usually portrayed as a small boy with wings and a bow and arrow.

Daphne. A nymph of Greco-Roman mythology, pursued by Apollo and saved from his assault through transformation into a laurel tree.

Darkskin. Translation of Spanish *moreno* (dark or brunette), often a polite substitute for *negro*. See also Translator's Note.

Darro. A small river that runs through Granada, Spain.

Defenestration. A punishment that involves hurling a person or thing through a window.

Democritus (fl. fifth century BCE). An ancient Greek philosopher whose writings have survived only in secondhand accounts.

Demosthenes (384–322 BCE). A famous statesman and orator of ancient Athens.

Deza, Don Pedro de (1520–1600). Named president of the Audiencia and Chancery Court of Granada in 1556, he was closely involved in Philip II's Morisco policy.

Diogenes (d. c. 320 BCE). An ancient Greek philosopher associated with the school of cynics.

Dionysius (c. 432–367 BCE). King of the city of Syracuse in Sicily, famous for receiving the philosopher Plato at his court.

Dominican. A member of the mendicant Order of Saint Dominic, founded in 1216.

Don/Doña. A title of respect that precedes a first name in Spanish, originally reserved for nobility.

Draco (fl. seventh century BCE). The first recorded legislator of ancient Athens. Plutarch (1932, 107) says he punished minor offenses such as theft and idleness with death.

Ducat. A gold coin used across Europe in the medieval and early modern periods.

Duchess. Female equivalent of a duke or the wife of a duke.

Duke. A title of nobility, below a prince and above a marquis.

Duke of Alba. See Alba.

Easter Eve. Eve of the most important holiday of the Christian calendar, marking the resurrection of Christ.

Eber. Great-great-grandson of Noah in the Hebrew Bible (Genesis 10–11).

Ebony. A black or dark brown timber.

Egmont, Count of (1522–1568). Along with the Count of Horne, an instigator of the Dutch revolt against Spanish authority, executed by order of the Duke of Alba. See also Low Countries.

Egypt (Egyptian). A North African country and ancient kingdom that dates back to the third millennium BCE. Part of the Muslim Ottoman Empire at the time of the Triad.

Emperor. A title held by ancient Roman rulers beginning with Augustus Caesar as well as by sovereigns of the Holy Roman Empire.

Enoch. Great-grandfather of Noah in the Hebrew Bible (Genesis 5:21–24). Traditionally considered the author of an ancient Hebrew text known as the Book of Enoch.

Ensign. The position of flag-bearer in early modern Spanish infantry or cavalry. The royal ensign served the king directly.

Espinosa, Cardinal (1502–1572). President of the Council of Castile and Inquisitor General under Philip II, he was closely involved in the king's Morisco policy.

Ethiopia (Ethiopian). A country of sub-Saharan Africa, Christianized in the fourth century. At the time of the Triad, it was often a synonym for Africa, as was Guinea, though Ethiopia's long Christian tradition allowed for more positive associations than the latter.

Eulalia, Saint (fl. third century). A Christian girl martyred in the Roman city that would become Mérida, where a convent in her name existed at the time of the Triad.

Euphrates. Along with the Tigris, one of the two great rivers of ancient Mesopotamia.

Europe. Together with Africa and Asia, one of the three continents known to the ancient world, a view that was coming undone at the time of the Triad.

Evadne. A woman of Greco-Roman mythology who hurled herself onto her husband's funeral pyre. Perhaps a symbol of fortitude.

Exemplum (exempla). An example or model, used especially in the Christian tradition to refer to moral lessons or exemplary tales.

Extremadura. A region of western Spain bordering Portugal, home to Mérida.

Favorite. A person who is specially loved, trusted, or provided with favors by someone of high rank such as a prince or king.

Ferdinand. King of Aragon who, together with his wife, Isabella of Castile, conquered Granada from the Moors in 1492. *Ferdinand* is the Anglicized form of *Fernando*, so the king is cited as a precedent to Don Fernando de Válor's coronation as king of the Moriscos in *JL*.

Fernando de Válor, Don. See Válor, Don Fernando de.

Flanders (Flemish, Fleming). A province of the Low Countries, today corresponding to the country of Belgium. A partial setting of *BBS*, it appears in the play's Spanish title.

France. A European country across the Pyrenees from Spain and a traditional rival of the latter.

Friar. A member of a mendicant religious order such as the Dominicans and Franciscans.

Friday of Sorrows. The Friday of the fifth week of Lent and traditional beginning of Holy Week, often marked by public penance and mortification of the flesh.

Frisian. Pertaining to the province of Friesland in the Low Countries or to the Frisian Islands of the North Sea. The Frisians were known for a breed of horses at the time of the Triad.

Galeotto. Unclear reference, perhaps to the fifteenth-century humanist Galeotto Marzio.

Galley. A long, low ship once common in Mediterranean trade and war, propelled by oars that were frequently manned by slaves known as galley slaves.

Gallo, Magister (1512–1579). Bishop of Orihuela and of Segovia. According to Mármol y Carvajal (1852, 161), an advisor to Philip II on his Morisco policy.

Garrote. A strangulation method used for execution in early modern Spain.

Garter. A band or ribbon that holds up a stocking, often symbolic of a woman's virginity.

Gentiles. In biblical sources, anyone who is not a Jew, including Christians. By the time of the Triad, a synonym for pagan or unbeliever.

Germany (German). A central European country, part of the Holy Roman Empire at the time of the Triad and often confused with the Low Countries.

Gerund. A verbal noun in Latin, English, and other languages.

Gestas. Name given in apocryphal writings to one of the thieves crucified with Jesus.

Golden calf. In the Hebrew Bible (Exodus 32), a statue of gold made by the Israelites during Moses's absence, which became a symbol of idolatry and heathenism.

Gonzalo, Don. See Aguilar, House of.

Granada. A city and province in southern Spain, site of the last Muslim kingdom on the Iberian peninsula and of an important university. Setting of *JL*.

Grandee. A nobleman, usually Spanish or Portuguese, of the highest rank.

Greece (Greek). A country of southeastern Europe, home to an influential civilization of the ancient Mediterranean.

Guadalquivir. A major Spanish river that runs through Seville, called Betis by the ancient Romans.

Guerrero, Archbishop (in office 1546–1576). Archbishop of Granada who was closely involved in Philip II's Morisco policy.

Guinea (Guinean). A country of sub-Saharan Africa. Like Ethiopia, it was often used at the time of the Triad to refer to the whole continent, usually without the positive connotations enabled by Ethiopia's long Christian history.

Hadrian (76–138). An emperor of ancient Rome, known for his admiration of Greek culture.

Hail Mary. A well-known Christian prayer, often recited as a form of penance.

Halberd. A pole weapon of the early modern period consisting of an axe blade topped by a spike and mounted on a long shaft. Often associated with the infantry rank of sergeant in early modern Spain.

Harquebus. A firearm of the musket family, invented in the fifteenth century.

Hebrew. A member of the ancient Hebrew people or the language spoken by them; a Jew.

Henna. A reddish-brown dye used especially for hair and temporary tattoos.

Herald. An official crier or messenger.

Holy Roman Empire (Holy Roman Emperor). A Central European state founded by Charlemagne in the late eighth century and ruled by an emperor modeled on that of ancient Rome. In 1516, Holy Roman Emperor Charles V became Charles I of Spain, initiating the Habsburg line of kings that would last until 1700.

Homer (fl. c. 700 BCE). An ancient Greek poet, author of the *Iliad* and the *Odyssey*.

Horace (65–27 BCE). An ancient Roman poet.

Horne, Count of (c. 1524–1568). Along with the Count of Egmont, an instigator of the Dutch revolt against Spanish authority, executed by order of the Duke of Alba. See also Low Countries.

House of Aguilar. See Aguilar, House of.

House of Austria. See Austria, House of.

Humors. Primary elements of the human body according to premodern medicine, which ascribed the origin of disease to their imbalance.

Hungary (Hungarian). A Central European country that, at the time of the Triad, was a Habsburg possession outside the Holy Roman Empire.

Indulgence. A remission of sin by the Catholic Church, often confirmed in an official document.

Inquisition. A tribunal created by the medieval Catholic Church to pursue and punish heresy. In Spain, where it was established in 1478, the crown was given the unique power of appointing inquisitors.

Italy. A country of southern Europe, home to Rome and a frequent travel destination for Spaniards at the time of the Triad.

Jacob. A patriarch of the Hebrew Bible, grandson of Abraham. Said to have bred speckled sheep from his uncle Laban's flock by placing mottled branches where the animals would see them while mating (Genesis 30:37–43).

Jasmine. A Eurasian shrub that produces a fragrant white flower, a frequent metaphor for feminine beauty at the time of the Triad.

Jasper. A type of opaque quartz, ranging in color from brownish red to blue.

Javelin. A light spear thrown as a weapon in war and hunting.

Jenovia. Unclear reference, perhaps a confusion with the third-century Syrian queen Zenobia.

Jet. A dark black gemstone, often polished and worn in jewelry.

Jineta sword. A uniquely carved Spanish sword associated with the infantry rank of captain.

Josephus (fl. first century). A Jewish priest and scholar of ancient Rome who wrote valuable histories of the Jewish people such as *Jewish Antiquities*.

Juan of Austria, Don (1547–1578). A member of the House of Austria, illegitimate son of Charles V and half brother of Philip II. He had a major role in suppressing the second Morisco revolt as well as in the Battle of Lepanto, and he is an important character in *JL*. See also Aguilar, House of.

Juan Latino. See Latino, Juan.

Jude, Saint. One of the twelve apostles and author of the New Testament Epistle of Jude.

Justin (fl. third century). An ancient Roman historian whose summary of an earlier work by Pompeius Trogus, now lost, provides insights into ancient Near Eastern history.

Kettledrum. A drum with a rounded base and adjustable membrane.

Laban. An uncle to Jacob in the Hebrew Bible (Genesis 24:29–60).

Lackey. A servant or otherwise obsequious follower. Lackeys were frequent comic characters in the Spanish *comedia*.

Lactantius (c. 250–c. 325). An early Christian author known for his *Divine Institutes* and referred to as the "Christian Cicero" at the time of the Triad.

Lady-in-waiting. A court attendant to a high-ranking noblewoman.

Lampoon. A harsh satire, often directed against an individual.

Latino, Juan. (c. 1516–c. 1597). An Afro-Spanish poet and scholar, originally known as Juan de Sessa, whose life forms the basis of *JL*. He was a slave to the second Duke of Sessa and accompanied his son Gonzalo to school, where he learned Latin, adopting the surname *Latino*. See also Aguilar, House of; Carlobal; and Villanueva, Magister.

Laurel. An evergreen tree native to the Mediterranean, sacred to the ancient Greek god Apollo and often symbolic of victory.

Leda. A princess of Greco-Roman mythology, seduced by Jupiter in the disguise of a swan. In *VOA*, the peasant girl Tirrena garbles the myth.

Leila. A Moorish dance.

Libya (Libyan). A country of North Africa, famous for its hot climate.

Lisbon. The capital of Portugal and home to Europe's largest Black slave population at the time of the Triad.

Litter. A covered couch outfitted with handles, used for transporting a single passenger.

Livy (c. 60 BCE–17 CE). An ancient Roman historian, source of much of our knowledge of early Rome.

Low Countries. A group of northwest European nations comprising modern Belgium, Luxembourg, and the Netherlands. Spanish possessions dating back to the inheritance of Charles V in 1516, the Low Countries revolted against Spanish authority in the 1560s, forming the backdrop to *BBS*. By the time the latter play was written (c. 1620), Flanders and the southern provinces had been pacified (beginning with the Duke of Alba's campaign), but war continued against the Dutch in the north.

Ludovico. Unclear reference, possibly to the poet Ludovico Ariosto (1474–1533) or to one of the various Ludovicos of Mantua's powerful House of Gonzaga.

Madrid. A city in central Spain, capital of the Spanish Empire from 1561 on (with the exception of 1601–1606, when the court relocated to Valladolid). Partial setting of *BBS*.

Magus (magi). A member of a priestly caste of ancient Persia. In the biblical story of Jesus, three magi follow a star to the site of the infant's birth in Bethlehem (Matthew 2:1–12). A long tradition, beginning as early as 800 and well developed in European visual art by the time of the Triad, represents one of the magi as a Black man. The three magi are celebrated on January 6, the Feast of the Epiphany.

Magister. The Latin title for a teacher or professor. See also Translator's Note.

Magister Gallo. See Gallo, Magister.

Magister Villanueva. See Villanueva, Magister.

Majordomo. The head steward of a large household or palace.

Mandinga. An ethnic group of West Africa (modern spelling *Mandinka*). At the time of the Triad, the term was a racial insult that sometimes appeared as a place name, as in the phrase "king of Mandinga and Zape" (Correas 1906, 478).

Manicongo. A traditional title of the ruler of the Kingdom of the Congo. At the time of the Triad, the term was also a place name and often functioned a racial insult.

Marquis. A title of nobility, below a duke and above a count. Also spelled *marquess*.

Marquis of Mondéjar. See Mondéjar, Marquis of.

Mars (martial). The ancient Roman god of war and father of Cupid by Venus. The adjective *martial* means warlike. In premodern astronomy, Mars was considered the fifth planet.

Martial (c. 40–c. 103). An ancient Roman poet known for a book of short poems, the *Epigrams*.

Maurice, Saint (fl. third century). A commander in the ancient Roman army, martyred for refusing to persecute Christians. In a famous sculpture completed for the Magdeburg Cathedral in the thirteenth century, he is portrayed as a fully armored knight with black skin, perhaps because of the relationship between his name and the Latin word *maurus* (Moor).

Meesieur. See Monsieur.

Melancholy. Sad or morose. Also an alternative word for black bile, one of the four humors of the body in premodern medicine, associated with a morose temperament.

Menchaca (d. 1571). A member of the Council of Castile under Philip II.

Merda. Portuguese word meaning "shit" (*mierda* in Spanish). It forms the basis of a pun on Juan de Mérida's name in *BBS*.

Mérida. A city in southwestern Spain, partial setting of *BBS* and an element of the main character's name.

Milan. A city in northern Italy, part of the Spanish Empire at the time of the Triad.

Minerva. The ancient Roman goddess of wisdom, justice, law, craft, and strategy, the latter of which associates her with war.

Minotaur. A monster of Greco-Roman mythology, sired by a bull to the Cretan queen Pasiphae.

Miscellany. A collection of diverse writings.

Mondéjar, Marquis of (Luis Hurtado de Mendoza, 1489–1566). A Spanish nobleman who held many important positions during the reigns of Charles V and Philip II.

Monsieur. A French title, analogous to English *Mister*. In *BBS*, Antón distorts it into *Meesieur*.

Moors (Moorish). Muslims who invaded Iberia in 711 and remained on the peninsula until their final defeat by Christian armies in Granada in 1492. See also Translator's Note.

Moriscos. Moors who remained in Spain after the defeat of Granada in 1492 and were forced to convert to Christianity. They twice rebelled against Spanish rule, in 1500 and 1568, the second revolt forming the backdrop to *JL*. They were finally expelled from the peninsula in 1609–1614, only a few years before the plays of the Triad were written. See also Translator's Note.

Moses. A major Jewish prophet who, as recounted in the Book of Exodus, led his people from captivity in Egypt.

Muhammad (c. 570–632). An Arab religious leader, founder and central prophet of Islam.

Muse. A source of inspiration, personified in ancient Greece as several sister deities who presided over poetry and the arts.

Naevia. A woman referenced in the poetry of the ancient Roman poet Martial.

Naples. A city in southern Italy, part of the Spanish Empire at the time of the Triad.

Narcissus. A beautiful youth of Greco-Roman mythology who fell in love with his own image in a pool of water. A frequent early modern metaphor for beauty.

Negro. Spanish word meaning "black" in reference to things and people. In the latter case it often meant "slave" and could be used offensively. See also Translator's Note.

Nile. A river in Egypt, the longest in the world and a principal source of papyrus.

Noah. A patriarch of the Hebrew Bible who built an ark to escape the great flood (Genesis 6:11–9:19). He sent out a raven as a first attempt to discover dry land, but it did not return.

Nominative. A grammatical case in Latin and other languages.

Numa Pompilius (fl. 700 BCE). The legendary second king of ancient Rome.

Olympus. The highest mountain in Greece, traditional home to the major gods of Greco-Roman mythology.

Orange. A county in the Low Countries and seat of William, Prince of Orange, who led the Dutch revolt against Spanish rule and who appears as a character in *BBS*.

Orcus. An ancient Roman deity of the underworld, often conflated with Pluto and Dis.

Orpheus. A famed musician and poet of Greco-Roman mythology, known for his failed attempt to rescue his wife, Eurydice, from the underworld.

Osuna. A town in southern Spain near Seville, home to the University of Osuna.

Our Father. A well-known Christian prayer, also known as the Pater Noster and Lord's Prayer.

Ovid (43 BCE–17 CE). An ancient Roman writer famous for his mythological and love poetry.

Page. A youth who attended a knight or another person of rank in the medieval and early modern periods.

Paleface. Translation of Spanish *blanco* or Portuguese *branco* in nominalized form, often used in parallel to negro and with a slight comic intent. See also Translator's Note.

Pantarbe jewel. A mythical precious stone associated with magical powers. It appears in various ancient sources including book 4 of Heliodorus's *An Ethiopian Story* (Heliodorus 2019, 506).

Papyrus. A reed native to the Nile River and cultivated for its use in an early form of paper.

Parchment. A smooth, durable paper made from the skin of a sheep or goat.

Parley. A conference called to discuss terms with an enemy.

Parnassus. A mountain of central Greece. According to ancient Roman writers, it was home to the muses and the Castalian Spring.

Pegasus. A winged horse of Greco-Roman mythology, used by Perseus to travel to Ethiopia and free Andromeda. Also said to have created the Castalian Spring with a kick of its hoof.

Pelasgians. An ancient people of the Aegean Sea and eastern Mediterranean, prior to the arrival of Greek-speaking peoples in the Bronze Age.

Pergamon. A powerful ancient Greek city near Troy. It was an important center of parchment production in the ancient Mediterranean, lending its name to the word.

Perseus. A major hero of Greco-Roman mythology, known for slaying the Gorgon Medusa and freeing Andromeda.

Phaon. A legendary boatman of the Greek island of Lesbos, with whom the poet Sappho supposedly fell in love. Ovid tells the story in his *Letters from Heroines*.

Philip II (1527–1598). A Spanish king, son of Charles V, who ruled 1556–1598. He is a character in *BBS*.

Phlegm (phlegmatic). One of the four humors of the body in premodern medicine, associated with a phlegmatic or sluggish temperament.

Phoenicia (Phoenician). A prosperous Semitic civilization of the ancient Mediterranean, known for developing an alphabet that became a model for the Greeks and Romans.

Phoenix. A mythical Arabian bird thought to achieve immortality through a perpetual cycle of regeneration from its own ashes.

Pike. A heavy spear with a long shaft used by European infantry in the medieval and early modern periods.

Pindar (c. 518–c. 438 BCE). An ancient Greek poet from Thebes. According to legend, when Alexander the Great demolished the city, he left Pindar's house standing.

Pitch. A black or dark-colored residue from organic materials such as tar.

Plato (c. 429–347 BCE). Together with Aristotle, one of the two great philosophers of the ancient world.

Plaza del Carmen. A public square in Granada near the cathedral.

Pliny ("the Elder," 23–79 CE). An ancient Roman natural historian, well-known at the time of the Triad.

Plutarch (46–c. 119). An ancient Greek writer, well-known at the time of the Triad for his biographies of Greeks and Romans.

Pompey the Great (106–48 BCE). An ancient Roman general and statesman, originally an ally of Julius Caesar but later his bitter enemy in a conflict that led to civil war and to the eventual downfall of both men.

Pope. The supreme leader of the Roman Catholic Church.

Porphyry. A hard igneous rock, usually red or purple rather than the black ascribed to it in *BBS*.

Portugal (Portuguese). Spain's neighbor on the Iberian peninsula and major slave-trafficking nation in the early modern period, annexed to Spain at the time of the Triad. The Portuguese were known for their poetic and musical talents.

Posidonius (c. 135–c. 51 BCE). An ancient Greek politician and stoic philosopher said to have influenced Cicero. Pompey the Great admired his work and allegedly visited him twice.

Preceptor. A teacher or tutor.

Prior. The highest or second-highest position at a monastery.

Proto. A prefix that often emphasizes what follows in a comic way, as in *protowoman* or *protonegro*.

Proverbs. A book of the Hebrew Bible that purports to collect the sayings of Solomon and other wise men. Juan Latino alludes to the proverb "Lazy hands make for poverty, but diligent hands bring wealth" (Proverbs 10:4).

Pyrrhus (319–272 BCE). An ancient Greek king of Epirus whose costly military triumphs gave rise to the term *pyrrhic victory*.

Pythagoras (c. 570–c. 495 BCE). An ancient Greek philosopher whose ideas, including the so-called Pythagorean theorem, are known entirely from secondhand sources.

Quijada, Luis (d. 1570). Attendant to Charles V and, later, tutor to Don Juan of Austria, with whom he participated in suppressing the second Morisco revolt. A minor character in *BBS*.

Rebus. A cryptic representation of a word or phrase through pictures, symbols, or arrangement of letters. In early modern Spain, slaves were often branded with a rebus that represented the Spanish word meaning "slave." See also Translator's Note.

Rhine. A major European river that flows from the Alps to the North Sea.

Rome (Roman). Principal city of Italy, seat of the ancient Roman Empire as well as the Roman Catholic Church, and origin of the Latin language. See also Holy Roman Empire.

Ronda. A city in southern Spain near Seville.

Royal Chamberlain. See Chamberlain.

Royal Ensign. See Ensign.

Saba. A kingdom mentioned in the Hebrew Bible, also written *Sheba*, whose queen is said to have visited the court of Solomon (I Kings 10:1–13 and II Chronicles 9:1–12). In *VOA*, the word indicates not a place but rather the queen of Ethiopia.

Sack-butt. A pun on *sackbut*, a late-medieval wind instrument and precursor to the trombone.

Saint John's Eve. A festival celebrated on June 23, the evening before the feast day of Saint John the Baptist. In Spain, it doubles as a midsummer celebration with ancient pagan elements such as bonfires and magic.

Santiago, Order of. A military-religious order established in medieval Spain. Being inducted into the order required proof of "pure" blood, meaning no trace of Jewish, Moorish, or African ancestry.

Sappho (fl. 600 BCE). An ancient Greek woman poet, native to the island of Lesbos.

Saraband. A stately court dance of the seventeenth and eighteenth centuries resembling the minuet.

Scepter. A staff or baton carried by a king or other sovereign as an emblem of authority.

Scimitar. A saber with a curved blade, originally used by Arabs and Turks.

Scipio (236–183 BCE). An ancient Roman general and statesman who led Rome to victory over Carthage in the Second Punic War.

Scythia (Scythian). A region of the Eurasian steppe, north of the Black and Caspian Seas, famous for its cold climate.

Semiramis (fl. ninth century BCE). A queen of the ancient Assyrian Empire, known as a strong ruler after her husband's death.

Sentinel. A person, often a soldier, who stands guard at a point of passage.

Sessa, Duke and Duchess of. See Aguilar, House of.

Sessa, Juan de. See Latino, Juan.

Seth. Third son of Adam and Eve in the Hebrew Bible (Genesis 5:3–8).

Seville (Sevillian). Capital of the Spanish region of Andalusia. Home to early modern Spain's largest Black slave population as well as two of the three Triad authors.

Shawm. A late medieval wind instrument, precursor to the oboe.

Sicily (Sicilian). A major Mediterranean island, across the Tyrrhenian Sea from mainland Italy and part of the Spanish Empire at the time of the Triad. Two important characters in *VOA* are Sicilian.

Sierra. A range of mountains, especially with a serrated or irregular outline.

Siren. In Greco-Roman mythology, one of several part-human, female creatures that lured sailors to destruction with their enchanting song.

Solomon. A son of David and king of Israel in the Hebrew Bible, traditionally considered the author of the Book of Proverbs. See also Saba.

Strabo (c. 64 BCE–21 CE). An ancient Greek geographer and historian, author of an extensive account of the ancient world.

Swabia (Swabian). A historical region of southwest Germany.

Swarthy. Translation of Spanish *prieto* or Portuguese *preto*. Like darkskin, it was a polite substitute for negro. See also Translator's Note.

Syria (Syrian). A country of southwest Asia, on the eastern edge of the Mediterranean, that dates back to the ancient Assyrian Empire.

Tamerlane (1336–1405). A Turk who conquered a wide swath of lands from the Mediterranean to India and Russia.

Tantalus. A figure of Greco-Roman mythology, punished with perpetual hunger and thirst only to have food and drink slip from his hands whenever he reached for them.

Tarpeia. A Vestal Virgin of ancient Roman mythology, known for betraying her country to the Sabines.

Teaching chair. A permanent teaching position, called thus after the elevated chair from which the instructor lectured.

Teuton (Teutonic). A member of a central European people, conflated in *BBS* with Flemish.

Thebes. A major ancient Greek city, home to mythological figures such as Cadmus and Oedipus as well as the Greek poet Pindar. Destroyed by Alexander the Great in 335 BCE.

Tiara. A three-tiered crown worn by both the pope and the Holy Roman Emperor.

Timanthes (fl. fourth century BCE). An ancient Greek painter, often associated with excellence in visual representation.

Timbuktu. An African city incorporated into the Mali Empire in the fourteenth century.

Toledo, Don Antonio de (d. 1579). A member of the Council of Castile under Philip II.

Troy. An ancient city of Asia Minor, conquered by the Greeks in a destructive war that inspired Homer's *Iliad* and *Odyssey*.

Turkey (Turk). A Muslim country of the eastern Mediterranean, seat of the Ottoman Empire at the time of the Triad.

Tyre. The capital of ancient Phoenician civilization.

Tyrrhenian Sea. A part of the Mediterranean bordered by mainland Italy and the islands of Corsica, Sardinia, and Sicily.

University of Osuna. See Osuna.

Valdelucero. Unclear geographical reference, presumably intended as a location in Albania.

Válor, Don Fernando de (c. 1546–1569). A Morisco town councilor of Granada who, under the Arabic name Aben Humeya, was proclaimed king of the Moriscos and led a revolt against Spanish authority in 1568. In *JL* he is a also suitor to Doña Ana Carlobal.

Varro (116–27 BCE). An ancient Roman writer and scholar, most of whose works are now lost.

Vassal. A person bound in service to a lord by a formal contract.

Vassalage. The state or condition of being a vassal.

Velasco (fl. sixteenth century). A member of the Council of Castile under Philip II.

Veni, vidi, vici. A Latin aphorism attributed to Julius Caesar that means "I came, I saw, I conquered." Often cited as a model of brevity.

Villanueva, Magister. An instructor who competed with the historical Juan Latino for a teaching position in Latin. Chief antagonist in *JL*.

Virgil (70–19 BCE). The most renowned poet of ancient Rome, author of the *Aeneid*, the *Eclogues*, and the *Georgics*. In the latter (1.145) he wrote that "work conquered everything."

William of Orange, Prince. See Orange.

Zambra. Originally a Moorish dance, today part of the flamenco style.

Zape. An obscure word that may reference a coastal area of Sierra Leone (von Germeten 2006, 218) and was probably a racial insult at the time of the Triad (see Mandinga). Also the Spanish term used to shoo a cat.